African American
Theater Buildings

ALSO BY ERIC LEDELL SMITH
AND FROM McFARLAND

*Blacks in Opera: An Encyclopedia of People
and Companies, 1873–1993* (1995)

*Bert Williams: A Biography
of the Pioneer Black Comedian* (1992)

African American Theater Buildings

An Illustrated Historical Directory, 1900–1955

ERIC LEDELL SMITH

McFarland & Company, Inc., Publishers
Jefferson, North Carolina, and London

The present work is a reprint of the illustrated case bound edition of African American Theater Buildings: An Illustrated Historical Directory, 1900–1955, *first published in 2003 by McFarland.*

LIBRARY OF CONGRESS CATALOGUING-IN-PUBLICATION DATA

Smith, Eric Ledell, 1949–
    African American theater buildings : an illustrated historical directory, 1900–1955 / Eric Ledell Smith.
       p.   cm.
    Includes bibliographical references and index.

    ISBN 978-0-7864-4922-4
    softcover : 50# alkaline paper ∞

    1. African American theater — History — 20th century.
2. Theaters — United States — Directories.   I. Title.
PN2270.A35S58   2011
792'.089'96073 — dc21   2003011177

BRITISH LIBRARY CATALOGUING DATA ARE AVAILABLE

© 2003 Eric Ledell Smith. All rights reserved

No part of this book may be reproduced or transmitted in any form or by any means, electronic or mechanical, including photocopying or recording, or by any information storage and retrieval system, without permission in writing from the publisher.

Cover photograph: Ritz Theater, Jacksonville, Florida (SoulofAmerica.com)

Manufactured in the United States of America

McFarland & Company, Inc., Publishers
  Box 611, Jefferson, North Carolina 28640
    www.mcfarlandpub.com

For my high school English
teacher, Nettie Kravitz

CONTENTS

Acknowledgments	ix
Preface	xi
Introduction	1
Alabama	9
Arizona	21
Arkansas	21
California	26
Colorado	34
Connecticut	34
Delaware	34
District of Columbia	35
Florida	46
Georgia	61
Illinois	73
Indiana	84
Iowa	88
Kansas	88
Kentucky	89
Louisiana	91
Maryland	101
Massachusetts	114
Michigan	115
Minnesota	122
Mississippi	122
Missouri	129
Nebraska	135
Nevada	136
New Jersey	136
New Mexico	138
New York	139
North Carolina	150
Ohio	163
Oklahoma	170
Pennsylvania	175
South Carolina	192
Tennessee	198
Texas	203
Virginia	222
Washington	235
West Virginia	235
Wisconsin	237
Appendix 1— Numbers of Theater Buildings	239
Appendix 2— Architects	241
Appendix 3— Owners and Managers	242
Appendix 4— African American Drive-in Theaters	247
Bibliography	249
Index	253

ACKNOWLEDGMENTS

I wish to thank the following individuals and institutions who assisted me in researching this book: Geraldine Duchow and her staff of the Theater Collection of the Free Library of Philadelphia; Paula Heiman and Sally Biel of the Pennsylvania Historical and Museum Library; the staff of the State Library of Pennsylvania; the staff of the Library of Congress; and the staff of the National Archives. Martin McCaffery and Robert K. Headley helped me many times with information on theaters.

I wish to acknowledge the assistance and support of the following individuals and institutions with the photographs for this book: Martin McCaffery, the Los Angeles Public Library; the Washingtoniana Division of the District of Columbia Library; the Historical Society of Washington, D.C.; the Middle Georgia Archives of the Washington Memorial Library, Macon, Georgia; Thomas Dorsey of SoulofAmerica.com; the Robert K. Headley Collection; the Maryland Historical Society; the Museum of the City of New York; the Schomberg Center for Research in Black History of the New York Public Library; the Tulsa Historical Society; the Athenaeum of Philadelphia; and Miriam Meislik of the Archives Service Center at the University of Pittsburgh.

I also thank all of my friends who gave me moral support during my research over the last three years, especially Barbara Barksdale, Larry Baume, India Garnett, Calobe Jackson, Dorothy King, Nettie Kravitz, Jacqu-e Pinn, Bruce Robertson, John W. Scott, and Georg Sheets.

PREFACE

African American Theater Buildings is an illustrated historical directory and bibliographic guide to more than 1500 theater buildings across the United States that were operated for an African American audience from 1900 through 1955. Such theaters were owned and managed by both blacks and whites. They included nickelodeons, vaudeville houses, musical houses, neighborhood movie theaters, and drive-ins.

Not included in this book are honky-tonks, nightclubs, taverns, black theater or performance spaces before 1900, or theaters for a predominately white audience.

It is a sad commentary on American race relations that some elements of African American culture and history, such as the African American theater building, are still virtually ignored by American scholars and historic preservationists. Although the popularity of motion pictures has spawned a number of books about famous "movie palaces," especially in New York City and Los Angeles, these books describe and celebrate theaters frequented by white audiences.

Although I have identified nearly 2000 African American theater buildings, only one such theater has been the subject of a book: the legendary Harlem Theater in Ted Fox's 1983 *Showtime at the Apollo*. Fox provides an in-depth look at the evolution and oral tradition of an important black theater in the North. Most African American theaters, however, were in the South. In fact, *all* of the known "black" drive-in theaters were located in the South, and the African American drive-in theater has received no attention from scholars.

One reason for the neglect of the African American theater building is the general perception of scholars that the public is interested only in the entertainment offered in a theater and not in the theater building itself. This is reflected in the literature now available on black theater. The literature deals with theatrical companies, playwrights, plays and productions that appeared in these houses rather than the history of the buildings. For example, James Haskins's book *Black Theater in America*, Edith Issacs's *The Negro in the American Theater*, and Erroll Hill's *The Theater of Black Americans* concern black drama, black dramatists, and black actors and productions.

Recently, several scholars have addressed the topic of the black theater building in outstanding reference books. The 1995 book *Blacks in Black and White*, by Henry T. Sampson, has an appendix on "theaters catering to Black Patronage, 1910–1950," but it merely reproduces previously published surveys of black theaters. Bernard L. Peterson's *The African American Theatre Directory, 1816–1960* is another commendable work, but despite his excellent coverage of many topics, Peterson is inconsistent when it comes to documenting theater buildings. Like Sampson, Peterson is largely concerned with documenting entertainers and shows rather than theater buildings.

Visual information has also been in short supply. Previous books on black theaters have generally not included photographs of the buildings, and when photographs are published, they tend to be of the same buildings (e.g., the Apollo in New York City). This lack of photographic evidence makes it extremely difficult to appraise the architectural styles of African American theaters.

Clearly there is a need for more research on black theater buildings. Good research tools are, however, hard to come by. Scholars in the past have had no standard bibliography to consult on black theater buildings. That is the main reason I have compiled this book, not only to document the existence of theater buildings, but to provide a central source of bibliographic information.

As the reader and critic will see, few primary sources exist for black theater buildings. What exists in the bibliography are secondary works such as books, articles from recent newspapers and magazines, and several dissertations. The few recent works on black theaters tend to cite the same sources or even cite one another. I have tried to identify as meticulously as possible the original sources on which these authors are basing their scholarship. Primary references are crucial in that often they provide the only clue that a theater building was in business in a certain community or when it operated. Secondary sources do sometimes name theater owners and managers, but only a few attempt to identify the architects or architecture of the theaters. When one compares the bibliographic literature of black theaters with that of white theaters, one perceives a huge information gap. *African American Theater Buildings* attempts to fill this gap.

This book identifies theaters alphabetically by state, then by city. Not all states are represented and the South is the most heavily represented because during much of the twentieth century, most of the African American population lived in the Southern United States. Throughout the United States both large and small communities had African American theaters, but invariably the best-known black theaters were in large urban areas such as Chicago, St. Louis, Philadelphia, Nashville, Birmingham, Atlanta, Detroit, New Orleans, and New York. The New York City entries are grouped under the names of the relevant boroughs, i.e., the Bronx, Brooklyn, and Manhattan. There are no known African theaters in Queens or Staten Island.

The index lists all cities and towns covered in this book. Spelling of the names of towns and cities has been verified by consulting the Geographic Names Information System (database).

Each numbered entry features the name of the theater building that was the predominant name when black audiences attended the theater and that is consistently cited in bibliographic references. Names and addresses of theaters were verified through telephone directories at the Library of Congress. Many theater names were common such as Harlem, Dunbar, and Lincoln. The names Gay and Gayety were also common but they do not describe theaters for homosexual audiences. Readers will find many theaters by these names and sometimes more than one in a single community.

Alternate names of theaters are given when known. These alternate names were cited either in trade publications like *Film Daily Yearbook* or in local theater surveys by authors such as Robert K. Headley or Stuart Galbraith. The names are cross-referenced both in the text and in the index. An alternate name was sometimes bestowed when a theater changed owners or managers or was renovated. In New York City, the focus for most theater scholars, theater name changes are well documented. Unfortunately, this is not true of the rest of the country, especially in the South. Southern communities with small black populations sometimes appear to have had several theaters; it is possible that in many cases these were the same building with different names. Local research might confirm the history of a building in question.

Whenever it is possible, I cite dates for when the theater was built and when it went out of business. Several black newspapers, such as the *Chicago Defender*, were especially valuable in noting the openings of African American theater houses. Because I consider the studies of historians who have focused on a single community valuable, I have quoted dates from these scholars, or, when available, newspaper articles about theater building openings.

Wherever the data are available, I have cited the name of the architect, the architectural style, and the seating capacity of the house. For this information I have relied upon theater historians who have done in-depth research into urban theaters. Architects were most often identified for buildings in New York, Washington, D.C., Indianapolis, Baltimore, Philadelphia, and Detroit. Seating capacity numbers were supplied through theater historians as well as sources such as *Film Daily Yearbook*. The citations of seating capacity were very inconsistent in bibliographic sources and the numbers given here are approximate.

When available, names of owners and managers are given along with the dates when they were employed, based upon available bibliographic references. If the sources indicate that the manager or owner is African American, this is indicated in the theater entry. Appendix 3 contains a complete alphabetical list of owners and managers identified in this book.

Each theater's entertainment type — vaudeville, drama, or film — is identified. Most African American theaters featured more than one type of entertainment. During the 1920s, a black theater could exhibit silent films and also feature TOBA vaudeville acts. The TOBA (Theater Owners Booking Association) is perhaps the most famous vaudeville circuit associated with African Americans. I have noted when the house was a member of this vaudeville circuit. Wherever I could find the information in local black newspapers, I have provided a description of typical entertainment in the theater's entry. I surveyed a number of African American newspapers and randomly selected dates of reviews, preferring those reviews that covered important movies and actors.

Each one of the entries in *African American Theater Buildings* has a bibliographic reference list. These lists cite reference works, dissertations, film industry publications, African American newspapers, autobiographies, and biographies, arranged alphabetically by author or title of publication. Sources are most abundant for the vaudeville houses that survived into the sound motion picture era. The Apollo in New York, the Grand in Chicago, and the Eighty-one in Atlanta are good examples of this type. These important film and vaudeville houses were reviewed regularly in black newspapers such as the *California Eagle, Louisiana Weekly, Chicago Defender, Norfolk Journal and Guide, Atlanta Daily World, Philadelphia Tribune, Pittsburgh Courier, Baltimore Afro-American,* and *Louisville Defender.*

On the other hand, advertisements and

reviews for movie houses are scarce for small communities, especially beyond the heyday of vaudeville in the 1920s. Most twentieth century mainstream or "white" newspapers did not carry advertisements for black theaters. Where documentation is available, it tends to be uneven in scope and often inconsistent.

I found that the main documentation of black theaters is based upon surveys. *Billboard, Motion Picture Herald, Film Daily Yearbook*, and the so-called "Negro" yearbooks or handbooks published statistics and lists of African American theaters based upon surveys, often the same ones. Surveys generally relied upon theater managers to return reports. Not all managers would consistently cooperate, however, and hence a theater might be reported one year and perhaps not the next year, even though the theater was still in business. This might explain why the 1937 survey of black theaters in *Motion Picture Herald* lists no Chicago theaters, although it is certain, from entertainers' autobiographies, that Chicago had African American theaters in the 1930s!

An abbreviated bibliographic citation is given in the references in each entry. The bibliography near the back of the book contains the full citation. Readers are cautioned that bibliographic sources such as *Film Daily Yearbook* provide vital clues as to the longevity of a given house, but this information alone does not necessarily indicate definitively when a house opened, when it was in business, or when it went out of business. In many communities, theaters must be licensed, and the municipal license department can possibly provide documentation of the longevity of a particular theater building.

The present work is, I believe, the first book to feature photographs of black theater buildings from around the country. As with theater entries themselves, unfortunately, not all towns and cities are represented with such illustrations. African American theater buildings were rarely photographed, and those that were represent only a fraction of the places that were actually in business. Conceivably, many African American theater buildings may still be standing but lack photographic documentation. Historical societies, libraries, individuals, web sites, and the Library of Congress supplied the photographs in this book.

I have employed several proper names in the text to describe people of African descent. The term I most commonly use is African American. However, the terms "Negro" and "colored," historically used to describe black people, are also used in this book. A small number of theaters were simply called "colored." Similarly, whenever I came across a bibliographic citation for an unnamed theater, for example in J.A. Jackson's or Monroe N. Work's surveys, I took the liberty of christening it as a "colored theater." I hope that this terminology does not offend the reader.

African American Theater Buildings is intended as a research guide to help people in local communities do research on black theaters. It also provides a broad introduction to the subject that I believe will be helpful to historians, architects, historic preservationists, and community leaders who might wish to preserve or at least document the history of these buildings, which were vital hubs of social and artistic life in their communities. Most of the theaters named in this book, I suspect, are no longer standing. Those of us interested in black film, theater, vaudeville, and architectural history need all the information we can get about these buildings. This is a fascinating and rich area of American popular culture history, crying out for scholarship. Scholars should be encouraged to turn their attention to African American theater buildings and provide richer documentation of the architecture, architects, business people, and entertainers who were associated with these structures. The present work is not the last word on the subject, but I hope that by being among the first, it will stimulate further work in this neglected area.

—Eric Ledell Smith
August 2003

INTRODUCTION

The American theater building, especially the African American theater building, is rapidly becoming an historical memory. With the wide use of radios, televisions, and videos for home entertainment, it is difficult for young people today to realize that at one time the theater was at the heart of American popular culture. The generations that enjoyed going out to the theater are diminishing. The documents and artifacts that symbolized the public memory of these theaters are also vanishing. The buildings themselves are crumbling or have succumbed to the wrecking balls of urban renewal. Yet these structures are worth remembering for the represented community life. Many theaters were works of architectural wonder. All were hallmarks of American entertainment venues of a past day.

By supplying information on hundreds of African American theater buildings, this book provides an overall perspective on the importance of such buildings in American society through the first half of the twentieth century. The focus is primarily on the buildings themselves—documenting their existence and location and whatever other facts could be ascertained—rather than on the entertainment or entertainers. There is already available a rich corpus of literature about theater entertainers and theatrical productions.

The African American theater building came into existence as a result of the change in American race relations that occurred at the end of the nineteenth century. In 1896, the United States Supreme Court handed down the infamous *Plessy v. Ferguson* decision. Homer Plessy filed a lawsuit against a Louisiana railroad that forced him to sit in a blacks-only car. The Supreme Court ruled that separate facilities for the races were acceptable.[1] This legal decision triggered the nationwide creation of what were known as "Jim Crow" establishments, places which relegated African Americans to separate spaces everywhere: trains, buses, theaters, and so forth. Even public water fountains and restrooms were designated "for whites" and "for colored." When entering an establishment such as a restaurant or theater, blacks had to enter from the side door or back entrance on an alley.

Historian Pearl Bowser emphasizes that Jim Crow was not just a Southern phenomenon: "In many northern communities, although Negroes had the legal rights to sit anywhere in the house, de facto segregation kept them confined to certain areas."[2] In 1921, a black state legislator who had purchased a ticket for the main floor of the Stanley Theater in Philadelphia was referred to the Jim Crow area. John C. Asbury told the press, "The usher looked at my ticket, looked at me, laughed in my face, and said, 'There is your seat up there,' pointing to the rear of the gallery."[3]

African Americans fought Jim Crow, however, suing theater managers who practiced racial discrimination. Mrs. S. Clarissa Evans won her lawsuit against a Proctor vaudeville theater in Troy, New

York, in 1911. "Mixed houses" or theaters that admitted both blacks and whites without discrimination did exist, but these establishments were few compared to the majority of theaters that were "lily white" or practiced Jim Crow customs. Even in "mixed houses" blacks were still under the pall of racism. "Not only were black patrons required to move at the whim of whites," but the management might have specific policies of assigning employees according to race, relegating blacks to more servile jobs such as messengers, maids, or porters rather than uniformed ushers or ticket-takers."[4]

The African American community reacted by promoting its own theaters. The right to enjoy theater shows without personal humiliation was important to black people, and the black press led the way in pressing for this civil right. "The *Birmingham (Ala.) Reporter* beseeched the 'colored people of Birmingham [to] make a practical settlement of their amusement problem as the colored people of Washington, New Orleans, and other Negro centers are doing by providing theaters of their own ... where they may march in through the front door without fear and trembling and occupy the best seats at a reasonable price of admission."[5]

Black entrepreneurs heeded the call. The first black businessman to establish a legitimate black theater was Robert Motts. Motts opened the Pekin Theater on 27th and State streets in Chicago on June 18, 1904. At first the Pekin featured musical shows, but later it switched to vaudeville.[6]

Motts' success with the Pekin may have influenced Sherman H. Dudley, a popular vaudeville performer associated with the Smart Set company. "In a letter published in the [*Indianapolis*] *Freeman* on 20 January 1912, he proposed to set up a chain of Negro theaters, which would be operated by black businessmen." His promotion asked, "How many colored men with money are willing to invest in theaters? The day is now ripe, the time has come; there is more profit in the show business than in any other business you can invest your money in, if properly managed. Why should you lose this opportunity?"[7] Two years later, the *Indianapolis Freeman* reported that Dudley owned or operated "fourteen theaters in thirteen cities." Several of these carried Dudley's name. "The *Freeman* reported that the Dudley Circuit had arrived 'in the nick of time' since a large number of the 'white houses' [had] closed their door to the colored performer.'"[8]

The acquisition or building of theaters oriented toward African American audiences stimulated the emerging black film industry. As historian Henry T. Sampson notes, "The movement toward the construction of black theaters by such men as Robert Motts [and] Sherman H. Dudley ... had resulted in a circuit of black owned and operated theaters which formed a stable but limited market for the Black film producer."[9]

There were a number of black producers and black film companies in the early twentieth century. Some of the better known ones include the Lincoln Motion Picture Company, the Foster Photoplay Company, the Colored Players Film Corporation and the Micheaux Film Corporation, owned by filmmaker Oscar Micheaux. According to Micheaux's biographer, "Micheaux saw the audience for his films in the growth of urban black communities and in smaller towns in the South, where Negroes were hungry for success stories and eager to see themselves in identifiable roles."[10]

By the 1920s, many black communities had a choice between frequenting Jim Crow houses, mixed houses and "race houses," or African American theaters. Most chose to attend the latter. Race loyalty or pride motivated many African Americans to patronize black oriented businesses. Theater owners knew this and exploited it in their advertisements.

A 1919 ad in an Atlanta newspaper featured a cartoon depicting a black couple debating where to go at night. The caption reads: "Why don't we go to that Colored theatre on Auburn Avenue. You see the same picture [as you do downtown] and do not go in from the alley. Let us go there. We can go in the front and sit anywhere we want and it is also run by a Colored man."[11] A similar argument was put forth by Dunbar Theater owner Edward C. Brown in a 1919 advertisement in the *Philadelphia Tribune*: "Colored people, like any other people, wish to spend their money where they are wanted. They know the very minute they enter the doors of a colored theater they are welcome. They know they can obtain any seat in the house they can pay for — they want to feel this way, and it is a natural feeling."[12] In Lexington, Kentucky, the management placed an advertisement in the newspaper urging, "Colored People Take Notice. Come where you are welcome and meet your friends. The Frolic Theater offers splendid pictures, excellent singing, and fine music."[13]

Race pride was reinforced by the presence of African Americans on theater staffs. The record shows that although most African American theaters were owned by white people, they tended to be managed by African Americans, and there were also a substantial number of African American theater owners. It is also noteworthy that some African Americans owned or managed more than one theater at a time. Rufus Byars and Sherman H. Dudley each operated four theaters in Washington, D.C. Lew Henry operated the Lincoln and the Lyceum in Cincinnati.

Some women operated African American theaters including Zelia N. Breaux, Bessie Foster, Marie Downes, Mrs. Minnie McAlfee, Mrs. A. E. Miller and Mrs. Lola Williams. Mrs. Williams ran a chain of three Oklahoma theaters, all of them called Dreamland.

Beginning in the 1920s, black people began to operate motion picture projectors. For instance, in 1925 Hewitt Bundy became the first African American projectionist at the Dunbar Theater in Philadelphia.[14]

Another factor boosting both race pride and theater attendance was the naming of theater buildings. African American theaters were often christened with the names of black heroes. The Douglass (for Frederick Douglass), the Dunbar (Paul Laurence Dunbar), the Lincoln (Abraham Lincoln), the Carver (George Washington Carver) and the Booker T (Booker T. Washington) were the most popular names for African American theaters. We know that some of these theaters celebrated these heroes in the façade or interior décor of the theater buildings. The Booker T Theater in Baltimore had a portrait of Booker T. Washington hung above the screen. The Carver Theater in Alexandria, Virginia, portrayed the life of George Washington Carver with hand painted murals on the auditorium walls. The Lincoln Theater in Baltimore had an outdoor neon sign in the shape of Abraham Lincoln's head.

Photographs of African American theater buildings show they were similar to other American theater buildings. Black audiences went to air domes, nickelodeons, storefront theaters, opera houses, vaudeville theaters, newsreel theaters, tent theaters, movie houses, and even drive-in theaters.

Open-air theaters, often called air domes, were popular in the days before air conditioning. "An air dome consisted of four walls, without a roof, and seats placed directly on the ground between a projector coop and a simple screen. Open to the sky, the air-dome structure was economical, requiring only an open lot with a high fence, and less of a fire hazard than enclosed theatres."[15] African American air domes were located in Hot Springs, Arkansas; Washington, D.C.; Florida; Atlanta; Columbus, Ohio; and Indianapolis. Some theaters, such as the Booker T. in Vicksburg, Mississippi, were remodeled into a theater from an air dome.

The storefront theater was also a common type of African American theater. They were exactly what the name implies, storefronts or one or two story structures with theater seating on the street level, a projection booth and makeshift screen and a sign hung above the door outside. The American and the New Albert in Baltimore, the Lincoln in New York City and the Alamo in Washington, D.C., all were storefront theaters. The Royal in Nashville was formerly a Masonic Temple and the Plymouth in Washington used to be a Plymouth car sales room!

Architecturally similar to the storefront was the nickelodeon, which tended to follow a standard layout. "Nickelodeons were small, typically measuring twenty by eighty feet, and usually had a center aisle leading to the screen; appointments usually included short straight rows of straight-back chairs or wooden benches and a projector located at the rear. There was no balcony."[16] As the name implies, admission cost a nickel. The Joy and York Street Palace in Philadelphia, the Standard in Cleveland, the Lincoln in New York City, and the Alamo in Washington, D.C., were originally nickelodeons. Detroit tops the list with five African American nickelodeons: the Bijou, the Columbia, the Gratiot, the Liberty, and the Rosebud.

Opera houses were also popular entertainment places in the African American community. An "opera house" might be designed specifically for opera, or (as was often the case in small communities) it might be simply a public hall, auditorium, or theater that hosted all types of entertainment — opera, operetta, musical comedies, legitimate plays, burlesque and vaudeville. Green's Opera House in Richmond, Virginia, Harlem Opera House in New York City, and Ford's Opera House in Washington are typical of urban area opera houses. Smaller communities such as Cairo, Illinois, and Franklin, Louisiana, also had opera houses.

Small communities found it economically feasible to have tent theaters erected to entertain African American theater audiences. Not much is known about these "theaters" but they were similar to air domes except that a tent covered the audience and projector and screen. They were probably used in the summertime. Tent theaters were used in Florida, Georgia, Mississippi, Missouri, North Carolina, South Carolina and Texas.

There were also African American drive-in theaters, all in the South. Alabama, Florida, Georgia, North Carolina, South Carolina, Tennessee, and Texas had drive-ins catering to African Americans. Virtually nothing is known about these theaters except that they existed. African American film history books have no information about them, and recent scholarship on drive-ins is likewise silent. It would be interesting to know whether the drive-in theater habits and tastes of African Americans differed from those of other audiences; who managed and owned these drive-ins; and what fate befell the theaters. This is a potential subject for scholarly research.¹⁷

In the days before television, specifically during World War II, there were so-called "newsreel theaters" specializing in or exhibiting newsreels. African American newsreel theaters were located in Long Beach, California; Los Angeles; Chicago, Illinois; and Detroit, Michigan.

African American theaters were sometimes the target of violence. For example, in 1932, whites in Headland, Alabama, forced theater owner Eddie Wilson to close down his African American theater. On December 22, 1921, the Dream Theater in St. Petersburg, Florida, was bombed, ostensibly because the white owner "took trade away from the Jim Crow section of white theaters." In 1921, the Dreamland Theater, operated by Mrs. Lola Williams, was torched during the Tulsa race riot. Mrs. Williams rebuilt and reopened her theater. The Park Theater in Baltimore was seriously damaged during the 1968 riots.

It is likely that other African American theaters experienced similar violence, and while the story of how Mrs. Lola Williams managed to rebuild the Dreamland Theater is documented, we know little if anything about how — and indeed, if — other theater owners rebuilt and reopened their houses. This social history of black theaters remains an fascinating but under-documented subject.¹⁸

Many American architects were involved in the design and construction of African American theaters. A complete list of known architects is presented in Appendix 2. All of the architects are white except one: Isaiah J. Hatton, an African American who designed the second Dunbar Theater in Washington, D.C. Further research into the work of these architects might yield more detailed information about the theaters they designed.

An intriguing fact about African American theaters is how they proliferated throughout the country. Appendix 1 contains a list of the states with the most African American theaters in the period 1900–1955. Texas had the most with a total of 215. Florida is next with 189. North Carolina follows with 157. Georgia had 114, followed closely by Virginia with 113.

The same appendix also has the statistical rankings for cities. New York City (Manhattan, Brooklyn, and the Bronx) tops the list with a total of 60 theaters. Chicago had 49; Detroit, 48; the District of Columbia and Baltimore tied with 34 each; and Philadelphia had 31.

For the period 1909 through 1955, the lowest number of African American theaters counted was 112 in 1909. The peak was 1,072 in 1952. The number of black theaters held steady during the early 1930s and then dropped dramatically to a low of 232 in 1937. The number of theaters increased thereafter until about 1953.

In the 1954 case *Brown v. Board of Education*, the Supreme Court ruled that "the separate but equal doctrine adopted in *Plessy v. Ferguson*, 163 U.S. 537 has no place in the field of public education."¹⁹ This court case signaled the end of *de jure* Jim Crow in the United States.

This did not mean that black theaters went out of existence after 1954. *Film Daily Yearbook* continued to list "Negro theaters" in its 1955 issue but ceased afterward. Probably for legal reasons, the editor chose not to count these theaters separately but instead to include them in the regular roster of theaters noted annually in the *Yearbook*.

Certainly after 1955, black theatergoers could attend the previously all-white theater downtown or continue to attend their own neighborhood theater that was now integrated, at least *de jure*. Because of de facto segregation in housing patterns, however, many "African American theaters" remained African American in audience after 1955. Nevertheless, the special *mission* of the African American theater was gone. Gone was the need for black entrepreneurs to beckon to a black audience in need of their own places of entertainment. Gone was the incentive for black audiences to promote their race loyalty by going to a "black theater." Racial pride could be asserted no matter where one went. Gone was the need for black film producers to exhibit their films in all-black theaters. They now, at least in theory, had access to regular film distribution networks. So the black theater went the way of the "black hospital." Integration eliminated the necessity for these separate black institutions.

The ultimate fate of a number of African American theaters is documented in this book. Most places have been demolished; those that have survived have been renovated for other businesses or boarded up. Several important theaters, particularly the Royal in Philadelphia and the Attucks in Norfolk, have recently been the focus of historic preservationists.[20] Lack of information about the history of African American theater buildings, lack of capital in the African American community, and lack of interest in historic preservation are some of the reasons why these buildings have not been restored.

African American theater buildings are a fascinating but overlooked legacy in our country's cultural heritage. Their walls echo with the performances of many prominent and lesser known entertainers. The buildings were often owned and managed by leaders in the black community. The theaters were truly centers of black community life in the early twentieth century. Their history is worth learning about. I hope that this reference book will help readers discover that special cultural tradition in their town called an "African American theater."

Notes

1. *Plessy v. Ferguson*, 163 U.S. 537 (1896) 163 U.S. 537.
2. Pearl Bowser and Louise Spence, *Writing Himself into History: Oscar Micheaux, His Silent Films, and His Audiences* (New Brunswick, N.J.: Rutgers University Press, 2002): 61.
3. *Philadelphia Tribune*, "Stanley Theater Regrets Insult to Hon. J.C. Asbury," March 12, 1921.
4. Mary Carbine, "The Finest Outside the Loop: Motion Picture Exhibition in Chicago's Black Metropolis, 1905–1928," *Camera Obscura* 23 (May 1990): 18.
5. Bowser and Spence, 63.
6. Henry T. Sampson, *Blacks in Blackface: A Source Book on Early Black Musical Shows* (Metuchen, N.J.: Scarecrow, 1980): 115.
7. Athella Knight, "In Retrospect: Sherman H. Dudley: He Paved the Way for T.O.B.A.," *The Black Perspective in Music* 15 no. 2 (Fall 1987): 173.
8. *Indianapolis Freeman*, December 28, 1912. Cited in Knight, 161.
9. Henry T. Sampson, *Blacks in Black and White: A Source Book on Black Films*, second edition (Lanham, Md.: Scarecrow, 1995): 7.
10. Bowser, 27. Sampson's *Blacks in Black and White* has an appendix giving a list of "individuals and corporations organized to produce black-cast films between 1919 and 1950."
11. *Atlanta Daily World*, December 13, 1919. Cited in Bowser, 63.
12. *Philadelphia Tribune*, February 15, 1919.
13. *Lexington [Kentucky] Leader*, November 30, 1907. Cited in Gregory A. Waller, *Main Street Amusements: Movies and Commercial Entertainment in a Southern City, 1896–1930* (Washington, D.C.: Smithsonian Institution Press, 1995): 169.
14. *Chicago Defender*, "Race Operator for Douglass Theater," November 21, 1925.
15. Maggie Valentine, *The Show Starts on the Sidewalk: An Architectural History of the*

Movie Theater, Starring S. Charles Lee (New Haven: Yale University Press, 1994): 22.

16. Valentine, 26.

17. For an excellent discussion of the history of the drive-in see Kerry Segrave, *Drive-in Theaters: A History from Their Inception in 1933* (Jefferson, N.C.: McFarland, 1992).

18. Bowser, 80–81; Alfred L. Brophy, *Reconstructing the Dreamland: The Tulsa Riot of 1921: Race, Reparations, and Reconciliation* (Oxford: Oxford University Press, 2002).

19. *Brown v. Board of Education*, 347 U.S. 483 (1954).

20. See, for example, Kendall Wilson, "Royal Theater Gets Federal Boost," *Philadelphia Tribune,* September 19, 2000.

ALABAMA

Abbeville

1. CARVER THEATER
Picture house.
References: *Film Daily Yearbook,* 1952–1955.

Alexander City

2. PEOPLES THEATER
Picture house.
References: *Film Daily Yearbook,* 1930–1933, 1947, 1948, 1949.

3. REX THEATER
Picture house.
References: *Film Daily Yearbook,* 1950–1955.

Anniston

4. GEM THEATER
517–519 W. 15th Street
Picture house. Manager in 1945: Alfred A. Burrell.
References: *Film Daily Yearbook,* 1945–1955.

5. NEW QUEEN THEATER
504 W. 15th Street
Vaudeville house. A TOBA theater. Owner in 1924: S. J. Reaves. It had a poolroom. The New Queen may well be the TOBA theater in Anniston that Ethel Waters played.
References: Cahn, *Julius Cahn-Gus Hill Theatrical Guide.* Hill, *Pages from the Harlem Renaissance.* Jackson, "List of Colored Theaters and Attractions," *Billboard,* August 6, 1921; "The Theater Owners' Booking Association," *Billboard,* December 16, 1922. Work, *Negro Yearbook, 1921–1922.* Waters, *His Eye Is on the Sparrow.*

6. STAR THEATER
Picture house.
References: *Film Daily Yearbook,* 1930–1933.

Auburn

7. COLORED HIGH SCHOOL THEATER
Picture house.
References: *Film Daily Yearbook,* 1930, 1931.

Bessemer

8. FAIRYLAND THEATER
Vaudeville house.
References: Cahn, *Julius Cahn-Gus Hill Theatrical Guide.* Jackson, "List of Colored Theaters and Attractions," *Billboard,* August 6, 1921. Work, *Negro Yearbook, 1921–1922.*

9. FROLIC THEATER
1914 1st Avenue
Vaudeville and picture house. 250–400 seats. Manager in 1924: Frank Stallworth. Manager in 1928: Ben Jaffee. A TOBA theater. Bessie Smith performed here in 1925. In October 1926, the Frolic offered a vaudeville bill consisting of Maggie Jones, Sledge and Sledge, and Hampton

and Hampton. The Frolic may have been the Bessemer theater that Ethel Waters mentions in her autobiography.

References: Albertson, *Bessie*. *Baltimore Afro-American*, October 31, 1926. *Film Daily Yearbook*, 1930–1932, 1940–1955. Jackson, "The Theater Owners Booking Association," *Billboard*, December 16, 1922. *Motion Picture Herald*, April 24, 1937; July 15, 1939. Peterson, *The African American Theatre Directory*. Sampson, *Blacks in Black and White; Blacks in Blackface. Official Theatrical World of Colored Artists*. Waters, *His Eye Is on the Sparrow*.

10. LINCOLN THEATER
1928 1st Street
Picture house. Manager in 1955: Sam J. Raine.
References: *Film Daily Yearbook*, 1950–1955.

11. NEW DIXIE THEATER
Picture house. Owner in 1921: W.J. Lovely.
References: Jackson, "List of Colored Theaters and Attractions," *Billboard*, August 6, 1921. Work, *Negro Yearbook, 1921–1922*.

12. STAR THEATER
221 N. 19th Street
Picture house. Manager in 1955: John C. Harwell.
References: *Film Daily Yearbook*, 1950–1955.

Birmingham

13. BIRMINGHAM THEATER
1817 N. 3rd Street
Picture house. Manager in 1952: R. Norris Hadaway.
References: *Film Daily Yearbook*, 1949–1955.

14. CARVER THEATER
322 N. 17th Street
Picture house. 469 seats. President in 1941: Fred Levi.
References: *Film Daily Yearbook*, 1943–1955.

15. CHAMPION THEATER
306 N. 18th Street
Picture house. 750 seats. Managers in 1921: Nathaniel Pressly and P.A. Engler. Owners in 1921: Gay Theater Properties, H. J. Hury. According to Chambers, in 1921 the house personnel consisted of Nathaniel Pressly, house manager, Money Gilreatii, assistant manager, James Lyon on piano, and Clarence White on drums. The theater showed feature pictures and serials. The Champion was located on the old site of the Frolic theater.
References: Cahn. *Julius Cahn-Gus Hill Theatrical Guide*. Chambers, "Colored Theaters in Birmingham, Alabama," *Billboard*, December 16, 1922. *Film Daily Yearbook*, 1930–1933, 1940–1955. Jackson, "List of Colored Theaters and Attractions," *Billboard*, August 6, 1921; "The Theater Owners Booking Association," *Billboard*, December 16, 1922. *Motion Picture Herald*, April 24, 1937; July 15, 1939. Work, *Negro Yearbook, 1921–1922*. Sampson, *Blacks in Black and White*.

16. DIXIE THEATER
Picture house.
References: *Film Daily Yearbook*, 1930–1932.

17. EIGHTH AVENUE THEATER
211 8th Avenue
Picture house. 652 seats. Manager in 1952: Willie Brown.
References: *Film Daily Yearbook*, 1945, 1947–1955.

18. FAMOUS THEATER
1717 N. 4th Street

Carver Theater, Birmingham, Alabama (SoulOfAmerica.com)

Picture and vaudeville house. 450 seats. Owner in 1922: P. A. Engler. According to Chambers, this theater was "owned by P. A. Engler (white) with a colored working staff."

References: Chambers, "Colored Theaters in Birmingham, Alabama," *Billboard*, December 16, 1922. *Film Daily Yearbook*, 1930–1933, 1940–1955. *Motion Picture Herald*, April 24, 1937; July 15, 1939. Sampson, *Blacks in Black and White*.

19. FROLIC THEATER
312–14 N. 18th Avenue
Vaudeville and picture house. 850 seats. Manager in 1921: P. A. Engler. Owner in 1921: Gay Theater Properties. Manager in 1928: H. J. Hury. A TOBA theater. According to Chambers, of the three black theaters in Birmingham — Famous, Champion, and Frolic — the Frolic "caters to the best of people." It boasts "a five-piece orchestra under the direction of Prof. Henry Callin (piano). The other members [of the group] are Walter Young, Shead Harris, Fred Moore, and John Ovelton. R. B. (Happy) Brown is stage manager." Blues singer Bessie Smith was here in 1923 and in 1925 blues singer Ma Rainey sang here. In 1927 Seals and Mitchell's Melody Lane Girls performed at the Frolic.

References: Albertson, *Bessie*. Bowser, *Writing Himself into History*. Chambers, "Colored Theaters in Birmingham, Alabama," *Billboard*, December 16, 1922. *Chicago Defender*, Chambers, "Frolic Theater," July 31, 1926; "Doings at the Frolic," October 2, 1927. Cahn, *Julius Cahn-Gus Hill Theatrical Guide. Film Daily Yearbook*, 1930, 1943–1955. Jackson, "List of Colored Theaters and Attractions," *Billboard*, August 6, 1921; "The Theater Owners' Booking Association," *Billboard*, December 16, 1922. Hill, *Pages from the Harlem Renaissance. Official Theatrical World of Colored Artists.* Work, *Negro Yearbook, 1921–1922*.

20. GAY THEATER
1722 N. 4th Avenue
Vaudeville house. A TOBA theater. Owner: H. J. Hury and Gay Theater Properties. The Kid Thomas Company played here in April 1921. The Gay might be one of the three Birmingham theaters mentioned in Ethel Waters's autobiography.

References: Cahn, *Julius Cahn-Gus Hill Theatrical Guide*. Jackson, "List of Colored Theaters and Attractions," *Billboard*, August 6, 1921. Work, *Negro Yearbook, 1921–1922*. Peterson, *The African American Theatre Directory*. Waters, *His Eye Is on the Sparrow*.

21. GRAND THEATER
1520 N. 4th Street
Picture house. 350 seats. Manager in 1941: Wilbert M. Kelly.

References: *Film Daily Yearbook*, 1940–1944. *Motion Picture Herald*, July 15, 1939.

22. PIKE THEATER
Picture house.
References: *Film Daily Yearbook*, 1943, 1944.

23. QUEEN THEATER
Vaudeville house. Manager in 1921: W. Savage. In 1922, Chambers reported that "some few years back the Queen, a vaudeville house, educated this city with smut. The management used barrel-house acts and the better class of colored folks did not patronize this house. But the fight for clean entertainment has been won and [today] acts playing the Queen have to come clean or stay away."

References: *Billboard*, August 8, 1921. Cahn, *Julius Cahn-Gus Hill Theatrical*

8th Avenue Theater, Birmingham, Alabama, 1999 (photograph © Martin McCaffery)

Guide. Chambers, "Colored Theaters in Birmingham, Alabama," *Billboard*, December 16, 1922. Work: *Negro Yearbook, 1921–1922.*

Camden

24. GEM THEATER
    Picture house.
    References: *Film Daily Yearbook*, 1940.

Camp Hill

25. CROWN THEATER
    Main Street
    Picture house. 252 seats.
    References: *Film Daily Yearbook*, 1949–1955.

Decatur

26. ELITE THEATER
    Picture house.
    References: *Film Daily Yearbook*, 1950 1954.

27. GALAX THEATER
    Picture house.
    References: *Film Daily Yearbook*, 1930–1932.

28. SYKES THEATER
    Picture house. Manager in 1921: Mr. Sykes (African American).
    References: Jackson, "List of Colored Theaters and Attractions," *Billboard*, August 6, 1921. Work: *Negro Yearbook, 1921–1922.*

Dothan

29. CARVER THEATER
    State Street
    Picture house. 500 seats.
    References: *Film Daily Yearbook*, 1947–1955.

30. DOTHAN THEATER
    Picture house.
    References: *Film Daily Yearbook*, 1930–1932.

Ensley

31. PALACE THEATER
    1810 D Avenue
    Vaudeville and picture house. 400–500 seats. A TOBA theater. Owner in 1928: Milton Starr. Manager in 1928: R. V. Rhinehart. In 1928 Milton Starr purchased it for $50,000. Bessie Smith played the Ensley.
    References: *Chicago Defender*, "New Theater," January 28, 1928. *Film Daily Yearbook*, 1930–1932, 1940–1954. *Motion Picture Herald*, July 15, 1939. *Official Theatrical World of Colored Artists*. Waters, *His Eye Is on the Sparrow*.

Fairfield

32. MILES THEATER
    5228 Commerce Avenue
    Picture house.
    References: *Film Daily Yearbook*, 1944–1955.

Fayette

33. RICHARDS THEATER
    Picture house. 350 seats.
    References: *Film Daily Yearbook*, 1949–1955.

Florence

34. BESSIE THEATER
    Picture house. Owner in 1921: Mrs. Bessie Foster (African American).
    References: Cahn, *Julius Cahn-Gus Hill Theatrical Guide*. Jackson, "List of Colored Theaters and Attractions," *Billboard*, August 6, 1921. Work, *Negro Yearbook, 1921–1922*.

35. RIALTO MUSICAL SHOW THEATER
    Musical house. Owner in 1921: J. J. Dunn.
    References: Work, *Negro Yearbook, 1921–1922*.

36. WILSON DAM THEATER
    Picture house.
    References: Cahn, *Julius Cahn-Gus Hill Theatrical Guide*. Jackson, "List of Colored Theaters and Attractions," *Billboard*, August 6, 1921. Work, *Negro Yearbook, 1921–1922*.

Fort Deposit

37. FORT DEPOSIT THEATER
    Picture house.
    References: *Film Daily Yearbook*, 1949–1955.

Gadsden

38. BAKER THEATER
    Vaudeville house.
    References: Work, *Negro Yearbook, 1921–1922*.

39. CARVER THEATER
    113 N. 6th Street
    Picture house. 475 seats.
    References: *Film Daily Yearbook*, 1947–1955.

40. DIXIE THEATER

Picture house.
References: *Film Daily Yearbook*, 1930–1932.

41. GEM THEATER
Picture house. 300 seats.
References: *Film Daily Yearbook*, 1940–1955. *Motion Picture Herald*, July 15, 1939.

42. QUEEN THEATER
Picture house. Owner in 1921: J. Elson.
References: Cahn, *Julius Cahn-Gus Hill Theatrical Guide*. Jackson, "List of Colored Theaters and Attractions," *Billboard*, August 6, 1921. Work, *Negro Yearbook, 1921–1922*.

Greenville

43. PALACE THEATER
Picture house. 200 seats.
References: *Film Daily Yearbook*, 1940–1947. *Motion Picture Herald*, April 24, 1937; July 15, 1939. Sampson, *Blacks in Black and White*.

Huntsville

44. COLORED THEATER
Picture house. Owner: Eddie Wilson. "In 1932, traveling showman Eddie Wilson built a theater in the Crattix quarter of Headland, Alabama, but was quickly forced out by whites."
References: Bowser, *Writing Himself into History*.

45. PHOTO THEATER
Picture house. Said to be white owned, black managed.
References: Cahn, *Julius Cahn-Gus Hill Theatrical Guide*. Jackson, "List of Colored Theaters and Attractions," *Billboard*, August 6, 1921. Work, *Negro Yearbook, 1921–1922*.

46. PICTO THEATER
Picture house.
References: *Film Daily Yearbook*, 1930–1932.

47. PRINCESS THEATER
Church Street
Picture house. 340 seats.
References: *Film Daily Yearbook*, 1940–1955. *Motion Picture Herald*, July 15, 1939.

48. REGAL DRIVE-IN
Picture house.
References: *Film Daily Yearbook*, 1952–1955.

Hurtsboro

49. GAY THEATER
Picture house. The Gay was listed closed in the 1949, 1950, and 1951 editions of *Film Daily Yearbook*.
References: *Film Daily Yearbook*, 1947–1948, 1952–1955.

Jackson

50. DIXIE THEATER
Picture house.
References: *Film Daily Yearbook*, 1930–1932.

Lanett

51. VALLEY DRIVE-IN
Picture house. 300 cars. Owner: T.W. Petray.
References: *Film Daily Yearbook*. 1952–1955.

Mobile

52. BOOKER T. THEATER
Davis Avenue and Belsaw Street
Picture house. 1,026 seats.

References: *Film Daily Yearbook*, 1947–1955.

53. GAYETY THEATER
Picture house. The Gayety was reported as white owned and Black managed.
References: Cahn, *Julius Cahn-Gus Hill Theatrical Guide*. Jackson, "List of Colored Theaters and Attractions," *Billboard*, August 6, 1921. Work, *Negro Yearbook, 1921–1922*.

54. HARLEM THEATER
650 Selma Avenue
Picture house. 600 seats. Manager in 1949: Charles B. Jones.
References: *Film Daily Yearbook*, 1947–1955.

55. LINCOLN THEATER
900 Selma Avenue
Picture house. 600–750 seats. Owner in 1949: Charles B. Jones.
References: *Film Daily Yearbook*, 1940–1955. *Motion Picture Herald*, July 15, 1939.

56. NEW THEATER
Picture house.
References: *Film Daily Yearbook*, 1942.

57. PIKE THEATER
256 Davis Avenue
Vaudeville house. 856 seats. Manager in 1921: C. C. Schreiner. Managers in 1922: J. H. King and C. B. King. Manager in 1928: C. B. King. The theater was originally part of the Southern Consolidated Circuit and later joined the newly reorganized TOBA circuit. In April, 1921, the vaudeville show featured the Willie Toosweet Company.
References: Cahn, *Julius Cahn-Gus Hill Theatrical Guide*. *Chicago Defender*, "Pike Theater," February 18, 1928; "Pike Theater," February 25, 1928; "Pike Theater," March 10, 1928, "Pike Theater," March 24, 1928. *Film Daily Yearbook*, 1930–1933, 1940–1955. Hill, *Pages from the Harlem Renaissance*. Jackson, "List of Colored Theaters and Attractions," *Billboard*, August 6, 1921; "The Theater Owners Booking Association," December 16, 1922. *Motion Picture Herald*, April 24, 1937; July 15, 1939. *Official Theatrical World of Colored Artists*. Peterson, *The African American Theatre Directory*. Sampson, *Blacks in Black and White*. Work, *Negro Yearbook, 1921–1922*.

58. SKY KING
Picture house. The Sky King was listed as closed in the 1949, 1950, and 1951 editions of *Film Daily Yearbook*.
References: *Film Daily Yearbook*, 1947, 1952–1955.

59. WASHINGTON THEATER
Picture house.
References: *Film Daily Yearbook*, 1947, 1948.

Monroeville

60. BAMBOO THEATER
Picture house. The Bamboo was listed as closed in the 1950 and 1951 editions of *Film Daily Yearbook*.
References: *Film Daily Yearbook*, 1949–1955.

Montgomery

61. ART THEATER
Picture house.
References: *Film Daily Yearbook*, 1952–1955.

62. CARVER THEATER
620 S. Holt Street
Picture house. 590 seats. Manager in 1954: Charles G. Stokes.
References: *Film Daily Yearbook*, 1945–1955.

63. GEM THEATER
W. Jefferson Davis and W. Hannon Streets
Picture house. In December 1927, "Holmes and his Peacock Track Strutters were the headline attractions with a company of ten performers and a nice four-piece jazz orchestra."
References: *Chicago Defender*, "Phil Dorsey Says," December 3, 1927. *Film Daily Yearbook*, 1930–1932.

64. MAJESTIC THEATER
212 Bibb Street
Vaudeville house. Manager in 1921: M. Barkett.
References: Cahn, *Julius Cahn-Gus Hill Theatrical Guide*. Hill, *Pages from the Harlem Renaissance*. Jackson, "List of Colored Theaters and Attractions," *Billboard*, August 6, 1921; "The Theater Owners Booking Association," December 16, 1922. Simms, *Simms' Blue Book*. Work, *Negro Yearbook, 1921–1922*.

65. PEKIN THEATER
30 N. Lawrence Street
Picture house. 825 seats. Owner in 1921: S. Baum. Manager in 1922: J. A. English (African American).
References: Cahn, *Julius Cahn-Gus Hill Theatrical Guide*. *Chicago Defender*, "Pekin Theater," February 12, 1927. *Film Daily Yearbook*, 1930–1933, 1940–1955. Jackson, "List of Colored Theaters and Attractions," *Billboard*, August 6, 1921. *Motion Picture Herald*, April 24, 1937; July 15, 1939. Sampson, *Blacks in Black and White*. Simms, *Simms' Blue Book*.

66. RITZ THEATER
5 Coosa Street
Picture house. Manager in 1954: Leon Long.
References: *Film Daily Yearbook*, 1930–1932, 1940–1955. *Motion Picture Herald*, July 15, 1939.

67. STATE THEATER
155 Highland Street
Picture house. 375 seats.
References: *Film Daily Yearbook*, 1942–1955.

North Birmingham

68. DUNBAR THEATER
Picture house.
References: *Film Daily Yearbook*, 1930–1932.

Opelika

69. DREAMLAND THEATER
Vaudeville house. The Dreamland is reported as managed by blacks.
References: Hill, *Pages from the Harlem Renaissance*. Peterson, *The African American Theatre Directory*.

70. GEORGIA–ALABAMA THEATER
Picture house. 200 seats. Also known as the Ga-Ala.
References: *Film Daily Yearbook*, 1940. *Motion Picture Herald*, April 24, 1937; July 15, 1939. Sampson, *Blacks in Black and White*.

Phoenix City

71. RAMONA THEATER
Picture house.
References: *Film Daily Yearbook*, 1951–1955.

Piedmont

72. PRINCESS THEATER
Centre Street
Picture house. 240 seats.
References: *Film Daily Yearbook*, 1949–1955.

18 Alabama

Pekin Theater, Montgomery, Alabama, 1986 (photograph © Martin McCaffrey)

Plateau

References: *Film Daily Yearbook*, 1930–1932.

73. WASHINGTON THEATER
Picture house.

Alabama 19

State Theater, Montgomery, Alabama, 1995 (photograph © Martin McCaffrey)

Pritchard

74. CARVER THEATER
Picture house.
References: *Film Daily Yearbook*, 1945–1955.

75. GEM THEATER
Wilson Avenue and Railroad Street
Picture house. 525 seats.
References: *Film Daily Yearbook*, 1943–1955.

Selma

76. ROXY THEATER
1200–1222 Broad Street
Picture house. 300 seats. Manager in 1947: David R. Regan.
References: *Film Daily Yearbook*, 1943–1955.

Sheffield

77. CARVER THEATER
Picture house. 500 seats.
References: *Film Daily Yearbook*, 1950–1955.

78. FIELDS THEATER
Vaudeville and picture house. Manager in 1921: Elijah. N. Fields (African American).
References: Cahn, *Julius Cahn-Gus Hill Theatrical Guide.* Jackson, "List of Colored Theaters and Attractions," *Billboard*,

August 6, 1921. Work, *Negro Yearbook, 1921–1922*.

79. RIALTO THEATER
Picture house. Owner and manager in 1921: J. J. Dunn.
References: Work, *Negro Yearbook, 1921–1922*.

Talladega

80. COLLEGE THEATER
Picture house.
References: *Film Daily Yearbook*, 1930–1932.

81. LIBERTY THEATER
Picture house.
References: Cahn, *Julius Cahn-Gus Hill Theatrical Guide*. Jackson, "List of Colored Theaters and Attractions," *Billboard*, August 6, 1921. Work, *Negro Yearbook, 1921–1922*.

Troy

82. DREAMLAND THEATER
Picture house.
References: Cahn, *Julius Cahn-Gus Hill Theatrical Guide*. Jackson, "List of Colored Theaters and Attractions," *Billboard*, August 6, 1921. Work, *Negro Yearbook, 1921–1922*.

Tuscaloosa

83. ACE THEATER
Picture house.
References: *Film Daily Yearbook*, 1947, 1948.

84. DIAMOND THEATER
23rd Avenue
Picture house. 500 seats.
References: *Film Daily Yearbook*, 1940–1955. *Motion Picture Herald*, July 15, 1939.

85. STAR THEATER
Picture house.
References: *Film Daily Yearbook*, 1930–1932.

Tuskegee

86. EIGHTY DRIVE-IN
Picture house.
References: *Film Daily Yearbook*, 1950–1955.

87. LINCOLN DRIVE-IN
Picture house. 250 cars. Owner: ABC Theatrical Enterprises.
References: *Film Daily Yearbook*, 1952–1955.

88. MACON THEATER
North Side Street
Picture house. 772 seats.
References: *Film Daily Yearbook*, 1940–1955. *Motion Picture Herald*, July 15, 1939.

89. TUSKEGEE INSTITUTE THEATER
Picture house.
References: *Film Daily Yearbook*, 1931–1933.

ARIZONA

Phoenix

90. RAMONA THEATER
Picture house. 800 seats.

References: *Film Daily Yearbook*, 1947–1955.

ARKANSAS

Arkadelphia

91. WEST END THEATER
Picture house. Owner in 1921: M. C. Smith.
References: Cahn, *Julius Cahn-Gus Hill Theatrical Guide*. Jackson, "List of Colored Theaters and Attractions," *Billboard*, August 6, 1921. Work, *Negro Yearbook, 1921–1922*.

Blythville

92. DIXIE THEATER
Picture house.
References: *Film Daily Yearbook*, 1930–1933.

93. SAVOY THEATER
Picture house.
References: *Film Daily Yearbook*, 1947–1955.

Camden

94. CIRCLE THEATER
Picture house. According to the *Film Daily Yearbook*, the Circle was closed from 1949 1951.
References: *Film Daily Yearbook*, 1947–1955.

95. HARLEM THEATER
Picture house. The Harlem was closed from 1949 to through 1951 according to the *Film Daily Yearbook*.
References: *Film Daily Yearbook*, 1949–1955.

Cotton Plant

96. JAMES THEATER
917 Main Street
Picture house. 342 seats.

References: *Film Daily Yearbook*, 1949–1955.

Crawfordsville

97. GAY THEATER
Picture house. 205 seats. The Gay was closed from 1949 to 1955 according to the *Film Daily Yearbook*.
References: *Film Daily Yearbook*, 1947–1955.

Earle

98. SAVOY THEATER
Picture house.
References: *Film Daily Yearbook*, 1949–1955.

El Dorado

99. FAIRVIEW THEATER
Picture house.
References: *Film Daily Yearbook*, 1930–1933.

100. SAVOY THEATER
Picture house. 350 seats.
References: *Film Daily Yearbook*, 1949–1955.

101. STAR THEATER
Picture house.
References: *Film Daily Yearbook*, 1946–1955.

Forest City

102. HARLEM THEATER
106 N. Rosser Street
Picture house. 285 seats.
References: *Film Daily Yearbook*, 1942–1955.

Fort Smith

103. TEMPLE THEATER
11th and B Streets
Picture house. 870 seats. It is possible that the Temple was the unnamed theater listed in the 1921 *Billboard* survey.
References: Cahn, *Julius Cahn-Gus Hill Theatrical Guide*. Jackson, "List of Colored Theaters and Attractions," *Billboard*, August 6, 1921. Work, *Negro Yearbook, 1921–1922*.

Greenville

104. LIBERTY THEATER
Vaudeville house. The Liberty was on the combined TOBA and Managers and Performers vaudeville CIRCUITS.
References: Hill, *Pages from the Harlem Renaissance*. Jackson, "The Theater Owners' Booking Association," *Billboard*, December 16, 1922. Peterson, *The African American Theatre Directory*.

Helena

105. MRS. WILLIAMS' THEATER
Picture house.
References: *Film Daily Yearbook*, 1931–1933.

106. PLAZA THEATER
116 Walnut Street
Picture house. 408 seats. Manager in 1921: Mrs. E. A. Miller (African American). References: Cahn, *Julius Cahn-Gus Hill Theatrical Guide. Film Daily Yearbook, 1940*–1955. Jackson, "List of Colored Theaters and Attractions," *Billboard*, August 6, 1921. *Motion Picture Herald*, April 24, 1937; July 15, 1939. Murray, *Negro Handbook*. Work, *Negro Yearbook, 1921–1922*. Sampson, *Blacks in Black and White*.

Hope

107. COMMUNITY THEATER
Picture house. Owner in 1921: A. E. Rankin.
References: Cahn, *Julius Cahn-Gus Hill Theatrical Guide*. Jackson, "List of Colored Theaters and Attractions," *Billboard*, August 6, 1921. Work, *Negro Yearbook, 1921–1922*.

108. PALACE THEATER
Picture house.
References: *Film Daily Yearbook*, 1947–1955.

Hot Springs

109. GEM THEATER
Vaudeville house. A TOBA theater. Manager in 1928: Stanley Lee.
References: *Official Theatrical World of Colored Artists*.

110. MAJESTIC THEATER
473 Willington Avenue
Vaudeville house. Manager in 1921: B. C. Trueman. (African American).
References: Cahn, *Julius Cahn-Gus Hill Theatrical Guide*. Hill, *Pages from the Harlem Renaissance*. Jackson, "Additions to Theater List," *Billboard*, December 31, 1921. Work, *Negro Yearbook, 1921–1922*.

111. TRUMAN THEATER
Vaudeville house. A TOBA theater. It is not known whether the unnamed Hot Springs theater referred to in the 1921 *Billboard* survey was actually the Truman.
Source: Hill, *Pages from the Harlem Renaissance*. Jackson, "List of Colored Theaters and Attractions," *Billboard*, August 6, 1921; "The Theater Owners' Booking Association," *Billboard*, December 16, 1922.

112. VENDOME THEATER
423 Malvern Avenue
Vaudeville house. A TOBA theater. Manager in 1923: R. A. Elliott. The Roscoe Montella Company played there in 1926.
References: *Baltimore Afro-American*, October 31, 1926. Peterson, *The African American Theatre Directory*. Sampson, *Blacks in Blackface*.

113. WILSON'S AIRDOME THEATER
Guelpha Street
Picture house. Also called the Airdome. Manager in 1921: Lucien Wilson (African American).
References: Cahn, *Julius Cahn-Gus Hill Theatrical Guide*. Jackson, "Additions to Theater List," *Billboard*, December 21, 1921.

Hughes

114. BEALE STREET THEATER
Railroad Street
Picture house. 250 seats.
References: *Film Daily Yearbook*, 1946–1955.

Little Rock

115. ARGANTA THEATER
Picture house.
References: *Film Daily Yearbook*, 1931–1933.

116. GEM THEATER
712 W. 9th Street
Picture house. 632 seats.
References: *Film Daily Yearbook*, 1941–1955. *Motion Picture Herald*, April 24, 1937; July 15, 1939. Sampson, *Blacks in Black and White*.

117. PLAZA THEATER
712 W. 9th Street
Vaudeville house. Manager in 1921: M. A. Lightman. A TOBA theater. In April 1921 the vaudeville Fisher's Fun Festival

headed the bill. In 1927, "Harry Hunt and George Murray's 'Sugarfoot Greene from New Orleans' closed a 24-week tour at the Plaza Theatre," according to the *Chicago Defender*.

References: Cahn, *Julius Cahn-Gus Hill Theatrical Guide*. *Chicago Defender*, "Sugarfoot Greene Co. Closes," December 3, 1927. *Film Daily Yearbook*, 1930. Hill, *Pages from the Harlem Renaissance*. Jackson, "List of Colored Theaters and Attractions," *Billboard*, August 6, 1921; "The Theater Owners' Booking Association," *Billboard*, December 16, 1922. Work, *Negro Yearbook, 1921–1922*.

Magnolia

118. RITZ THEATER
   Picture house. 400 seats.
   References: *Film Daily Yearbook*, 1948–1955.

Malvern

119. DIXIE THEATER
   401 E. First Street
   Picture house. Owner and manager in 1921: Virgil Calhoun.
   References: Cahn, *Julius Cahn-Gus Hill Theatrical Guide*. Jackson, "List of Colored Theaters and Attractions," *Billboard*, August 6, 1921. Work, *Negro Yearbook, 1921–1922*.

120. RIO THEATER
   Picture house.
   References: *Film Daily Yearbook*, 1948–1955.

Marianna

121. BLUE HEAVEN THEATER
   Chestnut Street
   Picture house. 400 seats.
   References: *Film Daily Yearbook*, 1942–1955.

Newport

122. HARLEM THEATER
   Picture house. 450 seats.
   References: *Film Daily Yearbook*, 1947–1955.

North Little Rock

123. RITZ THEATER
   Picture house.
   References: *Film Daily Yearbook*, 1942.

Osceola

124. GEM THEATER
   Picture house. 600 seats.
   References: *Film Daily Yearbook*, 1950–1955.

125. JOY THEATER
   Picture house. 200 seats.
   References: *Film Daily Yearbook*, 1949–1955.

Pine Bluff

126. ENTERPRISE THEATER
   Picture house. Manager in 1921: Enterprise Amusement Company. Owner in 1921: J. M. Rhone (African American).
   References: Cahn, *Julius Cahn-Gus Hill Theatrical Guide*. Jackson, "Additions to Theater List," *Billboard*, December 31, 1921. Work, *Negro Yearbook, 1921–1922*.

127. VESTER THEATER
   122 E. 22nd Street
   Picture house. 370 seats.
   References: *Film Daily Yearbook*, 1940–

1955. *Motion Picture Herald*, July 15, 1939.

Prescott

128. COMMUNITY THEATER
Picture house. Owner in 1921: E. A. Rankin.
References: Cahn, *Julius Cahn-Gus Hill Theatrical Guide*. Jackson, "List of Colored Theaters and Attractions," *Billboard*, August 6, 1921. Work, *Negro Yearbook, 1921–1922*.

Proctor

129. STRONG CIRCUIT THEATER
Picture house.
References: *Film Daily Yearbook*, 1949–1955.

Scotland

130. GREEN RIVER THEATER
Picture house.
References: *Film Daily Yearbook*, 1930–1933.

Smackover

131. COLORADO THEATER
Picture house.
References: *Film Daily Yearbook*, 1930–1933.

Stamps

132. DREAMLAND THEATER
Picture house.
References: *Film Daily Yearbook*, 1930–1933.

Stuttgart

133. INTERSTATE THEATER
N. Maple Street
Picture house. Also known as the Strand. 450 seats. Owner in 1921: G. F. Brown. References: Cahn, *Julius Cahn-Gus Hill Theatrical Guide*. Jackson, "List of Colored Theaters and Attractions," *Billboard*, August 6, 1921. Work, *Negro Yearbook, 1921–1922*.

Texarkana

134. BOOKER T. WASHINGTON THEATER
1311 Laurel Street
Vaudeville house. 500 seats. Manager in 1921: James S. Douglas (African American). The Booker T was the unnamed theater listed in the 1921 *Billboard* survey.
References: Cahn, *Julius Cahn-Gus Hill Theatrical Guide*. Hill, *Pages from the Harlem Renaisance*. Jackson, "List of Colored Theaters and Attractions," *Billboard*, August 6, 1921. Peterson, *The African American Theatre Directory*. Work, *Negro Yearbook, 1921–1922*.

135. COMMUNITY THEATER
Picture house. Manager in 1921: A. E. Rankin.
References: Cahn, *Julius Cahn-Gus Hill Theatrical Guide*. Jackson, "List of Colored Theaters and Attractions," *Billboard*, August 6, 1921. Work, *Negro Yearbook, 1921–1922*.

136. DREAMLAND THEATER
Picture house.
References: Hill, *Pages from the Harlem Renaissance*. Jackson, "The Theater Owners' Booking Association," *Billboard*, December 16, 1922. Peterson, *The African American Theatre Directory*.

Turrell

137. HARLEM THEATER
Picture house.
References: *Film Daily Yearbook,* 1947–1955.

138. TURRELL THEATER
Picture house.
References: *Film Daily Yearbook,* 1930, 1931.

Warren

139. PALACE THEATER
Picture house.
References: *Film Daily Yearbook,* 1930–1933.

140. REX THEATER
Picture house. According to *Film Daily Yearbook,* the Rex was closed from 1949 to 1951.
References: *Film Daily Yearbook,* 1949–1955.

West Helena

141. BLAIR'S THEATER
Picture house.
References: *Film Daily Yearbook,* 1941–1955.

142. JUG THEATER
Picture house.
References: *Film Daily Yearbook,* 1949–1955.

143. SILVER STAR THEATER
Picture house.
References: *Film Daily Yearbook,* 1949–1954.

West Memphis

144. HARLEM THEATER
Broadway and 9th Street
Picture house. 405 seats.
References: *Film Daily Yearbook,* 1946–1955.

CALIFORNIA

Bakerfield

145. VIRGINIA THEATER
Picture house. 450 seats.
References: *Film Daily Yearbook,* 1950–1955.

146. VISTA THEATER
Picture house.
References: *Film Daily Yearbook,* 1950–1955.

Fresno

147. BIJOU THEATER
Picture house.
References: *Film Daily Yearbook,* 1930–1932.

148. LYCEUM THEATER
Picture house.
References: *Film Daily Yearbook*, 1930–1932.

149. RYAN THEATER
1437 Tulave Street
Picture house. 400 seats.
References: *Film Daily Yearbook*, 1930–1932, 1947–1948, 1950–1955.

Long Beach

150. NEWSREEL THEATER
Picture house.
References: *Film Daily Yearbook*, 1947, 1948.

151. TRACY THEATER
Picture house.
References: *Film Daily Yearbook*, 1947, 1948.

Los Angeles

152. AILENA THEATER
Picture house. 700 seats.
References: *Film Daily Yearbook*, 1949–1955.

153. AVALON THEATER
5244 S. Park
Picture house. 400 seats.
References: *Film Daily Yearbook*, 1947–1955.

154. BARBARA THEATER
Picture house.
References: *Film Daily Yearbook*, 1947, 1948.

155. BILL ROBINSON THEATER
4219 S. Central Avenue
Picture and musical house. 850 seats. Also known as the Tivoli. According to Bette Cox, "one advertisement mentions Alton Redd and his band performing at the Tivoli." Musician Marshall Royal recalls that "I used to play there in my younger days…We'd have a six-piece band on stage at the Bill Robinson Theater just as a Sunday afternoon attraction. It packed the people in and it was very successful."
References: Djedje, *California Soul*. Cox, *Central Avenue: Its Rise and Fall*. *Film Daily Yearbook*, 1940–1955. *Motion Picture Herald*, July 15, 1939.

156. CENTRAL THEATER
17th and Central Avenue
Vaudeville and picture house. On January 22 and 23, 1920, the Central featured the film *Back to God's Country*, with Nell Shipma and "Wapie" the Killer. Also on the bill was the two-reel comedy *The Keystone Babies*. On January 24, the house exhibited the Rolin comedy *Why Go Home* and Elmo Lincoln in *Tarzan of the Apes*.
References: *California Eagle*, January 17, 1927. *Film Daily Yearbook*, 1930–1933.

157. DARKEL THEATER
Picture house.
References: *Film Daily Yearbook*, 1947, 1948.

158. DELUXE THEATER
West Jefferson Street
Picture house. 438 seats.
References: *Film Daily Yearbook*, 1947–1955.

159. FLORENCE MILLS THEATER
S. Central Avenue and 35th Street
Picture house. 700 seats. Also known as the Globe and the Amusio. Renamed in the 1930s after entertainer Florence Mills. Musician Marshall Royal recalls "it wasn't much of a theater. A very small theater, but they had some pretty good acts that came in there. A lot of show business people that got out in this area would get practically stranded and end up going

there for weekends or for two or three days at a time to make a little money to live on and get back to where they were going. And that's about the size of it." Singer Eddie Beal remembers that "I played piano all through the thirties. I started out playing in places like the Lincoln and the Florence Mills theaters."

References: Cox, *Central Avenue: Its Rise and Fall*. Djedje, *California Soul*. *Film Daily Yearbook*, 1940–1955. *Motion Picture Herald*, April 24, 1937. Sampson, *Blacks in Black and White*.

160. GAIETY THEATER
Picture house.
References: Djedje, *California Soul*. *Film Daily Yearbook*, 1930–1933.

161. HUB THEATER
10th Street and S. Central Avenue
Picture house. 500 seats.
References: *Film Daily Yearbook*, 1930–1933, 1947–1955.

162. JADE THEATER
Picture house. 250 seats.
References: *Film Daily Yearbook*, 1947, 1948.

163. LARGO THEATER
1827 E. 103rd Street
Picture house. 904 seats.
References: Djedje, *California Soul*. *Film Daily Yearbook*, 1940–1955. *Motion Picture Herald*, July 15, 1939.

164. LINCOLN THEATER
2300 S. Central Avenue
Picture, vaudeville, and legitimate house. 1960 seats. Architect: Adolph Ramish. Owner in 1927: Sam Kramer. Manager in 1927: Curtis W. Carpentier. Manager in 1943: Jimmy Marshall. Nicknamed the "West Coast Apollo," the Lincoln had all African Americans on its staff. According to Bette Cox, the Lincoln Theater was "the first on the West Coast for African Americans and the first in Southern California." It opened for business in 1927, offering movies, vaudeville, talent shows, and live performances. "Curtis Mosby's orchestra, the Dixieland Blue Blowers, opened the theater. The first show was Bill Russell's revue from the East Coast ... Bardu Ali from Louisiana was the master of ceremonies at the Lincoln Theater and blackface comedian Pigmeat Markham entertained there." The Lincoln had a Wurlitzer pipe organ which Haven Johnson or Sam Browne usually played. During the week of November 11, 1927, the Lincoln featured the Doc Straine play *The Liar* with Sam "Bibo" Russell. Featured films that week were *American Beauty* starring Billie Dove, and *Chinese Parrot* featuring Hobart Bosworth and Marion Nixon. Mosby's Blue Blowers appeared also during shows at 6:15 and 8:15 pm. This act featured singer Charles Willis, billed as "the colored John McCormack." Tickets on weekdays were 40 cents. Weekends and holidays cost 50 cents and the Saturday matinee 25 cents. Every Saturday night at 11:30 the Lincoln featured a "Big Midnite Ramble." The following week at the Lincoln, show dog Rin Tin Tin could be seen in the picture *Jaws of Steel*, and Norma Talmadge was starring in the film *Camille*. "In 1933 the black newspaper—the Los Angeles *Sentinel*—presented an annual Christmas show at the Lincoln Theater. Those who brought a couple of cans of food [for the needy] were admitted to enjoy the top talent of that era, such as the Rockettes, Pigmeat Markham and his revue and Benny Carter and his orchestra. In 1943, Jimmy Marshall became manager of the Lincoln and sought to take advantage of the Great Migration to the West. "I'd like to make an Apollo of the West Coast out of the Lincoln. With so many big-name bands and artists moving westward, that should not be too difficult," said Marshall. Many

Largo Theater, Los Angeles, California, 1960 (Photograph Collections/Los Angeles Public Library)

noted performers played the Lincoln: actors Clarence Muse and Leon Pass, actresses Nina McKinney, Evelyn Preer, and Sadie Thompson, the stock company the Lafayette Players; singers Ernie Andrews, Eddie Beal, Kitty Bilbrew, Charles Brown, Nat King Cole and Baby Mack; and the orchestras of Count Basie, Duke Ellington, Lionel Hampton and Les Hite and dancer Bill "Bojangles" Robinson. According to historian Bette Cox, the Lincoln "is now used as a church."

References: Cox, *Central Avenue: Its Rise and Fall*. *Chicago Defender*, "A New Theater," May 21, 1927; "Los Angeles Race Theater Soon To Open," October 1, 1927; "In Los Angeles," October 1, 1927. *California Eagle*, November 11, 25, 1927. Djedje, *California Soul. Film Daily Yearbook*, 1930–1933, 1932, 1940–1955. "Colored Play Cast Returns to LA Base," [About the Lafayette Players] *Hollywood Citizen News*, June 1, 1932; "Lincoln Theater Opens Doors Tonight," *Los Angeles Examiner*, October 7, 1927. *Los Angeles Sentinel*, "Grand Premiere at Lincoln Theater," July 3, 1946; "Sugar Chile Robinson Opens at Lincoln Theater Tuesday," July 25, 1946; "Lionel Hampton Band in Town to Play Lincoln Theater," August 8, 1946; "Lincoln's Weekly Kiddie Contest Proves Popular," September 4, 1946. *Motion Picture Herald*, April 24, 1937; July 15, 1939. Sampson, *Blacks in Black and White*.

Lincoln Theater, Los Angeles, California, 1960 (Photograph Collections/Los Angeles Public Library)

165. NEWSREEL THEATER
S. Broadway
Picture house. 1177 seats.
References: *Film Daily Yearbook,* 1947.

166. ROSEBUD THEATER
1940 S. Central Avenue
Picture house. 800 seats. During the week of January 12–18, 1920, the Rosebud featured a variety of motion pictures including *Fighting Colleen* with Bessie Leve, *Go West Young Man* starring Tom Moore, *A Woman There Was* starring Theda Bara, and *The Brute Maker* with Frank Mayo. According to jazz saxophonist Marshall Royal (1912–1995) "the Rosebud specialized in motion pictures usually. The Rosebud showed two or three movies a day. Movies at that time (before 1929) were still without sound. And each one of those theaters had an organ and an organist that played along with the picture. It was a big thing on a weekend, Saturdays and Sundays, not to have so much live shows, but things like amateur contests. I won one of one first amateur contests at the Rosebud Theater playing a ukulele, that was of the things of that particular era."
References: Cox, *Central Avenue: Its Rise and Fall. California Eagle,* January 10, 1920. Djedje, *California Soul. Film Daily Yearbook,* 1930–1933, 1942, 1940–1955. *Motion Picture Herald,* April 24, 1937; July 15, 1939. Sampson, *Blacks in Black and White.*

167. SAVOY THEATER
5326 S. Central Avenue

Rosebud Theater, Los Angeles, California, 1945 (Photograph Collections/Los Angeles Public Library)

Picture house. 800 seats.
References: *Film Daily Yearbook*, 1930–1932, 1940–1955. *Motion Picture Herald*, July 15, 1939.

168. TIVOLI THEATER
11523 Santa Monica Blvd.
Picture house. 873 seats.
References: *Film Daily Yearbook*, 1930–1933. *Motion Picture Herald*, April 24, 1937. Sampson, *Blacks in Black and White*.

169. VERNON THEATER
Vogue Street
Picture house. 490 seats.
References: *Film Daily Yearbook*, 1930–1932.

Monterey

170. STATE THEATER
417 Alvavado Street

Picture house. 1,429 seats.
References: *Film Daily Yearbook*, 1949–1955.

Oakland

171. EL REY THEATER
3520 San Pablo Avenue
Picture house. 700–900 seats.
References: *Film Daily Yearbook*, 1949–1955.

172. GEM THEATER
Picture house.
References: *Film Daily Yearbook*, 1930–1933.

173. LINCOLN THEATER
1620 7th Avenue
Picture house. 800–900 seats.
References: *Film Daily Yearbook*, 1930–1933, 1940–1955. *Motion Picture Herald*, July 15, 1939.

174. MARQUEE THEATER
Picture house.
References: *Film Daily Yearbook*, 1930–1933.

175. REX THEATER
1011 Broadway Street
Picture house. 600 seats.
References: *Film Daily Yearbook*, 1947–1955.

Pittsburg

176. PALACE THEATER
Picture house. 400 seats.
References: *Film Daily Yearbook*, 1949–1955.

Richmond

177. RIO THEATER
412 McDonald Avenue
Picture house. 500 seats.
References: *Film Daily Yearbook*, 1949–1955.

178. STUDIO THEATER
Picture house.
References: *Film Daily Yearbook*, 1947–1955.

Sacramento

179. ALAMEDA THEATER
Picture house.
References: *Film Daily Yearbook*, 1947, 1948.

180. LYRIC THEATER
Picture house.
References: *Film Daily Yearbook*, 1930–1932.

181. NIPPON THEATER
Picture house.
References: *Film Daily Yearbook*, 1930, 1931.

182. RIO THEATER
Picture house.
References: *Film Daily Yearbook*, 1949–1955.

183. SILVER PALACE
Picture house.
References: *Film Daily Yearbook*, 1930, 1931.

San Diego

184. AZTEC THEATER
Picture house.
References: *Film Daily Yearbook*, 1947, 1948.

185. PLAZA THEATER
Picture house.
References: *Film Daily Yearbook*, 1947, 1948.

186. VICTORY THEATER
2558 Imperial Avenue
Picture house. 450 seats.
References: *Film Daily Yearbook*, 1949–1955.

San Francisco

187. AMERICAN THEATER
1226 Fillmore Street
Picture house. 1,210 seats. It opened in 1909 as part of the Chutes Amusement Park. In 1915 it reopened as the Lyric. In 1925 it was alternately known as the New Progress and the American. It closed in 1959 and was later demolished.
References: *Film Daily Yearbook*, 1949–1955.

188. ELLIS THEATER
1671 Ellis Streeet
Picture house. 1,000 seats. Also known as the New Ellis.
References: *Film Daily Yearbook*, 1945–1955.

189. LEWIS THEATER
Picture house.
References: *Film Daily Yearbook*, 1941–1944.

190. LIBERTY THEATER
649 Broadway
Picture house. 700–750 seats.
References: *Film Daily Yearbook*, 1949–1955.

191. MAJESTIC THEATER
Picture house.
References: *Film Daily Yearbook*, 1930–1932.

192. PEERLESS THEATER
Picture house.
References: *Film Daily Yearbook*, 1930–1932.

193. SILVER THEATER
Picture house.
References: *Film Daily Yearbook*, 1930–1932.

194. TEMPLE THEATER
1749 S. Fillmore Street
Picture house. 350 seats. The Temple opened in 1918 as a "Class A" theater. It was closed in 1966 and torn down.
References: *Film Daily Yearbook*, 1949–1955.

195. UNIQUE THEATER
2115 Market Street
Picture house.
References: *Film Daily Yearbook*, 1930–1932.

San Jose

196. LYRIC THEATER
Picture house.
References: *Film Daily Yearbook*, 1930–1932.

San Pedro

197. GLOBE THEATER
204 W. 6th Street
Picture house. 415–560 seats.
References: *Film Daily Yearbook*, 1953–1955.

Stockton

198. LIBERTY THEATER
Picture house. In 1949 through 1953 the Liberty was closed, according to the *Film Daily Yearbook*. It apparently reopened in 1954.
References: *Film Daily Yearbook*, 1949–1955.

199. LINCOLN THEATER
Picture house.
References: *Film Daily Yearbook*, 1930–1932.

200. STRAND THEATER
Picture house.
References: *Film Daily Yearbook*, 1930–1932.

COLORADO

Denver

201. ROXY THEATER
2549–51 Welton Street
Picture house. 561 seats. Manager in 1945: Able Davis.

References: *Film Daily Yearbook*, 1940–1942, 1950–1955. *Motion Picture Herald*, April 24, 1937; July 15, 1939. Sampson, *Blacks in Black and White*.

CONNECTICUT

Bridgeport

202. STRAND THEATER
Picture house.
References: *Film Daily Yearbook*, 1930–1933.

New Haven

203. LYRIC THEATER
158 Dixwell Avenue
Picture house. 450 seats.
References: *Film Daily Yearbook*, 1930–1933, 1947–1955.

DELAWARE

Greenwood

204. GREENWOOD THEATER
Picture house. Manager in 1921: Mr. Coleman (African American).

References: Cahn, *Julius Cahn-Gus Hill Theatrical Guide*. Jackson, "Additions to Theater List," *Billboard*, December 31, 1921.

Laurel

205. NEW WALLER THEATER
Picture house. 60 seats.
References: *Film Daily Yearbook*, 1949–1955.

Milford

206. PLAZA THEATER
Picture house. 1,000 seats.
References: *Film Daily Yearbook*, 1949–1955.

Seaford

207. PALACE THEATER
Picture house. 600 seats.
References: *Film Daily Yearbook*, 1947–1955.

Wilmington

208. NATIONAL THEATER
810–12 French Street
Vaudeville and picture house. 600 seats. Manager in 1921–1942: John Hopkins (African American).
References: Cahn, *Julius Cahn-Gus Hill Theatrical Guide*. *Film Daily Yearbook,* 1931–1933, 1941–1955. Jackson, "List of Colored Theaters and Attractions," *Billboard,* August 6, 1921. Work, *Negro Yearbook, 1921–1922.*

DISTRICT OF COLUMBIA

209. AIRDOME THEATER
331–337 G Street SW
Picture house. According to Headley, "Jerry C. Barnes and Wiley Davis received a license to operate a moving picture park on this location in June 1915."
References: Cahn, *Julius Cahn-Gus Hill Theatrical Guide*. Headley, *Motion Picture Exhibition in Washington, D.C.* Jackson, "Additions to Theater List," *Billboard*, December 31, 1921.

210. ALAMO THEATER
1203 7th Street NW
Nickeldeon, vaudeville house. 229 seats. The now-demolished Alamo, as described by Headley, began as a white theater, underwent some renovations to enlarge it in the fall of 1916, and was an African-American theater by 1921. Jones says of the Alamo: "the ventilation is poor, although the ceiling is of average height. The movies and vaudeville are of low type and the patrons are uneducated and extremely emotional. There are four performances daily. The prices of admission are fifteen cents for adults and ten cents for children."
References: *Film Daily Yearbook*, 1940–1955. Headley, *Motion Picture Exhibition in Washington, D.C.* Jones, *Recreation and Amusement. Motion Picture Herald*, April 24, 1937; July 15, 1939. Sampson, *Blacks in Black and White*.

211. AMERICAN THEATER

1014 Pennsylvania Avenue

Vaudeville and picture house. Owners in 1914: Sherman H. Dudley and Andrew Thomas.

According to Headley, the American stood on the site of one of the first theaters built in the capitol and the site of a theater since 1804; Andrew Thomas and Sherman Dudley acquired the theater and renamed it the American in 1914. It opened as an African-American vaudeville and movie house on February 16, 1914, under the direction of the Orpheum Amusement Company, and was sold to the Empire Circuit in 1917.

References: Headley, *Motion Picture Exhibition in Washington, D.C.*

BAND BOX THEATER *see* Booker T. Washington Theater

212. 170. BLUE MOUSE
2819 26th Street NW

Vaudeville house. Also called the Mott. 400 seats. Architects: Julius Wenig and Hugh McAuley. A TOBA theater and member of the Dudley vaudeville circuit. Manager in 1921: M. Martin. Manager in 1922: S. H. Dudley (African American). Manager in 1941: Howard Derrick.

Headley writes: "In 1910 when this theater was built, the name Blue Mouse was a widespread one for movie theaters. There was one in Baltimore, one in St. Paul, Minnesota, and one in Portland, Oregon. The Washington Blue Mouse was a one story brick and cement theater that cost $5,000 to build. The Blue Mouse was an African-American theater as early as 1915. The name was changed to Mott, after the abolitionist Lucretia Mott, when Lichtman Theaters acquired it in 1932. In 1954, the closed Mott was leased by Georgetown-on-the-Aisle and live plays were put on. It has been demolished." Jones said of the Blue Mouse: "This theater is located at Twenty-sixth and M Street Northwest.... It has a Negro manager. The seating capacity is four hundred. The ventilation is direct, that is, from three or four windows on each side of the theater. The doors may be left open also as a means of ventilation. This theater is situated among a rather rough class of people. About two-thirds of the patrons are young boys. The entertainments here consist of both pictures and vaudeville, featuring local talent. The pictures are of the mediocre type, featuring such actors as 'Buck Jones,' 'Tom Mix,' etc. Occasionally a high-class picture is shown, but only after it has 'gone the rounds' elsewhere. The lavatories are located at the side of the stage so that those wishing to enter must pass to the front of the room before the audience. The price of admission is twenty cents.'

References: Cahn, *Julius Cahn-Gus Hill Theatrical Guide. Film Daily Yearbook*, 1930, 1940–1955. Headley, *Motion Picture Exhibition in Washington D.C.* Hill, *Pages from the Harlem Renaissance.* Jackson, "List of Colored Theaters and Attractions," *Billboard,* August 6, 1921; "The Theater Owners' Booking Association," *Billboard,* December 16, 1922. Jones, *Recreation and Amusement. Motion Picture Herald,* April 24, 1937; July 15, 1939. Work, *Negro Yearbook, 1921–1922.*

213. BOOKER T. THEATER
1431–1433 U Street NW

Picture house. 508 seats. Also known as the Olympic and the Band Box. Architect: George P. Hales. Owner in 1928: A. Makeover. Owner in 1929: Lichtman Theaters. Manager in 1941: Alvin Campbell. According to Headley, Lichtman Theaters acquired and renamed the theater in April 1929; as the Booker T., it became one of the three largest African-American theaters on U Street. An article in the *Baltimore Afro-American* states,

"The Olympic Theater, U Street west of Fourteenth, which has recently been purchased and renamed the Booker T, will undergo a complete renovation and redecoration. A new marquee will be built. A beautiful Claude Neon electric sign will be erected, and the entire front of the house will be changed. The box office will be moved out to the street line. New carpets will be laid. Western Electric sound equipment at a cost of $7000 will be installed and a new stage setting will be put in with a portrait of the late Booker T. Washington in a setting over the screen. Headley says, "after it closed as a movie house in late 1976, it was a church for several years. It has been demolished, and the Frank D. Reeves Municipal Center covers the site."

References: *Baltimore Afro-American*, July 27, 1929. *Film Daily Yearbook*, 1940–1955. Headley, *Motion Picture Exhibition in Washington, D.C. Motion Picture Herald*, April 24, 1937; July 15, 1939. Sampson, *Blacks in Black and White*.

214. BROADWAY THEATER
1515 7th Avenue NW

Picture house. 500 seats. Architects: Milburn, Heister and Company. Owner in 1921: J. S. Leatherman. Manager in 1921: Rufus G. Byars (African American). Manager in 1941: Sigman Heard. Owner in 1940s: Lichtman Theaters. Headley says "the Broadway opened as an African-American theater on December 19, 1921 under the direction of Rufus G. Byars." In 1927 Jones reported that the theater "is located on Seventh Street near P Streets [sic], Northwest. It is managed by the owner, a Negro, Mr. Rufus G. Byars. The manager stated that the average weekly attendance is 234,000. The pictures shown are second runs but of the best releases, and afford an excellent opportunity for those who have missed them at other theaters. During a portion of the year 1926–27 this theater featured monthly a Negro production. This program received the highest approval of the patrons. The prices of admission are as follows: week days — adults, fifteen cents; children, ten cents; Sundays and holidays — twenty cents." Headley describes the Broadway as "a handsome two-story, brick, and terra-cotta building." The theater was demolished in the 1980s.

References: *Film Daily Yearbook*, 1930–1933, 1940–1955. Headley, *Motion Picture Exhibition in Washington, D.C.* Jones, *Recreation and Amusement. Motion Picture Herald*, April 24, 1937; July 15, 1939. Sampson, *Blacks in Black and White*. Work, *Negro Yearbook, 1921–1922*.

215. CARVER THEATER
2405 Nichols Ave. SE

Picture house. 508 seats. Architect: John J. Zink. Headley says the Carver opened in 1948 and closed six years later.

References: *Film Daily Yearbook*, 1950–1955. Headley, *Motion Picture Exhibition in Washington, D.C.*

216. CHASE'S THEATER
1424 Pennsylvania Avenue, NW

Vaudeville house. Owner in 1910: Plimpton B. Chase. Manager: D. Gentry. Architects: W.B. Gray and Harvey. Also known as Albaugh's Opera House and Poli's. About 1939 it was torn down to make way for the Federal Triangle.

References: Peterson, *The African American Theatre Directory*. Headley, *Motion Picture Exhibition in Washington, D.C.*

217. CHELSEA THEATER
1913 M Street, NW

Vaudeville and picture house. Architect: Julius Wenig. Manager in 1914: D. Gentry. The Chelsea was part of the Dudley circuit. Headley, says "the Chelsea was a one-story brick moving picture theater 30 × 90 feet. It also had some live shows." In 1914, the vaudeville team of Chadwick and Crippen played here.

References: *Chicago Defender*, November 30, 1914. Headley: *Motion Picture Exhibition in Washington, DC. Indianapolis Freeman*, "What's What on the Dudley Circuit," January 31, 1914.

218. DIXIE THEATER
800–802 H Street NW
Picture house. 393 seats. Architects: C. Clark Jones and Stewart Charles.

References: Cahn, *Julius Cahn-Gus Hill Theatrical Guide*. Headley, *Motion Picture Exhibition in Washington, D.C.* Jackson, "List of Colored Theaters and Attractions," *Billboard*, August 6, 1921. Work, *Negro Yearbook, 1921–1922*.

219. DREAMLAND THEATER
2101–2105 14th Street NW
Picture house.

References: Headley, *Motion Picture Exhibition in Washington D.C. Film Daily Yearbook*, 1930–1933.

220. DUDLEY THEATER
1213 U Street, NW
Vaudeville house. 200 seats. Architect: F. A. Hurlehane. Opened in 1910 as the Minnehaha Theater. Owner in 1913–1920: S. H. Dudley. Manager in 1914: Lew Henry. It was part of the Dudley vaudeville circuit. In 1914, vaudvillians Owens and Owens were here with Bessie Cary. Headley says, "it cost about $5,000 to build. It was evidently operated by S. H. Dudley who changed the name [of the house] to Dudley between 1913 and 1920. …It … [was] still, as of 1992, standing. It is currently a restaurant."

Source: *Chicago Defender*, November 30, 1914. Headley, *Motion Picture Exhibition in Washington D.C.* Hill, *Pages from the Harlem Renaisssance*. *Indianapolis Freeman*, January 31, 1914. Jackson, "List of Colored Theaters and Attractions," *Billboard*, August 6, 1921; "The Theater Owners' Booking Association," *Billboard*, December 16, 1922. Peterson, *Profiles of African American Stage Performers*.

221. DUNBAR THEATER #1
1219 U. Street NW
Vaudeville and picture house. Probably built on the future site of the Lincoln, the Dunbar was the theater where African-American theater operator Rufus Byars began his career.

References: *Film Daily Yearbook*, 1930–1933. Headley, *Motion Picture Exhibition in Washington, D.C.*

222. DUNBAR THEATER #2
1901–1903 7th Street NW
Picture house. Between 346–395 seats. Architects: Isaiah J. Hatton (African American) and Reginald Geare. Manager in 1921: Rufus G. Byars (African American). Manager in 1927: Raymond H. Murray (African American). "The Dunbar was located in a four story office and apartment building built by the Southern Aid Society of Virginia. There is some indication that Reginald Geare was involved in designing the theater. It cost about $60,000. It opened on October 18, 1920. The opening was Oscar Micheaux's *The Brute*. It was always an African-American theater. Jones says of the Dunbar: "It is owned by the Crescent Amusement Company, a Negro corporation. It has a seating capacity of 395. The approximate attendance, except during the summer months, is 700 daily. This theater features motion pictures only, the western type chiefly. Ventilation and sanitary conditions are inadequate and the floors and furniture are not kept free from dust. The prices of admission are as follows: matinee, adults and children, ten cents; night-adults and children, fifteen cents." As of 2002, the theater building is still standing but boarded up.

Dunbar Theater No. 2, Washington, DC, 2000 (photograph © Martin McCaffrey).

References: Cahn, *Julius Cahn-Gus Hill Theatrical Guide. Film Daily Yearbook*, 1940–1955. Headley, *Motion Picture Exhibition in Washington, D.C.* Jackson, "List of Colored Theaters and Attractions," *Billboard*, August 6, 1921. Jones, *Recreation and Amusement. Motion Picture Herald*, July 15, 1939. Murray, *Negro Handbook, 1942.* Simms, *Simms' Blue Book.*

223. FAIRYLAND THEATER
1838 L Street, NW
Vaudeville house. 1909–1919. Architect: Julius Wenig. Owner in 1910s: S. H. Dudley. Headley says the one-story brick was most likely built for F.T. Kearney for about $1,500. In 1914, it was part of the Dudley vaudeville circuit.
References: *Chicago Defender*, November 30, 1914. Headley, *Motion Picture Exhibition in Washington, D.C.* Peterson, *The African American Theatre Directory.*

224. FAVORITE THEATER
62 H Street, N.W.
Picture house. 1913–1930. 400 seats. Architect: W.S. Plager. According to Headley "it was demolished in 1972."
References: *Film Daily Yearbook*, 1930–1933. Headley, *Motion Picture Exhibition in Washington, D.C.*

225. FLORIDA THEATER
1438 Florida Avenue NE
Picture house. 410 seats. Architect: C. Denny. Said to be Black owned and managed. Manager in 1921: Mr. Colfax. Headley describes the Florida as "a one story brick movie theater ... built at a cost of $10,000 by the Florida Amusement Company. It had become an African-American theater by the mid-twenties.... It was torn down to construct a high-rise apartment building in the 1970s."
References: Cahn, *Julius Cahn-Gus Hill Theatrical Guide.* Headley, *Motion Picture Exhibition in Washington, D.C.* Jackson, "List of Colored Theaters and Attractions," *Billboard*, August 6, 1921. Work, *Negro Yearbook, 1921–1922.*

226. FORAKER THEATER
1120–1122 20th Street NW
Vaudeville and picture house. 245–456 seats. Architects: James H. Warner and George R. Santmeyer. The Foraker was part of the Dudley and the TOBA vaudeville circuits. Owners in 1909: Fred Gosselin and I. H. Rowland. Managers in 1914: Davis Brothers. Managers in 1921: Sherman H. Dudley, Raymond H. Murray, and Rufus Byars (African Americans). The Foraker was enlarged in 1916, almost doubling its seating capacity, and in a few years was being advertised as the "Largest Theatre in Washington using Vaudeville and Pictures only." Jones says "The vaudeville consists of black-faced comedians, dancing girls, and jazz singers. The jokes are always within the universe of discourse of the class of patrons who attend. This theater has recently reopened under new management and is attracting rather large crowds. It has two or three shows an evening."
References: Cahn, *Julius Cahn-Gus Hill Theatrical Guide. Film Daily Yearbook*, 1930. Headley, *Motion Picture Exhibition in Washington D.C.* Hill, *Pages from the Harlem Renaissance. Indianapolis Freeman*, "What's What on the Dudley Circuit," January 31, 1914. Jackson, "List of Colored Theaters and Attractions," *Billboard*, August 6, 1921; "The Theater Owners' Booking Association," *Billboard*, December 16, 1922. Jones, *Recreation and Amusement.* Peterson, *The African American Theatre Directory.* Work, *Negro Yearbook, 1921–1922.*

227. FORD DABNEY THEATER
2001 9th Street
Vaudeville and picture house. 1910–1912. Owner in 1912: Ford Dabney. Man-

ager in 1912: James H. Hudnell. Ford Dabney was a songwriter whose music was performed by Bert Williams and other vaudevillians.

References: Headley, *Motion Picture Exhibition in Washington, D. C.* Smith, *Bert Williams.*

228. GEM THEATER
1131 7th Street NW

Picture house. 356 seats, Architects: William L. Speiden and Albert Speiden. According to Headley, "It opened in 1914. It was operated by the Gem Theater Company. It was a segregated theater with a low wall down the middle of the auditorium; whites sat on one side and African Americans on the other." About 1950, the Gem was listed in *Film Daily Yearbook* as a "Negro theater." Headley reports that "the Gem was demolished as part of the urban renewal of the 7th Street corridor."

References: *Film Daily Yearbook*, 1930, 1950–1955. Headley, *Motion Picture Exhibition in Washington, D.C.* Jackson, "List of Colored Theaters and Attractions," *Billboard*, August 6, 1921.

229. HIAWATHA THEATER
2006–2008 11th Street NW

Vaudeville and picture house. 224 seats. Architects: W. Sidney Pittman, Vaughan and Hattan. Managers in 1921: Raymond H. Murray and Rufus G. Byars (African Americans). "The theater had a galvanized iron and brick front. It probably opened on November 11, 1909. According to Headley in 1909, the Hiawatha was the oldest African-American-owned theater in the U.S. The theater was improved in the summer of 1910 by raising the roof and extending the back. The improvements cost about $4000. It was operated by the Hiawatha Amusement Co. and managed by Raymond H. Murray for many years.... The Hiawatha was a popular African-American theater throughout the teens. It closed in May 1922 because of poor business, but may have reopened for a short time later. One of the most popular entertainments at the Hiawatha were T. Spencer Finley's nightly monologues on current events, Prof. George E. Battle, who later went to the Dunbar, played the piano at the Hiawatha."

References: Cahn, *Julius Cahn-Gus Hill Theatrical Guide.* Headley, *Motion Picture Exhibition in Washington, D.C.* Jackson, "List of Colored Theaters and Attractions," *Billboard*, August 6, 1921. Moore, *Leading the Race.* Simms, *Simms' Blue Book.* Work, *Negro Yearbook, 1921–1922.*

230. HOWARD THEATER
620–624 T Street NW

Vaudeville house. Between 1,200 and 1,242 seats. Architect: J. Edward Storck. A TOBA theater. Manager in 1914: Andrew J. Thomas. Managers in 1921: Thomas Brothers. Manager in 1941: Edward Evans. In the early 20th century, the Howard was part of the Dudley vaudeville circuit. Many famous performers appeared at the Howard: Wilbur Sweatman and his band in 1922, Bessie Smith in 1924, the Whitman Sisters in 1926. Ethel Waters, Louis Armstrong, and Cab Calloway were crowd pleasers at the Howard in the 1930s. During the 1940s, Billie Holiday and the Willie Bryant Band were headliners. Charlie Parker appeared in 1952. The Howard was in business from about 1910 to 1970.

References: Albertson, *Bessie.* Cahn, *Julius Cahn-Gus Hill Theatrical Guide.* Calloway, *Of Minnie the Moocher and Me.* Collier, *Louis Armstrong.* Dance, *The World of Earl Hines. Film Daily Yearbook*, 1940–1955. Fitzpatrick, *The Guide to Black Washington.* Jackson, "List of Colored Theaters and Attractions" *Billboard*, August 6, 1921. *Motion Picture Herald*, April 24, 1937; July 15, 1939. George-

Howard Theater (Washingtoniana Division, D.C. Public Library)

Graves, *The Royalty of Vaudeville*. Gottschild, *Waltzing in the Dark*. Holiday, *Lady Sings the Blues*. *Official Theatrical World of Colored Artists*. Peterson, *Profiles of African American Stage Performers*. Russell, *Bird Lives!* Sampson, *Blacks in Black and White*. Waters, *His Eye Is on the Sparrow*. Work, *Negro Handbook, 1912*.

231. JEWEL THEATER
   4th ½ Street SW

Picture house. Between 250 to 300 seats. Architect: F. B. Proctor. The Jewel was said to be white owned and black managed. In 1927 Jones wrote of the Jewel: "It is managed by Negroes and the property is probably owned by Negroes. It has a seating capacity of approximately four hundred [sic]. The patrons are mostly of the shiftless class, mainly boys and young men who seek amusement in low class theaters and pool rooms. The shows consist principally of pictures of the 'wild west' type with an occasionally good picture. The price of admission is twenty cents for adults and children." According to Headley, the Jewel was bought by Lichtman Theaters around 1928 and in 1939 was razed for the construction of the Social Security Building.

References: Cahn, *Julius Cahn-Gus Hill Theatrical Guide*. *Film Daily Yearbook*, 1930, 1940–1955. Headley, *Motion Picture Exhibition in Washington, D.C.* Jones, *Recreation and Amusement*. *Motion Picture Herald*, April 24, 1937; July 15, 1939. Sampson, *Blacks in Black and White*.

232. LANGSTON THEATER
2501–2507 Benning Road NE
Picture house. 696 seats. Architect: John J. Zink. According to Headley, the Langston was in business from 1945 to 1977.
References: *Film Daily Yearbook*, 1947–1955. Headley, *Motion Picture Exhibition in Washington, D.C.*

233. LINCOLN THEATER
1215 U Street NW
Vaudeville and picture house. 1,600 seats. Owner in 1922: Crandall Theater Corporation. Manager in 1941: Jack Carter. According to Sandra Fitzpatrick, "the Lincoln Theater was opened in February 1922 under black management. In 1927, the 1,600-seat theater was sold to the Lincoln-Howard Corporation which operated both the Lincoln and Howard theaters." Louis N. Brown played the theater's Manuel Mohler organ in the 1920s. In 1939 during the screening of the movie *Gone With the Wind*, the Lincoln was picketed by African Americans, protesting the film's treatment of slavery.
References: *Film Daily Yearbook*, 1930–1933, 1940–1955. Fitzpatrick, *The Guide to Black Washington*. Hill, *Pages from the Harlem Renaissance*. *Motion Picture Herald*, April 24, 1937; July 15, 1939. Sampson, *Blacks in Black and White*.

234. MACEO THEATER
1939 11th Street N.W.
Vaudeville house. Architects: James H. Childs and W. Sidney Pittman. 200–300 seats. Said to be black owned. Although primarily oriented toward an African-American audience, the Maceo also welcomed whites. It opened in 1909, and its closing date is unknown.
References: Headley, *Motion Picture Exhibition in Washington D.C.* Hill, *Pages from the Harlem Renaissance*.

235. MAJESTIC THEATER
9th and C. St. NW
Vaudeville house. 1850–1931. 1,000 seats. Manager in 1914: Frank Brown (African American). Originally called Wall's Opera House or Ford's Opera House, it was reopened by Frank Brown as the Majestic for black audiences in 1914. On opening night, the show included vaudeville acts such as Miss Susie Sutton and T. Spencer Finley. The final act was an unnamed movie. The *Washington Bee* praised manager Frank Brown for hiring all African-American employees at the theater. But a year later the theater filed a petition in the District of Columbia Supreme Court asking for the appointment of a receiver for the Majestic. According to Headley, "the federal government bought it in 1929 and it was razed in 1931 to erect the Department of Justice Building."
References: Headley, *Motion Picture Exhibition in Washington, D.C.* Sampson, *Blacks in Blackface*.

236. MID–CITY THEATER
1223 7th Avenue NW
Vaudeville house. 200–250 seats. Architect: Samuel R. Turner. Manager in 1921: Sherman H. Dudley (African American). According to Headley, the now-demolished Mid-City originally cost $4,200 to convert to a theater and was sold in 1930 to a white-owned corporation. "It had become an African-American theater by 1919 when Sherman Dudley advertised it as the 'only vaudeville theater on the popular thoroughfare ... and the only theatre on Seventh Avenue catering to colored people that does not discriminate," writes Headley.
References: Bowser, *Writing Himself into History*. Cahn, *Julius Cahn-Gus Hill Theatrical Guide*. *Film Daily Yearbook*, 1930–1932, 1940–1955. Jackson, "List of Colored Theaters and Attractions," *Bill-*

Lincoln Theater, Washington, D.C., 1999 (photograph © Martin McCaffrey)

board, August 6, 1921; "The Theater Owners' Booking Association," *Billboard*, December 16, 1922. *Motion Picture Herald*, April 24, 1937; July 15, 1939. Peterson, *The African American Theatre Directory*. Sampson, *Blacks in Black and White*. Work, *Negro Yearbook, 1921–1922*.

MOTT THEATER *see* Blue Mouse Theater

237. PLYMOUTH THEATER
1365 H. Street NE
Picture house. Architect: Morris Hallett. Hallett designed the theater from a former Plymouth car salesroom. "Ike Weiner took it over in 1945 and remodeled it," according to Headley. The theater closed in 1952.
References: *Film Daily Yearbook*, 1945–1955. Headley, *Motion Picture Exhibition in Washington, D.C.*

238. RAPHAEL THEATER
1409 9th Street NW
Picture house. 400 seats. Owner: Lichtman Theaters. Manager in 1941: George Miller.
References: *Film Daily Yearbook*, 1940–1955. *Motion Picture Herald*, April 24, 1937; July 15, 1939. Sampson, *Blacks in Black and White*.

239. REPUBLIC THEATER
1133–1149 U Street NW
Picture house. 1,000 seats. Architect: Philip M. Julien. Owner: Lichtman Theaters. Manager in 1921: Walter Pinchback (African American). Manager in 1941: Thomas Bernard. According to Headley, the Republic was built in 1921, by Joseph Makeover's Globe Amusement Company. "The front of the Republic was of stucco work in imitation of buff Indiana

limestone. A Spanish tile roof topped the façade. The seating was stadium-style, on one floor with a loge level mid-way back from the screen. The broad entrance lobby led to a thirteen-foot foyer that extended across the entire width of the theater. The Republic installed a two-manual Moller organ, Opus 4075 in 1921," Headley writes. When the DC metro system was built, the Republic Theater was torn down.

References: Cahn, *Julius Cahn-Gus Hill Theatrical Guide. Film Daily Yearbook*, 1931, 1932, 1933, 1940–1955. Headley, *Motion Picture Exhibition in Washington, D.C.* Hill, *Pages from the Harlem Renaissance.* Jackson, "List of Colored Theaters and Attractions," *Billboard*, August 6, 1921. *Motion Picture Herald*, April 24, 1937; July 15, 1939. Sampson, *Blacks in Black and White*. Work, *Negro Yearbook, 1921-1922*.

240. ROSALIA THEATER
218–20 F Avenue SW
Picture house. 350 seats. Owner: Abe Lichtman. Manager in 1941: James Washington. References: *Film Daily Yearbook*, 1930–1933, 1940–1955. *Motion Picture Herald*, April 24, 1937; July 15, 1939. Peterson, *The African American Theatre Directory, 1816–1960.* Sampson, *Blacks in Black and White*.

241. SENATOR THEATER
3946–3956 Minnesota Avenue, NE
Picture house. 946 seats. Architect: John J. Zink. Owner: Berheimer Theaters. According to Headley, the Senator opened on February 19, 1942, with the Alfred Hitchcock film *Suspicion* starring Cary Grant and Joan Fontaine. "In late 1951, it was leased by the Bernheimer organization to operate as an African American theater." The auditorium was demolished in 1989 but the façade still stands.

References: *Film Daily Yearbook*, 1953–1955. Headley, *Motion Picture Exhibition in Washington, D.C.*

242. STRAND THEATER
5129–5131 Grant Street, N.E.
Picture and vaudeville house 1928–1959. Architect: James A. Dowride or J.A. Melby. Also known as the Deanwood. 550 seats. A TOBA theater. Manager in 1929: Ira J. LaMott.

References: *Film Daily Yearbook*, 1940–1955. Headley, *Motion Picture Exhibition in Washington, D.C. Motion Picture Herald*, April 24, 1937; July 15, 1939. Sampson, *Blacks in Black and White*.

243. SYLVAN THEATER
106–112 Rhode Island Avenue NW
Picture house 1914–1965. 450 seats. Architect: N.T. Haller. Also known as the American.

References: *Film Daily Yearbook*, 1952–1955. Headley, *Motion Picture Exhibition, Washington, D.C.*

244. YORK THEATER
3640–3648 Georgia Avenue NW
Picture house 1919–1954. Architect: Reginald W. Geare. 852–1,000 seats. Headley says it is now used as a church.

References: *Film Daily Yearbook*, 1952–1955. Headley, *Motion Picture Exhibition in Washington, D.C.*

FLORIDA

Apalachicola

245. HILLTOP THEATER
Picture house.
References: *Film Daily Yearbook*, 1947–1955.

Apopka

246. WASHINGTON THEATER
Picture house.
References: *Film Daily Yearbook*, 1930–1933.

Arcade

247. RITZ THEATER
Picture house. 250 seats.
References: *Film Daily Yearbook*, 1947–1955.

Auburndale

248. ACE THEATER
Picture house.
References: *Film Daily Yearbook*, 1952–1955.

249. TWINKLE DRIVE-IN
References: *Film Daily Yearbook*, 1953–1955.

Avon Park

250. AVON THEATER
Picture house.
References: *Film Daily Yearbook*, 1945–1955.

251. STRINGER THEATER
Picture house.
References: *Film Daily Yearbook*, 1930–1933.

Bartow

252. HARLEM THEATER
469 3rd Avenue
Picture house. 208–250 seats. Said to be Black owned and managed. This may be the unnamed Bartow theater listed in the 1921 *Billboard* survey. The Harlem was closed from 1949 to 1951, according to *Film Daily Yearbook*.
References: Cahn, *Julius Cahn-Gus Hill Theatrical Guide*. *Film Daily Yearbook*, 1940–1955. Jackson, "List of Colored Theaters and Attractions," *Billboard*, August 6, 1921. *Motion Picture Herald*, July 15, 1939. Work, *Negro Yearbook, 1921–1922*.

Belle Glade

253. ACE THEATER
Picture house. 400 seats.
References: *Film Daily Yearbook*, 1950–1955.

254. GOLDEN NUGGET THEATER,
Picture house.
References: *Film Daily Yearbook*, 1940–1953. *Motion Picture Herald*, July 15, 1939.

255. NEW FRAZIER THEATER
Picture house.
References: *Film Daily Yearbook*, 1950–1953.

256. SHOWBOAT THEATER
Picture house.
References: *Film Daily Yearbook*, 1949.

Bradentown

257. LINCOLN THEATER
Picture house. 500 seats.
References: *Film Daily Yearbook*, 1930, 1940–1955. *Motion Picture Herald*, April 24, 1937; July 15, 1939.

Bunnell

258. CHARLES THEATER
Picture house.
References: *Film Daily Yearbook*, 1949–1955.

Clearwater

259. DIXIE THEATER
Picture house. 300 seats.
References: *Film Daily Yearbook*, 1940–1955. *Motion Picture Herald*, April 24, 1937; July 15, 1939. Sampson, *Blacks in Black and White*.

260. HARLEM THEATER
Picture house.
References: *Film Daily Yearbook*, 1946–1948.

261. LINCOLN THEATER
Picture house.
References: *Film Daily Yearbook*, 1930.

262. PARK THEATER
N. Greenwood Avenue
Picture house. 397 seats.
References: *Film Daily Yearbook*, 1949–1955.

Clewiston

263. HARLEM THEATER
Picture house. 300 seats. According to *Film Daily Yearbook*, the Harlem was closed in 1949.
References: *Film Daily Yearbook*, 1940–1955. *Motion Picture Herald*, July 15, 1939.

264. LINCOLN THEATER
Picture house. The Lincoln was listed as closed from 1949 to 1951 by the *Film Daily Yearbook*.
Source: *Film Daily Yearbook*, 1940–1955. *Motion Picture Herald*, July 15, 1939.

265. QUEEN THEATER
Picture house.
References: *Film Daily Yearbook*, 1950–1955.

Cocoa

266. MAGNOLIA THEATER
Picture house.
References: *Film Daily Yearbook*, 1930.

267. PRINCESS THEATER
Picture house.
References: *Film Daily Yearbook*, 1930.

268. SKY VIEW DRIVE-IN
Picture house.
References: *Film Daily Yearbook*, 1955.
Coconut Grove

269. ACE THEATER
Picture house.
References: *Film Daily Yearbook*, 1947–1955.

270. GRAND THEATER
Picture house.
References: *Film Daily Yearbook*, 1930.

271. NEWS THEATER
Picture house.
References: *Film Daily Yearbook*, 1940–1946. *Motion Picture Herald*, July 15, 1939.

Coral Gables

272. AIRDOME THEATER
Picture house.
References: *Film Daily Yearbook*, 1930.

Cross City

273. PALACE THEATER
Picture house.
References: *Film Daily Yearbook*, 1940–1955. *Motion Picture Herald*, July 15, 1939.

Dade City

274. ROOSEVELT THEATER
Picture house.
References: *Film Daily Yearbook*, 1949.

Dania

275. CASE THEATER
Picture house. The Case was a portable tent theater.
References: *Film Daily Yearbook*, 1950–1955.

Daytona Beach

276. COLORED THEATER
Picture house.
References: Work, *Negro Yearbook*, 1921–1922.

277. MIDWAY THEATER
Picture house. 436 seats. Also known as the Crystal. Manager in 1921: J. H. Cuthbert (African American).
References: Cahn, *Julius Cahn-Gus Hill Theatrical Guide. Film Daily Yearbook*, 1930. Jackson, "List of Colored Theaters and Attractions," *Billboard*, August 6, 1921; "Additions to Theater List," *Billboard*, December 31, 1921.

278. PALM DRIVE-IN
Picture house.
References: *Film Daily Yearbook*, 1952–1955.

279. RITZ THEATER
577 2nd Avenue
Picture house. 475 seats.
References: *Film Daily Yearbook*, 1940–1955. *Motion Picture Herald*, April 24, 1937; July 15, 1939. Sampson, *Blacks in Black and White*.

Deland

280. WASHINGTON THEATER
254 Voorhis Avenue
Picture house. 200 seats.
References: *Film Daily Yearbook*, 1930, 1940–1955. *Motion Picture Herald*, July 15, 1939.

Delray Beach

281. CASE THEATER
Picture house. 380 seats. The Case was a portable tent theater.
References: *Film Daily Yearbook*, 1950–1955.

282. DELRAY THEATER
Picture house. 380 seats.
References: *Film Daily Yearbook*, 1940–1949. *Motion Picture Herald*, July 15, 1939.

283. LINCOLN THEATER
Picture house.
References: *Film Daily Yearbook*. 1952–1955.

Eustis

284. EGYPT THEATER
Picture house.
References: *Film Daily Yearbook*, 1930.

Florence Villa

285. ELITE THEATER
Picture house.
References: *Film Daily Yearbook*, 1949–1955.

Florida City

286. RITZ THEATER
Picture house. 247 seats.
References: *Film Daily Yearbook*, 1947–1955.

Fort Lauderdale

287. BROWN'S DRIVE-IN
Picture house.
References: *Film Daily Yearbook*, 1952–1955.

288. CASE THEATER
Picture house. The Case was a tent or portable theater.
References: *Film Daily Yearbook*, 1950–1955.

289. PALACE THEATER
Picture house. 300 seats.
References: *Film Daily Yearbook*, 1930, 1940–1946. Murray, *The Negro Handbook, 1942*. *Motion Picture Herald*, April 24, 1937; July 15, 1939. Sampson, *Blacks in Black and White*.

290. VICTORY THEATER
541 5th Street NW
Picture house. 525 seats.
References: *Film Daily Yearbook*, 1948–1955.

Fort Myers

291. GRAND THEATER
2107 Fowler Street
Picture house. 300 seats.
References: *Film Daily Yearbook*, 1930, 1940–1955. *Motion Picture Herald*, April 24, 1937; July 15, 1939. Sampson, *Blacks in Black and White*.

292. LINCOLN DRIVE-IN
Picture house.
References: *Film Daily Yearbook*, 1954, 1955.

293. PALACE THEATER
Picture house.
References: *Film Daily Yearbook*, 1930.

294. ROYAL THEATER
References: *Film Daily Yearbook*, 1929.

Fort Pierce

295. GRAND THEATER
Picture house.
References: *Film Daily Yearbook*, 1940–1950. *Motion Picture Herald*, July 15, 1939.

296. LINCOLN THEATER
Picture house. 400 seats.
References: *Film Daily Yearbook*, 1948–1955.

297. REX THEATER
Picture house.
References: *Film Daily Yearbook*, 1930.

Gainesville

298. LINCOLN THEATER
Picture house. 400 seats. The Lincoln was listed as closed in the 1950 and 1951 editions of *Film Daily Yearbook*.
References: *Film Daily Yearbook*, 1940–1955. *Motion Picture Herald*, July 15, 1939.

299. METTS THEATER
Picture house. 250 seats.
References: *Film Daily Yearbook*, 1930. *Motion Picture Herald*, April 24, 1937. Sampson, *Blacks in Black and White*.

300. PERRY THEATER
Picture house.
References: *Film Daily Yearbook*, 1948–1955.

301. ROSE THEATER
Picture house.
References: *Film Daily Yearbook*, 1950–1955.

302. W. E. LEE THEATER
Picture house.
References: *Film Daily Yearbook*, 1949–1955.

Goulds

303. DIXIE THEATER
Picture house.
References: *Film Daily Yearbook*, 1950–1955.

Haines City

304. BEN'S THEATER
Picture house.
References: *Film Daily Yearbook*, 1949–1955.

305. IMPERIAL THEATER

Picture house.
References: *Film Daily Yearbook*, 1930.

Hollandale

306. HYDE PARK DRIVE-IN
Picture house.
References: *Film Daily Yearbook*, 1953–1955.

Hollopaw

307. CENTRAL THEATER
Picture house.
References: *Film Daily Yearbook*, 1930–1933.

Hollywood

308. LIBERTY THEATER
Picture house.
References: *Film Daily Yearbook*, 1952–1955.

309. MODELLA THEATER
References: *Film Daily Yearbook*, 1930–1933.

Homestead

310. ACE THEATER
Picture house.
References: *Film Daily Yearbook*, 1950–1955.

311. LINCOLN THEATER
Picture house.
References: *Film Daily Yearbook*, 1930–1933.

Jacksonville

312. AIRDOME THEATER
106 Mytle Avenue
Vaudeville house. Owner in 1912: Clarence Muse (African American). According to Sampson, the famous film actor Clarence Muse was performing in Florida in 1912 when he met the owners of the Airdome Theater. "As the owners were in debt, Muse bought into the show using a large sum of money he had won playing cards." The Whitman Sisters performed at the Airdome in June 1910.
References: Peterson, *The African American Theatre Directory*; *Profiles of African American Stage Performers*. Sampson, *Blacks in Black and White*.

313. AUSTIN THEATER
612 W. Ashley
Vaudeville house. Manager in 1921: Buddy Austin (African American).
References: Cahn, *Julius Cahn-Gus Hill Theatrical Guide*. *Film Daily Yearbook*, 1942. Jackson, "List of Colored Theaters and Attractions," *Billboard*, August 6, 1921. Work, *Negro Yearbook, 1921–1922*.

314. EMPRESS THEATER
20 E. Forstythe
Vaudeville and picture house. 600 seats. Manager in 1921: R. Chase (African American).
References: Cahn, *Julius Cahn-Gus Hill Theatrical Guide*. Jackson, "Additions to Theater List," *Billboard*, December 31, 1921.

315. FROLIC THEATER
743 W. Ashley
Picture house. Also known as the New Frolic. 743 seats. Manager in 1921: Gus Seligman.
References: Cahn, *Julius Cahn-Gus Hill Theatrical Guide*. *Film Daily Yearbook*, 1930–1933, 1940–1955. Jackson, "List of Colored Theaters and Attractions," *Billboard*, August 6, 1921. *Motion Picture Herald*, April 24, 1937; July 15, 1939. Sampson, *Blacks in Black and White*. Work, *Negro Yearbook, 1921–1922*.

316. GEM THEATER
Picture house.

References: *Film Daily Yearbook*, 1930–1933.

317. GLOBE THEATER

Vaudeville and picture house. 1,000 seats. Managers: W.S. Sumter, Dr. J. Seth Hill, and Frank Crowd (African Americans). According to Peterson, the Globe was considered "the Southern anchor of the tour for black shows and vaudeville artists. It originally opened as the Bijou Theater on July 15, 1908. In January 1910, the name was changed to the Globe after the theater was completed remodeled." Peterson mentioned also that the theater was home to the Bijou Stock Company. In 1908, the play *Ephraim Johnson from Norfolk* was produced here.

References: Hill, *Pages from the Harlem Renaissance*. Peterson, *The African Americann Theatre Directory; Profiles of African American Stage Performers*. Peterson, *Profiles of African American Stage Performers*. Sampson, *Blacks in Black and White*.

318. LINCOLN THEATER

Vaudeville house. Owners: W. T. Clark, G. W. Walton, T. B. Pursley (African Americans). According to Sampson, the Lincoln opened in 1912.

References: Peterson, *The African American Theatre Directory*. Sampson, *Blacks in Blackface*.

319. PIX THEATER

Picture house.

References: *Film Daily Yearbook*, 1947–1955.

320. RITZ THEATER

825 Davis Street

Picture house. 654–970 seats.

References: *Film Daily Yearbook*, 1940–1955. *Motion Picture Herald*, April 24, 1937; July 15, 1939. Sampson, *Blacks in Black and White*.

321. ROOSEVELT THEATER

818 W. Ashley Street

Picture house. 1,150 seats.

References: *Film Daily Yearbook*, 1948–1955.

322. SKY VIEW DRIVE-IN

Picture house. 375 cars. Owner: Roy Benjamin.

References: *Film Daily Yearbook*, 1949–1955.

323. STRAND THEATER

701 W. Ashley Street

Vaudeville and picture house. 900 seats. A TOBA theater. Manager in 1921: Buddy Austin. The Strand was originally part of the Southern Consolidated Vaudeville circuit and later joined the combined TOBA and Managers and Performers circuit. Later it became a movie house.

References: Cahn, *Julius Cahn-Gus Hill Theatrical Guide*. *Film Daily Yearbook*, 1930–1933, 1940–1955. Hill, *Pages from the Harlem Renaissance*. Jackson, "The Theater Owners' Booking Association," *Billboard*, December 16, 1922. *Motion Picture Herald*, April 24, 1937; July 15, 1939. Peterson, *The African American Theatre Directory*. Sampson, *Blacks in Black and White*.

324. TOM BAXTER'S PLACE

Vaudeville house. According to Peterson, the house was in business from about 1900 to through the 1910s.

References: Peterson. *The African American Theatre Directory*.

Jasper

325. LINCOLN THEATER

Picture house.

References: *Film Daily Yearbook*, 1949–1955.

Key West

326. LINCOLN THEATER

Picture house.

References: *Film Daily Yearbook*, 1949–1955.

Ritz Theater, Jacksonville, Florida (SoulofAmerica.com)

Kissimmee

327. DUNBAR THEATER
Picture house.
References: *Film Daily Yearbook*, 1930–1933.

Lake City

328. CARVER THEATER
Picture house. 400 seats. According to *Film Daily Yearbook*, the Carver was closed in 1949.
References: *Film Daily Yearbook*, 1949–1955.

329. DESOTO THEATER
Picture house. 465 seats. According to the *Film Daily Yearbook*, the DeSoto was closed in 1950 and 1951.
References: *Film Daily Yearbook*, 1947–1955.

Lakeland

330. PRINCESS THEATER
Picture house.
References: *Film Daily Yearbook*, 1930–1933.

331. RAULERSON'S THEATER
Picture house.
References: *Film Daily Yearbook*, 1952–1955.

332. ROXY THEATER
902–904 N. Florida Avenue
Picture house. 400 seats. Manager in 1938: James W. Savage.
References: *Film Daily Yearbook*, 1940–1955. *Motion Picture Herald*, July 15, 1939.

Lake Wales

333. DELLA ROBA THEATER
Picture house. 150 seats.
References: *Film Daily Yearbook*, 1940–1955. *Motion Picture Herald*, April 24, 1937. *Motion Picture Herald*, July 15, 1939. Sampson, *Blacks in Black and White*.

334. REX THEATER.
Picture house.
References: *Film Daily Yearbook*, 1930–1933.

Leesburg

335. CARVER THEATER
Picture house.
References: *Film Daily Yearbook*, 1950–1955.

Liberty City

336. LIBERTY THEATER
Picture house.
References: *Film Daily Yearbook*, 1947, 1948.

Loughman

337. AVALON THEATER
Picture house.
References: *Film Daily Yearbook*, 1930–1933.

Miami

338. ACE THEATER
3608 Grand Avenue
Picture house. 250–300 seats. Manager in 1942: Delvin Wright.
References: *Film Daily Yearbook*, 1940–1955. *Motion Picture Herald*, July 15, 1939.

339. BUNCHE THEATER
22990 W. Bunch Park
Picture house. Manager in 1955: James F. Camp.
References: *Film Daily Yearbook*, 1952–1955.

340. HARLEM THEATER
322 14th Street NW
Picture house. 300–607 seats. Manager in 1942: Herman Polies.
References: *Film Daily Yearbook*, 1940–1955. *Motion Picture Herald*, April 24, 1937; July 15, 1939. Sampson, *Blacks in Black and White*.

341. LIBERTY THEATER
6700 15th Street NW
Picture house. 375 seats.
References: *Film Daily Yearbook*, 1945–1955.

342. LINCOLN THEATER
555 Lincoln Road
Picture house. 1,850 seats. Manager in 1942: John M. Shepard.
References: *Film Daily Yearbook*, 1930–1933. *Motion Picture Herald*, April 24, 1937. Sampson, *Blacks in Black and White*.

343. LYRIC THEATER
817 Second Avenue NW
Picture house. 605 seats. Manager: Karl K. Keyser.
References: *Film Daily Yearbook*, 1930–1933, 1940–1955. Hill, *Pages from the Harlem Renaissance*. Jackson, "The Theater Owners' Booking Association," *Billboard*, December 16, 1922. *Motion Picture Herald*, April 24, 1937; July 15, 1939. Sampson, *Blacks in Black and White*.

344. MODERN THEATER
1130 3rd Avenue NW
Picture house. 500 seats. Manager in 1942: Flore Marasco.
References: *Film Daily Yearbook*, 1940–1955. *Motion Picture Herald*, July 15, 1939.

345. MOONLIGHT THEATER
Picture house.
References: *Film Daily Yearbook*, 1930–1933.

346. RITZ THEATER
927 2nd Avenue NW
Picture house. 500 seats. Manager in 1942: Walter Toemnes.

54 Florida

Ritz Theater, Miami, Florida (SoulofAmerica.com)

References: *Film Daily Yearbook*, 1940–1955. *Motion Picture Herald*, July 15, 1939.

347. SKYDOME THEATER
Picture house.
References: *Film Daily Yearbook*, 1930–1933.

Moore Haven

348. TOBIAS THEATER
Picture house.
References: *Film Daily Yearbook*, 1950–1955.

Mulberry

349. HARLEM THEATER
Picture house.
References: *Film Daily Yearbook*, 1947–1955.

Nassau

350. SAVOY THEATER
Picture house. 350 seats.
References: *Motion Picture Herald*, April 24, 1937. Sampson, *Blacks in Black and White*.

Newberry

351. W. LEE THEATER
Picture house.
References: *Film Daily Yearbook*, 1949–1955.

New Smyrna Beach

352. STAR THEATER
Picture house.
References: *Film Daily Yearbook*, 1949–1955.

Ocala

353. BROADWAY THEATER
Picture house.
References: *Film Daily Yearbook*, 1930–1933.

354. FLORIDA THEATER
Picture house.
References: *Film Daily Yearbook*, 1930–1933.

355. LYRIC THEATER
Vaudeville house. The Lyric was part of the combined TOBA and Managers and Performers vaudeville circuit.
References: Hill, *Pages from the Harlem Renaissance*. Jackson, "The Theater Owners' Booking Association," *Billboard*, December 16, 1922.

356. ROXY THEATER
Picture house.
References: *Film Daily Yearbook*, 1949–1955.

357. WEST SIDE THEATER
Picture house. 250 seats.
References: *Film Daily Yearbook*, 1940–1955. *Motion Picture Herald*, April 24, 1937; July 15, 1939. Sampson, *Blacks in Black and White*.

Orlando

358. CARVER THEATER
701 W. Church Street
Picture house. Manager in 1955: Edward Gordon.
References: *Film Daily Yearbook*, 1952–1955.

359. LINCOLN THEATER
520 W. Church Street
Picture house. 684 seats. Manager in 1955: E. H. Pond.
References: *Film Daily Yearbook*, 1940–1955. *Motion Picture Herald*, July 15, 1939.

360. SKYVIEW DRIVE-IN
Picture house.
References: *Film Daily Yearbook*, 1953–1955.

361. STRAND THEATER
Picture house. 600 seats.
References: *Motion Picture Herald*, April 24, 1937. Sampson, *Blacks in Black and White*.

362. WASHINGTON SHORES DRIVE-IN
Picture house. 200 cars. Owner: Floyd Stowe.
References: *Film Daily Yearbook*, 1952–1955.

Pahokee

363. ACE THEATER
Picture house.
References: *Film Daily Yearbook*, 1940–1955. *Motion Picture Herald*, July 15, 1939.

364. GOLDEN NUGGET THEATER
Picture house. 150 seats.
References: *Film Daily Yearbook*, 1940–1944. *Motion Picture Herald*, July 15, 1939.

365. PLANTATION THEATER
Picture house. According to the *Film Daily Yearbook*, the Plantation was closed from 1949 to 1951.
References: *Film Daily Yearbook*, 1949–1955.

366. PRINCE THEATER
Picture house.
References: *Film Daily Yearbook*, 1940–1944. *Motion Picture Herald*, July 15, 1939.

367. SHOWBOAT THEATER
Picture house. 400 seats.
References: *Film Daily Yearbook*, 1949–1955.

Palatka

368. HOWELL THEATER

Picture house.
References: *Film Daily Yearbook,* 1949.

369. LINCOLN THEATER
Picture house.
References: *Film Daily Yearbook,* 1930–1933, 1946–1948.

370. MADISON THEATER
311 W. 11th Street
Picture house.
References: *Film Daily Yearbook,* 1949–1955.

Palmetto

371. REX THEATER
Picture house. 150 seats.
References: *Film Daily Yearbook,* 1940–1955. *Motion Picture Herald,* April 24, 1937; July 15, 1939. Sampson, *Blacks in Black and White.*

Panama City

372. LINCOLN THEATER
Picture house. 407 seats.
References: *Film Daily Yearbook,* 1952–1955.

373. ROYAL THEATER
Picture house.
References: *Film Daily Yearbook,* 1944–1955.

Pensacola

374. BELMONT THEATER
115 E. Belmont Street
Vaudeville house. Manager in 1927: Ernest L. Cummings. The Belmont was part of the combined TOBA and Managers and Performers vaudeville circuit. According to Hill, the Belmont did the opposite of what most African American theaters did: it originally catered exclusively to black audiences but opened its doors to white patrons on August 1, 1922. Under the new arrangement, "white people [were] seated in the balcony," while the colored patrons [occupied] the first floor." In 1927, Dusty Fletcher and his Harlem Strutters appeared here.
References: Bowser, *Writing Himself into History.* Cahn, *Julius Cahn-Gus Hill Theatrical Guide. Chicago Defender,* "Harlem Strutters," November 26, 1927. *Film Daily Yearbook,* 1930–1933. Hill, *Pages from the Harlem Renaissance.* Jackson, "List of Colored Theaters and Attractions," *Billboard,* August 6, 1921; "The Theater Owners' Booking Association," Billboard, December 16, 1922. Peterson, *The African American Theatre Directory.* Work, *Negro Yearbook,* 1921–1922.

375. EL DORADO THEATER
Vaudeville theater. According to Peterson and Sampson, the El Dorado was in business during the 1910s and 1920s.
References: Peterson, *The African American Theatre Directory.* Sampson, *Blacks in Black and White.*

376. ELECTRIC THEATER
Belmont Street
Vaudeville house. Manager: M. Jacoby.
References: Peterson, *The African American Theatre Directory.*

377. LINCOLN THEATER
505 N. Tarragona Street
Picture house. Manager in 1919: Peter Delano. Manager in 1921: Ernest L. Cummings. Owners: W. S. Sumter, Dr. J. Seth Hill, Frank Crowd (African Americans).
References: Cahn, *Julius Cahn-Gus Hill Theatrical Guide.* Hill, *Pages from the Harlem Renaissance.* Jackson, "List of Colored Theaters and Attractions," *Bill-*

Florida 57

board, August 6, 1921. Work, *Negro Yearbook, 1921–1922*.

378. RITZ THEATER
303 N. Tarragona Street
Picture house. 429 seats
Reference: *Film Daily Yearbook*, 1946–1955.

379. ROXY THEATER
Picture house.
References: *Film Daily Yearbook*, 1947, 1948.

Perrine

380. MIDWAY THEATER
Picture house. 260 seats.
References: *Film Daily Yearbook*, 1949–1955.

Perry

381. BROOKLYN THEATER
Picture house.
References: *Film Daily Yearbook*, 1949–1955.

382. LYRIC THEATER
Picture house.
References: *Film Daily Yearbook*, 1930–1933.

Plant City

383. HAZEL THEATER
Picture house. 250 seats.
References: *Film Daily Yearbook*, 1949–1955.

384. LINCOLN THEATER
Picture house.
References: *Film Daily Yearbook*, 1930–1933.

Pompano

385. CASE THEATER
Picture house. This was a portable or tent theater.
References: *Film Daily Yearbook*, 1950–1955.

386. LOVELAND THEATER
Picture house. 242 seats.
References: *Film Daily Yearbook*, 1952–1955.

387. POMPANO THEATER
Picture house. 350 seats.
References: *Film Daily Yearbook*, 1940–1955. *Motion Picture Herald*, July 15, 1939.

Port St. Joe

388. HARLEM THEATER
Port Reed Avenue
Picture house. 948 seats. According to *Film Daily Yearbook*, the Harlem was closed from 1949 to 1951.
References: *Film Daily Yearbook*, 1949–1955.

Punta Gorda

389. LINCOLN THEATER
Picture house.
References: *Film Daily Yearbook*, 1930–1933.

Quincy

390. ROXY THEATER
Picture house. 250 seats.
References: *Film Daily Yearbook*, 1940–1955. *Motion Picture Herald*, July 15, 1939.

Quitman

391. STAR THEATER

Picture house.
References: *Film Daily Yearbook*, 1955.

Saint Augustine

392. CARVER THEATER
Picture house.
References: *Film Daily Yearbook*, 1951–1955.

393. COLORED THEATER
Picture house. Owner in 1922: E. A. Martin (African American). It is possible but not certain that this may have been the Carver or the Rex.
References: Cahn, *Julius Cahn-Gus Hill Theatrical Guide*. Jackson, "List of Colored Theaters and Attractions," *Billboard*, August 6, 1921. Sampson, *Blacks in Black and White*. Work, *Negro Yearbook, 1921–1922*.

394. REX THEATER
Picture house.
References: *Film Daily Yearbook*, 1949, 1950.

Saint Petersburg

395. COMMUNITY THEATER
Picture house.
References: *Film Daily Yearbook*, 1952–1955.

396. DREAM THEATER
408 9th Street
Vaudeville and picture house. Also known as the Capitol. 614 seats. Owner in 1921: Jack Lively. The house was part of the combined TOBA and Managers and Performers vaudeville circuit.
References: Cahn, *Julius Cahn-Gus Hill Theatrical Guide*. Hill, *Pages from the Harlem Renaissance*. Jackson, "List of Colored Theaters and Attractions," *Billboard*, August 6, 1921; "The Theater Owners' Booking Association," *Billboard*, December 16, 1922. Work, *Negro Yearbook, 1921–1922*.

397. HARLEM THEATER
1017–1019 S. 3rd Avenue
Picture house. 500 seats.
References: *Film Daily Yearbook*, 1940–1955. *Motion Picture Herald*, April 24, 1937; July 15, 1939. Sampson, *Blacks in Black and White*.

398. LINCOLN THEATER
Picture house.
References: *Film Daily Yearbook*, 1930–1933.

399. PALACE THEATER
Picture house.
References: *Film Daily Yearbook*, 1930–1933.

400. REX THEATER
Picture house.
References: *Film Daily Yearbook*, 1952–1955.

401. ROYAL THEATER
1911 S. 22nd Street
Picture house. 700 seats.
References: *Film Daily Yearbook*, 1950–1955.

Sanford

402. ACE THEATER
Picture house.
References: *Film Daily Yearbook*, 1949.

403. AVENUE THEATER
Picture house.
References: *Film Daily Yearbook*, 1950–1955.

404. LINCOLN THEATER
Picture house.
References: *Film Daily Yearbook*, 1930–1933.

405. STAR THEATER
Picture house.

References: *Film Daily Yearbook*, 1949–1955.

Saratoga

406. ACE THEATER
Picture house. 400 seats.
References: *Film Daily Yearbook*, 1947–1955.

407. CENTRAL THEATER
Picture house.
References: *Film Daily Yearbook*, 1930–1933.

Sebring

408. AVON THEATER
Picture house.
References: *Film Daily Yearbook*, 1949–1955.

409. DIXIE THEATER
Picture house. 170 seats.
References: *Film Daily Yearbook*, 1930–1933, 1946–1955.

410. PALM THEATER
Picture house. 150 seats.
References: *Film Daily Yearbook*, 1945–1955.

411. RIDGE THEATER
Picture house.
References: *Film Daily Yearbook*, 1952–1955.

Seminole

412. ACE THEATER
Picture house.
References: *Film Daily Yearbook*, 1950–1955.

South Bay

413. LAKE THEATER
Picture house.
References: *Film Daily Yearbook*, 1949–1955.

Tallahassee

414. A AND M COLLEGE THEATER
Picture house. 500 seats.
References: *Film Daily Yearbook, 1940–1947. Motion Picture Herald*, April 24, 1937; July 15, 1939. Sampson, *Blacks in Black and White.*

415. CAPITOL THEATER
Picture house. 500 seats.
References: *Film Daily Yearbook*, 1930–1933, 1940–1955. *Motion Picture Herald*, July 15, 1939.

416. FAN THEATER
Picture house.
References: *Film Daily Yearbook*, 1930–1933.

417. LEON THEATER
525 W. Tennessee Street
Picture house. 435 seats.
References: *Film Daily Yearbook*, 1942–1955.

Tampa

418. BUCKINGHAM THEATER
Vaudeville house. Manger in 1901: Pat H. Chappelle (African American). Chapelle and his brothers James and Lewis managed the Chappelle Brothers' Circuit. According to Peterson, this was "one of the earliest black-controlled vaudeville circuits." It consisted of a chain of vaudeville houses in cities such as Savannah, Georgia; Jacksonville, Florida; and Tampa. The Buckingham was the Tampa house of the Chappelle Brothers. In 1906, the Buckingham hosted a "variety troupe" production called *The Funny Folks*.

References: Peterson, *The African American Theatre Directory*.

419. CARVER THEATER
Picture house.
References: *Film Daily Yearbook*, 1949–1955.

420. CENTRAL THEATER
1201 Central Avenue
Picture house. 774 seats. According to *Film Daily Yearbook*, the Central was closed from 1949 to 1951.
References: *Film Daily Yearbook*, 1930–1933, 1940–1955. *Motion Picture Herald*, April 24, 1937; July 15, 1939. Sampson, *Blacks in Black and White*.

421. LINCOLN THEATER
1109 Central Avenue
Picture house. 700 seats.
References: *Film Daily Yearbook*, 1946–1955.

422. MACEO THEATER
1310 Central Street
Picture house. Owner in 1921: C. A. Sappel.
References: Cahn, *Julius Cahn-Gus Hill Theatrical Guide*. *Film Daily Yearbook*, 1930–1933. Jackson, "List of Colored Theaters and Attractions," *Billboard*, August 6, 1921. Work, *Negro Yearbook*, 1921–1922.

423. PALACE THEATER
Tampa and Zack Streets.
Vaudeville and picture house. 1,381 seats. The house was part of the combined TOBA and Managers and Performers vaudeville circuit.
References: Cahn, *Julius Cahn-Gus Hill Theatrical Guide*. Hill, *Pages from the Harlem Renaissance*. Jackson, "List of Colored Theaters and Attractions," *Billboard*, August 6, 1921; "Theater Owners' Booking Association," *Billboard*, December 16, 1922.

424. PLAZA THEATER

Picture house. 650 seats.
References: *Film Daily Yearbook*, 1940–1949. *Motion Picture Herald*, July 15, 1939.

Vero Beach

425. REX THEATER
Picture house.
References: *Film Daily Yearbook*, 1949–1955.

Wauchula

426. ARCADE THEATER
Picture house.
References: *Film Daily Yearbook*, 1949–1955.

427. RITZ THEATER
Picture house.
References: *Film Daily Yearbook*, 1949–1955.

428. WAUCHULA THEATER
Picture house.
References: *Film Daily Yearbook*, 1949–1955.

West Palm Beach

429. DIXIE THEATER
Vaudeville and picture house. 485 seats. Owner in 1923: H. C. Bartholomew. Roscoe and Mitchell's Radio Girls performed at the Dixie in 1923.
References: *Chicago Defender,* "Dixie Theater," June 9, 1923. *Film Daily Yearbook*, 1930–1933.

430. GRAND THEATER
448 N. Rosemary Street
Vaudeville and picture house. 511–600 seats. In 1925, Kid Red was the featured performer. The *Chicago Defender* said the

show was "standing room only." Other performers included comedian Memphis Lewis, dancers Eldridge and Tidridge, saxaphonist T. J. Lee, pianist Little Buddy Farrar, and one-legged dancer Silver Fox.

References: *Chicago Defender*, "West Palm Beach," September 12, 1925. *Film Daily Yearbook*, 1930–1933, 1940–1955. *Motion Picture Herald*, April 24, 1937; July 15, 1939. Sampson, *Blacks in Black and White*.

Winter Garden

431. COLORED ANNEX THEATER
Picture house.
References: *Film Daily Yearbook*, 1949–1955.

Winter Haven

432. VILLA THEATER
Picture house.
References: *Film Daily Yearbook*, 1949–1955.

Ybor City

433. CAMPOBELLO THEATER
Picture house.
References: *Film Daily Yearbook*, 1930–1933.

GEORGIA

Albany

434. RITZ THEATER
225 S. Jackson Street
Picture house. 572 seats.
References: *Film Daily Yearbook*, 1943–1955.

435. STRAND THEATER
Vaudeville and picture house. 663 seats. Architects: Lockwood and Poundstone. Owner in 1928: Harry Hirschensohn. A TOBA theater. According to the *Chicago Defender*, the music in the house "was furnished by an automatic electrola with a volume ranging from a whisper to a full orchestra volume."
References: *Chicago Defender*, "Albany, Ga. Has New Theater," April 7, 1928.

Americus

436. HARLEM THEATER
Picture house. 600 seats.
References: *Film Daily Yearbook*, 1949–1955.

437. ROXY THEATER
Picture house.
References: *Film Daily Yearbook*, 1949–1955.

Athens

438. HARLEM THEATER
Picture house.
References: *Film Daily Yearbook*, 1952–1955.

439. MORTON THEATER
Vaudeville and picture house. 200 seats. Black owned and managed. The Morton was originally part of the Southern Consolidated Vaudeville Circuit and later joined the combined TOBA and Managers and Performers vaudeville circuit. In March 1920, the Morton featured the Oscar Micheaux film *Within Our Gates.*
References: Bowser, *Writing Himself into History.* Cahn, *Julius Cahn-Gus Hill Theatrical Guide.* Hill, *Pages from the Harlem Renaissance.* Jackson, "List of Colored Theaters and Attractions," *Billboard,* August 6, 1921; "The Theater Owners' Booking Association," *Billboard,* December 16, 1922. *Motion Picture Herald,* April 24, 1937. Peterson, *The African American Theatre Directory.* Riis, "Pink Morton's Theater." Sampson, *Blacks in Black and White.* Work, *Negro Yearbook, 1921–1922.*

440. STAR THEATER
Picture house.
References: *Film Daily Yearbook,* 1930–1933.

Atlanta

441. AIRDOME THEATER
Central Avenue
Vaudeville house. According to Peterson, this theater was in business during the 1910s.
References: Peterson, *The African American Theatre Directory.*

442. ARCADE THEATER
Decatur Street
Vaudeville house. According to Peterson, this theater was in business from about 1910 to 1930.
References: Peterson, *The African American Theatre Directory.* Sampson, *Blacks in Black and White.*

443. ASHBY THEATER
925 Hunter Street NW
Picture house. 480 seats. In October 1955, the Ashby was showing the films *Chief Crazy Horse,* starring Victor Mature, and *His Majesty O'Keefe,* starring Burt Lancaster.
References: *Atlanta Daily World,* October 2, 1955. *Film Daily Yearbook,* 1940–1955. *Motion Picture Herald,* April 24, 1937; July 15, 1939. Sampson, *Blacks in Black and White.*

444. AUDITORIUM THEATER
192 Auburn Avenue
Vaudeville and picture house. Also called Odd Fellows' Auditorium. 613 seats. Black owned and managed. Owner in 1921: S. L. Lockett. Built in 1914 by the Southern Amusement Company. This may have been the theater named in an advertisement run by the newspaper the *Atlanta Independent* in 1919. It showed black people saying to one another "Why don't we go to that Colored theatre on Auburn Avenue. You see the same picture and do not go in from the alley. Let us go there. We can go in the front and sit anywhere we want to and it is also run by a Colored man."
References: *Atlanta Independent,* November 29, December 6, 13, 1919. Bowser, *Writing Himself into History.* Cahn, *Julius Cahn-Gus Hill Theatrical Guide. Film Daily Yearbook,* 1931. Jackson, "List of Colored Theaters and Attractions," *Billboard,* August 6, 1921. Peterson, *The African American Theatre Directory.* Work, *Negro Yearbook, 1921–1922.*

445. CARVER THEATER
1295 Jonesboro Road NE
Picture house. 650 seats. Manager in 1955: Joseph A. Ellington. During Christmas week 1955, the Carver offered the films *Tall Man Riding,* starring Dorothy

Malone, and Randolph Scott and the Bowery Boys in *Crazy Over Horses*.

References: *Atlanta Daily World*, December 25, 1955. *Film Daily Yearbook*, 1952–1955.

446. EIGHTY-ONE THEATER
81 Decatur Street

Vaudeville house. 950 seats. Built circa 1908. Also known as Bailey's Eighty-One. A TOBA theater. Manager in 1921: Charles P. Robins. Manager in 1928: Tom Bailey. It was remodeled in 1925. Atlanta resident B. B. Beamon recalls, "A fellow owned the theater by the name of Tom Bailey. White man. Mr. Bailey was a black entrepreneur. He owned all the black theaters in Atlanta. Back then, all the [black] acts were coming into the 81 Theatre, Bessie Smith and Ma Rainey and them." Kate McTell recalls that "we'd all do the Charleston, Black Bottom, Twiggletoe and along in there. It was more socializing with the musicians than it is now. They were charging at the door, which was about twenty-five cents or fifty cents back in the Depression. It would be packed in there." All blacks did not patronize the Eighty-one. Atlanta resident Paulin Minniefield says: "Decent people were not supposed to go down there. I'm just telling you the way we were brought up." Around 1913, Bessie Smith got her start in show business here. In 1919 blues singer Margie Sipp sang here. On February 28, 1920, the Oscar Micheaux picture *Within Our Gates* was shown at the Eighty-One. Among the many TOBA performers appearing here were Ethel Waters and the Hill Sisters. In the 1930s, Count Basie and Gonzelle White's band performed here. By the 1950s, however, the theater featured regular Hollywood films. In October 1955, the Eighty-One offered a double feature: *Conquest of Space*, and *The Marauders*, starring Keenan Wynn. During Christmas week 1955, the theater had the movie *Tall Man Riding*, co-starring Dorothy Malone and Randolph Scott.

References: Albertson, *Bessie*. *Atlanta Daily World*, October 2, 1955, December 25, 1955. Basie, *Good Morning Blues*. Bowser, *Writing Himself into History*. Bradshaw, *Born with the Blues*. *Chicago Defender*, Sept. 16, 1922; "81 Theater Opens," December 5, 1925. *Film Daily Yearbook*, 1930, 1931, 1940–1955. Jackson, "List of Colored Theaters and Attractions," *Billboard*, August 6, 1921; "The Theater Owners' Booking Assocation," *Billboard*, December 16, 1922. Kuhn, *Living Atlanta: An Oral History of the City*. *Motion Picture Herald*, July 15, 1939. *Official Theatrical World of Colored Artists*. Peterson, *The African American Theatre Directory*. Waters, *His Eye Is On the Sparrow*. Work, *Negro Yearbook, 1921–1922*.

447. FAMOUS THEATER
Decatur Street

Vaudeville theater. Manager: J. B. Kelly. According to Peterson, the Famous was in operation from the 1910s through the 1930s.

References: Peterson, *The African American Theatre Directory*. Sampson, *Blacks in Black and White*.

448. FORREST THEATER
243 Forrest Avenue NE

Picture house. Manager in 1955: Charles Brewer. In October 1955, the Forrest was showing the motion pictures *Montana Belle*, co-starring Jane Russell and George Brent, and *Hell's Island*, co-starring John Payne and Mary Murphy. During Christmas week 1955, the theater offered the films *Rage at Dawn*, starring Randolph Scott, and *High Society* with the Bowery Boys.

References: *Atlanta Daily World*, October 3, 1955; December 25, 1955. *Film Daily Yearbook*, 1948–1955.

449. HARLEM THEATER
Picture house. 400 seats.
References: *Film Daily Yearbook*, 1940–1955. *Motion Picture Herald*, July 15, 1939.

450. LENOX THEATER
Picture house.
References: *Film Daily Yearbook*, 1940–1947. *Motion Picture Herald*, July 15, 1939.

451. LINCOLN THEATER
Picture house. 300 seats.
References: *Film Daily Yearbook*, 1940–1955. *Motion Picture Herald*, April 24, 1937; July 15, 1939. Sampson, *Blacks in Black and White*.

452. LUNA PARK THEATER
99 Decatur Street
Picture house. Manager in 1910: G. C. Garner. According to Peterson, the Luna Park was in operation during the 1910s and 1920s.
References: Peterson, *The African American Theatre Directory*.

453. NINETY-ONE THEATER
91 Decatur Street
Vaudeville house. Manager in 1921: Charles P. Bailey. Bessie Smith appeared here in 1920.
References: Albertson, *Bessie*. Cahn, *Julius Cahn-Gus Hill Theatrical Guide*. *Film Daily Yearbook*, 1931. Jackson, "List of Colored Theaters and Attractions," *Billboard*, August 6, 1921. Waters, *His Eye Is On the Sparrow*. Work, *Negro Yearbook, 1921–1922*.

ODDS FELLOWS AUDITORIUM see Auditorium Theater.

454. PALM GARDEN THEATER
Glenwood Avenue
Vaudeville house. Manager: Frank McKenzie. The Palm Garden was in business during the 1910s, according to Peterson.
References: *Peterson, The African American Theatre Directory*.

455. PARADISE THEATER
Peters Street
Vaudeville house. Manager: Elijah Davis. According to Peterson, the Paradise was in business during the 1910s.
References: Peterson, *The African American Theatre Directory*.

456. PARAMOUNT THEATER
Vaudeville house. Also known as the Howard Theater. Atlanta resident Jack Cathcart recalled that "at the Paramount Theatre, which was originally Howard Theatre, they used a larger band, anywhere from thirty to forty people. And for years that was under the direction of Enrico Leide."
References: *Chicago Defender*, "New Houses Opening on Starr Circuit," September 21, 1929. *Film Daily Yearbook*, 1930–1932. Kuhn, *Living Atlanta: An Oral History of the City*.

457. PICTORIAL THEATER
Picture house.
References: *Film Daily Yearbook*, 1940–1942. *Motion Picture Herald, July 15, 1939*.

458. RITZ THEATER
653 Fair Street SW
Picture house. Manager in 1955: Charles Brewer. In October 1955, the Ritz featured Alan Ladd in *Drum Beat* and the Bowery Boys in *Bowery to Bagdad*. During Christmas week 1955, moviegoers saw the movies *Son of Sinbad*, starring Dale Robertson, Sally Forrest, Lili St. Cyr, and Vincent Price, and *Santa Fe Passage*, starring John Payne.
References: *Atlanta Daily World*, October 2, 1955; December 15, 1955. *Film Daily Yearbook*, 1952–1955.

459. ROYAL THEATER

232 or 238 Auburn Avenue NE
Picture house. 450 seats. Also known as Bailey's Royal. In October 1955, moviegoers at the Royal were treated to the adventure-drama motion picture *River of No Return*, starring Robert Mitchum, Marilyn Monroe, and Rory Calhoun. During Christmas week 1955, the theater was showing Howard Hughes's *Son of Sinbad*, starring Dale Robertson, Sally Forrest, Lili St. Cyr, and Vincent Price.
References: *Atlanta Daily World*, October 3, 1955; December 25, 1955. *Film Daily Yearbook*, 1933, 1940–1955. *Motion Picture Herald*, April 24, 1937; July 15, 1939. Sampson, *Blacks in Black and White*.

460. STRAND THEATER
55 Decatur Street
Picture house. 300–500 seats.
References: *Film Daily Yearbook*, 1930–1933, 1940–1955. *Motion Picture Herald*, April 24, 1937; July 15, 1939. Sampson, *Blacks in Black and White*.

Attapulcus

461. HACK THEATER
Picture house.
References: *Film Daily Yearbook*, 1949–1955.

Augusta

462. HARLEM THEATER
Picture house.
References: *Film Daily Yearbook*, 1948–1955.

463. LENOX THEATER
1120 N. 9th Street
Vaudeville house. 800 seats. Built in 1922. A TOBA theater. Owner in 1921: J. A. Moffett (African American). Owner in 1925: Milton Starr. Manager in 1925: Earl Evans. Built in 1922, it was renovated in 1925 by Milton Starr at a cost of $100,000. The Oscar Micheaux film *Within Our Gates* was featured at the Lenox on February 28, 1920.
References: Bowser, *Writing Himself into History*. Cahn, *Julius Cahn-Gus Hill Theatrical Guide*. *Chicago Defender*, "Buys Theater," July 25, 1925; "$100,000 Theater Opened In Augusta, Ga., August 31," September 5, 1925. *Film Daily Yearbook*, 1930–1933, 1947–1955. Work, *Negro Yearbook, 1921–1922*.

464. PALACE THEATER
533 9th Street
Vaudeville house. Owner in 1921: George Angelos. Manager in 1921: James Patterson. The Palace was part of the combined TOBA and Managers and Performers vaudeville circuit.
References: Hill, *Pages from the Harlem Renaissance*. Jackson, "The Theater Owners' Booking Association," *Billboard*, December 16, 1922. Work, *Negro Yearbook, 1921–1922*.

465. RITZ THEATER
Picture house.
References: *Film Daily Yearbook*, 1945–1948.

466. SHOWCASE THEATER
Picture house.
References: *Film Daily Yearbook*, 1952–1955.

Bainbridge

467. DECATUR THEATER
Picture house.
References: *Film Daily Yearbook*, 1947.

Barnesville

468. DIXIE THEATER

Picture house.
References: *Film Daily Yearbook*, 1949–1955.

Baxley

469. BRANCH THEATER
Picture house.
References: *Film Daily Yearbook*, 1930–1933.

Blackshear

470. PARKER THEATER
Picture house.
References: *Film Daily Yearbook*, 1930–1933.

Brownsville

471. GEM THEATER
Picture house.
References: *Film Daily Yearbook*, 1947–1955.

Brunswick

472. JAXON THEATER
Picture house.
References: *Film Daily Yearbook*, 1930–1932.

473. LOEW'S PALACE
1406 Glocester Street
Also known as the Palace. Manager in 1921: James Buggs.
References: Simms, *Simms' Blue Book*.

474. PEKIN THEATER
1301 Glocester Street
Vaudeville house. Owner and manager in 1921: W. J. Stiles. (African American). The Oscar Micheaux film *Within Our Gates* was shown here in February 1920.
References: Bowser, *Writing Himself into History*. Cahn, *Julius Cahn-Gus Hill Theatrical Guide*. Jackson, "List of Colored Theaters and Attractions," *Billboard*, August 6, 1921. Work, *Negro Yearbook, 1921–1922*.

475. ROXY THEATER
1601 Albany Street
Picture house. 250 seats.
References: *Film Daily Yearbook*, 1941–1955.

476. VICTOR THEATER
Vaudeville house. Managers in 1915: George Barrett and Jim Buggs. In January 1915, the Victor vaudeville show featured Mexican singer, Priscilla Algretta, Sam Jones, standup comedian, magician Prince Ali Mona, and comedy singers Ada and Silas Green.
References: *Indianapolis Freeman*, "Notes from the Victor Theater, Brunswick, Ga.," January 2, 1915.

Camilla

477. PALACE THEATER
Picture house.
References: *Film Daily Yearbook*, 1950–1955.

Columbus

478. AIRDOME THEATER
Vaudeville house. According to Peterson, the Airdome "was owned by Ma Rainey after her retirement in 1935."
Source: Peterson, *The African American Theatre Directory*.

479. DIXIE THEATER
1024 1st Avenue
Picture house. 250–350 seats.
References: *Film Daily Yearbook*, 1940–1955. *Motion Picture Herald*, April 24, 1937; July 15, 1939. Sampson, *Blacks in Black and White*.

480. DREAM THEATER
1026 1st Avenue
Vaudeville house. Built circa 1907. Manager in 1921: G.S. Love. The house was part of the combined TOBA and Managers and Performers Vaudeville Circuit.
In March 1920, the Oscar Micheaux film *Within Our Gates* was shown and in 1921, blues singer Clara Smith performed.
References: Bowser, *Writing Himself into History*. Cahn, *Julius Cahn-Gus Hill Theatrical Guide. Film Daily Yearbook*, 1930–1932. Hill, *Pages from the Harlem Renaissance*. Jackson, "List of Colored Theaters and Attractions," *Billboard*, August 6, 1921; "The Theater Owners' Booking Association," *Billboard*, December 16, 1922. Peterson, *The African American Theatre Directory; Profiles of African American Stage Performers*. Work, *Negro Yearbook, 1921–1922*.

481. DUNBAR THEATER
Vaudeville house. The boxer Jack Johnson appeared here in 1925.
References: *Baltimore Afro-American*, October 31, 1926. Peterson, *The African American Theatre Directory*. Sampson, *Blacks in Blackface*.

482. JET DRIVE-IN
Picture house. 190 cars. Owner: Martin Theatres. Also called the Jive Drive-In.
References: *Film Daily Yearbook*, 1953–1955.

483. LIBERTY THEATER
821 8th Avenue
Picture house. 750 seats. Manager in 1925: Roy Martin.
References: *Film Daily Yearbook*, 1933, 1940–1955. *Motion Picture Herald*, July 15, 1939.

484. OKMULGEE PARK THEATER
Manager: W. M. Rainey. According to Peterson, Rainey is a relative of blues singer Ma Rainey. The Okmulgee was in business from the 1910s to the 1930s.
References: Peterson, *The African American Theatre Directory*.

Cordele

485. COLORED THEATER
Picture house.
References: Jackson, "Additions to Theater List," *Billboard*, December 31, 1921.

486. ELITE THEATER
Picture house. Oscar Micheaux's film *Within Our Gates* was shown here March 17, 1920.
References: Bowser, *Writing Himself into History*.

487. GLOBE THEATER
Picture house.
Source: Cahn, *Julius Cahn-Gus Hill Theatrical Guide. Film Daily Yearbook*, 1930–1933.

Covington

488. GEM THEATER
Picture house.
References: *Film Daily Yearbook*, 1947–1955.

489. MELROSE THEATER
Picture house.
References: *Film Daily Yearbook*, 1930–1933.

Dawson

490. STAR THEATER
Picture house.
References: *Film Daily Yearbook*, 1950–1955.

Decatur

491. CARVER THEATER

Picture house.
References: *Film Daily Yearbook,* 1950–1955.

492. EASTMAN THEATER
Picture house.
References: *Film Daily Yearbook,* 1947.

493. RITZ THEATER
Picture house. 250 seats. The Ritz was closed in 1949 according to *Film Daily Yearbook.*
References: *Film Daily Yearbook,* 1940–1949. *Motion Picture Herald,* April 24, 1937; July 15, 1939. Sampson, *Blacks in Black and White.*

494. STAR THEATER
Picture house.
References: *Film Daily Yearbook,* 1947.

Douglas

495. RIVOLI THEATER
Picture house. 700 seats.
References: *Film Daily Yearbook,* 1949–1955.

Dublin

496. CRYSTAL THEATER
Picture house. The Oscar Micheaux film *Within Our Gates* was shown here February 23–24, 1920.
References: Bowser, *Writing Himself into History.*

Eastman

497. DODGE THEATER
209 Railroad Avenue
Picture house. 824 seats.
References: *Film Daily Yearbook,* 1947–1955.

Fort Valley

498. CAROLINA THEATER
Picture house. The Carolina was a portable or tent theater.
References: *Film Daily Yearbook,* 1950–1955.

499. GEM THEATER
Picture house. In March 1920, the Oscar Micheaux film *Within Our Gates* was shown here.
References: Bowser, *Writing Himself into History.*

Gainesville

500. CARVER THEATER
Picture house.
References: *Film Daily Yearbook,* 1944–1948.

501. DIXIELAND THEATER
Picture house.
References: *Film Daily Yearbook,* 1930, 1931, 1932.

502. LINCOLN THEATER
Picture house. According to the *Film Daily Yearbook,* the Lincoln was closed from 1949 to 1951.
References: *Film Daily Yearbook,* 1949–1955.

503. REX THEATER
Picture house. 300 seats. Manager in 1921: G. M. Morgan.
References: Cahn, *Julius Cahn-Gus Hill Theatrical Guide. Film Daily Yearbook,* 1940–1943. Jackson, "List of Colored Theaters and Attractions," *Billboard,* August 6, 1921. *Motion Picture Herald,* April 24, 1937; July 15, 1939. Sampson, *Blacks in Black and White.* Work, *Negro Yearbook, 1921–1922.*

504. ROXY THEATER
Athens Street
Picture house. 250 seats.
References: *Film Daily Yearbook,* 1947–1955.

Gray

505. GRAY THEATER
Picture house.
References: *Film Daily Yearbook*, 1949.

Griffin

506. GRIFFIN THEATER
Vaudeville and picture house.
References: Work, *Negro Yearbook, 1921–1922*.

507. LIBERTY THEATER
Picture house.
References: *Film Daily Yearbook*, 1930–1932.

508. LINCOLN THEATER
Slaton Avenue
Picture house. 180 seats.
References: *Film Daily Yearbook*, 1940–1955. *Motion Picture Herald*, July 15, 1939.

Jackson

509. NEW COLORED THEATER
Picture house.
References: *Film Daily Yearbook*, 1950–1955.

LaGrange

510. PRINCESS THEATER
E. Depot Street
Picture house. 350 seats.
References: *Film Daily Yearbook*, 1940–1955. *Motion Picture Herald*, April 24, 1937; July 15, 1939. Sampson, *Blacks in Black and White*.

Lithonia

511. HARLEM THEATER
Picture house. 175 seats. According to the *Film Daily Yearbook*, the Harlem was closed from 1949 to 1951.
References: *Film Daily Yearbook*, 1949–1955.

Louisville

512. RUBY THEATER
Vaudeville house. According to Hill, the Ruby was part of the Dudley vaudeville circuit in 1911 and joined the Southern Consolidated circuit in 1916.
References: Hill, *Pages from the Harlem Renaissance*.

Macon

513. DIXIE THEATER
Picture house.
References: *Film Daily Yearbook*, 1946–1955.

514. DOUGLASS THEATER
355 Broadway Street
Vaudeville house. 512 seats. Also called the Old Douglass. Manager in 1921: C H. Douglass (African American). Manager in 1928: Ben Stein. The Oscar Micheaux motion picture *Within Our Gates* was shown here in March 1920. In spring of 1921, the Anita Bush Company and the Henry Dixon Jazzland Girls performed at the Douglass. In July 1923, blues singer Bessie Smith appeared here along with yodler Charlie Anderson and comics Harris and Harris. In March 1924, the vaudeville bill consisted of Okeh recording artist Sarah Martin, pianist Henry Callin, stuntman Dewyman Niles, comedians Lee and Wright, and the husband and wife singer/dancer team of Butterbeans and Susie. In October 1926, Dudley and Byrd, Prince and Connie, and Glasco and Glasco performed at the Douglass. Gonzelle White's band and Count Basie

Douglass Theater, Macon, Georgia (Middle Georgia Archives, Washington Memorial Library, Macon, Georgia)

appeared here in the 1930s. The Douglass was still in business in 2002.

References: *Baltimore Afro-American*, October 26, 1926. Basie, *Good Morning Blues*. Bowser, *Writing Himself into History*. Cahn, *Julius Cahn-Gus Hill Theatrical Guide*. *Chicago Defender*, "The Douglass," July 28, 1923; March 15, 21, and June 14, 1924. *Film Daily Yearbook*, 1930–1933, 1940–1955. Hill, *Pages from the Harlem Renaissance*. Jackson, "The Theater Owners' Booking Association," *Billboard*, December 16, 1922. *Motion Picture Herald*, April 24, 1937; July 15, 1939. Peterson, *Profiles of African American Stage Performers*. Sampson, *Blacks in Black and White*; *Blacks in Blackface*. Simms, *Simm's Blue Book*. Work, *Negro Yearbook 1921–1922*.

515. NEW DOUGLASS

Picture and vaudville house. Manager in 1921: C. H. Douglas.

References: Cahn, *Julius Cahn-Gus Hill Theatrical Guide*. Jackson, "List of Colored Theaters and Attractions," *Billboard*, August 6, 1921. Work, *Negro Yearbook, 1921–1922*.

516. PIC THEATER

Picture house.

References: *Film Daily Yearbook*, 1940–1942. *Motion Picture Herald*, July 15, 1939.

Moultrie

517. HARLEM THEATER

Picture house.

References: *Film Daily Yearbook*, 1947–1955.

518. STAR THEATER
Picture house.
References: *Film Daily Yearbook*, 1930–1932.

Newman

519. PAL THEATER
Picture house.
References: *Film Daily Yearbook*, 1947–1955.

Quitman

520. STAR THEATER
Picture house.
References: *Film Daily Yearbook*, 1947–1955.

Rome

521. BROADWAY THEATER
Picture house.
References: *Film Daily Yearbook*, 1930–1932.

522. CARVER THEATER
Picture house.
References: *Film Daily Yearbook*, 1949–1955.

Sandersville

523. DIXIE THEATER
Picture house. The Oscar Micheaux motion picture *Within Our Gates* was shown here February 26, 1920.
References: Bowser, *Writing Himself into History.*

Savannah

524. DREAMLAND THEATER
Picture and vaudeville house.
References: Cahn, *Julius Cahn-Gus Hill Theatrical Guide.* Jackson, "Additions to Theater List," *Billboard*, December 31, 1921.

525. DUNBAR THEATER
467 W. Broad Street
Picture house. 650 seats. Manager in 1921: Walter Scott (African American). Owner: Savannah Motion Picture Company. The theater opened as the New Dunbar in 1921 with a screening of the Oscar Micheaux film *Symbol of the Unconquered.*
References: Cahn, *Julius Cahn-Gus Hill Theatrical Guide. Film Daily Yearbook*, 1930, 1931, 1932, 1940–1955. *Chicago Defender*, March 15, 21, and June 14, 1924. Jackson, "List of Colored Theaters and Attractions," *Billboard*, August 6, 1921. *Motion Picture Herald*, April 24, 1937; July 15, 1939. Sampson, *Blacks in Blackface.* Simms, *Simms' Blue Book.* Work, *Negro Yearbook 1921–1922.*

526. EAST SIDE THEATER
722 E. Broad Street
Picture house. 857 seats.
References: *Film Daily Yearbook*, 1946–1955.

527. GLOBE THEATER
Picture house. Owner in 1921: A. S. Guggenheimer.
References: Cahn, *Julius Cahn-Gus Hill Theatrical Guide.* Jackson, "List of Colored Theaters and Attractions," *Billboard*, August 6, 1921. Work, *Negro Yearbook, 1921–1922.*

528. HIGHWAY 21 DRIVE-IN
Picture house. 200 cars. Owner: Gus Hayes.
References: *Film Daily Yearbook*, 1953–1955.

529. MELODY THEATER
Picture house.

References: *Film Daily Yearbook*, 1947–1955.

530. PEKIN THEATER
625 S. Broad Street
Vaudeville house. Manager in 1921: A. G. Monroe (African American). Manager in 1924: Josephine Jennings. The house was part of the combined TOBA and Managers and Performers vaudeville circuit.
References: Cahn, *Julius Cahn-Gus Hill Theatrical Guide*. Hill, *Pages from the Harlem Renaisssance*. Jackson, "List of Colored Theaters and Attractions," *Billboard*, August 6, 1921; "The Theater Owners' Booking Association," *Billboard*, December 16, 1922. Simms, *Simms' Blue Book*. Work, *Negro Yearbook, 1921–1922*.

531. RICO THEATER
Picture house.
References: *Film Daily Yearbook*, 1948.

532. STAR THEATER
508 W. Broad Street
Picture house. 750 seats. Owner in 1921: A. S. Guggenheimer.
References: Cahn, *Julius Cahn-Gus Hill Theatrical Guide*. *Film Daily Yearbook*, 1930–1933, 1940–1955. Jackson, "List of Colored Theaters and Attractions," *Billboard*, August 6, 1921. *Motion Picture Herald*, April 24, 1937. Sampson, *Blacks in Black and White*. Work, *Negro Yearbook, 1921–1922*.

Swainsboro

533. STAR THEATER
Picture house.
References: *Film Daily Yearbook*, 1949–1955.

Sycamore

534. HARLEM THEATER
Picture house.
References: *Film Daily Yearbook*, 1947, 1948.

Thomaston

535. Harlem Theater
Picture house.
References: *Film Daily Yearbook*, 1950–1955.

Thomasville

536. RITZ THEATER
200 Jackson Street
Picture house. 200 seats.
References: *Film Daily Yearbook*, 1940–1955. *Motion Picture Herald*, July 15, 1939.

Tifton

537. ROXY THEATER
Picture house.
References: *Film Daily Yearbook*, 1948–1955.

Valdosta

538. FRANK THEATER
Picture house. According to Cahn and Work, this theater was owned and operated by African Americans in the 1920s. The Frank may be the unnamed theater listed in the 1921 *Billboard* survey.
References: Cahn, *Julius Cahn-Gus Hill Theatrical Guide*. *Film Daily Yearbook*, 1941–1948. Work, *Negro Yearbook, 1921–1922*.

539. LIBERTY THEATER
110 Florida Avenue
Picture house. 676 seats.
References: *Film Daily Yearbook*, 1949–1955.

540. PALACE THEATER
Picture house. 593 seats.
References: *Film Daily Yearbook*, 1949–1955.

Vidalia

541. GEM THEATER
Picture house.
References: *Film Daily Yearbook*, 1949–1955.

Warwick

542. CAROLINA THEATER
Picture house. The Carolina was a portable or tent theater.
References: *Film Daily Yearbook*, 1951–1955.

Waycross

543. CARVER THEATER
Picture house.
References: *Film Daily Yearbook*, 1948–1955.

544. STAR THEATER
Vaudeville house. Manager in 1921: H. A. Bunts (African American). The Oscar Micheaux film *Within Our Gates* was shown at the Star on March 19, 1920.
References: Bowser, *Writing Himself into History*. Cahn, *Julius Cahn-Gus Hill Theatrical Guide*. Jackson, "List of Colored Theaters and Attractions," *Billboard*, August 6, 1921. Work, *Negro Yearbook, 1921–1922*.

Waynesboro

545. MAGNOLIA THEATER
Picture house.
References: *Film Daily Yearbook*, 1951–1955.

West Point

546. STRAND THEATER
Picture house.
References: *Film Daily Yearbook*, 1930–1932.

547. TENTH STREET THEATER
Picture house.
References: *Film Daily Yearbook*, 1949–1955.

ILLINOIS

Cairo

548. LINCOLN THEATER
224 8th Avenue
Picture house. 907 seats.
References: *Film Daily Yearbook*, 1949–1955.

549. OPERA HOUSE THEATER
Picture house
References: *Film Daily Yearbook*, 1940–1948. *Motion Picture Herald*, April 24, 1937; July 15, 1939.

550. STANDARD THEATER
Picture house. Manager in 1921: L. B. Curtis.
References: Cahn, *Julius Cahn-Gus Hill*

Theatrical Guide. Film Daily Yearbook, 1930–1932. Jackson, "List of Colored Theaters and Attractions," *Billboard*, August 6, 1921. Work, *Negro Yearbook*, 1921–1922.

551. UPTOWN THEATER
Picture house.
References: *Motion Picture Herald*, April 24, 1937.

Chicago

552. ADELPHIA THEATER
7074 N. Clark Street
Picture house. 1,000–1,312 seats. Architect: Mark D. Kalischer. Manager in 1921: Sam Goode. Manager in 1923: Sam Atkinson.
References: *Architectural Forum*, "Adelphi Theater, Chicago," Vol. 63 (July 1935): 56–57. Jackson, "List of Colored Theaters and Attractions," *Billboard*, August 6, 1921. Cahn, *Julius Cahn-Gus Hill Theatrical Guide*. Work, *Negro Yearbook, 1921–1922*.

553. AMO THEATER
436 E. 61st Street
Picture house. 723 seats.
References: *Film Daily Yearbook*, 1949–1955.

554. APOLLO THEATER
526 E. 47th Street
Picture and vaudeville house. 669 seats. Architects: Holabird and Roche. In 1921, the Apollo showed pictures daily from 5:30 to 11:00 p.m. Vaudeville shows were featured on Saturday and Sunday from 2 to 11 p.m.
References: *Architectural Record*, "Apollo Theater, Chicago, Ill.," Vol. 53 (June 1923): 533–43. *Chicago Defender*, "Apollo of Chicago T.O.B.A House," December 22, 1928. *Film Daily Yearbook*, 1930–1933, 1940–1955. *Motion Picture Herald*, July 15, 1939.

555. ATLAS THEATER
4711 S. State Street
Picture and vaudeville house. 650 seats. Owner and manager in 1921: H. Dooley (African American). In February 1920, the Atlas featured the Oscar Micheaux film *Within Our Gates*. In 1921, the Atlas had a house orchestra called the Atlas Orchestra. In March 1922, the Atlas showed the following films: *Poor Relations, Life's Darn Funny, The Marriage of William Ash, For His Mother's Sake, The Gilded Lily*, and *The End of the World*, starring Betty Compton.
References: Bowser, *Writing Himself into History*. Cahn, *Julius Cahn-Gus Hill Theatrical Guide. Film Daily Yearbook*, 1931, 1932. Jackson, "List of Colored Theaters and Attractions," *Billboard*, August 6, 1921. Work, *Negro Yearbook, 1921–1922*.

556. AVENUE THEATER
3110 Indiana Avenue
Vaudeville and picture house. 1,000 seats. Built in 1914. Owner in 1921: Panama Amusement Company. Manager in 1921: Louis Weinberg. According to Peterson, the Avenue was originally a Jim Crow house that became an all-black theater "after the white population moved from the area, and when black patronage began to be attracted away to the nearby Grand Theatre." In May 1921, the *Chicago Defender* advertised the following vaudeville acts at the Avenue: Morrella's Toy Shop, Margaret Ward Thomas, Rene and Florence, Folette's Monkeys, Gant and Perkins, Daniels and Walton, and Francis and Phillips. Admission on the main floor was 40 cents and 27 cents for the balcony. Children under 12 were admitted for 19 cents. In 1921, the Clarence Jones Orchestra performed. In March 1922, Avenue audiences were treated to *Little Lord*

Fauntleroy, starring Mary Pickford. The famed Lafayette Players performed here.

The Avenue was taken over in 1923 by the Follies Amusement Company, which owned a chain of Illinois theaters. The new company initiated a policy of a resident colored musical burlesque company in addition to three vaudeville acts. One of the acts booked in 1923 was blues singer Lucille Hegaman. In January 1924, blues singer Ethel Waters headlined the show. Joining Waters on the bill were pianist and dancer Ethel Williams, the singing and dancing team of Mason and Zudora, telepathist Mahandra, the DeBurg Sisters, and a musical comedy revue called *Make It Snappy*. During the same year, Bessie Smith performed here. In 1929, the *New York Age* praised Louis Armstrong's performance at the Lafayette: "Never before in the history of Harlem theatricals had any artist received a reception comparable to that accorded Louis Armstrong at the Lafayette Theatre. The audience simply rose in their chairs as this most remarkable of all cornetists drew from his golden trumpet music such as has never been heard before."

References: Albertson, *Bessie*. *Billboard*, August 8, 1921. Cahn, *Julius Cahn-Gus Hill Theatrical Guide*. *Chicago Defender*, "Avenue Theater Has New Policy," December 15, 1923; "Ethel Waters & Co. At the Avenue," January 5, 1924. *Film Daily Yearbook*, 1940. Hill, *Pages from the Harlem Renaissance*. *Motion Picture Herald*, July 15, 1939. *New York Age*, June 29, 1929. Peterson, *The African American Theatre Directory*. Work, *Negro Yearbook, 1921–1922*.

557. BLUE BIRD THEATER
3115 Indiana
Picture house. Manager in 1921: W. C. Gates and Sons (African Americans).
References: Cahn, *Julius Cahn-Gus Hill Theatrical Guide*. Jackson, "List of Colored Theaters and Attractions," *Billboard*, August 6, 1921. Work, *Negro Yearbook, 1921–1922*.

558. BROADWAY STRAND THEATER
Picture house.
References: *Film Daily Yearbook*, 1949–1954.

CARUSO'S VIRGINIA THEATER *see* Virginia Theater.

559. COLUMBIA THEATER
11 N. Clark Street
Vaudeville house. Owner: Robert T. Motts (African American).
References: Peterson, *The African American Theatre Directory*.

560. CORT THEATER
Picture house.
References: *Film Daily Yearbook*, 1949–1954.

561. ELBA THEATER
3115 Indiana Avenue
Picture house. Also called the New Elba. Owner in 1921: Fred Rosenthal. In May 1921, the Elba featured Eugene O'Brien in the motion picture *Worlds Apart*, along with a two-reel comedy and newsreel.
References: Cahn, *Julius Cahn-Gus Hill Theatrical Guide*. Jackson, "Additions to Theater List," *Billboard*, December 31, 1921. Work, *Negro Yearbook, 1921–1922*.

562. FOUNTAIN THEATER
344 E. 35th Street
Picture house. In January 1915 the Fountain featured *Shadows of the Past*.
References: Carbine, "The Finest Outside the Loop." Sylvester Russell, "Chicago Weekly Review," January 2, 1915.

563. FOUR STAR THEATER
Picture house.

References: *Film Daily Yearbook*, 1950–1954.

564. FRANKLIN THEATER
328 E. 31st Street
Picture house. 700 seats.
References: Jackson, "List of Colored Theaters and Attractions," *Billboard*, August 6, 1921. Work, *Negro Yearbook, 1921–1922*.

565. GLOBE THEATER
1145 Blue Island Avenue
Picture house. 850 seats.
References: *Film Daily Yearbook*, 1940–1948. *Motion Picture Herald*, July 15, 1939.

566. GRAND THEATER
3110–3112 S. State Street
Vaudeville house. 500–800 seats. A TOBA. theater. Manager in 1921: Mr. Johnson. Manager in 1928: H. B. Miller. One of the earliest black musical stock companies playing this house was that of Billy King. One of the earliest jazz bands at the Grand was that of Wilbur Sweatman. According to Tom Fletcher, Dave Peyton's orchestra also played at the Grand. In 1918 the Billy King Stock Company performed here. The *Chicago Defender* reported that two musicals played at the Grand in April 1921: *The Wiff Woff Wabblers*, starring Amon Davis and Eddie Stafford, and Irvin C. Miller's company in a new edition of *Broadway Rastus*. In May 1921, the Irvin C. Miller musical comedy *Alabama Bound* played at the Grand. In 1922, the show *Plantation Revue* was featured. Ethel Waters appeared here in April 1923 along with violinist James O'Brien. In 1924, the Whitman Sisters and Bessie Smith were a big hit at the Grand. In 1926 the show *Shufflin' Sam from Alabam'* played the Grand. Also in 1926, Andrew Bishop, Cleo Desmond, and the Lafayette Players were here. The Billy Butler Orchestra played this house in 1928. In 1932 the Grand exhibited the motion picture *Possessed*, starring Joan Crawford and Clark Gable.
References: Albertson, *Bessie*. *Baltimore Afro-American*, October 31, 1926. Bradshaw, *Born with the Blues*. Cahn, *Cahn-Gus Hill Theatrical Guide*. *Chicago Defender*, April 14, 1923; Langston, "Whitman Sisters Open Good Show at the Grand," June 21, 1924. Dance, *The World of Earl Hines*. *Film Daily Yearbook*, 1940–1951. Fletcher, *100 Years of the Negro in Show Business*. George-Graves, *The Royalty of Negro Vaudeville*. Harrison, *Black Pearls*. Hill, *Pages from the Harlem Renaissance*. Jackson, "List of Colored Theaters and Attractions," *Billboard*, August 6, 1921. *New York Age*, Slater, Bob. "Theatrical Jottings," January 30, 1926. *Motion Picture Herald*, July 15, 1939. Peterson, *Profiles of African American Stage Performers*. Sampson, *Blacks in Blackface*. *Official Theatrical World of Colored Artists*. Waters, *His Eye Is On the Sparrow*. Work, *Negro Yearbook 1921–1922*.

567. GROVELAND THEATER
31st and Cottage Grove Streets
Picture house. 400 seats.
References: *Film Daily Yearbook*, 1930–1932.

568. HARMONY THEATER
411 E. 43rd Street
Picture house. 593 seats.
References: *Film Daily Yearbook*, 1930–1933.

569. IMPERIAL THEATER
2329 Madison Street
Picture house. 1,000 seats.
References: *Film Daily Yearbook*, 1940–1948. *Motion Picture Herald*, July 15, 1939.

570. INDIANA THEATER
219 E. 43rd Street
Picture house. 786 seats. Manager in 1923: Manuel Fieldman.

References: *Film Daily Yearbook*, 1930–1933, 1940–1955. *Motion Picture Herald*, July 15, 1939.

571. IRVING THEATER
1310 S. Halsted Street
Picture house. 298 seats.
References: *Film Daily Yearbook*, 1940–1955. *Motion Picture Herald*, July 15, 1939.

572. JOY THEATER
9223 Commerce Avenue
Picture house. 299 seats.
References: *Film Daily Yearbook*, 1940–1952. *Motion Picture Herald*, July 15, 1939.

573. LAKE THEATER
3125 Cottage Grove
Picture house. Managers in 1921: King and Davis.
References: Cahn, *Julius Cahn-Gus Hill Theatrical Guide*. Jackson, "List of Colored Theaters and Attractions," *Billboard*, August 6, 1921. Work, *Negro Yearbook, 1921–1922*.

574. LINCOLN THEATER
3132–3134 State Street
Picture and vaudeville house. 299 seats. A TOBA theater. Manager in 1923: Joseph Nathan. In March 1922, the Lincoln featured the following films: *Play Square, Secret Four, Beautiful Liar, Touchdown, Call of the Wild, Blue Jacket's Honor, Tolerable David, The Scrapper, Arizona and the Horseman*, and the final episode of the serial *Blue Fox*. In October 1921, the Lincoln showed the film *Some Wild Oats*, advertised as "the greatest play on sex hygiene." The Lincoln advertised that "on account of the delicate subject and scenes, men and women will not be admitted together!" The Lincoln scheduled separate showings for mothers and daughters and for fathers and sons.
References: Cahn, *Julius Cahn-Gus Hill Theatrical Guide*. Jackson, "List of Colored Theaters and Attractions," *Billboard*, August 6, 1921. *Film Daily Yearbook*, 1931–1933.

575. LOUIS THEATER
108 E. 35th Street
Picture house. 700 seats.
Sources: *Film Daily Yearbook*, 1940–1955. *Motion Picture Herald*, July 15, 1939.

576. LYCEUM THEATER
3851 Cottage Grove
Picture house. 700 seats.
References: *Film Daily Yearbook*, 1930, 1932, 1951.

577. LYNN THEATER
1044 W. 63rd Street
Picture house. 299 seats.
References: *Film Daily Yearbook*, 1949–1955.

578. MADLIN THEATER
1910 W. Madison Street
Picture house. 790 seats.
References: *Film Daily Yearbook*, 1949–1955.

579. METROPOLITAN THEATER
4644 S. Parkway
Picture house. 1,400 seats. Owner in 1926: Jack Haag. Manager in 1926: Cary B. Lewis (African American). The Metropolitan was part of the Colored Consolidated vaudeville circuit. In 1914 Goodbar and Lewis, C. S. Thompson, and Tim and Hester Moore appeared here. Louis Armstrong played the Metropolitan in April 1927. Other famous musicians at the Metropolitan included Earl Hines, the Sammy Stewart Orchestra, Erskine Tate and his Orchestra, Fats Waller, and Charlie Carpenter. The theater was demolished in 1997.
References: Collier, *Louis Armstrong*. Dance, *The World of Earl Hines*. Film

78 Illinois

Daily Yearbook, 1930–1933, 1940–1955. *Indianapolis Freeman,* "On Colored Consolidated Time," January 31, 1914. *Motion Picture Herald,* July 15, 1939. Newman, "Metropolitan Theater." Jazz Age Chicago website: http://www.suba.com/~scottn/explore/sites/theaters/met.htm

580. MICHIGAN THEATER
110 E. 55th Street
Picture house. 1,345 seats.
References: *Film Daily Yearbook,* 1940–1947, 1949–1955. *Motion Picture Herald,* July 15, 1939.

581. MIDWAY THEATER
6246 Cottage Grove Avenue
Picture house. 850 seats.
References: *Film Daily Yearbook,* 1949–1955.

582. MONOGRAM THEATER
3520 S. Halstead Street
Vaudeville house. 432 seats. Manager 1921–1928: H. B. Miller. Manager in 1923: R. A. Healy. The Monogram was part of the Colored Consolidated and TOBA vaudeville circuits. Louis Armstrong, Ethel Waters, and the Hill Sisters were early performers at the Monogram. In 1914, LaBlanch Young and Webb and Simmons appeared here. In 1921, the Martin and Walker Company performed in a feature called *The Insurance Agents.* In March 1924, blues singer Clara Smith headlined the vaudeville bill with comics Brown and Struffin, juggler Jolly Saunders, and singers DeGaston and Yuen. Tom Fletcher recalls that bandleader Wilbur Sweatman played the Monogram.
References: Basie, *Good Morning Blues.* Cahn, *Julius Cahn-Gus Hill Theatrical Guide. Chicago Defender,* "The Monogram," March 1, 1924. *Film Daily Yearbook,* 1931, 1932. Fletcher, *100 Years of the Negro in Show Business.* Hill, *Pages from the Harlem Renaissance.* Jackson, "List of Colored Theaters and Attractions," *Billboard,* August 6, 1921; "The Theater Owners' Booking Association," *Billboard,* December 16, 1922. Kenney, *Chicago Jazz. Official Theatrical World of Colored Artists.* Waters, *His Eye Is on the Sparrow.* Work, *Negro Yearbook, 1921–1922.*

583. N.R.A. THEATER
5748 Prairie Avenue
Picture house. 750 seats.
References: *Film Daily Yearbook,* 1940–1953. *Motion Picture Herald,* July 15, 1939.

584. OAKLAND SQUARE THEATER
3947 Drexel Boulevard
Picture house. 1,424 seats. Managers in 1923: Ascher Brothers. The Oakland Square was one of many Chicago theaters owned by the Ascher brothers. It cost $200,000 to build and was equipped with an organ.
References: *Film Daily Yearbook,* 1949–1955.

585. OWL THEATER
4653–55 S. State Street
Picture house. 944 seats. Manager in 1921: Mr. Saulkins. Manager in 1923: Dirk Kemp. It was advertised in the *Chicago Defender* in 1921 as "the most popular theatre of the South Side." The house orchestra was that of Clarence M. Jones and His Select Orchestra, which played during the pictures. The Owl featured the Eddie Polo western serial *The Bull's Eye* in 1918. The audience saw the film *Outside the Law* starring Lon Chaney and Priscilla Dean in April 1921. During 1921, the Clarence Lee Orchestra performed at the Owl. In March 1922, the Owl featured Franklin Parnum in *Arizona and the Horseman, The Guttersnipe,* and *Square Deal Man.* As an added treat, the Jack Johnson-Stanley Ketchel boxing fight pictures, banned in the South, were shown. In 1923 the Owl featured the silent movie *Soft Boiled,* starring Tom

Mix. The Verona Biggs Orchestra played here in 1928.

References: Bowser, *Writing Himself into History*. Cahn, *Julius Cahn-Gus Hill Theatrical Guide*. *Film Daily Yearbook*, 1930–1933, 1940–1955. Jackson, "List of Colored Theaters and Attractions," *Billboard*, August 6, 1921. *Motion Picture Herald*, July 15, 1939. *Official Theatrical World*. Work, *Negro Yearbook, 1921–1922*.

586. PARK THEATER
5960 W. Lake Street
Picture house. 568 seats. Manager in 1923: George Miller.
References: *Film Daily Yearbook*, 1940–1955. *Motion Picture Herald*, July 15, 1939.

587. PEERLESS THEATER
3955 Grand Boulevard
Picture house. 904 seats. The Dave Peyton Orchestra performed here in 1926 and 1928.
References: *Chicago Defender*, May 15, 1926. *Film Daily Yearbook*, 1931–1933. *Official Theatrical World*.

588. PEKIN THEATER
27th and S. State Streets
Play and picture house. 1,200 seats. Also called Mott's Pekin Temple. Owner: Robert M. Motts. Manager in 1915: W. H. Smith. The Pekin is one of the most famous African American theater buildings. Motts opened the Pekin in 1905. A year later the Pekin Players — an 11-member black theater stock company — was founded. The Pekin Players presented comic plays. James Haskins claimed that the actors sometimes performed in "whiteface" to make their performances more realistic! In 1907, the comedians Miller and Lyles performed in the musical *The Mayor of Dixie*. In 1909 the Pekin featured the Joe Jordan band, Perry Bradford, and singer Alberta Perkins. The play *Panama* was also produced here that same year. In 1910, dancers Brown and Navarro appeared in the show *A Night In Chinatown*. In 1911, the Pekin featured the Jesse Shipp play *The Test*, but local newspapers reported that the management cut down the play in order to make room for films and wrestling matches! About this time, Motts encountered serious competition from white-run black theatres offering vaudeville. By 1926, the theater had become a precinct station for the Chicago Police Department. Among the many actors who performed at the Pekin are Abbie Mitchell and Charles Gilpin.

References: Bowser, *Writing Himself into History*. Bradshaw, *Born with the Blues*. *Chicago Defender*, "Theater They Once Played In Is Now Police Station," December 18, 1926. Fraden, *Blueprints for a Black Federal Theatre*. Harrison, *Black Pearls*. Haskins, *Black Theater in America*. Peterson, *Profiles of African American Stage Performers*.

589. PHOENIX THEATER
3104 N. 35th Street
Picture house. Owner in 1921: O. C. Hammond. Manager in 1921: Frank Hammond. In 1917, the Phoenix's management refused to play the film *A Natural Born Shooter* because it was considered "degrading low comedy." The Chicago firm Ebony Film Corporation produced the picture. In March 1922, the Phoenix featured the following motion pictures: *The Golden Gift, Shadows of the Sea, Received Payment, Call of Home, Wonderful Thing, Little Minister*, and *Two Kinds of Women*.
References: Bowser, *Writing Himself into History*. Cahn, *Julius Cahn-Gus Hill Theatrical Guide*. Jackson, "List of Colored Theaters and Attractions," *Billboard*, August 6, 1921. Work, *Negro Yearbook, 1921–1922*.

590. PICKFORD THEATER

108 N. 35th Street

Picture house. 600 seats. Also known as the Louis. Owner and Manager in 1921: O. C. Hammond. In 1921, the Pickford featured Clarence H. Black's Symphony Orchestra. In March 1922, the Pickford was showing the pictures *Why Announce Your Marriage, For His Mother's Sake, Hail the Woman, The Wonderful Thing*, and *Her Own Money*.

References: *Film Daily Yearbook*, 1930–1932. Jackson, "List of Colored Theaters and Attractions," *Billboard*, August 6, 1921. Work, *Negro Yearbook, 1921–1922*.

591. PUBLIC THEATER

4701 Prairie Avenue

Picture house. 600 seats.

References: *Film Daily Yearbook*, 1940–1955. *Motion Picture Herald*, July 15, 1939.

592. REGAL THEATER

4719 S. Parkway

Vaudeville and picture house. 3,000 seats. Architects: Alexander L. Levy and William J. Klein. The Regal opened for business in 1928. The *Chicago Defender* was impressed with the décor of the Regal: "The interior of the Regal presents one of the most beautiful and amazing spectacles ever exhibited in a public institution; a triumph of imaginative design that carries the theatergoers into an Oriental garden on a moonlight night. Overhead is stretched a mammoth polychrome canopy supported by huge poles of gold and fringed with a horizon-like vista of blue sky. Over the giant stage is the outline of an entrance to an Oriental pagoda, completing an effect that is almost enchanting in its romantic charm." The Regal gained a reputation as part of the so-called "chitlin' circuit" of rhythm and blues artists and remained one of the preeminent black theaters up to the 1970s. The Regal was popular in Chicago for its annual Bud Billiken Thanksgiving party for children. Among the notable African American vaudeville acts that played the Regal were the Whitman Sisters and comedienne Jackie "Moms" Mabley. In 1927 musician Lois Deppe was a headliner. In the 1930s jazz pianist Fats Waller had a run-in with gangsters in the theater. Also in the 1930s, the Dave Peyton Orchestra and musician Louis Armstrong entertained. Charlie Parker visited in 1941 and 1943. Count Basie entertained in 1942, and the Billy Eckstine Orchestra played here in 1944. In the 1960s many soul acts appeared at the Regal, including Darrow Fletcher, Jo Ann Garrett, the Five Stairsteps, the Artistics, the Vontastics, the Drew-vels, Major Lance, Gene Chandler, the Accents, the Sequins, the Marvelows, the Five Du-Tones, and the Dells. In 1961 Dizzy Gillespie and Dinah Washington performed with rhythm and blues disc jockey Al Benson. In 1973, the Regal was torn down.

References: Basie, *Good Morning Blues*. *Chicago Defender*, "Circus Days At the Regal Theater," March 17, 1928. Collier, *Louis Armstong*. Dance, *The World of Earl Hines*. *Film Daily Yearbook*, 1930–1933, 1940–1955. George-Graves, *The Royalty of Negro Vaudeville*. Gillespie, *To Be or Not to Bop*. Russell, *Bird Lives!* Gottschild, *Waltzing in the Dark*. Kenney, *Chicago Jazz*. *Motion Picture Herald*, July 15, 1939. Peterson, *Profiles of African American Stage Performers*. Pruter, *Chicago Soul*. Sampson, *Blacks in Blackface*. Waller, *Fats Waller*.

593. STAR THEATER

3847 S. State Street

Picture house.

References: *Film Daily Yearbook*, 1949–1955.

594. STATE-HARRISON THEATER

546 S. State Street

Regal Theater, Chicago, Illinois (SoulofAmerica.com)

Picture house. 305 seats.
References: *Film Daily Yearbook* 1952, 1953.

595. STATES THEATER
3607 State Street
Picture house. 675 seats. Manager in 1921: Mr. Paul. In 1921, the *Chicago Defender* advertised the States as "the home of great features." One of those features was E. M. Wyer's States Orchestra. In April 1921, the States was showing Lon Chaney and Priscilla Dean in *Outside the Law*. In March 1922, the audience at the States saw Hoot Gibson in *Headin' West*, and William B. Hart in *The Square Deal Man*.
References: *Film Daily Yearbook*, 1930–1933, 1940–1955. Harrison, *Black Pearls*. Jackson, "List of Colored Theaters and Attractions," *Billboard*, August 6, 1921. *Motion Picture Herald*, July 15, 1939. Work, *Negro Yearbook, 1921–1922*.

596. TERRACE THEATER
3108 S. Indiana Avenue
Picture house. 1,036 seats.
References: *Film Daily Yearbook*, 1941–1955.

597. VENDOME THEATER
3145–46 State Street
Picture house. 1,300 seats. Owner in 1921: O. C. Hammond. Manager in 1921: John Hammond. Managers in 1921: Frank and Johnny Hammond. The Vendome opened in 1919. The *Chicago Defender* described how it looked: "It will have a mezzanine floor, containing boxes only; a smoking room for gentlemen and a beautifully equipped ladies' retiring room. It is intended to have a ten-piece orchestra in addition to a $10,000 pipe organ, and all employees will be liveried, including a corps of competent usherettes. The attractions will be nothing but the finest productions, and those of the greater magnitude will be booked for runs lasting as long as four days." The Vendome's shows usually opened with Erskine Tate's Little Symphony playing an overture. Then followed the movie, and at intermission Tate's Jazz Syncopators would play a hot feature. Louis Armstrong played not only solos during the jazz number but frequently an operatic aria or standard solo piece. In the April 5, 1921 issue of the *Chicago Defender*, the Vendome was advertised as having a "mammoth pipe organ" and featuring Erskine Tate's Symphony Orchestra. In May 1921, the Vendome was showing the Oscar Micheaux film *The Gunsalus Mystery*. It starred Evelyn Preer, Lawrence Chenault, and Mattie Wilkes. In October 1921, the Hugo Ballin film *The Journey's End* was shown. It starred Wyndham Standing, Mabel Ballin, and George Bancroft. In March 1922, the Vendome showed the films *Grand Larceny*, *The Night Rose*, and *Get Rich Quick Wallingford*. The Clarence Jones Orchestra performed here in 1928. Later on jazz musician Earl Hines appeared at the Vendome.
References: Basie, *Good Morning Blues*. Bowser, *Writing Himself into History*. Cahn, *Julius Cahn-Gus Hill Theatrical Guide*. Carbine, "The Finest Outside the Loop." Collier, *Louis Armstrong*. Dance, *The World of Earl Hines*. *Film Daily Yearbook*, 1930–1933. Jackson, "List of Colored Theaters and Attractions," *Billboard*, August 6, 1921. Kenney, *Chicago Jazz*. Newman, "Vendome Theater." Jazz Age Chicago website: http://www.suba.com/~scottn/explore/sites/theaters/met.htm. Work, *Negro Yearbook, 1921–1922*.

598. VICTORY THEATER
91st Street and Cottage Grove
Picture house. 2,000 seats.
References: *Film Daily Yearbook*, 1949–1955.

599. VIRGINIA THEATER

210 E. 43rd Street
Picture house. 272 seats. Also known as Caruso's Virginia.
References: *Film Daily Yearbook*, 1949–1955.

600. WESTERN THEATER
2211 Lake
Picture house. Manager in 1921: S. L. Owens (African American).
References: Jackson, "List of Colored Theaters and Attractions," *Billboard*, August 6, 1921.

601. WILLARD THEATER
342 E. 51st Street
Nickelodeon and picture house. 600 seats. Owned by the Alfred Hamburger chain, the Willard had an orchestra pit and an organ. In 1928 the Sammy Stewart Orchestra played here.
References: *Film Daily Yearbook*, 1940–1952. *Motion Picture Herald*, July 15, 1939.

Colp

602. PLAZA THEATER
Picture house.
References: *Film Daily Yearbook*, 1930–1932.

East Saint Louis

603. AMERICAN THEATER
Picture house.
References: *Film Daily Yearbook*, 1930–1933.

604. BROADWAY THEATER
Picture house. 465 seats.
References: *Film Daily Yearbook*, 1940–1949. *Motion Picture Herald*, July 15, 1939.

605. DELORA THEATER
Picture house.
References: *Film Daily Yearbook*, 1949–1955.

606. DELUXE THEATER
1500 Walnut Street
Picture house. 400–500 seats.
References: *Film Daily Yearbook*, 1940–1955. *Motion Picture Herald*, April 24, 1937; July 15, 1939.

607. HARLEM THEATER
11 S. Main Street
Picture house. 500 seats.
References: *Film Daily Yearbook*, 1949–1955.

608. LINCOLN THEATER
Vaudeville house. A TOBA theater. Manager in 1928: Harry Hershenson.
References: *Film Daily Yearbook*, 1930. *Official Theatrical World of Colored Artists*.

609. LITTLE BROADWAY THEATER
1213 E. Broadway
Picture house. 600 seats.
References: *Film Daily Yearbook*, 1930–1933, 1949–1955.

610. OLYMPIA THEATER
11 Main Street
Picture house. Manager: M. L. Hawkins (African American).
References: Cahn, *Julius Cahn-Gus Hill Theatrical Guide*. *Film Daily Yearbook*, 1930–1933. Jackson, "List of Colored Theaters and Attractions," *Billboard*, August 6, 1921. Work, *Negro Yearbook*, 1921–1922.

Kinloch

611. KINLOCH THEATER
Picture house
References: *Film Daily Yearbook*, 1948.

Lovejoy

612. LIBERTY THEATER

Picture house. Manager in 1921: J. H. Sylvester.
References: Cahn, *Julius Cahn-Gus Hill Theatrical Guide*. Jackson, "List of Colored Theaters and Attractions," *Billboard*, August 6, 1921. Work, *Negro Yearbook, 1921–1922*.

Mounds

613. GRAND THEATER
Picture house. Manager: J. H. Crawford. This may have been the unnamed theater listed in the 1921 *Billboard* survey.
References: Cahn, *Julius Cahn-Gus Hill Theatrical Guide*. Jackson, "List of Colored Theaters and Attractions," *Billboard*, August 6, 1921. Work, *Negro Yearbook, 1921–1922*.

St. Clair County

614. JOY THEATER
Picture house.
References: *Film Daily Yearbook*, 1950–1955.

Springfield

615. PEKIN THEATER
815 E. Washington Street
Picture house. Manager in 1921: James Mason.
References: Cahn, *Julius Cahn-Gus Hill Theatrical Guide. Film Daily Yearbook*, 1930–1932. Jackson, "List of Colored Theaters and Attractions," *Billboard*, August 6, 1921. Work, *Negro Yearbook, 1921–1922*.

Venice

616. ROCK ISLAND THEATER
Picture house.
References: *Film Daily Yearbook*, 1948–1955.

INDIANA

East Chicago

617. MARS THEATER
Picture house.
References: *Film Daily Yearbook*, 1949–1955.

Gary

618. BROADWAY THEATER
1678 Broadway
Vaudeville house. 600 seats. A TOBA theater. Manager in 1928: Vern U. Young.
References: *Film Daily Yearbook*, 1931–1933. *Official Theatrical World of Colored Artists*.

619. ROOSEVELT THEATER
1446 Broadway
Picture house. 800–1,000 seats.
References: *Film Daily Yearbook*, 1940–1955. *Motion Picture Herald*, July 15, 1939.

620. STRAND THEATER
1631 Broadway
Vaudeville house. Manager in 1921: Walter Smith.
References: Cahn, *Julius Cahn-Gus Hill Theatrical Guide*. *Film Daily Yearbook*, 1930–1933. Jackson, "List of Colored Theaters and Attractions," *Billboard*, August 6, 1921. Work, *Negro Yearbook, 1921–1922*.

Indiana Harbor

621. BROADWAY THEATER
2205 Broadway
Picture house. 440 seats.
References: *Film Daily Yearbook*, 1949, 1950.

622. GARDEN THEATER
3424 Main Street
Picture house. 750 seats.
References: *Film Daily Yearbook*, 1949, 1950.

Indianapolis

623. AIRDOME THEATER
Indiana Avenue
Vaudeville house. Owner: R. S. Geyser. According to Peterson, the Airdome was in business during the 1910s.
References: Peterson, *The African American Theatre Directory*.

624. AVENUE THEATER
Picture house.
References: *Film Daily Yearbook*, 1949–1955.

625. CAPITOL THEATER
Picture house.
References: *Film Daily Yearbook*, 1930–1932.

626–27. COLUMBIA THEATER
Picture house. Also known as the Empire. Owner in 1910: Hill Brothers. Manager in 1921: Bert Zarrigg.
References: Cahn, *Julius Cahn-Gus Hill Theatrical Guide*. *Film Daily Yearbook*, 1930–1932. Jackson, "List of Colored Theaters and Attractions," *Billboard*, August 6, 1921. Peterson, *The African American Theatre Directory*. Work, *Negro Yearbook, 1921–1922*.

628. DOUGLAS THEATER
1403 E. 19th Street
Vaudeville and picture house. 460 seats. Built in 1914 as the Atlas; renamed Douglas in 1922. Manager in 1921: Charles English.
References: *Film Daily Yearbook*, 1930–1933, 1940–1955. *Motion Picture Herald*, April 24, 1937; July 15, 1939. Sampson, *Blacks in Black and White*. Work, *Negro Yearbook, 1921–1922*.

629. DUNICK THEATER
1320 E. 16th Street
Vaudeville house. Manager in 1921: J. Nicholson.
References: Cahn, *Julius Cahn-Gus Hill Theatrical Guide*. Jackson, "List of Colored Theaters and Attractions," *Billboard*, August 6, 1921. Work, *Negro Yearbook, 1921–1922*.

EMPIRE THEATER *see* Columbia Theater.

630. EMROE THEATER
Picture house.
References: *Film Daily Yearbook*, 1930–1932.

631. ENGLISH THEATER
Picture house.
References: *Film Daily Yearbook*, 1930–1932.

632. GEM THEATER
Picture house.

86 Indiana

References: *Film Daily Yearbook*, 1930–1932.

633. HORTENSE THEATER
Picture house.
References: *Film Daily Yearbook*, 1931–1933.

634. INDIANA THEATER
134 W. Washington Street
Picture and vaudeville house. 3,133 seats. Architects: Rubish and Hunter. Manager in 1921: Dr. O. Puryear (African American). Manager in 1955: Alvin W. Hendricks.
References: Cahn, *Julius Cahn and Gus Hill Theatrical Guide*. *Film Daily Yearbook*, 1930–1933, 1940–1955. Jackson, "List of Colored Theaters and Attractions," *Billboard*, August 6, 1921. *Motion Picture Herald*, April 24, 1937; July 15, 1939. Sampson, *Blacks in Black and White*. Shortridge, "The Indiana Theatre: Post Past, Uncertain Future," *Marquee* 7 (Fourth Quarter 1975): 3–8. Work, *Negro Yearbook, 1921–1922*.

635. JEWELL THEATER
Picture house.
References: *Film Daily Yearbook*, 1930–1932.

636–37. LIDO THEATER
786 Indiana Avenue
Picture house. 300–500 seats. Manager in 1940: Otis Bell.
References: *Film Daily Yearbook*, 1940–1955. *Motion Picture Herald*, April 24, 1937; July 15, 1939. Sampson, *Blacks in Black and White*.

638. PARK THEATER
2441 Martindale Avenue
Picture house. 765 seats. Manager in 1955: Amanda L. Brown.
References: *Film Daily Yearbook*, 1948–1955.

639. PIONEER THEATER
513–515 Indiana Avenue
Picture house. Manager in 1922: Mrs. Anna Bowman. The Pioneer opened in 1916.
References: Cahn, *Julius Cahn-Gus Hill Theatrical Guide*. Jackson, "List of Colored Theaters and Attractions," *Billboard*, August 6, 1921. Work, *Negro Yearbook, 1921–1922*.

640. REGAL THEATER
2464 Northwestern Avenue
Picture house. 370 seats. Manager in 1940: Shedrick S. Stephens. The Regal opened in 1927 as the Northwestern and in 1933 it was renamed the Regal.
References: *Film Daily Yearbook*, 1930–1933. *Film Daily Yearbook*, 1940–1955. *Motion Picture Herald*, April 24, 1937. Sampson, *Blacks in Black and White*.

641. SENATE THEATER
1327–1329 N. Senate Avenue
Vaudeville house. Manager in 1921: James Hill and Lewis Hill.
References: Cahn, *Julius Cahn and Gus Hill Theatrical Guide*. *Film Daily Yearbook*, 1930–1933. Jackson, "List of Colored Theaters and Attractions," *Billboard*, August 6, 1921. Work, *Negro Yearbook, 1921–1922*.

642. TWO JOHNS THEATER
786 Indiana Avenue
Vaudeville house. Owners: John A. Hubert and John H. Victor.
References: *Film Daily Yearbook*, 1930–1933. Peterson, *The African American Theatre Directory*.

643. WALKER THEATER
603–607 Indiana Avenue
Vaudeville and picture house. 1,085 seats. Architects: Rubish and Hunter. Manager in 1955: Joseph W. Barr. The

Walker Theater, Indianapolis, Indiana (SoulofAmerica.com)

theater was named for owner Madame C. J. Walker, the African American beautician mogul.

References: *Film Daily Yearbook*, 1930–1933, 1940–1955. *Motion Picture Herald*, April 24, 1937; July 15, 1939. Sampson, *Blacks in Black and White*. Work, *Negro Yearbook*, 1912.

644. WASHINGTON THEATER
521 Indiana Avenue

Vaudeville and picture house. Managers: Tim Owsley and Emsirdell S. Stone. The Washington opened in 1910 as the Geye Lew, was renamed the Crown Garden in 1911 and became the Washington in 1916. The Crown Garden was part of the Colored Consolidated vaudeville circuit. In 1914 the Butlers, Roy Bailey, and Jones and Jones played here. It was part of the Managers and Performers and the TOBA vaudeville circuits. In April 1921, the Washington featured Frank Montgomery's musical *Hello 1921*.

References: Cahn, *Julius Cahn-Gus Hill Theatrical Guide*. *Film Daily Yearbook*, 1930. Hill, *Pages from the Harlem Renaissance*. Jackson, "List of Colored Theaters and Attractions," *Billboard*, August 6, 1921; "The Theater Owners' Booking Association," *Billboard*, December 16, 1922. Peterson, *The African Amer-*

ican Theatre Directory. Work, *Negro Yearbook, 1921–1922.* Indianapolis Freeman, "On Colored Consolidated Time," January 31, 1914.

IOWA

Carroll

645. GEM THEATER
Vaudeville house. Owner: Charles Luting. According to Peterson, the Gem was in operation during the 1900s.
References: Peterson, *The African American Theatre Directory.*

Des Moines

646. LINCOLN THEATER
788 12th Street
Picture house. 500 seats. Manager in 1921: Walter Smith. Manager in 1922: M. A. Ferdon.
References: Cahn, *Julius Cahn-Gus Hill Theatrical Guide.* Jackson, "List of Colored Theaters and Attractions," *Billboard,* August 6, 1921. Work, *Negro Yearbook, 1921–1922.*

KANSAS

Kansas City

647. CASTLE THEATER
Picture house.
References: *Film Daily Yearbook,* 1947, 1948.

648. PRINCESS THEATER
1918 W. 5th Street
Picture house. 782 seats. Also known as the New Princess.
References: *Film Daily Yearbook,* 1930–1933, 1940–1955. *Motion Picture Herald,* April 24, 1937; July 15, 1939. Sampson, *Blacks in Black and White.*

649. REGAL THEATER
1612 N. 10th Street
Picture house. 600 seats.
References: *Film Daily Yearbook,* 1940–1955. *Motion Picture Herald,* July 15, 1939.

Topeka

650. APEX THEATER
Picture house.
References: *Film Daily Yearbook*, 1930–1933.

651. RITZ THEATER
122 E. 4th Street
Picture house. 429–550 seats.
References: *Film Daily Yearbook*, 1940–1955. *Motion Picture Herald*, April 24, 1937; July 15, 1939. Sampson, *Blacks in Black and White.*

Wichita

652. DUNBAR THEATER
1007 Cleveland Avenue
Picture house. 467 seats.
References: *Film Daily Yearbook*, 1943–1955.

KENTUCKY

Frankfort

653. KENTUCKY STATE COLLEGE THEATER
Picture house.
References: *Film Daily Yearbook*, 1952–1955.

Henderson

654. DOXEY THEATER
210 Elm Street
Picture house. Manager in 1921: F. B. Doxey.
References: Cahn, *Julius Cahn-Gus Hill Theatrical Guide.* Jackson, "List of Colored Theaters and Attractions," *Billboard*, August 6, 1921. Work, *Negro Yearbook, 1921–1922.*

Lexington

655. ADA MEADE THEATER
Picture house.
References: *Film Daily Yearbook*, 1930–1932.

656. LYRIC THEATER
Picture house. 924 seats.
References: *Film Daily Yearbook*, 1948–1955.

657. ORPHEUM THEATER
Picture house.
References: *Film Daily Yearbook*, 1930–1932.

Louisville

658. DIXIE THEATER
Preston and Caldwell Streets
Picture house. 280 seats.
References: *Film Daily Yearbook*, 1930–1932, 1941–1955. *Motion Picture Herald*, April 24, 1937; July 15, 1939. Sampson, *Blacks in Black and White.*

659. GRAND THEATER
611 W. Walnut Street

Picture house. 665–700 seats. In January 1955, the Grand excelled in showing action pictures such as *Gambler From Natchez* starring Dale Robertson, *Dawn at Socorro*, starring Rory Calhoun, *Naked Alibi*, starring Sterling Hayden and Gloria Grahame, and *Four Guns to the Border*, starring Rory Calhoun.

References: *Film Daily Yearbook*, 1931–1933, 1940–1955. *Motion Picture Herald*, April 24, 1937; July 15, 1939. Sampson, *Blacks in Black and White*. *Louisville Defender*, January 13, 1955.

660. LINCOLN THEATER
914 W. Walnut Street

Vaudeville and picture house. 677 seats. A TOBA theater. Management in 1921: F. O. Dillon (African American) and William Warley. In April 1921, the vaudeville bill featured the Sandy Burns company, Roy White's Stylish Slippers, Little Clarence Foster, John Mason's Dixie Beach Girls, and Edwards and Edwards. In March 1924, the Lincoln featured juggler Lane Drew, comics Jines and Jacqueline, dancers Rastus and Jones, and blues singer Ida Cox with pianist Jesse Crump.

References: Cahn, *Julius Cahn-Gus Hill Theatrical Guide*. *Film Daily Yearbook*, 1930–1933. Hill, *Pages from the Harlem Renaissance*. Jackson, "List of Colored Theaters and Attractions," *Billboard*, August 6, 1921; "The Theater Owners' Booking Association," *Billboard*, December 16, 1922. *Chicago Defender*, Jines, "Lincoln Theater," March 15, 1925. *Film Daily Yearbook*, 1931. Hill, *Pages from the Harlem Renaissance*. *Official Theatrical World of Colored Artists*. Simms, *Simms' Blue Book*. Work, *Negro Yearbook, 1921–1922*.

661. LYRIC THEATER
604 W. Walnut Street

Picture house. Also known as the New Lyric. 700 seats. During the week of January 13, 1955, the Lyric was showing the films *A Woman's Face*, starring Joan Crawford, and *The Bigamist*, starring Joan Fontaine, Edmond O'Brien, and Ida Lupino. Also showing was the Otto Preminger film *Carmen Jones*, starring Dorothy Dandridge, Pearl Bailey, and Harry Belafonte.

References: *Film Daily Yearbook*, 1930–1933, 1940–1955. *Louisville Defender*, January 13, 1955.

662. PALACE THEATER
122 W. Walnut Street

Vaudeville and picture house. 923 seats. Also known as the Palace Picture House and the United Artists Theater. Managers in 1921: Mr. Sanders and Mrs. Minnie McAfee. (African Americans). In a desperate move to lure customers, the management hired African American orators to entertain the audience in 1917. For just forty-five cents, moviegoers could get into the Palace in January 1955 to see the "adults only" picture *Wages of Sin* plus the sensational second feature *Marihuana*. Also shown that month was *Dead End* starring Humphrey Bogart and the Original Dead End Boys, and *Bright Road*, starring Dorothy Dandridge and Harry Belafonte. The Palace offered a kiddie show every Saturday.

References: Bowser, *Writing Himself into History*. Cahn, *Julius Cahn and Gus Hill Theatrical Guide*. *Film Daily Yearbook*, 1930–1933, 1941–1955. Jackson, "List of Colored Theaters and Attractions," *Billboard*, August 6, 1921. *Louisville Defender*, January 13, 1955. Simms, *Simms' Blue Book*. Work, *Negro Yearbook, 1921–1922*.

663. RUBY THEATER

Vaudeville house. The Ruby was part of the Colored Consolidated Time vaudeville circuit. In 1914 the Kinky Doo Trio and Johnson and Johnson appeared here.

References: *Indianapolis Freeman*, "On Colored Consolidated Time, January 31, 1914.

664. VICTORY THEATER
Vaudeville house. Manager in 1921: Steven Bell (African American).
References: Cahn, *Julius Cahn-Gus Hill Theatrical Guide*. Jackson, "List of Colored Theaters and Attractions," *Billboard*, August 6, 1921. Work, *Negro Yearbook, 1921–1922*.

Mayfield

665. UNIQUE THEATER
Picture house. Manager in 1921: O. Neile.
References: Cahn, *Julius Cahn-Gus Hill Theatrical Guide*. Jackson, "List of Colored Theaters and Attractions," *Billboard*, August 6, 1921. Work, *Negro Yearbook, 1921–1922*.

Owensboro

666. PLAZA THEATER
Picture house. According to *Film Daily Yearbook*, the Plaza was closed in 1950 and 1951.
References: *Film Daily Yearbook*, 1949–1955.

Paducah

667. HIAWATHA THEATER
432 S. 7th Street
Picture house. Manager in 1920: S. H. George (African American).
References: Cahn, *Julius Cahn-Gus Hill Theatrical Guide*. Jackson, "List of Colored Theaters and Attractions," *Billboard*, August 6, 1921. Work, *Negro Yearbook, 1921–1922*.

Pikesville

668. LIBERTY THEATER
Picture house.
References: *Film Daily Yearbook*, 1949.

Winchester

669. LINCOLN THEATER
Picture house. Manager in 1921: Mrs. Curry.
References: Cahn, *Julius Cahn-Gus Hill Theatrical Guide*. Jackson, "List of Colored Theaters and Attractions," *Billboard*, August 6, 1921. Work, *Negro Yearbook, 1921–1922*.

LOUISIANA

Alexandria

670. ACE THEATER
Picture house.
References: *Film Daily Yearbook*, 1946–1955.

671. GRAND THEATER
Vaudeville house. Said to be white owned, black managed. Owner: Saenger Amusement Company.
References: Cahn, *Julius Cahn-Gus Hill Theatrical Guide*. Jackson, "List of Col-

ored Theaters and Attractions," *Billboard*, August 6, 1921. Work, *Negro Yearbook, 1921–1922*.

672. HIPPODROME THEATER
Vaudeville house.
References: Hill, *Pages from the Harlem Renaisssance*. Work, *Negro Yearbook, 1921–1922*.

673. LIBERTY THEATER
821 Lee Street
Vaudeville and picture house. 500 seats. Manager in 1921: R. W. Cole.
References: *Film Daily Yearbook*, 1930–1932. Peterson, *The African American Theatre Directory*.

674. RITZ THEATER
819 Lee Street
Picture house. 600 seats.
References: *Film Daily Yearbook*, 1940–1955. *Motion Picture Herald*, July 15, 1939.

675. SILVER CITY THEATER
Picture house.
References: *Film Daily Yearbook*, 1949–1955.

Amite

676. BONNIE THEATER
Picture house. 250 seats.
References: *Film Daily Yearbook*, 1949–1955.

Baldwin

677. ARCADE THEATER
Picture house.
References: *Film Daily Yearbook*, 1949–1955.

Bastrop

678. BROWN THEATER
Picture house.
References: *Film Daily Yearbook*, 1949–1955.

Baton Rouge

679. EAST END THEATER
1101 Eureka Street
Picture house. 300 seats. Manager in 1955: Carl T. Wethers.
References: *Film Daily Yearbook*, 1946–1955.

680. GRAND THEATER
133 Liberty Street.
Vaudeville and picture house. 475 seats. A TOBA theater. Manager in 1922: E. S. Moorman. Manager in 1928: Ernest Boehringer.
References: *Film Daily Yearbook*, 1930–1932. Jackson, "List of Colored Theaters and Attractions," *Billboard*, August 6, 1921. *Official Theatrical World of Colored Artists*. Work, *Negro Yearbook, 1921–1922*.

681. MCKINLEY THEATER
1362 East Boulevard
Picture house. 450 seats. Manager in 1955: Timothy P. Norris.
References: *Film Daily Yearbook*, 1940–1955. *Motion Picture Herald*, April 24, 1937; July 15, 1939. Sampson, *Blacks in Black and White*. *Official Theatrical World of Colored Artists*. Work, *Negro Yearbook, 1921–1922*

682. TEMPLE THEATER
337 North Boulevard
Picture house. 391 seats. Manager in 1955: Marvin E. Hall.
References: *Film Daily Yearbook*, 1930–1933, 1940–1955. *Motion Picture Herald*, April 24, 1937; July 15, 1939. Sampson, *Blacks in Black and White*.

Bogalusa

683. FOX THEATER

Vaudeville theater. 350 seats.
References: Hill, *Pages from the Harlem Renaissance.* Work, *Negro Yearbook, 1921–1922.*

684. PRINCESS THEATER
Picture house.
References: *Film Daily Yearbook,* 1930–1932.

Coushatta

685. WATERS THEATER
Picture house.
References: *Film Daily Yearbook,* 1951–1955.

Crowley

686. FUN THEATER
Picture house.
References: *Film Daily Yearbook,* 1941, 1942.

687. STAR THEATER
Picture house.
References: *Film Daily Yearbook,* 1949–1955.

De Ridder

688. HARLEM THEATER
Picture house.
References: *Film Daily Yearbook,* 1941–1955.

689. REALART THEATER
Picture house.
References: *Film Daily Yearbook,* 1949.

Donaldsonville

690. HARLEM THEATER
719 Lessard Street
Picture house. 350 seats.
References: *Film Daily Yearbook,* 1942–1955.

Eunice

691. F AND M LIBERTY THEATER
200 W. Park Avenue
Picture house. 500 seats.
References: *Film Daily Yearbook,* 1949–1955.

Ferriday

692. ACE THEATER
Picture house.
References: *Film Daily Yearbook,* 1947–1955.

693. ARCADE THEATER
Picture house.
References: *Film Daily Yearbook,* 1949.

Franklin

694. OPERA HOUSE THEATER
Picture house. 400 seats.
References: *Film Daily Yearbook,* 1950–1955.

695. TETCHE THEATER
Picture house.
References: *Film Daily Yearbook,* 1949–1955.

Hammond

696. ACE THEATER
Picture house.
References: *Film Daily Yearbook,* 1950–1955.

697. RITZ THEATER
120 S. Cypress Street
Picture house. 684 seats.
References: *Film Daily Yearbook,* 1949–1955.

Homer

698. COLORED THEATER

Picture house. Said to be Black owned and managed. This may have been the unnamed theater listed in the 1921 *Billboard* survey.

References: Cahn, *Julius Cahn-Gus Hill Theatrical Guide.* Jackson, "List of Colored Theaters and Attractions," *Billboard,* August 6, 1921. Work, *Negro Yearbook, 1921–1922.*

699. STAR THEATER
Picture house.
References: *Film Daily Yearbook,* 1949–1955.

Houma

700. BOND THEATER
Picture house.
References: *Film Daily Yearbook,* 1947–1955.

701. GRAND THEATER
Picture house.
References: *Film Daily Yearbook,* 1950–1955.

Lafayette

702. FUN THEATER
Picture house.
References: *Film Daily Yearbook,* 1941, 1942.

703. GIL THEATER
221 S. Antoine Street
Picture house. 750 seats.
References: *Film Daily Yearbook,* 1951–1955.

704. LIBERTY THEATER
Picture house. 300 seats.
References: *Film Daily Yearbook,* 1940–1955. Hill, *Pages from the Harlem Renaissance. Motion Picture Herald,* April 24, 1937; July 15, 1939. Peterson, *The African American Theatre Directory.* Sampson, *Blacks in Black and White.*

705. MCCOMB THEATER
Picture house. 350 seats.
References: *Film Daily Yearbook,* 1949–1955.

Lake Charles

706. BOULEVARD THEATER
Picture house. Manager in 1921: S. B. Mancusco.
References: Cahn, *Julius Cahn-Gus Hill Theatrical Guide.* Jackson, "List of Colored Theaters and Attractions," *Billboard,* August 6, 1921. Work, *Negro Yearbook, 1921–1922.*

707. DIXIE THEATER
Picture house. 350 seats.
References: *Film Daily Yearbook,* 1941–1955.

708. LAKE THEATER
Picture house.
References: *Film Daily Yearbook,* 1949–1955.

709. LOUISIANNE THEATER
Picture house. 350 seats.
References: Hill, *Pages from the Harlem Renaissance. Film Daily Yearbook,* 1940. *Motion Picture Herald,* July 15, 1939. Work, *Negro Yearbook, 1921–1922.*

710. PALACE THEATER
405 Boulevard
Picture house. 300–553 seats.
References: *Film Daily Yearbook,* 1931, 1932, 1933, 1940–1947. *Motion Picture Herald,* April 24, 1937; July 15, 1939. Sampson, *Blacks in Black and White.* Work, *Negro Yearbook, 1921–1922.*

711. PRINCE THEATER
Vaudeville house. 560 seats.
References: Hill, *Pages from the Harlem Renaissance.* Jackson, "List of Colored Theaters and Attractions," *Billboard,* August 6, 1921. Hill, *Pages from the Harlem Renaissance.*

Lake Providence

712. HARLEM THEATER
Picture house.
References: *Film Daily Yearbook*, 1949–1955.

713. LAKE THEATER
Picture house. 500–600 seats.
References: *Film Daily Yearbook*, 1948–1955.

La Place

714. LA PLACE THEATER
Picture house. 400 seats.
References: *Film Daily Yearbook*, 1949–1955.

Lutcher

715. WEST END THEATER
Picture house.
References: *Film Daily Yearbook*, 1930–1932.

Mansfield

716. ROXY THEATER
Picture house.
References: *Film Daily Yearbook*, 1949–1955.

Marrero

717. GOLDEN TERRACE THEATER
Picture house. The Golden Terrace was closed from 1949 to 1951 according to *Film Daily Yearbook*.
References: *Film Daily Yearbook*, 1949–1955.

Mindlin

718. TOWER THEATER
Picture house.
References: *Film Daily Yearbook*, 1947.

Monroe

719. DREAMLAND THEATER
Picture house.
References: Cahn, *Julius Cahn-Gus Hill Theatrical Guide*. *Film Daily Yearbook*, 1930–1933. Jackson, "List of Colored Theaters and Attractions," *Billboard*, August 6, 1921. Work, *Negro Yearbook, 1921–1922*.

720. RITZ THEATER
911 De Siavd Street
Picture house. 600 seats.
References: *Film Daily Yearbook*, 1940–1955. *Motion Picture Herald*, July 15, 1939.

New Iberia

721. MUSU THEATER
Picture house.
References: *Film Daily Yearbook*, 1941–1955.

New Orleans

722. ACE THEATER
323 S. Rampart Street
Picture house. 465–555 seats. Manager in 1955: Clifford LaFrance. In January 1955, the Ace offered moviegoers the following films: *Human Desire*, starring Glenn Ford, *Sins of Rome*, starring Massimo Giroffi, *Saracen Blade*, starring Ricardo Montalban, *Guerilla Girl*, starring Helmut Dantino, *Station West*, starring Dick Powell, and *Safari Drums*, starring Johnny Sheffield. Also shown were the serial films *Trader Tom of China, Chapter 2* and *Batman Chapter 1* and cartoons.

References: *Film Daily Yearbook*, 1940–1955. *Louisiana Weekly*, January 8, 1955. *Motion Picture Herald*, July 15, 1939.

723. BORDEAUX THEATER

Picture house. Managers: Bordeaux and Camp (African Americans).

References: Cahn, *Julius Cahn-Gus Hill Theatrical Guide*. Hill, *Pages from the Harlem Renaissance*. Jackson, "List of Colored Theaters and Attractions," *Billboard*, August 6, 1921. Work, *Negro Yearbook, 1921–1922*.

724. CARVER THEATER

2101 Orleans Avenue

Picture house. 1,050 seats. The Carver featured many films during the month of January 1955 including: *Desiree*, starring Marlon Brando and Jean Simmons, *Ma and Pa Kettle At Home*, starring Marjorie Main and Percy Kilbride, *The Black Widow*, starring Gene Tierney and Van Heflin, *Private Hell 36*, starring Ida Lupino and Steve Cochran, and *Jesse James' Women*, featuring Don Barry and Peggy Castle.

References: *Film Daily Yearbook*, 1951–1955. *Louisiana Weekly*, January 8, 1955.

725. CIRCLE THEATER

1709 N. Galvez Street

Picture house. 550–1800 seats. Manager in 1940: Abraham Goldberg. During Christmas week 1940, the Circle had the following lineup of pictures: *Let Freedom Ring*, starring Nelson Eddy and Lionel Barrymore, *Twenty Mule Team*, starring Wallace Berry, *Irene*, co-starring Anna Neagle and Ray Millard, *Phantom Riders*, starring Walter Pigeon, and *Lillian Russell*, starring Alice Faye, Don Ameche, and Henry Fonda. Also shown that week were an *Our Gang* comedy and a Mills Brothers musical. In January 1955, the Circle boasted a "new giant screen" to show its main attractions, including the film *Betrayed*, starring Clark Gable, Lana Turner, and Victor Mature, and *Ruby Gentry*, starring Charleston Heston, Jennifer Jones, and Karl Malden.

References: *Film Daily Yearbook*, 1941–1955. *Louisiana Weekly*, December 28, 1940, January 8, 1955.

726. DIXIE THEATER

1311 S. Rampart Street

Picture house. 350 seats. Manager in 1940: Paul H. Brunet. In January 1955, the Dixie featured a musical short and cartoon along with a double feature: *Cat Women of the Moon* starring Sonny Tufts, and the George Stevens picture *Shane*, co-starring Alan Ladd, Jean Arthur, and Van Heflin.

References: *Film Daily Yearbook*, 1941–1955. *Louisiana Weekly*, January 8, 1955.

727. GALLO THEATER

2122 S. Clairborne Avenue

Picture house. 500 seats. In January 1955, the Gallo was showing *Johnny Guitar*, starring Sterling Hayden, *Desiree*, starring Marlon Brando and Jean Simmons, as well as cartoons and news.

References: *Film Daily Yearbook*, 1947–1955. *Louisiana Weekly*, January 8, 1955.

728. GEM THEATER

3938 Thalia

Picture house. 850 seats. In January 1955, the Gem seems to offer something for everyone. It had the comedies *Here We Go Again* and *No Adults Allowed*. It offered the cartoon *The Milky Waif*. Hollywood films included *Drums Across the River*, co-starring Audie Murphy and Lisa Gaye, *Top Hat*, starring Ginger Rogers and Fred Astaire, *Border River*, starring Yvonne DeCarlo and Joel McCrea, and *White Fire*, starring Scott Brady and Mary Castle. Also advertised was an "all colored cast" in the picture *Lying Lips*.

References: *Film Daily Yearbook*, 1948, 1950–1955. *Louisiana Weekly*, January 8, 1955.

729. IROQUOIS THEATER
  413 S. Rampart Street
  Vaudeville house. Manager in 1921: G. Ford (African American).
  References: Jackson, "List of Colored Theaters and Attractions," *Billboard*, August 6, 1921. Work, *Negro Yearbook, 1921–1922*.

730. JOLLY THEATER
  Picture house.
  References: *Film Daily Yearbook*, 1940. *Motion Picture Herald*, July 15, 1939.

731. LINCOLN THEATER
  2514 Washington Avenue
  Picture house. 600 seats. Managers in 1921: Howard and Louisiana. Manager in 1940: Jacques A. Dicharry. The Whitman Sisters appeared here in 1932. During Christmas week 1940 the Lincoln was showing three films: *Island of Lost Men*, co-starring Anna Mae Wong and J. Carroll Nash, *Jeepers Creepers* with the Weaver Brothers and Roy Rogers, and *Silver on the Sage*, co-starring Bill Boyd and Gabby Hayes. In January 1955, the Lincoln featured *Human Desire*, starring Glenn Ford, *Sangaree*, starring Fernando Lamas, *Broken Lance*, starring Spencer Tracy and Richard Widmark, and *House on Telegraph Hill*, starring Richard Basehart. In addition, moviegoers could see a Three Stooges comedy and a Little Herman cartoon.
  References: Cahn, *Julius Cahn-Gus Hill Theatrical Guide*. *Film Daily Yearbook*, 1930–1933, 1940–1955. George-Graves, *The Royalty of Negro Vaudeville*. Jackson, "List of Colored Theaters and Attractions," *Billboard*, August 6, 1921. *Louisiana Weekly*, December 28, 1940; January 8, 1955. *Motion Picture Herald*, April 24, 1937; July 15, 1939. Sampson, *Blacks in Black and White* Work, *Negro Yearbook, 1921–1922*.

732. LUTHER K. MITCHELL THEATER
  Picture house. Manager: Luther K. Mitchell (African American).
  References: Cahn, *Julius Cahn-Gus Hill Theatrical Guide*. Jackson, "List of Colored Theaters and Attractions," *Billboard*, August 6, 1921. Work, *Negro Yearbook, 1921–1922*.

733. LYRIC THEATER
  201 Burgundy Street
  Vaudeville house. TOBA member. Manager in 1921: Luke S. Bordeaux. Managers: Beaudreaux and Bennett. In April 1921, the Willie Toosweet Company, Jack Ginger Wiggins, and the All Star Review Company with Charles Hightower performed at the Lyric: The theater also ran the musical *Chicago Follies*. In August 1923, blues singer Bessie Smith headlined a show with comedians Ferbee and McCann, actor Paul Carter, yodeler Charles Anderson, and comic singers Harris and Harris. In March 1924, the vaudeville bill included the benders Boyd and Boyd, singers Ferguson and Ferguson, comedians Cutout and Willie Eldridge, the piano cabaret act of Jackson, Wilson and Johnson, comedians DeLoach and Corbin, and blackface comedians Matthews and Matthews. In October 1926, the Lyric featured the vaudevillians Thomas and Breeden, Green and Lane, Jones and Chatman, Fritz Jazz Lips Jr., and Billy Arnet. In November 1927, Seals and Mitchell's Melody Lane Girls came to the Lyric. During the 1930s, Gonzelle White's band and Count Basie appeared at the theater.
  References: *Baltimore Afro-American*, October 31, 1926. Basie, *Good Morning Blues*. *Chicago Defender,* Browne, " Stage Jottings," August 11, 1923; Davis, "Amon's Pen," Cahn, *Julius Cahn-Gus Hill Theatrical Guide*. November 5, 1927; Sessions, "At the Lyric," March 1, 1924.

George-Graves, *The Royalty of Negro Vaudeville*. Hill, *Pages from the Harlem Renaissance*. Jackson, "List of Colored Theaters and Attractions," *Billboard*, August 6, 1921; "The Theater Owners' Booking Association," *Billboard*, December 16, 1922. Sampson, *Blacks in Blackface*. Work, *Negro Yearbook, 1921–1922*.

734. OTHELLO THEATER
235 S. Rampart Street
Picture house. 600 seats. Managers: the Knights of Pythias Lodge (African American).
References: Cahn, *Julius Cahn-Gus Hill Theatrical Guide*. Hill, *Pages from the Harlem Renaissance*. Jackson, "Additions to Theater List," *Billboard*, December 31, 1921. Work, *Negro Yearbook, 1921–1922*.

735. PALACE THEATER
201 Dauphine Street
Picture house. 1,110 seats. Manager in 1940: J. H. Moser. During the week of December 14, 1940, the Palace showed the pictures *The Man Who Wouldn't Take*, starring Ralph Cooper and Pigmeat Markham, and *Typhoon*, starring Dorothy Lamour and Robert Preston. In January 1955, the Palace featured Johnny Weismuller and Judy Walsh in *Cannibal Attack*, Gary Cooper in *The Westerner*, Donald O'Connor in *Francis Joins the WACs*, Ronald Reagan and Barbara Stanwyck in *Cattle Queen of Montana*, and Leo Gorcey and Huntz Hall in *Jungle Gents*.
References: *Film Daily Yearbook*, 1940–1955. *Louisiana Weekly*, December 14, 1940; January 8, 1955. *Motion Picture Herald*, April 24, 1937; July 15, 1939. Sampson, *Blacks in Black and White*.

736. PYTHIAN TEMPLE
238 S. Saratoga Street
Vaudeville house. Owners in 1921: Knights of Pythias Lodge (African American).
References: Cahn, *Julius Cahn-Gus Hill Theatrical Guide*. Jackson, "List of Colored Theaters and Attractions," *Billboard*, August 6, 1921.

737. RITZ THEATER
1809 LaSalle Street
Picture house. 600 seats. Manager in 1940: W. J. Roeach. In January 1955, the Ritz exhibited the following pictures: *Saskatchewan*, starring Alan Ladd and Shirley Winters, *Ride Vaquero*, starring Robert Taylor and Ava Gardner, *Gog*, starring Richard Egan, *Hot News*, starring Stanley Clements, and *Badman's Territory*, starring Randolph Scott. References: *Film Daily Yearbook*, 1941–1955. *Louisiana Weekly*, advertisement, January 8, 1955. *Motion Picture Herald*, July 15, 1939.

738. TEMPLE THEATER
Vaudeville and picture house. In 1920, the New Orleans police department asked the Temple to stop showing the Oscar Micheaux film *Within Our Gates* because of racial tensions in the city.
References: Bowser, *Writing Himself into History*. Hill, *Pages from the Harlem Renaissance*. Peterson, *The African American Theatre Directory*.

New Roads

739. ALAMO THEATER
Picture house.
References: *Film Daily Yearbook*, 1940. *Motion Picture Herald*, July 15, 1939.

740. STAR THEATER
Picture house. 215 seats.
References: *Film Daily Yearbook*, 1942–1955.

Opelousas

741. ALAMO THEATER
Picture house.

References: *Film Daily Yearbook*, 1930–1932.

742. BON AMI THEATER
Vaudeville and picture house. 240 seats.
References: Hill, *Pages from the Harlem Renaissance*. Work, *Negro Yearbook, 1921–1922*.

743. LOU ANN THEATER
Picture house.
References: *Film Daily Yearbook*, 1949–1955.

744. ROSEDALE THEATER
Picture house.
References: *Film Daily Yearbook*, 1949–1955.

Patterson

745. ARCADE THEATER
Picture house.
References: *Film Daily Yearbook*, 1949.

Plaquemine

746. GREATER OSAGE THEATER
Picture house.
References: *Film Daily Yearbook*, 1949–1955.

Reserve

747. MAURIN THEATER
Picture house. 300 seats.
References: *Film Daily Yearbook*, 1949–1955.

Rustin

748. LINCOLN THEATER
Picture house.
References: *Film Daily Yearbook*, 1947–1955.

Saint Martinsville

749. REX THEATER
Picture house. According to the *Film Daily Yearbook*, the Rex was closed in 1949.
References: *Film Daily Yearbook*, 1943–1955.

Scotlandville

750. COLORED THEATER
Picture house. Said to be owned and managed by African Americans.
References: Cahn, *Julius Cahn-Gus Hill Theatrical Guide*. Jackson, "List of Colored Theaters and Attractions," *Billboard*, August 6, 1921.

751. COOK'S SCENIC HIGHWAY THEATER
Picture house. 296 cars. This was most likely a drive-in theater.
References: *Film Daily Yearbook*, 1940–1955. *Motion Picture Herald*, July 15, 1939.

Shreveport

752. HIPPODROME THEATER
Vaudeville house.
References: Cahn, *Julius Cahn-Gus Hill Theatrical Guide*. Jackson, "List of Colored Theaters and Attractions," *Billboard*, August 6, 1921. Work, *Negro Yearbook, 1921–1922*.

753. RITZ THEATER
1705 Milan Street
Picture house. 560 seats. Manager in 1942: Syd Levy.
References: *Film Daily Yearbook*, 1941–1955.

754. STAR THEATER
1045–1050 Texas Avenue
Vaudeville house. 800–967 seats. A

TOBA theater. Manager in 1920: Charles F. Gordon. Manager in 1921: Jack S. Welch. Manager in 1928: Arthur Cunningham. According to Bowser, Gordon did not like the subject matter of the Oscar Micheaux film *Within Our Gates* and refused to show the movie at the Star.
References: Bowser, *Writing Himself into History*. Cahn, *Julius Cahn-Gus Hill Theatrical Guide. Film Daily Yearbook*, 1931–1933, 1940–1955. Hill, *Pages from the Harlem Renaissance*. Jackson, "List of Colored Theaters and Attractions," *Billboard*, August 6, 1921; "The Theater Owners' Booking Association," *Billboard*, December 16, 1922. *Motion Picture Herald*, April 24, 1937; July 15, 1939. *Official Theatrical World of Colored Artists*. Sampson, *Blacks in Black and White*. Work, *Negro Yearbook, 1921–1922*.

Sulphur

755. GREEN THEATER
Picture house.
References: *Film Daily Yearbook*, 1949–1955.

756. HARLEM THEATER
Picture house.
References: *Film Daily Yearbook*, 1947–1955.

Tallulah

757. BAILEY THEATER
Picture house. 500 seats.
References: *Film Daily Yearbook*, 1940–1944. *Motion Picture Herald*, July 15, 1939.

758. GREEN FROG THEATER
Picture house.
References: *Film Daily Yearbook*, 1949–1955.

759. RITZ THEATER
Picture house.
References: *Film Daily Yearbook*, 1945–1955.

760. ROXY THEATER
References: *Film Daily Yearbook*, 1946, 1947, 1948.

Thibodaux

761. HARLEM THEATER
Picture house. 259–263 seats.
References: *Film Daily Yearbook*, 1940–1955. *Motion Picture Herald*, July 15, 1939.

Vidalia

762. VIDALIA THEATER
Picture house. 250 seats.
References: *Film Daily Yearbook*, 1947–1955.

Vinton

763. ALICE THEATER
Picture house.
References: *Film Daily Yearbook*, 1949–1955.

764. JULIAN THEATER
Picture house.
References: *Film Daily Yearbook*, 1949–1955.

Welsh

765. ROSENWALD SCHOOL THEATER
Picture house.
References: *Film Daily Yearbook*, 1930–1932, 1946–1955.

Winnfield

766. WINN THEATER

Winnfield, Louisiana
Picture house. 350 seats.
References: *Film Daily Yearbook*, 1949–1955.

Winsboro

767. HARVARD THEATER
Picture house.
References: *Film Daily Yearbook*, 1952–1955.

MARYLAND

Annapolis

768. BOOKER T. THEATER
Picture house. 500 seats.
References: *Film Daily Yearbook*, 1940–1943. *Motion Picture Herald*, April 24, 1937; July 15, 1939. Sampson, *Blacks in Black and White.*

769. CLAY STREET THEATER
Picture house. Manager in 1921: John Costi.
References: Cahn, *Julius Cahn-Gus Hill Theatrical Guide.* Jackson, "List of Colored Theaters and Attractions," *Billboard*, August 6, 1921. Work, *Negro Yearbook, 1921–1922.*

770. STAR THEATER
71–75 Calvert Street
Picture house. 500 seats. Management in 1921: JML Amusement Co.
References: Cahn, *Julius Cahn-Gus Hill Theatrical Guide. Film Daily Yearbook*, 1931–1933, 1940–1955. Jackson, "Additions to Theater List," *Billboard*, December 31, 1921. *Motion Picture Herald*, April 24, 1937; July 15, 1939. Sampson, *Blacks in Black and White.*

Avenue

771. PARADISE THEATER
Picture house.
References: *Film Daily Yearbook*, 1950–1955.

Baltimore

ALBERT AUDITORIUM *see* New Albert Theater

772. AMERICAN THEATER
941–43 Pennsylvania Avenue
Picture house. 250–300 seats. Also known as Lincoln Number 2 and AM. Manager in 1921: A. Rosen. According to Headley, "this theater was built for Kalem Flaks around 1920 in a remodeled store. It was renamed Lincoln Number Two, probably in order to distinguish it from the other Lincoln, around 1928. It closed soon thereafter. In May 1921, the *Baltimore Afro-American* featured advertisements for the American for the films *The Jungle Princess*, featuring Juanita Hanen, *The Flame of Youth*, starring Shirley Mason, and *The Road Demon* with Tom Mix.
References: Cahn, *Julius Cahn-Gus Hill Theatrical Guide.* Jackson, "List of Colored Theaters and Attractions," *Billboard*, August 6, 1921. *Film Daily Yearbook*, 1931, 1932. Headley, *Exit: A History of Movies in Baltimore.* Work, *Negro Yearbook, 1921–1922.*

773. ANTHONY THEATER
103 S. Main Street
Picture house. 600 seats. Architect: David Harrison. Manager in 1945: Robert R. Lee. The Anthony "was the first real movie theater in the black steelworker's community of Turner's Station near Dundalk," according to Headley.
References: *Film Daily Yearbook*, 1949–1955. Headley, *Exit: A History of Movies in Baltimore*.

774. ARENA PLAYHOUSE
Drama house. 314 seats. From 1953 to the present. Resident theater of the Arena Players Company.
References: Peterson, *The African American Theatre Directory*.

ARGONNE THEATER *see* Goldfield Theater

775. BIDDLE THEATER
1235 Biddle Street
Picture house. Architect: James Kourkoulis. Manager: Mr. Lee. "It was formerly a garage with a hall on the second floor," notes Headley. The Biddle was built in 1947 and closed about 1970.
References: *Film Daily Yearbook*, 1955. Headley, *Exit: A History of Movies in Baltimore*.

776. BOOKER T. THEATER
930–932 W. Baltimore Street
Picture house. Also known as the Aladdin and the New Queen. 400 seats. Architect: James A. Bowers. Headley reports that the Booker T. was sporadically called the New Aladdin from 1918–20 and in 1930, when it was called the New Queen. It reopened as the Booker T. after closing around 1930, but permanently closed again in 1938.
References: *Film Daily Yearbook, 1940–1943*. Headley. *Exit: A History of Movies in Baltimore. Motion Picture Herald*, April 24, 1937; July 15, 1939. Sampson, *Blacks in Black and White*.

BROADWAY GARDEN THEATER *see* Park Theater.

777. CAREY THEATER
1440 N. Carey Street
Picture house. 275 seats. Architect: Stanislaus Russell. Owner: J. C. Cremen. Managers: William George, Harry Duvall. According to Headley, "the Carey was an early black movie house which opened in early 1916. It cost about $15,000. It was advertised as 'the best ventilated colored theater in the city' in 1920. The theater seated about 4450 persons, and was built of red brick." The theater closed in about 1953, and the building was briefly used as a church before being demolished in the 1970s. The *Baltimore Afro-American* advertised the following films at the Carey for the week of January 3, 1921: *Twenty-three and One-half Hours Leave*, with Douglas McLean and Doris May, *Mystery of 13*, featuring Francis Ford and Rosemary Theby, *The Rough House*, a two act comedy starring Fatty Arbuckle, and *Doing Time*, featuring Little Sambo.
References: Cahn, *Julius Cahn-Gus Hill Theatrical Guide*. Jackson, "List of Colored Theaters and Attractions," *Billboard*, August 6, 1921. *Film Daily Yearbook*, 1930–1933, 1940–1955. Headley, *Exit: A History of Movies in Baltimore. Motion Picture Herald*, April 24, 1937; July 15, 1939. Sampson, *Blacks in Black and White*. Work, *Negro Yearbook, 1921–1922*.

CARVER THEATER *see* Diane Theater

778. DALY THEATER
936 Pennsylvania Avenue
Picture house. According to Headley, this open-air theater, one of the earliest black theaters in Baltimore, was run by William H. Daly from about November 1909 to 1913 or 1914, when he moved it to 1115 Pennsylvania Avenue. "One of the

Arena Playhouse, Baltimore, Maryland (SoulofAmerica.com)

interesting features of Daly's was a live electric wire atop the outside fence, which could be activated by a switch in the projection booth. Its purpose was to discourage kids from sneaking over the fence." writes Headley.

References: Headley, *Motion Picture Exhibition in Washington, D.C.* Peterson, *The African American Theatre Directory.*

779. DIANE THEATER

1429–1431 Pennsylvania Avenue

Picture house. 500 seats. According to Headley, "The Diane was opened in 1935 by the Hornstein family. In the mid-fifties it became the Carver, and, in 1959 or 1960, it became the New Carver. [As of 1972] it is still operating under the latter name with the brightest chrome yellow front in town. The marquee was removed around 1971."

References: *Film Daily Yearbook*, 1930, 1940–1955. *Motion Picture Herald*, April 24, 1937; July 15, 1939. Sampson, *Blacks in Black and White.*

DOUGLAS THEATER *see* Royal Theater.

780. DUNBAR THEATER

619–621 N. Central Avenue

Picture house. 500 seats. Architects: Callis and Callis. Manager in 1921: Josiah Diggs (African American). The movies *The Damel in Distress* and *Sahara*, starring Louise Glaum, were the big draws at the Dunbar the week of August 23, 1920. The *Baltimore Afro-American* advertised the following films at the Dunbar for the week of January 4, 1921: *The Veiled Mystery*, starring Antonio Moreno, *The Prince Chap*, starring Thomas Meighan, and *Thunderbolt Jack*, featuring Jack Hoxey. Built for the Crown Amusement Company in 1916, the Dunbar was planned as a one-story brick and stucco building, seating 250–300, for about $25,000. By

1923, he continues, when renovations raised the seating capacity to 500 or 1,000, according to differing reports, the Dunbar was presenting films by Paramount, Fox, Metro Goldwyn, Warner Brothers, and First National. "The Dunbar lasted until 1957 in spite of a serious fire in June 1945, which destroyed much of the building. The theater was razed to make room for a housing project," writes Headley.

References: Cahn, *Julius Cahn-Gus Hill Theatrical Guide.* Jackson, "List of Colored Theaters and Attractions," *Billboard,* August 6, 1921. *Film Daily Yearbook,* 1930–1933, 1940–1955. Headley, *Exit: A History of Movies in Baltimore*; *Motion Picture Herald,* April 24, 1937; July 15, 1939. Sampson, *Blacks in Black and White.* Work, *Negro Yearbook,* 1921–1922.

781. Eden Theater
1401 Monument Street
Picture house. Also known as the National. 1,000 seats. Architects: E. A. Lockart and Oliver B. Wight. Manager in 1921: C. Robert Moore. Always a black heater, the venue was built as a triangle with a mirror screen across one wall and the entrance in the opposite corner, with 1,000 mahogany-finished seats in a semicircle; the theater also boasted two Powers 6-B projectors. The National had what was described as "the largest colored dancing hall in the state ... Samuel Crawford conducted the orchestra of violin, banjo, piano, and drums," writes Headley, who reports that the National closed in 1925 and reopened about 20 years later as the Eden, with a seating capacity of about 450. It closed permanently in 1952, and building was demolished.

References: *Film Daily Yearbook,* 1930, 1950–1955. Headley. *Exit: A History of Movies in Baltimore.*

782. Fremont Theater
615–617 N. Fremont Avenue
Picture house. 275 seats. Architects: Greenbaum and Evatt. Manager: Charles H. Imwold. Headley says "the Fremont's career lasted over forty years from early 1909 to about 1951. It may have been opened by a local druggist who tore out a couple of houses to build it [or] two gentlemen named Greenbaum and Evatt had something to do with building it. Charles H. Imwold operated it until 1921. The Fremont Amusement Company (Charles E. Nolte, President) acquired the Fremont after Imwold lost the lease."

References: *Film Daily Yearbook,* 1930, 1940–1955. Headley, *Exit: A History of Movies in Baltimore. Motion Picture Herald,* April 24, 1937; July 15, 1939. Sampson, *Blacks in Black and White.*

783. Fulton Theater
1563 N. Fulton Avenue
Picture house. Also called the Gertrude McCoy. 500 seats. Architect: F.E. Tormey. Active from 1915 to 1951. According to Headley, the Fulton was a theater designed "in the Italian Renaissance style of architecture with a spacious sixteen-foot deep vestibule and light gray stucco exterior. The interior of the house was finished in ivory and sky blue .... In 1927 the name was changed to Fulton.... The Fulton closed down in 1951. It was a food market for many years, but has recently been converted into a church."

References: *Film Daily Yearbook,* 1949–1955. Headley, *Exit: A History of Movies in Baltimore.*

784. Gilmore Theater
314 N. Gilmore Street
Picture house. Managers: Oscar Schlen, Gilmore, and Saratoga. Also known as the Gilmore-Douglass. Singers Bessie Smith and Hazel Green played here in 1918.

References: Albertson, *Bessie.* Bowser, *Writing Himself into History.* Cahn, *Julius*

Cahn-Gus Hill Theatrical Guide. Headley, *Exit: A History of Movies in Baltimore.* Jackson, "List of Colored Theaters and Attractions," *Billboard,* August 6, 1921. Work, *Negro Yearbook, 1921–1922.*

785. GOLDFIELD THEATER
924 S. Sharp Street.
Picture house. 600 seats. Originally called the Argonne. Later renamed the New Goldfield. Sometimes called the Goldfield number 2. Architect: Edward Storck. Manager in 1921: J.L. Rome. Headley reports that the one-story brick building was built by the Guilford Building Company in 1921 or 1922, from plans by Edward Storck at a cost of about $15,000. Renamed in 1926, the movie house was operated by both George Jacobs and Rome Theaters. "It had a small stage with a narrow rectangular addition to the roof where the curtain and scenery could be stored. As of 1972, the Goldfield was still standing, but it was in the way of an interstate expressway and will no doubt be destroyed. It has been closed since about 1960," writes Headley.
References: Cahn, *Julius Cahn-Gus Hill Theatrical Guide. Film Daily Yearbook,* 1930–1933, 1940–1955. Headley, *Exit: A History of Movies in Baltimore.* Hill, *Pages from the Harlem Renaissance.* Jackson, "List of Colored Theaters and Attractions," *Billboard,* August 6, 1921. *Motion Picture Herald,* April 24, 1937; July 15, 1939. Sampson, *Blacks in Black and White.* Work, *Negro Yearbook, 1921–1922.*

786. HARLEM THEATER
616 N. Gilmore Street
Picture house. 1,500 seats. Architect: Wilson Porter Smith. According to Headley, "the Harlem was built for the Rome organization in 1932. The building was originally the Harlem Park Methodist Episcopal Church. Wilson Porter Smith was the architect and Gus Schoenlein was the contractor of the theater conversion. When it was being converted into a movie house, local views held that it would probably be struck by lightning. The building is stone. It was originally atmospheric with a Spanish décor, but, in the fifties, the first floor walls were draped. The tile roofs and other atmospheric touches are still visible in the balcony. The blinking stars on the ceiling went out a long time ago. The interior color scheme, originally cream and blue, is now (1972) uniform blue. Up until fairly recently the Harlem could put on stage shows, but the curtain is now nailed down. It opened on 7 October 1932 with *Chandu the Magician* starring Edmund Lowe. Opening day ceremonies included a huge parade that featured floats, local organizations such as Elks, Pythians, Penrose Club, Antler Club, Vondell Club, and the South Baltimore Club, and many other civic leaders. T. Finley Wilson, Grand Exalted Ruler of the Elks, gave an address in flowing oratory inside the theater. The original marquee was 65 feet long and contained 900 fifty-watt bulbs to light the pavement beneath. The Harlem seats about 1,488 persons. Under the skillful management of Mr. Harold Grott, it is still going strong."
References: *Film Daily Yearbook,* 1940–1955. Headley, *Exit: A History of Movies in Baltimore. Motion Picture Herald,* April 24, 1937; July 15, 1939. Sampson, *Blacks in Black and White.*

787. HILL THEATER
610 Cherry Hill Road
Picture house. 929 seats. Architect: Julius Myerberg. Headley mentions the unusual clock tower on the roof of the Hill Theater.
References: *Film Daily Yearbook,* 1949–1955. Headley, *Exit: A History of Movies in Baltimore.*

Harlem Theater, Baltimore, Maryland, 1974 (Robert K. Headley Collection)

788. HIPPODROME THEATER
12 N. Eutaw Street
Vaudeville house. Built in 1914. Architect: Thomas W. Lamb. Count Basie and his orchestra performed here in the 1930s.
References: Basie, *Good Morning Blues*. Cahn, *Julius Cahn-Gus Hill Theatrical Guide*. Headley, *Exit: A History of Movies in Baltimore*.

789. HOME THEATER
2211 Pennsylvania Avenue
Picture house. Owners: Amazon Amusement Company. According to Headley, the theater operated between 1909 and 1910.
References: Bowser, *Writing Himself into History*. Headley, *Exit: A History of Movies in Baltimore*.

790. JEAN THEATER
913 Warner Street
Picture house. 200 seats. Also called the Goldfield number 1. This apparently was the first Baltimore theater called the Goldfield and it is not identical with the New Goldfield or Goldfield number 2 on S. Sharp Street. Headley describes the Jean Theater as "a rectangular brick structure with a square, shallow storm lobby." The Jean operated under the name Goldfield from 1915 to about 1928. It then apparently reopened as the Jean in 1946. *Film Daily Yearbook* reports that the Jean was closed from 1949 to 1951.
References: *Film Daily Yearbook*, 1949–1955. Headley, *Exit: A History of Movies in Baltimore*.

KANE THEATER *see* Park Theater

791. LAFAYETTE THEATER
1433 W. Lafayette Avenue
Vaudeville and picture house. 300 seats. Architect: John Cowan. According to Headley, "the building was two stories high, of brick and stone, with a wide, fancy metal façade, and measured 40 × 125 feet. It was enlarged and renovated in 1919. Peter Oletsky acquired it in the fall of 1925 by which time it had become a black theater. [It] lasted until 1952...."
References: *Film Daily Yearbook*, 1940–1955. Headley, *A History of Movies in Baltimore. Motion Picture Herald*, April 24, 1937; July 15, 1939. Sampson, *Blacks in Black and White*.

792. LENOX THEATER
2115–2117 Pennsylvania Ave.
Picture house. 375 seats. Architect: George S. Childs. Owner in 1919: Benjamin Sachs. Manager in 1919: George Woodlen. Headley reports that there is conflicting information regarding the building of the Lenox. According to him, "the Lenox opened as the Rainbow 2 in 1919. It was designed by George S. Childs, and was described as a one-story, 32-× 154 foot, brick theater. It was to cost about $12,000. According to another source, it was designed by W. O. Sparklin as a 150 × 28 foot, brick and stucco theater that would cost $25,000. Benjamin Sachs was the owner and George Woodlen was the manager when the Rainbow opened. The Rainbow was a white theater. It was rebuilt by the Hornstein organization as the Lenox in 1936 after a break in operation since about 1925 during which it was a garage." The Lenox catered to African American audiences through the 1970s and around 1973 was converted into a church.
References: Headley, *Exit: A History of Movies in Baltimore. Film Daily Yearbook*, 1940–1955. *Motion Picture Herald*, April 24, 1937; July 15, 1939. Sampson, *Blacks in Black and White*.

793. LINCOLN THEATER
936 Pennsylvania Avenue
Vaudeville and picture house. 500 seats. Architect: Theodore W. Pietch. A TOBA theater. Also known as Lincoln Theater Number 1. Manager in 1921: M. Flaks. This house is not to be confused another Lincoln Theater at 941 Pennsylvania Avenue better known as the American. In August 1920, the Lincoln hosted Frank Montgomery's musical review *Hello 1920*. In January 1921, the *Baltimore Afro-American* advertised the following vaudeville acts at the Lincoln: "Smith and King Plays — the Wonder Music Co., the originators of Syncopation, Jazz Comedy and Wonder Steppers." In February 1924, the Lincoln's vaudeville show included singers and dancers Struffin and Brown, novelty act Stemmons and Stemmons, and singers and dancers Williams and Brown. According to Headley, "the Lincoln was built on the site of the old African Methodist Episcopal Zion Church of Baltimore by the Mutual Amusement Company. Designed by Theodore W. Pietsch, it was planned [for] vaudeville and motion pictures and to cater exclusively to black patronage." Opened in 1915 and soon purchased by Kalman Flaks, the Lincoln began with about 400 seats and enlarged to 900 seats, though it was originally designed to seat 1,300. "The Lincoln was integrated to some degree just after it opened. It was divided down the middle by an aisle. Whites sat on one side and blacks sat on the other. Otto 'Dutch' Niquet was one of the early operators there. The Lincoln may have been the only black movie house to employ behind the screen talkers. Music was provided by Professor Charles Harris's orchestra. The

Lenox Theater, Baltimore, Maryland, circa 1935 (Robert K. Headley Collection)

exterior of the Lincoln was nondescript with the exception of the unusual neon sign in the shape of Abraham Lincoln's head, which hung outside," writes Headley, adding that the theater was closed and demolished in 1971.

References: Cahn, *Julius Cahn-Gus Hill Theatrical Guide*. *Chicago Defender*, "Baltimore Notes," February 9, 1924. *Film Daily Yearbook*, 1930–1933, 1940–1955. Headley, *Exit: A History of Movies in Baltimore*. Hill, *Pages from the Harlem Renaissance*. Jackson, "List of Colored Theaters and Attractions," *Billboard*, August 6, 1921; "The Theater Owners' Booking Association," *Billboard*, December 16, 1922. *Motion Picture Herald*, April 24, 1937; July 15, 1939. Sampson, *Blacks in Black and White*. Work, *Negro Yearbook, 1921–1922*.

794. MADISON THEATER
818 Madison Avenue
Picture house. 400 seats. Probably this theater has been demolished.
References: *Film Daily Yearbook*, 1949–1955. Headley, *Exit: A History of Movies in Baltimore*.

795. MORGAN THEATER
2426 Pennsylvania Avenue
Picture house. 430 seats. Architect: Paul Emmart. Manager in 1945: Samuel Shoubin. Also known as the Schanze and the Uptown. It was built in 1912.

According to Headley, it was made of "reinforced concrete with granite and marble trim. There was a dance hall on the second floor for many years. Dr. Schanze's pharmacy was next door to the theater." The house was renamed the Morgan after remodeling in 1938 and then became the Uptown in 1940 before reverting back to the Morgan in 1949–1952. The Morgan closed in the early 1950s.

References: *Film Daily Yearbook*, 1947–1955. Headley: *Exit: A History of Movies in Baltimore.*

796. NATIONAL THEATER
Picture house.
References: *Film Daily Yearbook*, 1931, 1932.

797. NEW ALBERT THEATER
1230 Pennsylvania Avenue
Picture house. 600–800 seats. Also called the Renard Moving Picture Parlor until 1915. The New Albert was in business from about 1908 to 1960. According to Headley, The New Albert Theater was an auditorium, complete with dance-hall and a forty-car garage, built around what was probably once a storefront, according to Headley. In 1944 the garage was converted into a movie theater. It was demolished in 1971.
References: *Film Daily Yearbook*, 1944–1955. Headley, *Exit: A History of Movies in Baltimore.*

NEW CARVER THEATER *see* Diane Theater

NEW GOLDFIELD THEATER *see* Argonne Theater

NEW KANE *see* Park Theater

798. PARK THEATER
1105–1107 N. Broadway
Picture house. 400 seats. Architect: J.E. Laferty. This theater opened under the name Plaza. In 1921 it became the Broadway Garden and in 1929 it became the Park. Headley comments: "It was strictly a five-cent movie house... As the Park it lasted up to April 1968 when it was damaged by rioters' torches. It was reopened as the Kane or New Kane but lasted only about a year."
References: *Film Daily Yearbook*, 1945–1955. Headley, *Exit: A History of Movies in Baltimore.*

799. QUEEN THEATER
666 W. Lexington Street
Picture and vaudeville house. 300 seats. 1909–1933. Also known as the New Queen. Architects: Edward T. Bates and Harry Morstein. Owners in 1909: Queen Amusement Company. Manager in 1909: Henry H. Lee. Manager in 1916: Charles Moseley. According to Headley, advertised as "a refined place for refined people entertaining as many whites as colored," the Queen was one of the first movie theaters catering to blacks in Baltimore, with shows from seven to eleven weekdays and from four to eleven on Saturdays. It also gave vaudeville performances." It closed in 1933, and a factory now exists on the site.
References: *Film Daily Yearbook*, 1931–1933. Headley, *Exit: A History of Movies in Baltimore.*

800. RADIO THEATER
629 N. Eden Street
Picture house. 600 seats. Built in 1939 and torn down about 1957. Also known as the Star. According to Headley it was torn down to make way for a housing project.
References: *Film Daily Yearbook*, 1944–1955. Headley, *Exit: A History of Movies in Baltimore.*

801. RAINBOW THEATER
2115–17 Pennsylvania Avenue
Picture and vaudeville house. Also known as the New Rainbow. Owner in

1921: Benjamin Sachs. Manager in 1921: George H. Woolden. The *Baltimore Afro-American* advertised the following films at the Rainbow for the week of August 23, 1920: *The Dare Devil*, starring Tom Mix, *The Notorious Mrs. Sands*, featuring Bessie Barriscale, *The Woman Gives*, starring Norma Talmadge, and *Men of the West*, starring Harry Corey. The vaudeville shows that week included Grice and Coleman, Dude McDow, and the Boisy Legge Trio. During the week of January 3, 1921, the Rainbow was showing the Oscar Micheaux film *The Symbol of the Unconquered*, starring Lawrence Chenault, Mattie Wilkes, Walter Thompson, and Leigh Whipper.

References: Cahn, *Julius Cahn-Gus Hill Theatrical Guide. Film Daily Yearbook*, 1931, 1932. Jackson, "List of Colored Theaters and Attractions," *Billboard*, August 6, 1921. Work, *Negro Yearbook, 1921–1922*.

802. REGENT THEATER
1619–1629 Pennsylvania Avenue
Vaudeville and picture house. 1,400 seats. A TOBA theater. Owner in 1921: C. Simmons. Manager in 1921: M. Hornstein. Vaudeville performers at the Regent for the week of August 23, 1920 were Aaron and Robinson, jazz pianists, and Clifford and Jackson, dancers. Paul Harris led the Regent Theater orchestra. The *Baltimore Afro-American* listed the vaudeville team of Simms and Warfield as heading the vaudeville show for the 1921 Memorial Day weekend. Films shown that week included *Bubbles*, starring Mary Anderson, *The Breaking Point*, *Silk Hosiery* with Edith Bennett, and Paul Laurence Dunbar's *The Sport of the Gods*, with an all-black cast directed by Henry Vernot. Cab Calloway remembers the black shows at the Regent in his autobiography: "The revues at the Regent usually consisted of bands that would play instrumentals or accompany singers like me doing pop tunes. Then the chorus line would come in." The Sunshine Sammy Revue played here in 1925.

References: Cahn, *Julius Cahn-Gus Hill Theatrical Guide*. Calloway, *Of Minnie the Moocher and Me. Film Daily Yearbook*, 1930–1933, 1940–1949. Hill, *Pages from the Harlem Renaissance*. Jackson, "List of Colored Theaters and Attractions," *Billboard*, August 6, 1921. *Motion Picture Herald*, April 24, 1937; July 15, 1939. *New York Age*, Bob Slater, "Theatrical Jottings," November 28, 1925. Sampson, *Blacks in Black and White. Theatrical World of Colored Artists*. Work, *Negro Yearbook, 1921–1922*.

RENARD MOVING PICTURE PARLOR *see* New Albert Theater

RIO THEATER *see* Star Theater

803. ROOSEVELT THEATER
512 W. Biddle Street
Picture house. 400–500 seats. Active from 1921 to mid-1960s. Also known as the Deluxe Roosevelt. Managers in 1921: Jacob Friedlander and George Douglass. According to Headley, the Roosevelt's "interior featured lighting by means of large, disc-like varied colored globes set in the ceiling.... The building has been demolished."

References: Cahn, *Julius Cahn-Gus Hill Theatrical Guide. Film Daily Yearbook*, 1931–1933, 1940–1955. Headley, *Exit: A History of Movies in Baltimore*. Jackson, "List of Colored Theaters and Attractions," *Billboard*, August 6, 1921. *Motion Picture Herald*, April 24, 1937; July 15, 1939. Sampson, *Blacks in Black and White*.

804. ROYAL THEATER
1329 Pennsylvania Avenue
Vaudeville house. 1,349 seats. Also

Regent Theater, Baltimore, Maryland, circa 1919 (Robert K. Headley Collection)

called the Douglas. Owner: Abe Lichtman. Manager: C. Simmons. Headley describes the enormous, block-long theater: there was a large balcony, a big stage, several boxes — including a set of false boxes — and a tiny projection booth that had to be entered by climbing up an iron ladder at the rear of the building."

112 Maryland

Royal Theater, formerly known as the Douglass; Baltimore, Maryland (Maryland Historical Society, Baltimore)

According to the *Baltimore Afro-American*, the opening of the theater as the Douglass marked "an epoch in the history of Baltimore ... the promoters of this gigantic enterprise involving nearly half a million dollars, deserve great credit in putting over this wonderful monument to Negro genius and advancement, and I miss my guess if the colored people of Baltimore do not show by their support and hearty cooperation that their efforts are appreciated." Performers at the Royal included Louis Armstrong, Blanche Calloway, Nat King Cole, Count Basie, Stan Kenton, Bessie Smith, and Duke Ellington. The building was demolished in 1971.

References: Albertson, *Bessie*. *Baltimore Afro-American*, February 10, 1922. Bowser, *Writing Himself into History*. Calloway, *Of Minnie the Moocher and Me*. *Film Daily Yearbook*, 1930–1932, 1940–1955. Gottschild, *Waltzing in the Dark*. Headley, *Exit: A History of Movies in Baltimore*. Hill, *Pages from the Harlem Renaissance*. Holiday, *Lady Sings the Blues*. *Motion Picture Herald*, April 24, 1937; July 15, 1939. Peterson, *The African American Theatre Directory*. Sampson, *Blacks in Black and White*. Work, *Negro Yearbook, 1921–1922*.

SCHANZE THEATER *see* Morgan Theater

805. STAR THEATER
1529–1531 Monument Avenue
Vaudeville and picture house. 327–400 seats. Architect: F. E. Beall. A TOBA theater. Manager in 1921: Monument Bond. It opened as the Star in 1911, and became the Rio in 1939. Vaudeville entertainment including acts by Billy Walker and "Babe" Brown and the "peer act of colored vaudeville," Ernest Watt and Muriel Ringgold, was given at the Star in its early years. In August 1920, the Star had a vaudeville show consisting of the acts Williams and Richardson, singers and dancers; Maggie Graham, singer, and Dick and Dick, singers and dancers. In January 1921, the *Baltimore Afro-American* advertised the vaudeville act Henry Wooden's Bon Tons — King of Jazz and the Syncopated Orchestra. Films shown that week included *Phantom Foe*, *Thunderbolt Jack*, *Tiger Band*, and *Son of Tarzan*. In

February 1924, the vaudeville show included the Roscoe and Mitchell Radio Girls. In the 1940s and 1950s, the house featured motion pictures.

References: Cahn, *Julius Cahn-Gus Hill Theatrical Guide*. *Chicago Defender*, "Baltimore Notes," February 9, 1924. *Film Daily Yearbook*, 1930–1933, 1955. Headley, *Exit: A History of Movies in Baltimore*. Hill, *Pages from the Harlem Renaissance*. Jackson, "List of Colored Theaters and Attractions," *Billboard*, August 6, 1921; "The Theater Owners' Booking Association, *Billboard*, December 16 1922. *Motion Picture Herald*, July 15, 1939. Sampson, *Blacks in Black and White*.

UPTOWN THEATER *see* Morgan Theater

Barton

806. NEW THEATER
Picture house. 500 seats.
References: *Film Daily Yearbook*, 1940–1955. *Motion Picture Herald*, April 24, 1937; July 15, 1939. Sampson, *Blacks in Black and White*.

Berlin

807. REX THEATER
Picture house.
References: *Film Daily Yearbook*, 1949–1955.

Cambridge

808. MONOGRAM THEATER
228 Pine Street
Vaudeville house. 200 seats. Manager in 1915: Arthur E. Benjamin (African American). During the week of April 12, 1915, the New York Follies performed at the Monogram.
References: *Indianapolis Freeman*, April 15, 1915.

Crisfield

809. LINCOLN THEATER
Picture house.
References: *Film Daily Yearbook*, 1949–1955.

Pocomoke City

810. DIXIE THEATER
Picture house.
References: *Film Daily Yearbook*, 1949–1955.

Princess Anne

811. AUDITORIUM THEATER
Somerset Avenue
Picture house. 301 seats.
References: *Film Daily Yearbook*, 1949–1955.

Rockville

812. LINCOLN PARK THEATER
Picture house.
References: *Film Daily Yearbook*, 1950–1955.

St. Inigoes

813. BUTLER THEATER
Picture house.
References: *Film Daily Yearbook*, 1949–1955.

Salisbury

814. RITZ THEATER

Outen's Colored Theater (Jerry Gerlitzki for the Worcester County, Maryland, Tourism Office)

Salisbury, Maryland
Picture house. 460 seats.
References: *Film Daily Yearbook*, 1947–1955.

Snow Hill

815. OUTTEN'S COLORED THEATER
Picture house. Owner and manager: Rudolph Outten.
References: Paul Touart, "African American Heritage in Worcester County, Maryland: Segregation."

816. RIO THEATER
Picture house.
References: *Film Daily Yearbook*, 1949–1955.

Waldorf

817. WALDORF THEATER
Picture house. 400 seats.
References: *Film Daily Yearbook*, 1949–1955.

MASSACHUSETTS

Roxbury

818. ROXBURY THEATER
2170 Washington Street
Picture house. 650 seats.
References: *Film Daily Yearbook*, 1954–1955.

MICHIGAN

Bay City

819. ROXY THEATER
521 Washington Street
Picture house. 1,273 seats.
References: *Film Daily Yearbook*, 1949–1955.

Detroit

820. ALHAMBRA THEATER
9428 Woodwood Avenue
Picture house. 1,475 seats. Architect: C. Howard Crane. According to Galbraith, this house was built in 1915. The Alhambra advertised itself as the "aristocrat of neighborhood theaters." During August 1945, the theater featured the motion pictures *Here Come the Waves*, with Bing Crosby and Betty Hutton, *American Romance*, starring Brian Donlevy, *Tarzan and the Amazons*, with Johnny Weismuller, and *White Savage*, starring Maria Montez and Jon Hall. Gypsy Rose Lee is said to have performed here.
References: *Michigan Chronicle*, August 4, 1945. Galbraith, *Motor City Marquees*.

821. APOLLO THEATER
1150 Clay Street
Picture house. 390 seats. 1912–1949. Also known as the Clay.
References: *Film Daily Yearbook*, 1944–1955. Galbraith, *Motor City Marquees*.

822. ARCADE THEATER
2416 Hastings Street
Picture house. 430 seats. Also called the Detroit Arcade. Architect: B. C. Wetzell. According to Galbraith, the Arcade was built in 1913.
References: *Film Daily Yearbook*, 1930–1933, 1940–1955. Galbraith, *Motor City Marquees*. *Motion Picture Herald*, April 24, 1937; July 15, 1939. Sampson, *Blacks in Black and White*.

823. BEECHWOOD THEATER
5010 W. Warren Avenue
Picture house. 1915–1940s. 400 seats. Architect: C. Howard Crane. The Beechwood had a full stage, orchestra pit, and dressing rooms.
References: *Film Daily Yearbook*, 1930–1933. Galbraith, *Motor City Marquees*.

824. BIJOU THEATER
62 Monroe Street
Picture house. 314 seats. Architects: Mildner and Eisen. Also known as the Cent Odeon. Built as the Cent Odeon in 1906, the house was the second permanent movie house to open in Detroit. It was a nickelodeon for a while and became the Bijou in 1909. According to Galbraith, the Bijou closed in the mid-1970s.
References: *Film Daily Yearbook*, 1949–1955. Galbraith, *Motor City Marquees*.

825. BOOKER T. THEATER
1020 Holbrook Street
Picture house. Owner in 1954: Korman Theatres.
References: *Film Daily Yearbook*, 1950–1955. Galbraith, *Motor City Marquees*.

826. BROADWAY STRAND
Picture house.
References: *Film Daily Yearbook*, 1931–1933.

CARVER THEATER *see* Catherine Theater

827. CASTLE THEATER
3412 Hastings Street
Picture house. 1,000 seats. Built in 1915. Owner: Korman Theaters. The Castle was open all night Monday, Wednes-

day, Friday, and Saturday with "bargain midnite shows." Moviegoers got four features for the price of one. In July 1946 some of the pictures at the Castle included *Gentlemen with Guns*, starring Buster Crabbe, *Dakota*, with John Wayne and Vera Ralston, and *Behind Prison Walls*. Another feature film, possibly a newsreel, *Ring Champs of Yesteryear*, was shown featuring boxing champions Jack Johnson, Joe Gans, and Jess Willard.

References: *Film Daily Yearbook*, 1930–1933, 1940–1955. Galbraith, *Motor City Marquees*. *Michigan Chronicle*, July 13, 27, 1946. *Motion Picture Herald*, April 24, 1937; July 15, 1939. Sampson, *Blacks in Black and White*.

828. CATHERINE THEATER
1700 Chene
Picture house. 398 seats. Architect: C. Howard Crane. Also known as the Carver. According to Galbraith, this theater was built in 1913.

References: *Film Daily Yearbook*, 1940–1955. Galbraith, *Motor City Marquees*. *Motion Picture Herald*, April 24, 1937; July 15, 1939. Sampson, *Blacks in Black and White*.

CENT ODEON *see* Bijou Theater

829. CHIC THEATER
Picture house.
References: *Film Daily Yearbook*, 1949–1955.

CINEX THEATER *see* National Theater

830. COLORED THEATER
2201 St. Aubin Street
Picture and vaudeville house.
References: Cahn, *Julius Cahn-Gus Hill Theatrical Guide*. Jackson, "List of Colored Theaters and Attractions," *Billboard*, August 6, 1921. Work, *Negro Yearbook*, 1921–1922.

831. COLUMBIA THEATER
50 Monroe Street
Picture house. 1911–1956. 1,006 seats. Architect: C. Howard Crane. It opened as one of the first nickeldeons in town to have an orchestra and pipe organ. During the week of September 21, 1947, the Columbia featured three hit films: *Tall, Tan and Terrific*, starring Mantan Moreland, *Ebony Parade*, starring Cab Calloway, Count Basie and his band, and the Mills Brothers, and the western *Stars Over Texas*. In April 1948, the Columbia hosted the first Detroit showing of *The Fight Never Ends*, starring Joe Louis, the Mills Brothers, and Ruby Dee. In November 1948, the big draw at the Columbia was *Look Out Sister*, featuring Louis Jordan and an "all colored cast."

References: *Michigan Chronicle*, September 20, 1947; April 26, November 8, 1948. *Film Daily Yearbook*, 1949–1955. Galbraith, *Motor City Marquees*.

DAVISON THEATER *see* New Davison

832. DUKE THEATER
1000 Eight Mile Road
Picture house. 1,500 seats. Manager: Chester Owen. The house was named for musician Edward "Duke" Ellington. According to Galbraith, this theater opened in 1947. The early films shown at the Duke included *Lady in the Lake*, starring Robert Montgomery, *The Man I Love*, starring Ida Lupino, and *Margie*, starring Jeanne Crain. In December 1948, the Duke featured the Judy Canova film *Singing in the Corn*. Todd Rhodes and his orchestra performed on stage on February 17, 1948. Galbraith states that the Duke closed in 1953 and later became a warehouse.

References: *Michigan Chronicle*, May 10, 17, 24, and December 6, 1947. *Film Daily Yearbook*, 1949–1955. Galbraith, *Motor City Marquees*.

833. DUNBAR THEATER
2814 Hastings Street
Vaudeville and picture house. 1921–

1936. 658 seats. Manager in 1926: E. B. Dudley. Peterson tells us that E. B. Dudley and his wife were entertainers who performed in Florida with the Russell-Ownes-Brooks Stock Company. According to Galbraith, this was originally "a theater for the city's Yiddish community (as became evident when the site became the Yiddish in 1921) on the Lower East Side. Although primarily concerned with stage productions, the Circle did exhibit films for a time. The theater became the Dunbar in 1926, catering to African American audiences. It closed around 1936."

References: *Chicago Defender*, "New Theater," April 10, 1926. *Film Daily Yearbook*, 1930–1933, 1940. Galbraith, *Motor City Marquees*. *Motion Picture Herald*, April 24, 1937; July 15, 1939. Peterson, *The African American Theatre Directory*. Sampson, *Blacks in Black and White*.

834. EAST SIDE THEATER
2717 Gratiot Avenue
Picture house. 1910–1955. 650 seats.
Architect: George V. Pottle.
References: *Film Daily Yearbook*, 1949–1955. Galbraith, *Motor City Marquees*.

835. ECHO THEATER
8962 Oakland Avenue
Picture house. 689 seats.
References: *Film Daily Yearbook*, 1940–1955. *Motion Picture Herald*, April 24, 1937; July 15, 1939. Sampson, *Blacks in Black and White*.

836. FARFIELD THEATER
Picture house.
Source: *Film Daily Yearbook*, 1940.

837. FOREST THEATER
4635 Woodward Avenue
Picture house. 592 seats. Architects: Fuller Clafflin and C. Howard Crane. According to Galbraith, the Forest was built by Claffin in 1914 and remodeled in 1935 by Crane.

References: *Film Daily Yearbook*, 1949–1955. Galbraith, *Motor City Marquees*.

838. GRANADA THEATER
5330 W. Warren Avenue
Picture house. 1,750 seats. In August 1944, there was a special matinee featuring the film *The Negro Soldier*, "with Uncle Sam's all star cast." The regular weekly fare consisted of *Riding High* with Dorothy Lamour and Dick Powell, *Ali Baba and the 40 Thieves* with Maria Montez and Jon Hall, and *Three Russian Girls*, featuring Anna Sten and Kent Smith. On Wednesday, the house gave away free dishes to women patrons. Audiences at the Granada during the week of August 21, 1948, enjoyed the Saturday matinee features *Winter Meeting*, starring Bette Davis, and *Joe Palooka Fighting Mad*, starring Joe Kirkwood. The midnight shows on Tuesday and Saturday were Judy Garland and Gene Kelly in *The Pirate*, and the western *Four Faces West*, with Joel McCrea, Frances Dee, and Charles Bickford.
References: *Film Daily Yearbook*, 1944–1955. *Michigan Chronicle*, June 24, 1944, August 21, 1948.

839. GRANDE THEATER
8024 W. Jefferson Avenue
Picture and vaudeville house. 1,837 seats. According to Galbraith the Grande was built in 1909 and was torn down in 1951.
References: *Film Daily Yearbook*, 1940–1943. Galbraith, *Motor City Marquees*.

840. GRANT THEATER
2240 Hastings Street
Picture house. 304–764 seats.
References: *Film Daily Yearbook*, 1930–1933, 1944–1955. *Motion Picture Herald*, July 15, 1939.

841. GRATIOT THEATER
2306–12 Gratiot Avenue
Nickeldeon, picture house. 1910–1930.

References: *Film Daily Yearbook*, 1930–1932. Galbraith, *Motor City Marquees*.

842. HIPPODROME THEATER
Picture house.
References: *Film Daily Yearbook*, 1930–1932,

843. HOLBROOK THEATER
Picture house.
References: *Film Daily Yearbook*, 1930–1933.

844. JEWEL THEATER
1450 Gratiot Avenue
Picture house. Built in 1914. Architect: William B. Stratton. 800 seats. According to Galbraith, "this larger theater lasted until the early days of talkies, closing in 1931.
References: *Film Daily Yearbook*, 1930–1933. Galbraith, *Motor City Marquees*.

845. KOPPIN THEATER
528–30 Gratiot Avenue
Nickelodeon and vaudeville house. A TOBA theater. Manager 1921–1928: Henry S. Koppin. In February 1924, blues singer Clara Smith headlined the bill at the Koppin, accompanied by pianist Stanley Miller. Others on the program were comedian Boots Hope, singers and dancers Brown and Struffin, and entertainers Jenkins and Jenkins.
References: Cahn, *Julius Cahn-Gus Hill Theatrical Guide. Chicago Defender*, E.S. Dudley, "The Koppin," February 9, 1924. *Film Daily Yearbook*, 1930–1932. Galbraith, *Motor City Marquees*. Harrison, *Black Pearls*. Hill, *Pages from the Harlem Renaissance*. Jackson, "List of Colored Theaters and Attractions," *Billboard*, August 6, 1921; "The Theater Owners' Booking Association," *Billboard*, December 16, 1922. Peterson, *The African American Theatre Directory. Theatrical World of Colored Artists*. Work, *Negro Yearbook*, 1921–1922.

846. KUM-C THEATER
1807 Concord Street
Picture house. 427 seats.
References: *Film Daily Yearbook*, 1949–1955.

847. LENOX THEATER
Picture house.
References: *Film Daily Yearbook*, 1949–1955.

848. LIBERTY THEATER
1020 Farmer Street
Nickeldeon and picture house. 500 seats. Owners in 1922: Arthur Benjamin and William R. Patterson (African Americans). According to Galbraith, the Liberty lasted from 1913 to 1926.
References: *Billboard*, "Two New Theaters," December 16, 1922. Galbraith, *Motor City Marquees*.

849. MAYFAIR THEATER
3424 Woodward Avenue
Picture house. 1,200 seats.
References: *Film Daily Yearbook*, 1949.

850. MONROE THEATER
204 Monroe Avenue
Picture house. 280 seats. According to the *Film Daily Yearbook*, the Monroe was closed in 1950 and 1951.
References: *Film Daily Yearbook*, 1949–1955.

851. NATIONAL THEATER
116 Monroe Street
Vaudeville and picture house. 972 seats. Architects: Albert Kahn and Ernest Wilby. Also called the Cinex.
References: *American Architect* "The National Theatre, Detroit, Michigan," 1912. *Film Daily Yearbook*, 1949–1955. Galbraith, *Motor City Marquees*.

852. NEW DAVISON THEATER
Picture house. 329 seats. Also called the Davison.
References: *Film Daily Yearbook*, 1949–1955.

OLIVE THEATER *see* Vaudette Theater

Paradise Theater, also known as Orchestra Hall, Detroit, Michigan (Library of Congress, Prints and Photographs Division)

ORCHESTRA HALL *see* Paradise Theater

853. PARADISE THEATER
3711 Woodward Avenue
Musical and picture house. Also known as Orchestra Hall. Among the bands at the Paradise in 1943 were the female orchestra International Sweethearts of Rhythm, the Erskine Hawkins orchestra, Cab Calloway and his Cotton Club Orchestra, Count Basie and his Orchestra, and Lucky Millinder and his orchestra. The motion picture *Stormy Weather*, starring Lena Horne, Cab Calloway, and Bill Robinson had a first run at the Paradise in October 1943. The Nat King Cole Trio, Benny Carter and his Orchestra, the Mills Brothers, and the Duke Ellington Orchestra played here in late 1944. Louis Armstrong and Orchestra, the Jean Parks Orchestra, and the singing group The Red Caps performed in 1945. Other famous orchestras such as those of Billy Eckstein and Earl "Fatha" Hines appeared at the Paradise in 1946. According to *Film Daily Yearbook*, the Paradise was closed in 1950 and 1951.

References: *Film Daily Yearbook*, 1949–1955. Holiday, *Lady Sings the Blues*. *Michigan Chronicle* February 20, March 13, 20, 27, April 24, 1943; September 16, 30, December 30, 1944; February 3, May 12, 1945; March 16, September 7, 1946.

854. PARK THEATER
2626 E. Davison Avenue
Picture house. 1921–1949. 676 seats. Architect: Harry T. Smith.

References: *Film Daily Yearbook,* 1949–1955. Galbraith, *Motor City Marquees.*

855. PIX THEATER
Picture house.
References: *Film Daily Yearbook,* 1949–1955.

856. PRISCILLA THEATER
2946 Mount Elliott Avenue
Picture house. 474 seats.
References: *Film Daily Yearbook,* 1949–1955.

857. ROGERS THEATER
3646 W. Warren Avenue
Picture house. 750 seats.
References: *Film Daily Yearbook,* 1949–1955.

858. ROSEBUD THEATER
429 Gratiot Avenue
Nickeldeon and picture house. 1915–1930.
References: *Film Daily Yearbook,* 1930–1932. Galbraith, *Motor City Marquees.*

859. ROXY THEATER
2745 Woodward Avenue
Picture house. 1,200 seats. Built in 1932. According to Galbraith, the Roxy closed in 1972.
References: *Film Daily Yearbook,* 1949. Galbraith, *Motor City Marquees.*

860. RUPERT THEATER
713 St. Aubin Street
Picture house. 285 seats.
References: *Film Daily Yearbook,* 1949–1955.

861. RUSSELL THEATER
5335 Russell Street
Vaudeville and picture house. 1917–1949. 1,046 seats. Architect: C. Howard Crane. The Russell had a balcony, full stage, orchestra pit and theater organ. The motion picture *Stormy Weather* played in the fall of 1944. It starred Lena Horne, Bill Robinson, and Cab Calloway.
References: *Film Daily Yearbook,* 1941–1955. Galbraith, *Motor City Marquees. Michigan Chronicle,* September 16, 1944. *Motion Picture Herald,* April 24, 1937; July 15, 1939. Sampson, *Blacks in Black and White.*

862. SAVOY THEATER
1515 Chene Street
Picture house. 365 seats.
References: *Film Daily Yearbook,* 1944–1948.

863. SHOOK THEATER
2814 Hastings Street
Vaudeville house. Manager in 1921: Ben Shook (African American).
References: Cahn, *Julius Cahn-Gus Hill Theatrical Guide.* Jackson, "List of Colored Theaters and Attractions," *Billboard,* August 6, 1921. Work, *Negro Yearbook, 1921–1922.*

864. STONE THEATER
2511 Woodward Avenue
Picture house. 250 seats.
References: *Film Daily Yearbook,* 1949–1955.

865. UNIQUE THEATER
Vaudeville house. Manager in 1914: E. H. Johnson. According to Sampson, the Unique opened in 1914. That year, Jake Hellens and the Claybrooks performed here.
References: *Indianapolis Freeman,* "On Colored Consolidated Time," January 31, 1914. Peterson, *The African American Theatre Directory.* Sampson, *Blacks in Blackface.*

866. VAUDETTE THEATER
674–76 Gratiot Avenue
Vaudeville house. 1910–1922. Member of the Dudley and TOBA circuits. Owner and Manager in 1921: E. B. Dudley (African American). According to Peterson, "This nickelodeon and pre-talkie theater had numerous name changes and owners. It was renamed the Dudley from

1916–1917, then returned to Vaudette in 1918, reverted to Dudley 1918–1921 and reincarnated as Vaudette from 1921–1922. In 1922 it was renamed the Olive." In 1921, the Vaudette featured Clarence Lee's Orchestra and John Mason's Dixie Beach Girls.

References: Cahn, *Julius Cahn-Gus Hill Theatrical Guide*. Galbraith, *Motor City Marquees*. Jackson, "List of Colored Theaters and Attractions," *Billboard*, August 6, 1921. Peterson, *The African American Theatre Directory*.

867. WARFIELD THEATER
5126 Hastings Street
Picture house. 376 seats. Built in 1914. Architects: Albert Kahn or William Brothers. According to Galbraith, "this theater closed in 1949, though it briefly reopened in the early fifties."

References: *Film Daily Yearbook*, 1933, 1944–1955. Galbraith, *Motor City Marquees*. *Motion Picture Herald*, April 24, 1937; July 15, 1939. Sampson, *Blacks in Black and White*.

868. WILLIS THEATER
4190 Hastings Street
Picture house. 399 seats.

References: *Film Daily Yearbook*, 1930–1933, 1940–1955. *Motion Picture Herald*, April 24, 1937; July 15, 1939. Sampson, *Blacks in Black and White*.

Flint

869. RICHARDS THEATER
929 Leith Street
Picture house. 468 seats.

References: *Film Daily Yearbook*, 1947–1955

870. TILDEN THEATER
Picture house.

References: *Film Daily Yearbook*, 1947–1955.

Grand Rapids

871. FRANKLIN THEATER
Picture house. 520 seats.

References: *Film Daily Yearbook*, 1949–1955.

Jackson

872. FAMILY THEATER
113 N. Otsego Street
Picture house. 500–822 seats.

References: *Film Daily Yearbook*, 1949–1955.

Port Huron

873. RITZ THEATER
215 Huron Street
Picture house. 350–400 seats.

References: *Film Daily Yearbook*, 1947–1955.

River Rouge

874. ELLIOTT THEATER
546 Elliott Street
Picture house. 400 seats.

References: *Film Daily Yearbook*, 1947–1955.

Saginaw

875. GEM THEATER
1221 N. 6th Street
Picture house. 350 seats.

References: *Film Daily Yearbook*, 1947–1955.

MINNESOTA

Minneapolis

876. LIBERTY THEATER
　Picture house.
　References: *Film Daily Yearbook*, 1930–1932.

Saint Paul

877. NEW BAY THEATER
　Picture house.
　References: *Film Daily Yearbook*, 1930–1932.

MISSISSIPPI

Belzoni

878. HARLEM THEATER
　Picture house. 300 seats.
　References: *Film Daily Yearbook*, 1940–1950. *Motion Picture Herald*, July 15, 1939.

Biloxi

879. HARLEM THEATER
　Picture house.
　References: *Film Daily Yearbook*, 1942–1955.

Brandon

880. TENT SHOW
　Picture house.
　References: *Film Daily Yearbook*, 1950–1955.

Brookhaven

881. PEOPLE'S THEATER
　Picture house.
　References: *Film Daily Yearbook*, 1930–1932.

882. REX THEATER
　Main Street
　Picture house. 300 seats.
　References: *Film Daily Yearbook*, 1940–1955. *Motion Picture Herald*, July 15, 1939.

Canton

883. HARLEM THEATER

106 Hickory Street
Picture house. 200 seats.
References: *Film Daily Yearbook*, 1942–1955. *Motion Picture Herald*, July 15, 1939.

Cauger

884. CAUGER THEATER
Picture house.
References: *Film Daily Yearbook*, 1946–1948.

Charleston

885. DIXIE THEATER
Picture house.
References: *Film Daily Yearbook*, 1949–1955.

Clarksdale

886. HARLEM THEATER
Picture house.
References: *Film Daily Yearbook*, 1949–1955.

887. QUEEN THEATER
Picture house.
References: Cahn, *Julius Cahn-Gus Hill Theatrical Guide*. Jackson, "List of Colored Theaters and Attractions," *Billboard*, August 6, 1921. Work, *Negro Yearbook, 1921–1922*.

888. ROXY THEATER
357 Isaquena Street
Picture house. 348 seats.
References: *Film Daily Yearbook*, 1949–1955.

889. SAVOY THEATER
Frisco Street
Picture house. 320–345 seats.
References: *Film Daily Yearbook*, 1940–1955. *Motion Picture Herald*, April 24, 1937; July 15, 1939. Sampson, *Blacks in Black and White*.

Cleveland

890. BOOKER T. THEATER
Christman Street
Picture house. 400 seats.
References: *Film Daily Yearbook*, 1950–1955.

Columbia

891. JOHN'S THEATER
Picture house. According to *Film Daily Yearbook*, this theater was closed from 1949 to 1951.
References: *Film Daily Yearbook*, 1949–1955.

Columbus

892. JOY THEATER
1820 Alton Street
Picture house. 400 seats.
References: *Film Daily Yearbook*, 1949–1955.

Crystal Springs

893. FOLLY THEATER
Picture house.
References: *Film Daily Yearbook*, 1946–1948.

Electric Mills

894. WASHINGTON THEATER
Picture house.
References: *Film Daily Yearbook*, 1940. *Motion Picture Herald*, July 15, 1939.

Greenville

895. HARLEM THEATER
920 Nelson Street
Picture house. 280–315 seats.
References: *Film Daily Yearbook*, 1940–1955. *Motion Picture Herald*, July 15, 1939.

896. LINCOLN THEATER
110 North Street
Picture house. 432–540 seats.
References: *Film Daily Yearbook*, 1940–1955. *Motion Picture Herald*, July 15, 1939.

897. REX THEATER
Picture house.
References: *Film Daily Yearbook*, 1949–1955.

898. ROYAL PALM THEATER
Vaudeville house. TOBA theater.
References: Peterson, *The African American Theatre Directory*.

Greenwood

899. BIJOU THEATER
Vaudeville house. Owner: B. F. Seals. According to Peterson, the Bijou was in business from the 1910s to the 1920s.
References: Peterson, *The African American Theatre Directory*.

900. DIXIE THEATER
Picture house. 500 seats.
References: *Film Daily Yearbook*, 1940–1955. *Motion Picture Herald*, April 24, 1937; July 15, 1939. Sampson, *Blacks in Black and White*.

901. WALTHALL THEATER
Walthall Street
Picture house. 699 seats.
References: *Film Daily Yearbook*, 1949–1955.

Grenada

902. GEM THEATER
Picture house.
References: *Film Daily Yearbook*, 1940. *Motion Picture Herald*, July 15, 1939.

903. UNION THEATER
Picture house. 349 seats.
References: *Film Daily Yearbook*, 1949–1955.

Gulfport

904. RITZ THEATER
314 20th Street
Picture house. 251 seats.
References: *Film Daily Yearbook*, 1943–1955.

905. ROYAL THEATER
Picture house.
References: *Film Daily Yearbook*, 1941, 1942.

906. STAR THEATER
Vaudeville house. The house was part of the combined TOBA and Managers and Performers vaudeville circuit.
References: *Hill, Pages from the Harlem Renaissance*. Jackson, "The Theater Owners' Booking Association," *Billboard*, December 16, 1922.

Hattiesburg

907. DIXIE THEATER
Picture house.
References: *Film Daily Yearbook*, 1940.

908. STAR THEATER
313 Mobile Street
Picture house. 340 seats.
References: *Film Daily Yearbook*, 1947–1955.

Hollandale

909. BOOTH THEATER
Picture house.
References: *Film Daily Yearbook*, 1949–1955.

Indianola

910. DIXIE THEATER
Picture house. 300 seats.
References: *Film Daily Yearbook*, 1940–1955. *Motion Picture Herald*, July 15, 1939.

Inverness

911. DIXIE THEATER
Picture house.
References: *Film Daily Yearbook*, 1946–1955.

912. LITTLE HARLEM THEATER
Picture house.
References: *Film Daily Yearbook*, 1949–1955.

Itta Bena

913. DIXIE THEATER
Picture house.
References: *Film Daily Yearbook*, 1949–1955.

Jackson

914. ALAMO THEATER
Picture house. 600 seats. Manager in 1921: R. A. Bell.
References: Cahn, *Julius Cahn-Gus Hill Theatrical Guide*. Jackson, "List of Colored Theaters and Attractions," *Billboard*, August 6, 1921. *Film Daily Yearbook*, 1930–1933, 1940–1955. *Motion Picture Herald*, April 24, 1937; July 15, 1939. Sampson, *Blacks in Black and White Work, Negro Yearbook, 1921–1922*.

915. AMERICAN THEATER
Vaudeville house. 2,000 seats. Owners: C. C. Simms and L.K. Atwood. According to Peterson, the American "was opened by African Americans after the white-owned Century Theater in Jackson refused to book Negro troupes and made Negro patrons use the fire escape to reach the gallery." Black Patti's Troubadours played the American during its opening performance in 1905.
References: Peterson, *The African American Theatre Directory*.

916. AMITE THEATER
123 W. Amite Street
Picture house. 550 seats.
References: *Film Daily Yearbook*, 1950–1955.

917. BOOKER T. THEATER
Picture house.
References: *Film Daily Yearbook*, 1940–1955. *Motion Picture Herald*, July 15, 1939.

918. GRAND THEATER
Picture house.
References: *Film Daily Yearbook*, 1949–1955.

919. LYRIC THEATER
Vaudeville house. A TOBA theater. In April 1921, the Willie Toosweet Company was the first TOBA act to appear at the Lyric.
References: *Chicago Defender*, April 23, 1921.

920. NEW THEATER
Picture house.
References: *Film Daily Yearbook*, 1945.

921. RITZ THEATER
Picture house. 405 seats.

126 Mississippi

References: *Film Daily Yearbook*, 1945–1955.

922. 35 DRIVE-IN
Picture house.
References: *Film Daily Yearbook*, 1953–1955.

Jonestown

923. GREEN THEATER
Picture house. 200 seats.
References: *Film Daily Yearbook*, 1950–1955.

Kosciusko

924. ROSE THEATER
Jackson Street
Picture house. 160 seats.
References: *Film Daily Yearbook*, 1946–1955.

Laurel

925. JOY THEATER
Picture house.
References: *Film Daily Yearbook*, 1955.

926. LINCOLN THEATER
Church at Maple Streets
Picture house. 500 seats.
References: *Film Daily Yearbook*, 1940–1955.

927. SAVOY THEATER
428 Front Street
Vaudeville house. Manager in 1921: Thomas Armstead.
References: Cahn, *Julius Cahn-Gus Hill Theatrical Guide*. Jackson, "List of Colored Theaters and Attractions," *Billboard*, August 6, 1921. Work, *Negro Yearbook*, 1921–1922.

Leland

928. HARLEM THEATER
Picture house. 176 seats.
References: *Film Daily Yearbook*, 1948–1955.

929. REX THEATER
Picture house. Also called the Pix Theater. In 1939, the Rex featured the films *Trigger Smith*, starring Jack Randall, *Thundering West*, and the Joe Louis and Bob Pastor fight for the heavyweight boxing title.
References: *Film Daily Yearbook*, 1940–1955. *Motion Picture Herald*, July 15, 1939.

Louisville

930. ALEWINE THEATER
Picture house.
References: *Film Daily Yearbook*, 1950–1955.

Macon

931. SAVOY THEATER
Picture house.
References: *Film Daily Yearbook*, 1949–1955.

McComb

932. LIBERTY THEATER
Picture house.
References: *Film Daily Yearbook*, 1949–1955.

933. LYRIC THEATER
Picture house. 150–250 seats.
References: *Film Daily Yearbook*, 1940–1955. *Motion Picture Herald*, April 24, 1937; July 15, 1939. Sampson, *Blacks in Black and White*.

Rex Theater, Leland, Mississippi, June 1937; photograph by Dorothea Lange (Library of Congress, Prints and Photographs Division)

Meridian

934. ALAMO THEATER
Picture house.
References: Cahn, *Julius Cahn and Gus Hill Theatrical Guide*. Jackson, "List of Colored Theaters and Attractions," *Billboard*, August 6, 1921. Work, *Negro Yearbook, 1921–1922*.

935. RITZ THEATER
2305 5th Avenue
Picture house. 400 seats.
References: *Film Daily Yearbook*, 1945–1955.

936. STAR THEATER
2408 5th Avenue
Vaudeville and picture house. 498–350 seats. A TOBA theater. The Star may have been the unnamed theater listed in the 1921 *Billboard* survey.
References: *Film Daily Yearbook*, 1940–1955. Hill, *Pages from the Harlem Renaissance*. Jackson, "List of Colored Theaters and Attractions," *Billboard*, August 6, 1921; "The Theater Owners' Booking Association," *Billboard*, December 16, 1922. *Motion Picture Herald*, April 24, 1937; July 15, 1939. Sampson, *Blacks in Black and White*.

Mount Bayou

937. CASINO THEATER
Negro City district
Picture house. Manager in 1921: Fred Miller (African American).

References: Cahn, *Julius Cahn-Gus Hill Theatrical Guide*. Jackson, "List of Colored Theaters and Attractions," *Billboard*, August 6, 1921. Work, *Negro Yearbook, 1921–1922*.

938. MELBA THEATER
   Picture house.
   References: *Film Daily Yearbook*, 1949–1955.

Natchez

939. ACE THEATER
   Picture house. 500 seats.
   References: *Film Daily Yearbook*, 1949–1955.

940. HAMILTON THEATER
   Picture house.
   References: *Film Daily Yearbook*, 1930–1932.

941. STAR THEATER
   Picture house.
   References: *Film Daily Yearbook*, 1946–1950.

Pascagoula

942. STAR THEATER
   Picture house.
   References: *Film Daily Yearbook*, 1947–1955.

Picayune

943. ROYAL THEATER
   Picture house.
   References: *Film Daily Yearbook*, 1949–1955.

Ruleville

944. ANNEX THEATER
   Picture house. Also called the Delta Annex
   References: *Film Daily Yearbook*, 1943–1948.

945. HARLEM THEATER
   Picture house.
   References: *Film Daily Yearbook*, 1949–1955.

Shelby

946. STAR THEATER
   Picture house.
   References: *Film Daily Yearbook*, 1947, 1948.

Shore

947. STAR THEATER
   Picture house.
   References: *Film Daily Yearbook*, 1949–1955.

Starkville

948. LUX THEATER
   Picture house. 400 seats.
   References: *Film Daily Yearbook*, 1949–1955.

Sunflower

949. DIXIE THEATER
   Picture house.
   References: *Film Daily Yearbook*, 1949–1955.

Tchula

950. TCHULA THEATER
   Main Street
   Picture house. 180–325 seats.
   References: *Film Daily Yearbook*, 1949–1955.

Tunica

951. SAVOY THEATER
Picture house. 290 seats.
References: *Film Daily Yearbook,* 1940–1955. *Motion Picture Herald,* July 15, 1939.

Tupelo

952. DIXIE BELLE THEATER
Picture house. 300 seats.
References: *Film Daily Yearbook,* 1949–1955.

Vicksburg

953. BOOKER T. WASHINGTON THEATER
Picture house. Owner: Charles H. Turpin. (African American). The Booker T. began as an airdome theater in 1923 and was later renovated into a traditional theater.
References: Peterson, *Profiles of African American Performers.*

954. COLORED THEATER
Picture house.
References: Cahn, *Julius Cahn-Gus Hill Theatrical Guide.* Jackson, "List of Colored Theaters and Attractions," *Billboard,* August 6, 1921.

955. PALACE THEATER
1615 Washington Street
Picture house. 589 seats.
References: *Film Daily Yearbook,* 1946–1955.

Winona

956. FRAN THEATER
Picture house. According to *Film Daily Yearbook*, the Fran was closed from 1949 to 1951.
References: *Film Daily Yearbook*, 1949–1955.

Yazoo City

957. NEW REN THEATER
Picture house.
References: *Film Daily Yearbook*, 1949–1955.

958. REX THEATER
Picture house.
References: *Film Daily Yearbook*, 1947, 1948.

MISSOURI

Charleston

959. RENFRO THEATER
Picture house.
References: *Film Daily Yearbook*, 1948.

Columbia

960. BOONE THEATER
15–17 N. 8th Street
Picture house. 430 seats.

Independence

961. GILLIS THEATER
Picture house.
References: *Film Daily Yearbook*, 1930–1932.

Kansas City

962. CARVER THEATER
Picture house.
References: *Film Daily Yearbook*, 1955.

963. CASTLE THEATER
1200 E. 12th Street
Picture house. 600–782 seats.
References: *Film Daily Yearbook*, 1940–1955. *Motion Picture Herald*, July 15, 1939.

964. COLUMBIA THEATER
716 Independence Avenue
Picture house. 425–611 seats. Manager in 1921: James M. Koupolis.
References: Cahn, *Julius Cahn-Gus Hill Theatrical Guide*. Jackson, "List of Colored Theaters and Attractions," *Billboard*, August 6, 1921. *Film Daily Yearbook*, 1930–1933. *Motion Picture Herald*, April 24, 1937. Sampson, *Blacks in Black and White*. Work, *Negro Yearbook, 1921–1922*.

965. EBLON THEATER
Picture house. Count Basie played organ here in the 1930s.
References: Basie, *Good Morning Blues*. *Film Daily Yearbook*, 1930–1932.

966. GEM THEATER
1615 E. 18th Street
Picture house. 600–1,200 seats. Also known as the Star. Manager in 1921: Gem Amusement Company.
References: Cahn, *Julius Cahn-Gus Hill Theatrical Guide*. *Film Daily Yearbook*, 1930–1933, 1940, 1955. Jackson, "Additions to Theater List," *Billboard*, December 31, 1921. *Motion Picture Herald*, July 15, 1939.

967. HOLLYWOOD THEATER
Picture house. 600 seats.
References: *Motion Picture Herald*, April 24, 1937. Sampson, *Blacks in Black and White*.

968. LINCOLN THEATER
1334 E. 10th Street
Vaudeville and picture house. 800–1,000 seats. A TOBA theater. Manager in 1921: L. Goldman. Manager in 1928: Rubin Finklestein. In 1923, Johnnie Lee Long and his Dixiana Girls and the Drake Walker Bombay Girls played here. In 1926 the William Benbow Company was at the Lincoln. Bessie Smith appeared here in the 1927 revue *Harlem Frolics*. In the 1930s Gonzelle White and the Big Jazz Jamboree and Count Basie played here.
References: Albertson, *Bessie*. *Baltimore Afro-American*, October 31, 1926. Basie, *Good Morning Blues*. Cahn, *Julius Cahn-Gus Hill Theatrical Guide*. *Film Daily Yearbook*, 1930–1933, 1940–1955. Jackson, "List of Colored Theaters and Attractions," *Billboard*, August 6, 1921. *Chicago Defender*, Jines, "Lincoln Theater," October 6, 1923; Jines, "Johnny's Show," December 8, 1923. *Motion Picture Herald*, April 24, 1937; July 15, 1939. Peterson, *The African American Theatre Directory*. Sampson, *Blacks in Black and White*; *Blacks in Blackface*. *Theatrical World of Colored Artists*. Work, *Negro Yearbook 1921–1922*.

969. LINCOLN SQUARE THEATER
Vaudeville and picture house. The Lincoln was part of the Managers and Performers circuit.

References: Peterson, *The African American Theatre Directory*.

970. LOVE'S THEATER
24th and Vine Streets
Picture house. Manager in 1921: G. W. K. Love.
References: Cahn, *Julius Cahn-Gus Hill Theatrical Guide*. Jackson, "List of Colored Theaters and Attractions," *Billboard*, August 6, 1921. Work, *Negro Yearbook*, 1921–1922.

971. LYRIC THEATER
622 Main Street
Picture and vaudeville house. 350 seats. Managers in 1921: Billy Kling, Charles T. Phelps (African Americans).
References: Cahn, *Julius Cahn-Gus Hill Theatrical Guide*. Jackson, "List of Colored Theaters and Attractions," *Billboard*, August 6, 1921. Work, *Negro Yearbook*, 1921–1922.

972. PANAMA THEATER
1711 E. 11th Street
Picture house. Manager: Lawrence E. Goldman.
References: Jackson, "List of Colored Theaters and Attractions," *Billboard*, August, 6, 1921. Cahn, *Julius Cahn-Gus Hill Theatrical Guide*. Work, *Negro Yearbook, 1921–1922*.

973. PRINCESS THEATER
3rd and Parallel Streets
Picture house.
References: Work, *Negro Yearbook*, 1921–1922.

974. TENT THEATER
Vaudeville house. Manager in 1921: Billy Kling (African American).
References: Cahn, *Julius Cahn-Gus Hill Theatrical Guide*. Jackson, "List of Colored Theaters and Attractions," *Billboard*, August 6, 1921. Work, *Negro Yearbook, 1921–1922*.

Kinloch Park

975. HARLEM THEATER
Picture house.
References: *Film Daily Yearbook*, 1949.

976. LINCOLN THEATER
Picture house.
References: *Film Daily Yearbook*, 1949–1955.

Saint Joseph

977. CHARWOOD THEATER
Picture house.
References: *Film Daily Yearbook*, 1933.

978. DUDLEY THEATER
211 N. 2nd Street
Picture house. Owner and manager in 1917: Charles T. Phelps (African American).
References: Cahn, *Julius Cahn-Gus Hill Theatrical Guide*. Jackson, "List of Colored Theaters and Attractions," *Billboard*, August 6, 1921. *Film Daily Yearbook*, 1930–1932. Work, *Negro Yearbook*, 1921–1922.

979. LOUIS THEATER
Picture house.
References: *Film Daily Yearbook*, 1940–1948.

980. PALACE THEATER
Picture house.
References: *Film Daily Yearbook*, 1930–1933.

Saint Louis

981. AMYTIS THEATER
4300 Saint Ferdinand Street

Picture house. 525 seats. The dance team of Norton and Margot played here the week of March 10, 1935.

References: *Film Daily Yearbook*, 1940–1955. Gottschild, *Waltzing in the Dark. Motion Picture Herald*, April 24, 1937; July 15, 1939. Sampson, *Blacks in Black and White*.

982. ASSEMBLY THEATER
Jefferson Street
Picture house. Manager in 1921: Richard Barrett (African American).

References: Cahn, *Julius Cahn-Gus Hill Theatrical Guide*. Jackson, "List of Colored Theaters and Attractions," *Billboard*, August 6, 1921. Work, *Negro Yearbook, 1921–1922*.

983. AUBERT THEATER
4949 Easton Avenue
Picture house. 1,064 seats.
References: *Film Daily Yearbook*, 1952–1955.

984. BOOKER T. WASHINGTON THEATER
2248 Market Street
Vaudeville and picture house. Also known as the Booker T. Washington Airdome. Manager in 1921–1928: Charles H. Turpin, a ragtime pianist (African American). According to Sampson it opened in 1913. The following year, Edwards and Hardee, Bessie Edington, and Glenn and Bogsdale appeared here. The Booker T. was part of the Colored Consolidated Time and TOBA vaudeville circuits. Charles's brother, ragtime composer Thomas M. J. Turpin, was at one time a manager of he Booker T. The theater was "where music was composed and arranged by Tom Turpin, Joe Jordan, and Artie Matthews." Josephine Baker performed here in vaudeville as a young girl. The vaudeville features during April 1921 included the McGarr-DeGaston Ragtime Steppers and Mary Mack's Merry Makers of Mirth. In 1923, Johnnie Lee Long and his Dixiana Girls, blues singer Sarah Martin, and Drake Walker's Bombay Girls came to the Booker T. In October 1926, the vaudeville show consisted of Clifford Ross, Long and Jackson, Dooley and Robinson, Bessie Smith, and the Sam Gray Company. Singer Bessie Smith returned to the Booker T. in 1927. Also in 1927, Johnny Lee Long's Dixiana Company performed. In the 1930s and 1940s, Count Basie and his orchestra entertained here.

References: Albertson, *Bessie. Baltimore Afro-American*, October 31, 1926. Baker, *Josephine*. Basie, *Good Morning Blues*. Bowser, *Writing Himself into History*. Cahn, *Julius Cahn-Gus Hill Theatrical Guide. Chicago Defender*, "At Turpins," June 9, 1923; Jines, Henry "Gang," "Booker Washington Theater," September 1, 1923; "Johnnie's Show," December 8, 1923; "Dixiana Company," October 8, 1927. *Film Daily Yearbook*, 1930–1932. Hill, *Pages from the Harlem Renaissance. Indianapolis Freeman*, "On Colored Consolidated Time," January 31, 1914. Jackson, "List of Colored Theaters and Attractions," *Billboard*, August 6, 1921; "The Theater Owners' Booking Association," *Billboard*, December 16, 1922. Jasen, *Rags and Ragtime*. Peterson, *Profiles of African American Performers*; *The African American Theatre Directory*. Sampson, *Blacks in Blackface*. Simms, *Simms' Blue Book. Theatrical World of Colored Artists*. Work, *Negro Yearbook 1921–1922*.

985. CARVER THEATER
1310 Franklin Avenue
Picture house. 652 seats.
References: *Film Daily Yearbook*, 1945–1955.

986. CASINO THEATER
Picture house.

References: *Film Daily Yearbook*, 1930–1932.

987. CIRCLE THEATER
4470 Easton Streeet
Picture house. 585 seats.
References: *Film Daily Yearbook*, 1952–1955.

988. COMET THEATER
4106 Finney Avenue
Picture house. 900 seats.
References: *Film Daily Yearbook*, 1930–1933, 1941–1955.

989. CRITERION THEATER
2644 Franklin Avenue
Picture house. 654 seats. Manager in 1921: Thomas James.
References: Cahn, *Julius Cahn-Gus Hill Theatrical Guide. Film Daily Yearbook*, 1930–1933, 1940–1955. Jackson, "List of Colored Theaters and Attractions," *Billboard*, August 6, 1921. *Motion Picture Herald*, July 15, 1939. Work, *Negro Yearbook, 1921–1922*.

990. DOUGLAS THEATER
4201 Finney Street
Picture house. 700 seats.
References: *Film Daily Yearbook*, 1930–1933, 1940–1955. *Motion Picture Herald*, April 24, 1937; July 15, 1939. Sampson, *Blacks in Black and White*.

991. GLOBE THEATER
Franklin Street
Picture house. 750 seats.
References: *Film Daily Yearbook*, 1940, 1941. *Motion Picture Herald*, July 15, 1939.

992. JEST-A-MERE THEATER
4201 Finney Avenue
Picture house. Manager in 1921: Tom Jones. Manager in 1923: C. Pitman.
References: Cahn, *Julius Cahn-Gus Hill Theatrical Guide*. Jackson, "List of Colored Theaters and Attractions," *Billboard*, August 6, 1921. Simms, *Simms' Blue Book*. Work, *Negro Yearbook, 1921–1922*.

993. JOY THEATER
Picture house.
References: *Film Daily Yearbook*, 1952–1955.

994. LACLEDE THEATER
3116 Laclede Avenue
Picture house. 550 seats.
References: *Film Daily Yearbook*, 1952–1955.

995. LINCOLN THEATER
3045 Olive Street
Picture house. 592 seats.
References: *Film Daily Yearbook*, 1952–1955.

996. MARQUETTE THEATER
1806 Franklin Avenue
Picture house. 650–975 seats.
References: *Film Daily Yearbook*, 1949–1955.

997. MOVIE THEATER
2620 Market Street
Picture house. 268 seats. Manager in 1921: Tom James.
References: Cahn, *Julius Cahn-Gus Hill Theatrical Guide. Film Daily Yearbook*, 1930–1933. Jackson, "List of Colored Theaters and Attractions," Billboard, August 6, 1921. Sampson, *Blacks in Black and White*. Work, *Negro Yearbook, 1921–1922*.

998. NEW MOVIE THEATER
Picture house.
References: *Film Daily Yearbook*, 1940–1955. *Motion Picture Herald*, April 24, 1937, July 15, 1939.

999. OLYMPIA THEATER
Picture house.
References: *Film Daily Yearbook*, 1930–1933.

1000. PALACE THEATER
Picture house.
References: *Film Daily Yearbook*, 1930–1933.

Missouri

1001. PENDLETON THEATER
4246 Finney Avenue
Picture house. Manager in 1922: Benjamin F. Austin.
References: Cahn, *Julius Cahn-Gus Hill Theatrical Guide*. Jackson, "List of Colored Theaters and Attractions," *Billboard*, August 6, 1921. Simms, *Simms' Blue Book*.

1002. QUEENS THEATER
4704 Muffit Street
Picture house. 650 seats.
References: *Film Daily Yearbook*, 1951, 1952.

1003. REGAL THEATER
3142 Easton Street
Picture house. 900 seats.
References: *Film Daily Yearbook*, 1943–1955. *Motion Picture Herald*, July 15, 1939.

1004. RETINA THEATER
Picture house.
References: *Film Daily Yearbook*, 1930–1932.

1005. ROOSEVELT THEATER
317 N. Leffingwell Street
Picture house. 500–646 seats.
References: *Film Daily Yearbook*, 1930–1933, 1940–1955. *Motion Picture Herald*, April 24, 1937; July 15, 1939. Sampson, *Blacks in Black and White*.

1006. STAR THEATER
16 S. Jefferson Street
Picture house. 521 seats. Manager in 1921: Chris Efigan.
References: *Film Daily Yearbook*, 1930–1933, 1940–1955. Jackson, "List of Colored Theaters and Attractions," *Billboard*, August 6, 1921. *Motion Picture Herald*, April 24, 1937; July 15, 1939. Sampson, *Blacks in Black and White*. Work, *Negro Yearbook, 1921–1922*.

1007. STRAND THEATER
2000 Market Street
Picture house. 279–500 seats.
References: *Film Daily Yearbook*, 1940–1955. *Motion Picture Herald*, April 24, 1937; July 15, 1939. Sampson, *Blacks in Black and White*.

1008. SUN THEATER
Picture house.
References: *Film Daily Yearbook*, 1952–1955.

1009. UPTOWN THEATER
4938 Delmar Avenue
Picture house. 839 seats.
References: *Film Daily Yearbook*, 1952–1955.

1010. VENDOME THEATER
Market Street
Vaudeville house. Owner: Mrs. Noah Warrington.
References: Peterson, *The African American Theatre Directory*.

1011. VENUS THEATER
Picture house.
References: *Film Daily Yearbook*, 1930–1933.

Springfield

1012. PALACE THEATER
325 Booneville Street
Picture house. Manager in 1921: H. L. Horne.
References: Cahn, *Julius Cahn-Gus Hill Theatrical Guide*. Jackson, "List of Colored Theaters and Attractions," *Billboard*, August 6, 1921. Work, *Negro Yearbook, 1921–1922*.

NEBRASKA

Omaha

1013. ALHAMBRA THEATER
Picture house.
References: *Film Daily Yearbook*, 1930–1932.

1014. CAMERPHONE THEATER
Douglass Street
Vaudeville house. Manager: M. M. Aronson.
References: Peterson, *The African American Theatre Directory*.

1015. DIAMOND THEATER
2410 Lake Street
Picture house. Manager in 1921: Mrs. Peterson. Manager in 1923: George Adams. The Oscar Micheaux film *The Homesteader* was shown here in 1919.
References: Bowser, *Writing Himself into History*. Cahn, *Julius Cahn-Gus Hill Theatrical Guide*. Jackson, "List of Colored Theaters and Attractions," *Billboard*, August 6, 1921. Work, *Negro Yearbook, 1921–1922*.

1016. FRANKLIN THEATER
1624 N. 24th Streeet
Picture house. Manager in 1921: Henry C. Melcher.
References: Work, *Negro Yearbook, 1921–1922*.

1017. LAKE THEATER
Picture house.
References: *Film Daily Yearbook*, 1930–1932.

1018. LOYAL THEATER
Picture house. Managers in 1921: Walker and Dorsey. The Loyal was advertised, according to Bowser, as "the first and only colored theatre in Nebraska." The Loyal charged 15 cents admission and emphasized this in advertisements: "See the same photo-plays downtown that you can see at the Loyal for 50% less." Early films featured here were Mack Sennett's comedy *Tillie's Punctured Romance*, starring Mabel Normand and Charlie Chaplin, and the 1919 Lincoln Motion Picture film, *A Man's Duty*. Oscar Micheaux's motion pictures *Within Our Gates* and *The Homesteader* played the Loyal in 1920.
References: Bowser, *Writing Himself into History*. Cahn, *Julius Cahn-Gus Hill Theatrical Guide*. Jackson, "List of Colored Theaters and Attractions," *Billboard*, August 6, 1921. Work, *Negro Yearbook, 1921–1922*.

1019. RITZ THEATER
2041 N. 24th Street
Picture house. 600 seats.
References: *Film Daily Yearbook*, 1933, 1940–1955. *Motion Picture Herald*, April 24, 1937; July 15, 1939. Sampson, *Blacks in Black and White*.

1020. ROYAL THEATER
Picture house. 398 seats. Managers in 1921: Walker and Dorsey.
References: Work, *Negro Yearbook, 1921–1922*.

NEVADA

Reno

1021. EMPIRE THEATER
Picture house.
References: *Film Daily Yearbook*, 1930.

1022. NEVADA THEATER
Picture house.
References: *Film Daily Yearbook*, 1930.

1023. RENO THEATER
Picture house.
References: *Film Daily Yearbook*, 1930.

NEW JERSEY

Asbury Park

1024. ROYAL THEATER
1206 Springwood Avenue
Vaudeville house. Manager in 1921: Mr. Fletcher.
References: Cahn, *Julius Cahn-Gus Hill Theatrical Guide*. Jackson, "List of Colored Theaters and Attractions," *Billboard*, August 6, 1921.

1025. STATE THEATER
Picture house. According to *Film Daily Yearbook*, the State was closed from 1949 to 1952.
References: *Film Daily Yearbook*, 1947–1955.

Atlantic City

1026. ALAN THEATER
1615 Arctic Avenue
Picture house. 600 seats.
References: *Film Daily Yearbook*, 1940–1955. *Motion Picture Herald*, July 15, 1939.

1027. APOLLO THEATER
Vaudeville house. 1,700 seats. The Irvin C. Miller show *Broadway Rastus* performed here in 1915.
References: Sampson, *Blacks in Blackface*.

1028. EARLE THEATER
Picture house. 1,985 seats.
References: *Film Daily Yearbook*, 1940. *Motion Picture Herald*, July 15, 1939.

Camden

1029. LYRIC THEATER
Picture house. 2,145 seats.
References: *Film Daily Yearbook*, 1949–1955.

1030. ROXY THEATER
Picture house.
References: *Film Daily Yearbook*, 1949–1955.

Morristown

1031. PALACE THEATER
Picture house.
References: *Film Daily Yearbook*, 1949–1955.

Newark

1032. ADAMS THEATER
Branford Place
Picture house. 1,900 seats. Jazz musicians Howard McGhee and Earl "Fatha" Hines were some of the entertainers booked here.
References: Dance, *The World of Earl Hines*. *Film Daily Yearbook*, 1949–1955. Russell, *Bird Lives!*

1033. COURT THEATER
16 Breintall Street
Picture house. 500–790 seats.
References: *Film Daily Yearbook*, 1940–1955. *Motion Picture Herald*, April 24, 1937; July 15, 1939. Sampson, *Blacks in Black and White*.

1034. ESSEX THEATER
Springfield Avenue
Picture house. 1,000 seats.
References: *Film Daily Yearbook*, 1940–1955. *Motion Picture Herald*, April 24, 1937; July 15, 1939. Sampson, *Blacks in Black and White*.

1035. GARDEN THEATER
Picture house.
References: *Film Daily Yearbook*, 1940–1955. *Motion Picture Herald*, April 24, 1937; July 15, 1939. Sampson, *Blacks in Black and White*.

1036. LUXOR THEATER
Market Street
Picture house. 570 seats.
References: *Film Daily Yearbook*, 1940–1955. *Motion Picture Herald*, July 15, 1939.

1037. LYRIC THEATER
211 Market Street
Picture house. 900–1200 seats. Architects: George W. Backoff and T. Cecil Hughes.
References: *Architects' and Builders Magazine*, "The Lyric Theatre, Newark, N.J.," 41 (December 1908). *Film Daily Yearbook*, 1940–1955. *Motion Picture Herald*, April 24, 1937; July 15, 1939. Sampson, *Blacks in Black and White*.

1038. METROPOLITAN THEATER
115 Montgomery Street
Vaudeville and picture house. 700 seats. Manager in 1921: Mr. Ross.
References: Cahn, *Julius Cahn-Gus Hill Theatrical Guide*. Jackson, "List of Colored Theaters and Attractions," *Billboard*, August 6, 1921. Work, *Negro Yearbook, 1921–1922*.

1039. MONTICELLO THEATER
Picture house.
References: *Film Daily Yearbook*, 1940–1948. *Motion Picture Herald*, July 15, 1939.

1040. NATIONAL THEATER
182 Belmont Avenue
Picture house. 500 seats.
References: *Film Daily Yearbook*, 1940–1955. *Motion Picture Herald*, April 24, 1937; July 15, 1939. Sampson, *Blacks in Black and White*.

1041. ORPHEUM THEATER
Washington Street
Vaudeville and picture house. 1,800 seats. Manager in 1925: Leigh Whipper (African American). The Orpheum opened in 1925 with the husband and

wife singing and dancing team Butterbeans and Susie. The Orpheum had a seven-piece orchestra and five local girls as ushers. The Orpheum's stage crew was recruited from the Lafayette Theater in New York. Bessie Smith also appeared here in 1925. In January 1926, Leonard Harper's Revue, featuring Giles and Gulfport, performed at the Orpheum.

References: Albertson, *Bessie. Chicago Defender*, "New Theater," July 18, 1925; "New Orpheum Theater Opens In Newark, N.J.," September 5, 1925. *Film Daily Yearbook*, 1931–1933. *New York Age*, Slater, Bob, "Theatrical Jottings," January 30, 1926.

1042. PARAMOUNT THEATER
195 Market Street
Picture house. 1,200–2,000 seats. In the 1930s, Count Basie and his orchestra appeared here.
References: Basie, *Good Morning Blues. Film Daily Yearbook*, 1949–1955.

1043. SAVOY THEATER
101 Springfield Avenue
Picture house. 1,472 seats.
References: *Film Daily Yearbook*, 1949–1955.

1044. STATION THEATER
Market Street
Picture house. 2,036 seats.
References: *Film Daily Yearbook*, 1940–1948. *Motion Picture Herald*, April 24, 1937; July 15, 1939. Sampson, *Blacks in Black and White*.

Trenton

1045. GARDEN THEATER
150 N. Broad Street
Picture house. 470 seats.
References: *Film Daily Yearbook*, 1949.

1046. NEW LINCOLN THEATER
Picture house.
References: *Film Daily Yearbook*, 1940. *Motion Picture Herald*, July 15, 1939.

NEW MEXICO

Carlsbad

1047. CAVERN THEATER
Picture house. 400 seats.
References: *Film Daily Yearbook*, 1954.

Hobbs

1048. SCOUT THEATER
Picture house. 744 seats.
References: *Film Daily Yearbook*, 1954.

NEW YORK

Buffalo

1049. BROADWAY THEATER
Picture house.
References: *Film Daily Yearbook*, 1930–1933.

1050. LYCEUM THEATER
Picture house.
References: *Film Daily Yearbook*, 1930–1933.

1051. MCCLAIN'S THEATER
Vaudeville house. The opening night show on December 25, 1926, featured S. H. Dudley's *Darktown Frolics* and Gibson's Famous Midgets.
References: *Chicago Defender*, "Buffalo's New Theater," December 25, 1926. *Film Daily Yearbook*, 1930.

1052. MCEVOY THEATER
Vaudeville house. Manager in 1921: Robert B. Joplin (African American).
References: Cahn, *Julius Cahn-Gus Hill Theatrical Guide*. Jackson, "Additions to Theater List," *Billboard*, December 31, 1921.

1053. PLAZA THEATER
William Street
Picture house. 1,000 seats.
References: *Film Daily Yearbook*, 1930–1933, 1940–1955. *Motion Picture Herald*, July 15, 1939.

1054. SAVOY THEATER
Picture house.
References: *Film Daily Yearbook*, 1930–1933.

1055. STAR THEATER
Picture house.
References: *Film Daily Yearbook*, 1933.

Corona

1056. PALACE THEATER
Picture house.
References: *Film Daily Yearbook*, 1949–1955.

Mount Vernon

1057. BILTMORE THEATER
Picture house. 620 seats.
References: *Film Daily Yearbook*, 1950–1955.

New Rochelle

1058. ASTOR THEATER
Picture house.
References: *Film Daily Yearbook*, 1950–1953.

New York City: Bronx

1059. BOSTON ROAD THEATER
1472 Boston Road
Picture house. 1,500 seats.
References: *Film Daily Yearbook*, 1949–1955.

1060. BRONX THEATER
440 E. 149th Street
Picture house. 1,500 seats.
References: *Film Daily Yearbook*, 1940–1955. *Motion Picture Herald*, July 15, 1939.

1061. FENWAY THEATER
1576 Washington Avenue
Picture house. 1,400 seats.
References: *Film Daily Yearbook*, 1949–1955.

1062. TOWER THEATER
1175 Boston Road
Picture house. 1,693 seats.
References: *Film Daily Yearbook*, 1949–1955.

1063. WILLIS THEATER
138 Street and Willis Avenue
Picture house. 2,150 seats.
References: *Film Daily Yearbook*, 1940–1955.

New York City: Brooklyn

1064. APOLLO THEATER
1531 Fulton Street
Picture house. 1,500 seats.
References: *Film Daily Yearbook*, 1940–1955. *Motion Picture Herald*, April 24, 1937; July 15, 1939. Sampson, *Blacks in Black and White*.

1065. ART THEATER
419 7th Avenue
Picture house. 450 seats.
References: *Film Daily Yearbook*, 1940–1948. *Motion Picture Herald*, April 24, 1937; July 15, 1939. Sampson, *Blacks in Black and White*.

1066. BANCO THEATER
Picture house.
References: *Film Daily Yearbook*, 1950–1955.

1067. BREVOORT THEATER
1274 Bedford Avenue
Picture house. 2,000 seats. Also known as Loew's Brevoort.
References: *Film Daily Yearbook*, 1940–1955. *Motion Picture Herald*, April 24, 1937; July 15, 1939. Sampson, *Blacks in Black and White*.

1068. CAPITOL THEATER
286 Saratoga Avenue
Picture house. 1,800 seats.
References: *Film Daily Yearbook*, 1941–1955. *Motion Picture Herald*, July 15, 1939.

1069. COMET THEATER
856 Gates Avenue
Picture house. 500 seats.
References: *Film Daily Yearbook*, 1949–1955.

1070. HOWARD THEATER
Picture house.
References: *Film Daily Yearbook*, 1940–1948. *Motion Picture Herald*, July 15, 1939.

1071. KISMET THEATER
785 De Kalb Avenue
Picture house. 842 seats.
References: *Film Daily Yearbook*, 1940–1955. *Motion Picture Herald*, July 15, 1939.

1072. LINDY THEATER
118 Graham Avenue
Picture house. 600 seats.
References: *Film Daily Yearbook*, 1949–1955.

1073. NEW UNITED THEATER
207 Myrtle Avenue
Picture house.
References: *Film Daily Yearbook*, 1940–1948. *Motion Picture Herald*, July 15, 1939.

1074. PEERLESS THEATER
433 Myrtle Avenue
Picture house. 560 seats.
References: *Film Daily Yearbook*, 1940–1955. *Motion Picture Herald*, July 15, 1939.

1075. PUTNAM THEATER
966–972 Fulton Street
Brooklyn, New York
Vaudeville house. Also known as the Supreme. Managers in 1924: Jones Gresham and David Lark. The Putnam was part of the Quality Amusement Company owned by Edward C. Brown. Gresham and Lark renovated the theater and reopened it as the Supreme Theater on March 5, 1924.

References: *Film Daily Yearbook*, 1930, 1931, 1932. "Putnam Theatre, Brooklyn, Re-Opened as the Supreme Theatre Under New Lessees," *New York Age*, March 8, 1924. Peterson, *The African American Theatre Directory*.

1076. REGENT THEATER
1217 Fulton Street
Brooklyn, New York
Picture house. 500 seats.
References: *Film Daily Yearbook*, 1940–1955. *Motion Picture Herald*, July 15, 1939.

1077. REO THEATER
375 Stone Avenue
Picture house. 596 seats.
References: *Film Daily Yearbook*, 1950–1955.

1078. ROGERS THEATER
333 Rogers Avenue
Picture house. 500 seats.
References: *Film Daily Yearbook*, 1949–1955.

1079. STATE THEATER
492 De Kalb Avenue
Picture house. 1,004 seats.
References: *Film Daily Yearbook*, 1940–1955. *Motion Picture Herald*, July 15, 1939.

1080. SUBWAY THEATER
158 Myrtle Avenue
Picture house. 600 seats.
References: *Film Daily Yearbook*, 1949–1955. *Motion Picture Herald*, July 15, 1939.

1081. SUMNER THEATER
265 Sumner Avenue
Picture house. 100 seats.
References: *Film Daily Yearbook*, 1949–1955. *Motion Picture Herald*, July 15, 1939.

1082. TIFFANY THEATER
357 Chester Street
Picture house. 680 seats.
References: *Film Daily Yearbook*, 1949–1955.

1083. TOMPKINS THEATER
534 Gates Avenue
Picture house. 600 seats.
References: *Film Daily Yearbook*, 1940–1955. *Motion Picture Herald*, July 15, 1939.

New York City: Manhattan

1084. ALHAMBRA THEATER
2110 7th Avenue
Vaudeville and picture house. 1,435 seats. Architect: Percy G. Williams. The Alhambra was active from about 1905 to 1964. According to Peterson, "it was one of the houses on the Keith Vaudeville Circuit, which booked some black acts, but had a regular policy of discrimination. This policy began to change, however, after the theater treasurer was arrested in 1920 for refusing to sell orchestra seats to two black customers; and with the change of management and the growth of the black Harlem population, the Alhambra...began to actively compete for black clientele." Famous acts and shows playing the Alhambra included Bert Williams, Aida Overton Walker, Florence Mills, Dewey "Pigmeat" Marham, Tim Moore, Count Basie and his orchestra, Bessie Smith's movie *St. Louis Blues*, Clara Smith, the Whitman Sisters, comedians Miller and Lyles, dancer Bill Robinson, blues singer Edith Wilson, Edgar Hayes and His Symphonic Harmonists and the musicals *Blackbirds of 1926*, "*Blackbirds of 1929*," and *Hot Chocolates*.
References: Albertson, *Bessie*. Basie, *Good Morning Blues*. Brown, *A History of the New York Stage*. Driggs, *The Sound of Harlem. Film Daily Yearbook,* 1930–1932, 1940–1955. George-Graves, *The Royalty*

of *Negro Vaudeville*. Harrison, *Black Pearls*. Kellner, *The Harlem Renaissance*. *Motion Picture Herald,* April 24, 1937; July 15, 1939. *Motion Picture Herald,* January 24, 1942. *New York Age,* August 6, 1918. Pfeffer, *My Harlem Reverie*. Sampson, *Blacks in Black and White*. Peterson *American Theatre Directory; Profiles of African American Stage Performers*. Sampson, *Blacks in Black and White*. Smith, *Bert Williams*.

1085. ANCO THEATER
 354 W. 42nd Street
 New York, New York
 Picture house. 572 seats.
 References: *Film Daily Yearbook*, 1950–1952.

1086. APOLLO THEATER
 256 125th Street
 Vaudeville, picture, musical house. 1,500 seats. Owners: Frank Schiffman and Leo Brecher. Also known as Hurtig and Seamon's Music Hall and later Hurtig and Seamon's Burlesque. Among the famous black performers at Hurtig and Seamons' as the vaudeville act of Williams and Walker. In March 1924, Liza and her Shuffling Band played here. According to Driggs, "The theater was renamed the Apollo when the Frank Schiffman family (then operating the Lafayette) bought it in 1934. Stage shows then began to build around the name jazz bands to compete with [those of] the Harlem Opera House." The Apollo is probably the best known historical African American theater, and it was part of the chitlin' circuit, a string of black theaters in the Northeast where soul acts appeared during the 1960s. The Apollo was famous for its amateur night. Many winners such as Sarah Vaughn and Ella Fitzgerald went on to international fame. The TOBA revue *Raisin' Cain* played here in 1929. Bessie Smith performed here in January 1934 with dancers Meer and Meer, comedians Dusty Fletcher and Galle DeGaston, fan dancer Noma, and blues singer Ida Cox. Fats Waller was a staple here in the 1930s. In the 1940s jazz musicians like the Count Basie Orchestra, Jay McShann Orchestra, the Earl Hines Orchestra, Billie Holiday, Charlie Parker, and Sarah Vaughan entertained at the Apollo. During the week of June 20, 1941, the dance team of Norton and Margot was on the program. In the 1960s, Chicago-based soul acts such as the Dells, the Marvelows, the Five DuTones, and Simtec and Wylie appeared here, along with artists from Motown Records, Atlantic Records, and Stax Records. Schiffman and Fox describe the experiences of Apollo performances in two books about the theater. According to Peterson, "in 1981, the Apollo was purchased by Percy Sutton and the Inner City Broadcasting Corp., which has tried to preserve it as one of the landmark Harlem theatres."

References: Albertson. *Bessie*. Anderson, *This Was Harlem*. Basie, *Good Morning Blues*. Dance, *The World of Earl Hines*. Driggs, *The Sound of Harlem*. *Film Daily Yearbook, 1940–1955*. Fox, *Showtime at the Apollo*. Green, *Show Biz*. George-Graves, *The Royalty of Negro Vaudeville*. Gottschild, *Waltzing in the Dark*. Harrison, *Black Pearls*. Holiday, *Lady Sings the Blues*. Hughes, *Black Magic*. Kellner, *The Harlem Renaissance*. *Motion Picture Herald*, April 24, 1937; July 15, 1939; January 24, 1942. *New York Age,* March 22, 1924. Peterson, *The African American Theatre Directory; Profiles of African American Stage Performers*. Pruter, *Chicago Soul*. Russell, *Bird Lives!* Sampson, *Blacks in Black and White*. Schiffman, *Uptown: the Story of Harlem's Apollo Theatre*. Dodson, *The Black New Yorkers*. Smith, *Bert Williams*. Waller, *Fats Waller*.

1087. BLUE BIRD THEATER

Apollo Theater, New York, New York (SoulofAmerica.com)

1763 Amsterdam Avenue
Picture house. 600 seats.
References: *Film Daily Yearbook*, 1940–1948. *Motion Picture Herald*, April 24, 1937; July 15, 1939; January 24, 1942. Sampson, *Blacks in Black and White*.

1088. BURLAND THEATER
Picture house.
References: *Film Daily Yearbook*, 1949–1952.

1089. CHATHAM THEATER
5 Chatham Square
Picture house. Also called the Governor. 591 seats.
References: *Film Daily Yearbook*, 1941–1955. *Motion Picture Herald*, July 15, 1939; January 24, 1942.

1090. COLUMBIA THEATER
1324 Amsterdam Avenue
Picture house. 590 seats.
References: *Film Daily Yearbook*, 1940–1955. *Motion Picture Herald*, April 24, 1937; July 15, 1939; January 24, 1942. Sampson, *Blacks in Black and White*.

1091. CRESCENT THEATER
42 W. 135th Street
Vaudeville, musical and picture house. Owners in 1909: Martinson and Nibur. Manager in 1921: Eugene Elmore. Comedian Eddie Hunter played the Crescent in 1900. The H. Lawrence Freeman opera *The Tryst* was produced here in 1909. The Muse and Pugh Stock Company was in residence at the Crescent, presenting plays from 1914 to 1915. Tom Fletcher, the veteran vaudevillian, recalls that Wilbur Sweatman and his orchestra performed at the Crescent.
References: Bowser, *Writing Himself into History*. Cahn, *Julius Cahn-Gus Hill Theatrical Guide*. *Film Daily Yearbook*,

1931, 1932. Fletcher, *100 Years of the Negro in Show Business*. Jackson, "List of Colored Theaters and Attractions," *Billboard*, August 6, 1921. Peterson, *The African American Theatre Directory*; *Profiles of African American Stage Performers*. Pfeffer, *My Harlem Reverie*. Work, *Negro Yearbook, 1921–1922*.

1092. DELUXE THEATER
Picture house.
References: *Film Daily Yearbook*, 1940–1948. *Motion Picture Herald*, April 24, 1937; July 15, 1939; January 24, 1942. Sampson, *Blacks in Black and White*.

1093. DOUGLAS THEATER
640 Lenox Avenue
Picture house. Also known as the New Douglas. Manager in 1921: Mr. Sovini. In June 1921, Anita Bush appeared in the motion picture *Crimson Skull*, and Constance Talmadge starred in *A Woman's Place*. In 1926 the films *The Auction Block*, starring Eleanor Boardman, and *The Song and Dance Man*, co-starring Tom Moore and Bessie Love, were shown. Count Basie performed here in the 1930s.
References: Basie, *Good Morning Blues*. Bowser, *Writing Himself into History*. Cahn, *Julius Cahn-Gus Hill Theatrical Guide*. *Film Daily Yearbook*, 1930–1932. Hill, *Pages from the Harlem Renaissance*. Jackson, "List of Colored Theaters and Attractions," *Billboard*, August 6, 1921. Kellner, *The Harlem Renaissance*. *New York Age*, April 3, 1926. Pfeffer, *My Harlem Reverie*. Work, *Negro Yearbook, 1921–1922*.

1094. EAGLE THEATER
1852 3rd Avenue
Picture house. 1200 seats.
References: *Film Daily Yearbook*, 1950–1955.

1095. FRANKLIN THEATER
440 Lenox Avenue
Picture house. 650 seats. Owner in 1921: Peter Eckert.
References: Cahn, *Julius Cahn-Gus Hill Theatrical Guide*. *Film Daily Yearbook*, 1930–1933, 1940–1955. Jackson, "List of Colored Theaters and Attractions," *Billboard*, August 6, 1921. *Motion Picture Herald*, April 24, 1937; July 15, 1939; January 24, 1942. Peterson, *The African American Theatre Directory*. Sampson, *Blacks in Black and White*. Work, *Negro Yearbook, 1921–1922*.

1096. GEM THEATER
523 8th Avenue
Picture house. According to Peterson, the Gem "was primarily a film house that catered to slum audiences and was noted for its unsanitary conditions." Smoking and spitting tobacco juice was common. Author Wallace Thurman recalled that babies would cry in time to music from the piano accompanying silent films and that patrons talked during the films, using a lot of vulgarity.
References: Kellner, *The Harlem Renaissance*. Peterson, *The African American Theatre Directory*. Thurman, *Negro Life in New York's Harlem*.

1097. HAMILTON THEATER
3560 Broadway
Picture house. 890 seats. Also known as Keith's Hamilton.
References: *Film Daily Yearbook*, 1949–1955.

1098. HARLEM OPERA HOUSE
205–211 W. 125th Street
Vaudeville and picture house. 1,540–1,700 seats. Built circa 1889. Demolished in 1959. Owner in 1890: Oscar Hammerstein I. Owners in 1922: Frank Schiffman and Leo Brecher. The Harlem Opera House was the first legitimate theater to be built north of Central Park in New York City. Under Hammerstein's

Harlem Opera House, 125th Street, New York (undated; Museum of the City of New York, Gift of Mrs. Eugenie Thierry, 43.316.123)

management, the house featured opera. When Schiffman bought the building in 1922, he changed the entertainment from opera to vaudeville. According to Driggs, "by 1930, the Harlem Opera House had a different name swing band on stage each week and inaugurated the famous Wednesday night amateur hour contest." Some contest winners such as Ella Fitzgerald went on to become famous. In 1934 Bessie Smith appeared here with twelve dancing mermaids in the revue *Christmas Revels*. She returned the following year with a cast of 50 and Don Redman and his band. Ralph Cooper served as master of ceremonies for a while here. "Around 1935," says Driggs, " the Harlem Opera House began showing films." The building was demolished in December 1959 to make way for a 33-lane bowling alley.

References: Albertson, *Bessie*. Brown, *A History of the New York Stage*. Colin, *Ella*. Dance, *The World of Earl Hines*. Driggs, *The Sound of Harlem*. *Film Daily Yearbook*, 1940–1955. Gottschild, *Waltzing in the Dark*. *Motion Picture Herald*, April 24, 1937; July 15, 1939; December 24, 1942. Peterson, *Profiles of African American Stage Performers*. Pfeffer, *My Harlem Reverie*. Sampson, *Blacks in Black and White*.

1099. JEFFERSON THEATER
214 E. 14th Street
Picture house. 1,885 seats.
References: *Film Daily Yearbook*, 1950–1952.

1100. JEWEL THEATER
11 W. 116th Street
Picture house. 700–800 seats.
References: *Film Daily Yearbook*, 1940–1949. *Motion Picture Herald*, July 15, 1939; January 24, 1942.

1101. LAFAYETTE THEATER
2227 7th Avenue

Vaudeville, picture, and drama house. 1,245–2,000 seats. Managers in 1921: Lester Walton, the Murray Brothers (African Americans). During its early years, the Lafayette was apparently a Jim Crow house or one with segregated seating for blacks. However, in the 1920s, it became the home of the Lafayette dramatic troupe. Bill "Bojangles" Robinson played here in 1915. According to Driggs, "when the Coleman Brothers took over the house, they began to concentrate on musical shows." Among the earliest black acts appearing here was the Duke Ellington band in 1922. During this period, one of the Lafayette's prominent organ players was jazz musician Fats Waller. In 1928, the revue *Mississippi Days*, starring Bessie Smith, came to the Lafayette. She also played here in the 1929 shows *Pansy* and *Late Hour Dancers*. The big band known as the Missourians played here in 1930 with Cab Calloway. In 1931, the Whitman Sisters appeared on a show including the Bennie Moten orchestra, Count Basie, and the motion picture *The Yellow Ticket*, starring Lionel Barrymore and Elissa Landi. During this period, one of the Lafayette's prominent organ players was jazz musician Fats Waller. In 1933 headliners included Bessie Smith, singers Jules Bledsoe and Mandy Lou, band leader, Willy Bryant, and comedian Dusty Fletcher. Other noted Lafayette performers in the 1930s included opera singer Minto Cato, comedian Garbage Jones, singer Alice Harris, The Four Bobs, the Alabama Tin Band, Ethel Waters, Ted Blackmon's Chorus, and the dance team of Wells, Mordecai, and Taylor. As part of the Federal Theater Program of the Works Progress Administration, black productions such as *Macbeth* and *The Hot Mikado* were performed here to capacity audiences.

References: Albertson, *Bessie*. Anderson, *This Was Harlem*. Basie, *Good Morning Blues*. Jackson, "List of Colored Theaters and Attractions," *Billboard*, August 6, 1921. *The Inter-State Tattler*, Butler, "The Whitman Sisters and Moten's Band at Lafayette," December 17, 1931. *Julius Cahn-Gus Hill Theatrical Guide*. Calloway, *Of Minnie the Moocher and Me*. Collier, *Duke Ellington*. Driggs, *The Sound of Harlem*. *Film Daily Yearbook*, 1930–1933, 1940–1949. Gottschild, *Waltzing in the Dark*. Harrison, *Black Pearls*. Hill, *Pages from the Harlem Renaissance*. *Motion Picture Herald*, April 24, 1937; July 15, 1939; January 24, 1942. Peterson, *Profiles of African American Stage Performers*; *African American Theatre Directory, 1816–1960*. Pfeffer, *My Harlem Reverie*. Simms, *Simms' Blue Book*. Mitchell, *Black Drama*. Sampson, *Blacks in Black and White*; *Blacks in Blackface*. Dodson, *The Black New Yorkers*. Thompson, *The Lafayette Players*. Thurman, *Negro Life in New York's Harlem*. Waller, *Fats Waller*. Work, *Negro Yearbook, 1921–22*. Waters, *His Eye Is On the Sparrow*. Young, *Lester Walton*.

1102. LIDO THEATER
Picture house.

References: *Film Daily Yearbook*, 1949–1955.

1103. LINCOLN THEATER
508 W. 135th Street

Vaudeville and picture house. 830–1250 seats. Built in 1909. Manager in 1921: Mrs. Marie Downes (African American). The Lincoln opened as a nickelodeon in a storefront building. Marie Downes, however, replaced this structure in 1915 with a better theater that could seat more than 1,000 persons. The Lincoln was famous for its organ, purchased in 1915 for allegedly $10,000. As a young man, Fats Waller began in show business

Exterior view of the Lafayette Theater during a performance of the WPA production of *Macbeth*, 1930s. (Photographs and Prints Division, Schomberg Center for Research in Black Culture, The New York Public Library, Astor, Lenox and Tilden Foundations)

playing the Lincoln's organ. According to Tom Fletcher it was Mamie Mullins who taught Waller to how play organ and Waller in turn taught Count Basie how to play. It is said that Marie Downes originally booked only white acts but later switched to exclusively black acts such as the Whitman Sisters. Downes's taste for Southern acts made her theater the Northern showcase of the T.O.B.A. Composer Perry Bradford's revue *Made in Harlem* played here in the 1920s. In 1924, the William Fox motion picture *Temple of Venus*, starring David Butler, Phyllis Haver, and Mary Philbin, was shown in February. Other "photo play attractions" during that same period included *Rosita*, starring Mary Pickford, and *West of the Water Tower*, featuring Glen Hunter. In 1926, Lucille Hagamin and Her Sunny Land Cotton Pickers came to the Lincoln. The classic blues singer Bessie Smith was a regular attraction, appearing here in 1927 in *Bessie Smith and Her Yellow Girl Revue*, and in 1929 in the revues *Harlem Frolics* and *Late Hour Dancers*. Blues queen Victoria Spivey played here in 1927. The Lincoln was a black motion picture house in the 1940s and 1950s, but was converted into a church in the 1960s.

References: Albertson, *Bessie*. Anderson, *This Was Harlem*. Basie, *Good Morning Blues*. Bowser, *Writing Himself into History*. Cahn, *Julius Cahn-Gus Hill Theatrical Guide*. Collier, *Duke Ellington*. Driggs, *The Sound of Harlem. Film Daily Yearbook*, 1930–1933, 1940–1955. Fletcher, *100 Years of the Negro in Show*

Business. George-Graves, *The Royalty of Negro Vaudeville.* Harrison, *Black Pearls.* Jackson, "Colored Theaters and Attractions," *Billboard,* August 6, 1921. Kellner, *The Harlem Renaissance.* Mitchell, *Black Drama. Motion Picture Herald,* April 24, 1937; July 15, 1939; January 24, 1942. Newman, "The Lincoln Theatre," *American Visions,* August 1991. *New York Age,* "At the Lincoln," February 9, 1924. Peterson, *The African American Theatre Directory; Profiles of African American Stage Performers.* Pfeffer, *My Harlem Reverie.* Sampson, *Blacks in Black and White.* Dodson, *The Black New Yorkers.* Thurman, *Negro Life in New York's Harlem.* Waller, *Fats Waller.*

1104. MORNINGSIDE THEATER
   2139 8th Avenue
   Picture house. 600 seats.
   References: *Film Daily Yearbook,* 1940–1955. *Motion Picture Herald,* July 15, 1939; January 24, 1942.

1105. ODEON THEATER
   256 W. 145th Street
   Picture house. 835 seats. According to Driggs, "for many years this was a movie house belonging to a chain that also owned the Douglas and Roosevelt theatres. These houses used a four-piece pit band and an occasional stage act. During the late 1920s, the musical groups were under the overall direction of J. T. Bymn."
   References: Driggs, *The Sound of Harlem. Film Daily Yearbook,* 1930–1933, 1940–1955. *Motion Picture Herald,* April 24, 1937; July 15, 1939; January 24, 1942. Pfeffer, *My Harlem Reverie.* Sampson, *Blacks in Black and White.*

1106. 116TH STREET THEATER
   132 W.116th Street
   Picture house. 1,809 seats. Also known as Loew's 116th Street.
   References: *Film Daily Yearbook,* 1949–1955. *Motion Picture Herald,* January 24, 1942.

1107. ORIENT THEATER
   111 W. 125th Street.
   Picture house. 850 seats. According to Driggs, "Willie the Lion Smith and cornetist June Clark had a band on stage in 1922." *Film Daily Yearbook* reported that the Orient was closed from 1953 to1955. The house was converted into a store and finally shut down in 1964.
   References: Driggs, *The Sound of Harlem. Film Daily Yearbook,* 1940–1955. *Motion Picture Herald,* April 24, 1937; July 15, 1939; January 24, 1942. Pfeffer, *My Harlem Reverie.* Sampson, *Blacks in Black and White.*

1108. PARK WEST THEATER
   113 W. 99th Street
   Picture house. 580 seats.
   References: *Film Daily Yearbook,* 1940–1955. *Motion Picture Herald,* April 24, 1937; July 15, 1939; January 24, 1942. Sampson, *Blacks in Black and White.*

1109. REGENT THEATER
   1906 Seventh Avenue
   Picture house. 1,845–2,460 seats. Architect: Thomas W. Lamb.
   References: *Architecture and Building* 45 (March 1913), "The Regent Theatre, 116th Street and 7th Avenue, New York," *Film Daily Yearbook,* 1940–1955. *Motion Picture Herald,* July 15, 1939; January 24, 1942.

1110. REGUN THEATER
   60–62 W. 116th Street
   Picture house. 700–1000 seats.
   References: *Film Daily Yearbook,* 1949–1955.

1111. RENAISSANCE THEATER
   2343 7th Avenue
   Vaudeville and picture house. 850 seats. Built circa 1920. Also known as the

Renaissance Casino. Manager in 1921: William C. Roach (African American). According to Peterson, the Renaissance was "the first black-controlled theatre in New York City." It was part of the Renaissance Casino complex, which consisted of the theater on the first floor and a ballroom on the second floor. Motion pictures exhibited at the Renaissance in 1926 included Cecil De Mille's *The Ten Commandments, Stage Struck*, starring Gloria Swanson, and *The Eagle*, starring Rudolph Valentino. The Oscar Micheaux picture, *After Thirty Years*, played the Renaissance in 1928. The film concerned a boy born of black parents who thought himself white.

References: Cahn, *Julius Cahn-Gus Hill Theatrical Guide*. *Chicago Defender*, "Race Theater Sold," May 8, 1926; "Micheaux's New Picture," March 31, 1928. *Film Daily Yearbook*, 1930–1933, 1940–1955. Hill, *Pages from the Harlem Renaissance*. Jackson, "List of Colored Theaters and Attractions," *Billboard*, August 6, 1921. Kellner, *The Harlem Renaissance*. Mitchell, *Black Drama*. *Motion Picture Herald*, April 24, 1937; July 15, 1939; January 24, 1942. *New York Age*, February 27, April 26, 1926. Sampson, *Blacks in Black and White*. Simms, *Simms' Blue Book*. Thurman, *Negro Life in New York's Harlem*. Work, *Negro Yearbook, 1921–1922*.

1112. ROOSEVELT THEATER
2497 7th Avenue
Picture house. 1,450 seats. Manager in 1921: Mr. Sovini. According to Driggs, "during the Twenties this movie house operated in conjunction with the Douglas and Odeon. Thomas 'Fats' Waller won an amateur night contest playing James P. Johnson's 'Carolina Shout.'"

References: Cahn, *Julius Cahn-Gus Hill Theatrical Guide*. Driggs, *The Sound of Harlem*. *Film Daily Yearbook*, 1930–1933, 1940–1955. Jackson, "List of Colored Theaters and Attractions," *Billboard*, August 6, 1921. Kellner, *The Harlem Renaissance*. *Motion Picture Herald*, April 24, 1937; July 15, 1939; January 24, 1942. Sampson, *Blacks in Black and White*. Work, *Negro Yearbook, 1921–1922*.

1113. SAVOY THEATER
112 34th Street
Picture house. 735 seats.
References: *Film Daily Yearbook*, 1930–1932. Kellner, *The Harlem Renaissance*.

1114. SUNSET THEATER
316 W. 125th Street
Picture house. 598 seats.
References: *Film Daily Yearbook*, 1940–1955. *Motion Picture Herald*, April 24, 1937; July 15, 1939; January 24, 1942. Sampson, *Blacks in Black and White*.

1115. VICTORIA THEATER
233 125th Street
Picture house. 982 seats.
References: *Film Daily Yearbook*, 1940–1955. *Motion Picture Herald*, April 24, 1937; July 15, 1939; January 24, 1942. Sampson, *Blacks in Black and White*.

1116. VICTORY THEATER
3rd Avenue and 146 Street
Picture house. 1,750 seats.
References: *Film Daily Yearbook*, 1950–1955.

1117. WASHINGTON THEATER
Picture house.
References: *Film Daily Yearbook*, 1940–1955. *Motion Picture Herald*, April 24, 1937; July 15, 1939; January 24, 1942. Sampson, *Blacks in Black and White*.

1118. WEST END THEATER
362 125th Street
Picture house. 670–2000 seats.
References: *Film Daily Yearbook*, 1949–1955.

South Jamaica, Long Island

1119. PLAZA THEATER
Picture house.
References: *Film Daily Yearbook*, 1940–1955. *Motion Picture Herald*, April 24, 1937; July 15, 1939. Sampson, *Blacks in Black and White*.

NORTH CAROLINA

Aberdeen

1120. BERKLAND THEATER
Picture house.
References: *Film Daily Yearbook*, 1931, 1932.

Albemarle

1121. VICTORY THEATER
Picture house.
References: *Film Daily Yearbook*, 1949–1955.

Asheboro

1122. STRAND THEATER
Picture house.
References: *Film Daily Yearbook*, 1950–1955.

Asheville

1123. BOOKER T. THEATER
Picture house. 300 seats.
References: *Film Daily Yearbook*, 1940–1945. *Motion Picture Herald*, July 15, 1939.

1124. EAGLE THEATER
Vaudeville and picture house. 350 seats. A TOBA theater. Manager in 1928: Harry Roth.
References: *Film Daily Yearbook*, 1930–1933, 1940–1955. *Motion Picture Herald*, July 15, 1939. *Official Theatrical World of Colored Artists*.

1125. PRINCESS THEATER
Picture house.
References: *Film Daily Yearbook*, 1940–1945. *Motion Picture Herald*, July 15, 1939.

1126. STAR THEATER
Picture house. The Oscar Micheaux film *Within Our Gates* was shown at the Star January 29, 1920.
References: Bowser, *Writing Himself into History*, Cahn, *Julius Cahn-Gus Hill Theatrical Guide*. Jackson, "List of Colored Theaters and Attractions," *Billboard*, August 6, 1921. Work, *Negro Yearbook*, 1921–1922.

Aulander

1127. LEVON THEATER
Picture house.

References: *Film Daily Yearbook*, 1949–1955.

Ayden

1128. MYERS THEATER
Picture house.
References: *Film Daily Yearbook*, 1949.

Baden

1129. DREAMLAND THEATER
Vaudeville house. Manager in 1921: W. T. Edding.
References: Cahn, *Julius Cahn-Gus Hill Theatrical Guide*. *Film Daily Yearbook*, 1931, 1932. Jackson, "List of Colored Theaters and Attractions," *Billboard*, August 6, 1921. Work, *Negro Yearbook*, 1921–1922.

Bailey

1130. BAILEY THEATER
Picture house.
References: *Film Daily Yearbook*, 1949–1955.

Bath

1131. DIXIE THEATER
Picture house.
References: *Film Daily Yearbook*, 1931, 1932.

Beaufort

1132. AUDITORIUM THEATER
Vaudeville house. Manager in 1914: Allen Parker. The Auditorium was part of the Dudley vaudeville circuit. In 1914, the Colemans and the Hill Sisters appeared here.
References: *Indianapolis Freeman*, "What's What on the Dudley Circuit," January 31, 1914.

1133. COLORED THEATER
Picture house. 200 seats.
References: *Motion Picture Herald*, April 24, 1937. Sampson, *Blacks in Black and White*.

1134. REX THEATER
Picture house.
References: *Film Daily Yearbook*, 1949–1955.

1135. SEA BREEZE THEATER
Picture house.
References: *Film Daily Yearbook*, 1940–1955. *Motion Picture Herald*, July 15, 1939.

Bladenboro

1136. WONIT THEATER
Picture house.
References: *Film Daily Yearbook*, 1949–1955.

Burlington

1137. ACE THEATER
Picture house.
References: *Film Daily Yearbook*, 1947–1955.

1138. DIXIE THEATER
Picture house.
References: *Film Daily Yearbook*, 1931, 1932.

1139. LINCOLN THEATER
Picture house.
References: *Film Daily Yearbook*, 1946.

Cameron

1140. STARLIGHT THEATER

Picture house.
References: *Film Daily Yearbook*, 1931, 1932.

Chapel Hill

1141. HOLLYWOOD THEATER
Picture house. 200 seats.
References: *Film Daily Yearbook*, 1949–1955.

1142. STANDARD THEATER
Picture house. 250 seats.
References: *Film Daily Yearbook*, 1931, 1932, 1940–1950. *Motion Picture Herald*, July 15, 1939.

Charlotte

1143. ASTOR THEATER
Picture house.
References: *Film Daily Yearbook*, 1949–1955.

1144. BROOKDALE DRIVE-IN
Picture house.
References: *Film Daily Yearbook*, 1949–1955.

1145. DIXIE THEATER
Vaudeville house. According to Peterson, the Dixie was in operation in the 1920s.
References: Peterson, *The African American Theatre Directory*.

1146. GRAND THEATER
Picture house. 300 seats.
References: *Film Daily Yearbook*, 1940–1955. *Motion Picture Herald*, April 24, 1937; July 15, 1939. Sampson, *Blacks in Black and White*.

1147. LINCOLN THEATER
Picture house. 600 seats.
References: *Film Daily Yearbook*, 1933, 1940–1955. *Motion Picture Herald*, April 24, 1937; July 15, 1939. Sampson, *Blacks in Black and White*.

1148. PALACE THEATER
Picture house.
References: Cahn, *Julius Cahn-Gus Hill Theatrical Guide*. Jackson, "List of Colored Theaters and Attractions," *Billboard*, August 6, 1921. Work, *Negro Yearbook*, 1921–1922.

1149. REX THEATER
Vaudeville house. A TOBA theater. Manager in 1928: S. W. Craver.
References: *Film Daily Yearbook*, 1931, 1932. Hill, *Pages from the Harlem Renaissance*. Jackson, "The Theater Owners' Booking Association," *Billboard*, December 16, 1922. *Official Theatrical World of Colored Artists*.

1150. ROYAL THEATER
Picture house.
References: *Film Daily Yearbook*, 1931–1933.

1151. SAVOY THEATER
Picture house. 600 seats.
References: *Film Daily Yearbook*, 1946–1955.

Clinton

1152. RITZ THEATER
Picture house.
References: *Film Daily Yearbook*, 1946–1955.

Coleran

1153. MYERS THEATER
Picture house.
References: *Film Daily Yearbook*, 1949.

Concord

1154. ALPINE THEATER

Vaudeville house. Said to be Black owned and managed.
References: Cahn, *Julius Cahn–Gus Hill Theatrical Guide.* Jackson, "List of Colored Theaters and Attractions," *Billboard,* August 6, 1921. Work, *Negro Yearbook, 1921–1922.*

1155. ROXY THEATER
Picture house.
References: *Film Daily Yearbook,* 1949–1955.

1156. WESTMORE THEATER
Picture house.
References: *Film Daily Yearbook,* 1931–1933.

Durham

1157. BOOKER T. THEATER
Picture house.
References: *Film Daily Yearbook,* 1949–1955.

1158. CARVER THEATER
Picture house.
References: *Film Daily Yearbook,* 1948.

1159–60. REGAL THEATER
Picture house. 350 seats.
References: *Film Daily Yearbook,* 1940–1955. *Motion Picture Herald,* April 24, 1937; July 15, 1939. Sampson, *Blacks in Black and White.*

1161. REX THEATER
Pettigrew Street
Vaudeville house. Manager in 1921: F. K. Watkins (African American). The Oscar Micheaux film *Within Our Gates* was shown here on January 26, 1920.
References: Bowser, *Writing Himself into History.* Jackson, "List of Colored Theaters and Attractions," *Billboard,* August 6, 1921.

1162. WONDERLAND THEATER
Pettigrew Street
Vaudeville and picture house. A TOBA theater. Owner and manager in 1921: F. K. Watkins (African American). Manager in 1928: G. W. Logan.
References: Bowser, *Writing Himself into History.* Cahn, *Julius Cahn–Gus Hill Theatrical Guide. Film Daily Yearbook,* 1931–1933. Jackson, "List of Colored Theaters and Attractions," *Billboard,* August 6, 1921. Simms, *Simms' Blue Book. Official Theatrical World of Colored Artists.* Work, *Negro Yearbook, 1921–1922.*

East Hickory

1163. NORWOOD THEATER
Picture house.
References: *Film Daily Yearbook,* 1931, 1932.

Edenton

1164. TAYLOR THEATER
Picture house.
References: *Film Daily Yearbook,* 1949.

Elizabeth City

1165. GAIETY THEATER
Picture house. 200 seats.
References: Cahn, *Julius Cahn–Gus Hill Theatrical Guide. Film Daily Yearbook,* 1931–1933, 1940–1955. *Motion Picture Herald,* July 15, 1939.

1166. NEW THEATER
Picture house. 200 seats.
References: *Motion Picture Herald,* April 24, 1937. Sampson, *Blacks in Black and White.*

1167. WASHINGTON THEATER
Picture house.
References: Work, *Negro Yearbook, 1921–1922*.

Elizabethtown

1168. LEMCONE THEATER
Picture house.
References: *Film Daily Yearbook*, 1949–1955.

Elm

1169. ELM THEATER
Picture house.
References: *Film Daily Yearbook*, 1949.

Enfield

1170. LERON THEATER
Picture house.
References: *Film Daily Yearbook*, 1949.

Fairmont

1171. FAIRMONT TENT THEATER
Picture house.
References: *Film Daily Yearbook*, 1950–1955.

Farmsville

1172. HOPKINS THEATER
Vaudeville house.
References: Work, *Negro Yearbook, 1921–1922*.

Fayetteville

1173. PALACE THEATER
Picture house.
References: *Film Daily Yearbook*, 1931, 1932.

Gadsden

1174. CARVER THEATER
Picture house.
References: *Film Daily Yearbook*, 1947.

1175. GAIETY THEATER
Picture house.
References: *Film Daily Yearbook*, 1947, 1948.

Garysburg

1176. BUFFALO THEATER
Picture house.
References: *Film Daily Yearbook*, 1944, 1945, 1949–1955.

Gastonia

1177. HIGHLANDS THEATER
Picture house.
References: *Film Daily Yearbook*, 1931, 1932.

1178. PALACE THEATER
Picture house.
References: *Film Daily Yearbook*, 1948–1955.

Goldsboro

1179. COLORED THEATER
Picture house.
References: Cahn, *Julius Cahn-Gus Hill Theatrical Guide*. Jackson, "List of Col-

ored Theaters and Attractions," *Billboard*, August 6, 1921.

1180. JAMES THEATER
Picture house. 325 seats.
References: *Film Daily Yearbook*, 1946–1955.

Greensboro

1181. COLLEGE THEATER
Picture house.
References: *Film Daily Yearbook*, 1931, 1932.

1182. GEM THEATER
Picture house.
References: *Film Daily Yearbook*, 1948–1955.

1183. PALACE THEATER
Vaudeville house. 300 seats. A TOBA theater. Manager in 1928: Charles Roth.
References: *Film Daily Yearbook*, 1931–1933, 1940–1950. *Motion Picture Herald*, April 24, 1937; July 15, 1939. *Official Theatrical World of Colored Artists*. Sampson, *Blacks in Black and White*.

1184. SUN DRIVE-IN
Picture house.
References: *Film Daily Yearbook*, 1952–1955.

Greenville

1185. COLONIAL THEATER
Picture house.
References: *Film Daily Yearbook*, 1931–1933.

1186. COLORED THEATER
Vaudeville and picture house.
References: Jackson, "List of Colored Theaters and Attractions," *Billboard*, August 6, 1921.

1187. LIBERTY THEATER
Vaudeville and picture house. Manager in 1921: O. T. Wilson.
References: Cahn, *Julius Cahn-Gus Hill Theatrical Guide*. Work, *Negro Yearbook*, 1921–1922.

1188. PLAZA THEATER
Picture house. 400 seats.
References: *Film Daily Yearbook*, 1946–1955.

1189. ROXY THEATER
Picture house.
References: *Film Daily Yearbook*, 1950–1955.

Henderson

1190. DIXIE THEATER
Picture house.
References: *Film Daily Yearbook*, 1931, 1932.

1191. STAR THEATER
Picture house.
References: *Film Daily Yearbook*, 1931, 1932.

1192. STARLITE DRIVE-IN
Picture house. 100 cars. Owner: B. R. Pless.
References: *Film Daily Yearbook*, 1952–1955.

Hertsford

1193. STATE THEATER
Picture house. 496 seats. Said to be "owned by Negro and white."
References: Murray, *The Negro Handbook, 1942*.

Hickory

1194. EMBASSY THEATER

Picture house.
References: *Film Daily Yearbook*, 1950–1955.

High Point

1195. DELANO THEATER
Picture house. 400 seats.
References: *Motion Picture Herald*, April 24, 1937. Sampson, *Blacks in Black and White*.

1196. EAGLE THEATER
Picture house.
References: *Film Daily Yearbook*, 1931–1933.

1197. RITZ THEATER
700 E. Washington Street
Picture house. 400 seats.
References: *Film Daily Yearbook*, 1946–1955.

Jackson

1198. JACKSON THEATER
Picture house.
References: *Film Daily Yearbook*, 1949.

Jacksonville

1199. STARR THEATER
Picture house. According to *Film Daily Yearbook*, the Starr was closed from 1949 to 1951.
References: *Film Daily Yearbook*, 1949–1955.

Kannapolis

1200. PALACE THEATER
Picture house.
References: *Film Daily Yearbook*, 1946–1955.

Kelford

1201. SPENCER THEATER
Picture house. According to *Film Daily Yearbook*, the Spencer was closed from 1949 to 1951.
References: *Film Daily Yearbook*, 1949–1955.

Kingston

1202. COLORED THEATER
Picture house.
References: Jackson, "List of Colored Theaters and Attractions, *Billboard*, August 6, 1921.

1203. GLOBE THEATER
Picture house.
References: Cahn, *Julius Cahn-Gus Hill Theatrical Guide*. Work, *Negro Yearbook, 1921–1922*.

1204. PALACE THEATER
Picture house. The Oscar Micheaux film *Within Our Gates* was exhibited here February 11, 1920.
References: Bowser, *Writing Himself into History*.

Kinston

1205. CARVER THEATER
Picture house.
References: *Film Daily Yearbook*, 1949–1955.

1206. LINCOLN THEATER
Picture house. 250 seats.
References: *Motion Picture Herald*, April 24, 1937. Sampson, *Blacks in Black and White*.

1207. PEOPLE'S THEATER
Picture house.
References: *Film Daily Yearbook*, 1931–1933.

1208. ROOSEVELT THEATER
Picture house.
References: *Film Daily Yearbook*, 1948.

1209. STATE THEATER
Picture house. 255 seats.
References: *Film Daily Yearbook*, 1940–1955. *Motion Picture Herald*, July 15, 1939.

Lake Washington

1210. COLORED THEATER
Picture house.
References: Jackson, "List of Colored Theaters and Attractions," *Billboard*, August 6, 1921.

1211. ELIZABETH THEATER
Picture house.
References: Cahn, *Julius Cahn-Gus Hill Theatrical Guide*.

Laurinburg

1212. ROXY THEATER
Picture house. According to *Film Daily Yearbook*, the Roxy was closed from 1949 to 1951.
References: *Film Daily Yearbook*, 1949–1955.

Leaksville

1213. HENRY THEATER
Picture house.
References: *Film Daily Yearbook*, 1947–1955.

Lenoir

1214. WEST END THEATER
Picture house.
References: *Film Daily Yearbook*, 1931, 1932.

Lincolnton

1215. MOTZ THEATER
Picture house.
References: *Film Daily Yearbook*, 1931, 1932.

Lumberton

1216. BROOKLYN THEATER
Picture house.
References: *Film Daily Yearbook*, 1931, 1932.

1217. ROBESON THEATER
Picture house.
References: *Film Daily Yearbook*, 1947–1955.

Mount Airy

1218. ELMONT THEATER
Picture house.
References: *Film Daily Yearbook*, 1931, 1932.

New Bern

1219. BERN THEATER
Picture house.
References: *Film Daily Yearbook*, 1947, 1948.

1220. COLORED THEATER
Picture house.
References: Jackson, "List of Colored Theaters and Attractions," *Billboard*, August 6, 1921.

1221. DIXIE THEATER
Picture house. Said to be Black owned and managed.
References: Cahn, *Julius Cahn-Gus Hill Theatrical Guide*. Work, *Negro Yearbook, 1921–1922*.

North Carolina

1222. FORD'S THEATER
Vaudeville house. Manager: R. F. Johnson. The theater was part of the Dudley vaudeville circuit in 1914.
References: *Chicago Defender*, November 30, 1914. Peterson, *The African American Theatre Directory*. Sampson, *Blacks in Blackface*.

1223. GLOBE THEATER
Vaudeville house. A TOBA theater. Manager in 1928: E. L. Lewis. The Oscar Micheaux motion picture *Within Our Gates* was featured on February 9, 1920.
References: Bowser, *Writing Himself into History*. *Film Daily Yearbook*, 1931, 1932. *Official Theatrical World of Colored Artists*.

1224. PALACE THEATER
Broad Street
Picture house.
References: *Film Daily Yearbook*, 1931–1933, 1940–1949, 1952–1955. *Motion Picture Herald*, July 15, 1939.

1225. RITZ THEATER
Picture house.
References: *Film Daily Yearbook*, 1949–1955.

Oxford

1226. CASINO THEATER
Picture house. Manager in 1921: C. I. Jones.
References: Cahn, *Julius Cahn-Gus Hill Theatrical Guide*. Jackson, "List of Colored Theaters and Attractions," *Billboard*, August 6, 1921. Work, *Negro Yearbook, 1921–1922*.

Pinehurst

1227. ADAMS THEATER
Picture house.
References: *Film Daily Yearbook*, 1931, 1932.

Plymouth

1228. DIXIE THEATER
Picture house.
References: *Film Daily Yearbook*, 1931, 1932.

Raeford

1229. NEW COLORED THEATER
Picture house.
References: *Film Daily Yearbook*, 1950–1955.

Raleigh

1230. BURGESS THEATER
Picture house.
References: *Film Daily Yearbook*, 1931, 1932.

1231. LIBERTY THEATER
Picture house.
References: *Film Daily Yearbook*, 1931–1933.

1232. LIGHTNER ARCADE THEATER
Vaudeville house. Managers: Lightner Brothers (African Americans).
References: Work, *Negro Yearbook, 1921–1922*.

1233. LINCOLN THEATER
Picture house.
References: *Film Daily Yearbook*, 1946–1955.

1234. RALEIGH THEATER
Picture house.
References: *Film Daily Yearbook*, 1940–1948.

1235. ROYAL THEATER

117 E. Hargett Street
Vaudeville and picture house. 350 seats. Manager in 1921: W. T. Jonn. The Royal was bought by Milton Starr in 1929.
References: Cahn, *Julius Cahn-Gus Hill Theatrical Guide*. *Chicago Defender*, "New Houses Opening on Starr Circuit," September 21, 1929. *Film Daily Yearbook*, 1940–1955. Jackson, "List of Colored Theaters and Attractions," *Billboard*, August 6, 1921. *Motion Picture Herald*, April 24, 1937; July 15, 1939. Sampson, *Blacks in Black and White*. Work, *Negro Yearbook, 1921–1922*.

Reidsville

1236. BOOKER T. THEATER
Picture house.
References: *Film Daily Yearbook*, 1949–1955.

1237. GEM THEATER
Picture and vaudeville house. Manager in 1921: J. B. McGehoe (African American).
References: Cahn, *Julius Cahn-Gus Hill Theatrical Guide*. *Film Daily Yearbook*, 1931–1933. Jackson, "Additions to Theater List," *Billboard*, December 31, 1921. Work, *Negro Yearbook, 1921–1922*.

1238. NEW COLORED THEATER
Picture house.
References: *Film Daily Yearbook*, 1940–1945. *Motion Picture Herald*, July 15, 1939.

1239. PENN THEATER
Picture house. 250 seats.
References: *Film Daily Yearbook*, 1940–1942. *Motion Picture Herald*, April 24, 1937; July 15, 1939. Sampson, *Blacks in Black and White*.

Roanoke Rapids

1240. CARVER THEATER
Picture house.
References: *Film Daily Yearbook*, 1950–1955.

Rocky Mount

1241. BOOKER T. THEATER
Picture house. 500 seats.
References: *Film Daily Yearbook*, 1940–1955. *Motion Picture Herald*, July 15, 1939.

1242. MANHATTAN THEATER
Picture house. 400 seats.
References: *Film Daily Yearbook*, 1931, 1932. *Motion Picture Herald*, April 24, 1937. Sampson, *Blacks in Black and White*.

1243. PENN THEATER
Picture house.
References: *Film Daily Yearbook*, 1943–1945.

1244. RITZ THEATER
Picture house.
References: *Film Daily Yearbook*, 1946–1955.

1245. SAVOY THEATER
Picture house.
References: *Film Daily Yearbook*, 1933.

Roxboro

1246. STAR THEATER
Vaudeville and picture house. Owner and manager in 1921: J. Bolden (African American).
References: Cahn, *Julius Cahn-Gus Hill Theatrical Guide*. Jackson, "Additions to Theater List," *Billboard*, December 31, 1921. Work, *Negro Yearbook, 1921–1922*.

Salisbury

1247. RITZ THEATER
Picture house.
References: *Film Daily Yearbook*, 1949–1955.

Sanford

1248. CAROLINA THEATER
Picture house.
References: *Film Daily Yearbook*, 1949–1955.

1249. DUNBAR THEATER
Picture house.
References: *Film Daily Yearbook*, 1931, 1932.

Seaboard

1250. JEAN THEATER
Picture house.
References: *Film Daily Yearbook*, 1949–1955.

Selma

1251. ROYAL THEATER
Picture house.
References: *Film Daily Yearbook*, 1931, 1932.

Shelby

1252. WASHINGTON THEATER
Picture house.
References: *Film Daily Yearbook*, 1950–1955.

Southern Pines

1253. AMITH HALL
Picture house.
References: *Film Daily Yearbook*, 1931, 1932.

Spindale

1254. BELLS THEATER
Picture house.
References: *Film Daily Yearbook*, 1950–1955.

Spring Hope

1255. JOYCE THEATER
Picture house.
References: *Film Daily Yearbook*, 1949.

Statesville

1256. DUNBAR THEATER
Picture house.
References: *Film Daily Yearbook*, 1931–1933.

Tarboro

1257. DIXIE THEATER
Picture house.
References: *Film Daily Yearbook*, 1949–1955.

Wadesboro

1258. HIGHLANDS THEATER
Picture house.
References: *Film Daily Yearbook*, 1931, 1932.

Washington

1259. LENOX THEATER
Picture house.

References: *Film Daily Yearbook*, 1949–1955.

1260. RITZ THEATER
Picture house.
References: *Film Daily Yearbook*, 1949–1955.

1261. VICTORIA THEATER
Picture house. The Oscar Micheaux film *Within Our Gates* was shown at the Victoria on February 10, 1920.
References: Bowser, *Writing Himself into History*.

Whiteville

1262. LINCOLN THEATER
Picture house. According to *Film Daily Yearbook*, the Lincoln was closed from 1950 to 1951.
References: *Film Daily Yearbook*, 1949–1955.

1263. OPPOLO THEATER
Picture house.
References: *Film Daily Yearbook*, 1950–1955.

Wilkesboro

1264. RENDEZVOUS THEATER
Picture house.
References: *Film Daily Yearbook*, 1949–1955.

Williamston

1265. CARVER THEATER
Picture house.
References: *Film Daily Yearbook*, 1950–1955.

Wilmington

1266. BROOKLYN THEATER

Vaudeville house. A TOBA theater. Manager in 1921: L. Wheeler. Manager in 1928: Robert Herring.
References: Cahn, *Julius Cahn-Gus Hill Theatrical Guide*. Jackson, "List of Colored Theaters and Attractions," *Billboard*, August 6, 1921. *Official Theatrical World of Colored Artists*. Work, *Negro Yearbook, 1921–1922*.

1267. LYRIC THEATER
Vaudeville house. Manager in 1914: Morris Whippler. The Lyric was part of the Dudley vaudeville circuit. In January 1914, Watts and Willis appeared here.
References: *Indianapolis Freeman*, "What's What on the Dudley Circuit," January 31, 1914.

1268. PALACE THEATER
Picture house.
References: *Film Daily Yearbook*, 1948.

1269. RITZ THEATER
Picture house.
References: *Film Daily Yearbook*, 1946–1955.

Wilson

1270. GLOBE THEATER
Vaudeville and picture house. Manager in 1914: J. J. Privett. This may have been the unnamed theater listed in the 1921 *Billboard* survey. In January 1914, Harris and Turner played here. The Oscar Micheaux film *Within Our Gates* opened here January 27, 1920.
References: Bowser, *Writing Himself into History*. Cahn, *Julius Cahn-Gus Hill Theatrical Guide*. *Film Daily Yearbook*, 1931–1933. Jackson, "List of Colored Theaters and Attractions," *Billboard*, August 6, 1921. Work, *Negro Yearbook, 1921–1922*.

1271. RITZ THEATER

Picture house. 500 seats.

References: *Film Daily Yearbook*, 1940–1955. *Motion Picture Herald*, April 24, 1937; July 15, 1939. Sampson, *Blacks in Black and White*.

Winston-Salem

1272. DUNBAR THEATER
Vaudeville house. Manager: R. A. Bottom.

References: Cahn, *Julius Cahn-Gus Hill Theatrical Guide*. Jackson, "List of Colored Theaters and Attractions," *Billboard*, August 6, 1921. Work, *Negro Yearbook, 1921–1922*.

1273. LAFAYETTE THEATER
Vaudeville house. 450 seats. Owner and manager in 1921: W.S. Scales (African American). A TOBA theater. The vaudeville headliners at the Lafayette in April 1921 were the Billy Young Shoulder Shakers.

References: Cahn, *Julius Cahn-Gus Hill Theatrical Guide*. *Film Daily Yearbook*, 1931, 1946–1955. Hill, *Pages from the Harlem Renaissance*. Jackson, "List of Colored Theaters and Attractions," *Billboard*, August 6, 1921; "The Theater Owners' Booking Association," *Billboard*, December 16, 1922. Peterson, *The African American Theatre Directory*. Work, *Negro Yearbook, 1921–1922*.

1274. LINCOLN THEATER
Vaudeville and picture house. 700 seats. A TOBA theater. Manager in 1928: W.S. Scales.

References: *Film Daily Yearbook*, 1931–1933, 1940–1955. *Motion Picture Herald*, April 24, 1937; July 15, 1939. Sampson, *Blacks in Black and White. Official Theatrical World of Colored Artists*.

1275. NEW REX THEATER
Fourth and Church Streets
Picture house. 600 seats. The New Rex was to be a two-story white face brick structure with interiors featuring historic Spanish scenery. It would have a modern cooling system and a $10,000 Wurlitzer organ. It is not clear whether it was actually built since all further bibliographic sources refer to the Rex rather than the New Rex.

References: *Chicago Defender*, "Winston-Salem to Have New Theater," March 10, 1928.

1276. PARK-VU DRIVE-IN
Picture house.

References: *Film Daily Yearbook*, 1952–1955.

1277. REX THEATER
Fourth and Church Streets
Picture house.

References: Cahn, *Julius Cahn-Gus Hill Theatrical Guide*. Jackson, "List of Colored Theaters and Attractions," *Billboard*, August 6, 1921. *Motion Picture Herald*, April 24, 1937. Sampson, *Blacks in Black and White*. Work, *Negro Yearbook, 1921–1922*.

1278. ROOSEVELT THEATER
Picture house.

References: *Film Daily Yearbook*, 1940–1945. *Motion Picture Herald*, July 15, 1939.

OHIO

Akron

1279. RITZ THEATER
407 E. Market Street
Picture house. 400 seats.
References: *Film Daily Yearbook*, 1950–1955.

Cincinnati

1280. BEECHER THEATER
870 Beecher Street
Picture house. 750 seats.
References: *Film Daily Yearbook*, 1931–1933, 1940–1955. *Motion Picture Herald*, April 24, 1937; July 15, 1939. Sampson, *Blacks in Black and White.*

1281. DIXIE THEATER
229 W. 5th Street
Picture house. 300 seats.
References: *Film Daily Yearbook*, 1933, 1940–1948. *Motion Picture Herald*, July 15, 1939.

1282. FREEMAN THEATER
1548 Freeman Street
Picture house. 447 seats.
References: *Film Daily Yearbook*, 1949–1955.

1283. GAITHER THEATER
W. 5th Street
Vaudeville house. Owner: Major Edward G. Gaither.
References: Dabney, *Cincinnati's Colored Citizens*. Peterson, *The African American Theatre Directory.*

1284. GEM THEATER
Picture house.
References: *Film Daily Yearbook*, 1931, 1932.

1285. HIPPODROME THEATER
843 W. 19th Street
Picture house. 1,000 seats.
References: *Film Daily Yearbook*, 1931, 1932, 1949, 1950.

1286. LINCOLN THEATER
500 W. 5th Street
Vaudeville and picture house. 500–1,000 seats. Built about 1914. A TOBA theater. Manager in 1921: Lew Henry (African American). In 1923 Piedmont and Caswell appeared here.
References: Dabney, *Cincinnati's Colored Citizens. Chicago Defender*, Murray, "Cinci Notes," October 27, 1923. *Film Daily Yearbook*, 1931–1933, 1940–1955. Hill, *Pages from the Harlem Renaissance.* Jackson, "List of Colored Theaters and Attractions, *Billboard,* August 6, 1921; "The Theater Owners' Booking Association," *Billboard,* December 16, 1922. *Motion Picture Herald,* April 24, 1937; July 15, 1939. Peterson, *Profiles of African American Stage Performers; The African American Theatre Directory.* Sampson, *Blacks in Black and White.* Work, *Negro Yearbook 1921–1922.*

1287. LYCEUM THEATER
Vaudeville house. Owner in 1921: T. S. Tinley. Manager in 1921: Lew Henry (African American). A TOBA theater. In April 1921, the vaudeville show featured Mary Mack's Merry Makers of Mirth, the Sandy Burns Company, and the Carter and Mitchell Company.

References: Cahn, *Julius Cahn-Gus Hill Theatrical Guide*. Dabney, *Cincinnati's Colored Citizens*. Hill, *Pages from the Harlem Renaissance*. Jackson, "List of Colored Theaters and Attractions," *Billboard*, August 6, 1921. Work, *Negro Yearbook 1921–1922*.

1288. PEKIN THEATER
336 W. 5th Street
Vaudeville and picture house. 229 seats. Owner and manager in 1921: Oscar Hawkins (African American). The Pekin was part of the Colored Consolidated Time vaudeville circuit. In January 1914, the Pekin show consisted of the Arrants, and Crampton and Bailey. In January 1915, the Pekin's vaudeville offerings included H. H. Puggsley, monologist, Josephine Tobias, singer, Gray and Dunlop, comedians, and Marjorie Lorraine, dancer.

References: Julius Cahn, *Julius Cahn-Gus Hill Theatrical Guide*. Dabney, *Cincinnati's Colored Citizens. Film Daily Yearbook*, 1931, 1932, 1940–1955. Hill, *Pages from the Harlem Renaissance*. *Indianapolis Freeman*, "The Show at Cincinnati, O," January 16, 1915; "On Colored Consolidated Time," January 31, 1914. *Motion Picture Herald*, July 15, 1939. Work, *Negro Yearbook 1921–1922*.

1289. REGAL THEATER
1201 Linn Street
Picture house. 1,400 seats.
References: *Film Daily Yearbook*, 1949–1955

1290. REX THEATER
Picture house.
References: *Film Daily Yearbook*, 1931, 1932.

1291. ROOSEVELT THEATER
425 Central Avenue
Vaudeville house. 800–926 seats. A TOBA theater. Manager in 1920: Lew Henry. Manager in 1928: Jack Lustgarten. In October 1923, Billie McLaurin and Tillie Marshall appeared in a vaudeville farce called "The Speedmakers." In March 1924, the Roosevelt's vaudeville show featured comedians Johnson and Lee, blackface singer Anna White, comedians Jines and Jacqueline, dancers Happy Ferguson and Mary Hicks, and blues singer Bessie Smith. Smith also played here in 1927.

References: Albertson, *Bessie*. Cahn, *Julius Cahn-Gus Hill Theatrical Guide*. *Chicago Defender*, Murray, "Cinci Notes," October 27, 1923; "Roosevelt Theater," March 8, 1924. Dabney, *Cincinnati's Colored Citizens. Film Daily Yearbook*, 1931–1933, 1940–1955. Jackson, "List of Colored Theaters and Attractions," *Billboard*, August 6, 1921. *Motion Picture Herald*, April 24, 1937; July 15, 1939. Peterson, *Profiles of African American Stage Performers*. Sampson, *Blacks in Black and White*.

1292. STATE THEATER
1504–1506 Central Avenue
Picture house. 1,000 seats.
References: *Film Daily Yearbook*, 1949–1955.

1293. VICTORIA THEATER
Picture house.
References: *Film Daily Yearbook*, 1931, 1932.

Cleveland

1294. ALPHA THEATER
Vaudeville house. The Alpha was part of the Colored Consolidated Time circuit. During the week of February 2, 1914, the McCarvers, Stone and Stone, and Marie Bostwick appeared here.
References: *Indianapolis Freeman*, "On Colored Consolidated Time," January 31, 1914.

Ohio 165

1295. APOLLO THEATER
Picture house.
References: *Film Daily Yearbook*, 1948.

1296. CARTER THEATER
2071 E. 9th Street
Picture house. 700 seats.
References: *Film Daily Yearbook*, 1949–1955,

1297. CEDAR THEATER
7500 Cedar Street
Picture house. 850 seats.
References: *Film Daily Yearbook*, 1931–1933, 1940–1955. *Motion Picture Herald*, April 24, 1937; July 15, 1939. Sampson, *Blacks in Black and White*.

1298. CROWN THEATER
945 E. 105th Street
Picture house. 604–650 seats.
References: *Film Daily Yearbook*, 1949–1955

1299. ERIE THEATER
E. 32nd Street and Woodland Avenue
Picture house. 450 seats.
References: *Film Daily Yearbook*, 1931–1933, 1940. *Motion Picture Herald*, April 24, 1937. Sampson, *Blacks in Black and White*.

1300. FAMILY THEATER
Picture house.
References: *Film Daily Yearbook*, 1931–1933.

1301. FOUNTAIN THEATER
Picture house.
References: *Film Daily Yearbook*, 1931, 1932.

1302. GLOBE THEATER
5217 Woodland Avenue
Vaudeville and picture house. 450 seats. A TOBA theater. Manager in 1921: Louis Israel. Manager in 1928: M. B. Hortwicz. In 1923, the Drake-Walker Bombay Girls appeared here. Doc Cheatham's Jazz Syncopators and Bessie Smith were here in 1923. Comedians Whitney and Tutt performed at the Globe in October 1926. Bessie Smith returned to the Globe in 1929 with the show *Steamboat Days*.
References: Albertson, *Bessie*. *Baltimore Afro-American*, October 31, 1926. Cahn, *Julius Cahn-Gus Hill Theatrical Guide*. *Film Daily Yearbook*, 1931, 1932, 1940–1955. Hill, *Pages from the Harlem Renaissance*. Jackson, "The Theater Owners' Booking Association," *Billboard*, December 16, 1922. Jines, *Chicago Defender*, "Globe Theater, Cleveland," July 28, 1923; August 22, 1925. *Motion Picture Herald*, April 24, 1937; July 15, 1939. Sampson, *Blacks in Black and White*. Sampson, *Blacks in Blackface*.

1303. GRAND CENTRAL THEATER
3543 Central Avenue
Vaudeville house. 300–400 seats. A TOBA theater and part of the South Consolidated circuit. Owner in 1921: Mr. Kaplan. Manager in 1921: O. T. Harris (African American). References: Cahn, *Julius Cahn-Gus Hill Theatrical Guide*. *Film Daily Yearbook*, 1931–1933, 1940–1948. Hill, *Pages from the Harlem Renaissance*. Jackson, "List of Colored Theaters and Attractions, *Billboard*, August 6, 1921; "The Theater Owners' Booking Association," *Billboard*, December 16, 1922. *Motion Picture Herald*, April 24, 1937; July 15, 1939. Peterson, *The African American Theatre Directory*. Sampson, *Blacks in Black and White*. Work, *Negro Yearbook 1921–1922*.

1304. HALTNORTH THEATER
2571 E. 55th Street
Picture house. 1,398 seats.
References: *Film Daily Yearbook* 1931–1933, 1940–1955. Hill, *Pages from the Harlem Renaissance*. *Motion Picture Herald*, April 24, 1937. Sampson, *Blacks in Black and White*.

166 Ohio

Karamu House Theater, Cleveland, Ohio (SoulofAmerica.com)

1305. KARAMU HOUSE THEATER
Drama and musical house.
This theater is home to the Arena Players and the Karamu Players.
References: Berry, *Langston Hughes*. Hughes, *Black Magic*. Kellner, *The Harlem Renaissance*. Peterson, *The African American Theatre Directory; Profiles of African American Stage Performers*.

1306. KING THEATER
2804 E. 79th Street
Picture house. 300 seats.
References: *Film Daily Yearbook*, 1949–1955.

1307. MAIN THEATER
Picture house.
References: *Film Daily Yearbook*, 1931, 1932, 1949–1955.

1308. QUINCY THEATER
8312 Quincy Street
Picture house. 700–750 seats.
References: *Film Daily Yearbook*, 1931–1933, 1940–1955. *Motion Picture Herald*, April 24, 1937; July 15, 1939. Sampson, *Blacks in Black and White*.

1309. RIVOLI THEATER
Picture house.
References: *Film Daily Yearbook*, 1931–1933.

1310. STANDARD THEATER
811 Prospect Avenue
Nickeldeon and picture house. 600–704 seats. In 1915, the Standard installed a Wurlitzer organ, Opus #68, that replaced its Wurlitzer Hope-Jones unit orchestra organ.
References: Bowser, *Writing Himself into History*. *Film Daily Yearbook*, 1949–1955.

1311. SUNBEAM THEATER
Picture house.
References: *Film Daily Yearbook*, 1949–1955.

1312. TEMPLE THEATER
2322 E. 55th Street

Picture house. 500–580 seats. Manager in 1921: Bernard E. Bolansy.
References: *Film Daily Yearbook*, 1940–1948. Jackson, "List of Colored Theaters and Attractions," *Billboard*, August 6, 1921. *Motion Picture Herald*, April 14, 1937; July 15, 1939. Sampson, *Blacks in Black and White*. Work, *Negro Yearbook 1921–1922*.

1313. U.S. THEATER
Picture house.
References: *Film Daily Yearbook*, 1931, 1932.

Columbus

1314. CROWN GARDEN THEATER
Long and 9th Streets
Vaudeville house. Built in 1916. Manager: Billy Smith.
References: Peterson, *The African American Theatre Directory*.

1315. DUNBAR THEATER
1287 Mount Vernon Avenue
Vaudeville house. Owner in 1915: James H. Barrett. Manager in 1921: J. A. Jackson (African American). Jackson was a popular black journalist for the entertainment weekly *The Billboard* from 1921 to 1925. The Dunbar was part of the Colored Consolidated Time vaudeville circuit. The newspaper *Indianapolis Freeman* reported in April 1915 that "Mr. James H. Clark has just opened the Dunbar Theater of Columbus, Ohio, with the Clark Stock Company." Future plays included *School Days* and *On the Reservation*. In February 1924, the Dunbar's vaudeville show had comics Johnson and Lee, blackface singer Anna White, comics Jines and Jacqueline, and novelty act Seals and White.
References: Cahn, *Julius Cahn-Gus Hill Theatrical Guide. Chicago Defender*, February 23, 1924. Hill, *Pages from the Harlem Renaissance*. Jackson, "List of Colored Theaters and Attractions," *Billboard*, August 6, 1921. Murray, *The Negro Handbook, 1942*. Peterson, *The African American Theatre Directory, 1816–1960*. Work, *Negro Yearbook, 1921–1922*.

1316. EMPRESS THEATER
768 E. Long Street
Picture and vaudeville house. 600 seats. Also known as the Gayety and the Knickerbocker. Owner and manager in 1921: J. A. Jackson (African American).
References: Cahn, *Julius Cahn-Gus Hill Theatrical Guide. Film Daily Yearbook*, 1931–1933, 1940–1955. Hill, *Pages from the Harlem Renaissance*. Jackson, "List of Colored Theaters and Attractions," *Billboard*, August 6, 1921. *Motion Picture Herald*, April 24, 1937; July 15, 1939. Murray, *The Negro Handbook, 1942*. Sampson, *Blacks in Black and White*. Work, *Negro Yearbook, 1921–1922*.

1317. EXHIBIT THEATER
Picture house.
References: *Film Daily Yearbook*, 1931, 1932.

GAYETY THEATER *see* Empress Theater

1318. GOODALE THEATER
Picture house.
References: *Film Daily Yearbook*, 1949.

1319. HIPPODROME THEATER
Picture house.
References: *Film Daily Yearbook*, 1931, 1932.

KNICKERBOCKER THEATER *see* Empress Theater.

MARTIN LUTHER KING PERFORMING ARTS CENTERS *see* Pythian Theater

1320. NEW THEATER
Picture house.

168　Ohio

References: *Film Daily Yearbook*, 1931–1933.

1321. NEW WONDER THEATER
Picture house.
References: *Film Daily Yearbook*, 1931–1933.

1322. OGDEN THEATER
Picture house. 1,000 seats.
References: *Film Daily Yearbook*, 1931–1933, 1947. *Motion Picture Herald*, April 24, 1937; July 15, 1939. Sampson, *Blacks in Black and White*.

1323. PYTHIAN THEATER
Vaudeville, picture house. Built by the Knights of Pythians, the Pythian opened as a theater in 1926. It is now known as the Martin Luther King Performing Arts Center.
References: *Film Daily Yearbook*, 1931, 1932, 1940–1955. *Motion Picture Herald*, July 15, 1939. Sampson, *Blacks in Blackface*.

1324. RIALTO THEATER
Picture house.
References: *Film Daily Yearbook*, 1931, 1932.

1325. ROYAL THEATER
Picture house.
References: *Film Daily Yearbook*, 1931, 1932.

1326. SAVOIA THEATER
Picture house.
References: *Film Daily Yearbook*, 1931, 1932.

Dayton

1327. CLASSIC THEATER
817 W. 5th Street
Picture house. 500–599 seats.
References: *Film Daily Yearbook*, 1931–1933, 1940–1946, 1949–1955. *Motion Picture Herald*, April 24, 1937; July 15, 1939. Sampson, *Blacks in Black and White*.

1328. EDGEMONT THEATER
Picture house.
References: *Film Daily Yearbook*, 1931, 1932.

1329. MIDGET THEATER
W. 3rd Street
Picture house. 350 seats. Manager in 1921: R. C. Krapf.
References: Cahn, *Julius Cahn-Gus Hill Theatrical Guide*. *Film Daily Yearbook*, 1931, 1932. Hill, *Pages from the Harlem Renaissance*. Jackson, "List of Colored Theaters and Attractions," *Billboard*, August 6, 1921. Work, *Negro Yearbook, 1921–1922*.

1330. PALACE THEATER
1125 W. 5th Street
Vaudeville and picture house. 600 seats. Manager in 1928: Lloyd H. Cox. Manager in 1941: John S. Henderson.
References: *Film Daily Yearbook*, 1931–1933, 1947–1955. *Official Theatrical World of Colored Artists*.

1331. PEKIN THEATER
Vaudeville house. Also known as the New Pekin. The Pekin was part of the Colored Consolidated Time vaudeville circuit. During the week of February 2, 1914, Bert Whitman and the Sunbeams performed here along with Sam Davis. Comedians Price and Jones appeared here in 1915.
References: *Indianapolis Freeman*, " On Colored Consolidated Time," January 31, 1914; "Pekin Theater, Dayton, O," January 9, 1915.

1332. REGAL THEATER
1314 Germantown Street
Picture house. 300 seats.
References: *Film Daily Yearbook*, 1949–1955.

Goodale

1333. ROYAL THEATER
Picture house.
References: *Film Daily Yearbook*, 1952–1955.

Hamilton

1334. LYRIC THEATER
Picture house.
References: *Film Daily Yearbook*, 1931, 1932.

1335. VENDOME THEATER
Picture house. Owner: Lee Richardson.
References: Peterson, *The African American Theatre Directory*.

Lockland

1336. DUNBAR THEATER
Picture house. 275 seats.
References: *Film Daily Yearbook*, 1940–1948. *Motion Picture Herald*, April 24, 1937; July 15, 1939. Murray, *The Negro Handbook, 1942*. Sampson, *Blacks in Black and White*.

1337. NEW HEIGHTS THEATER
Picture house.
References: *Film Daily Yearbook*, 1949–1955.

1338. ROXY THEATER
Picture house.
References: *Film Daily Yearbook*, 1949–1955.

Middletown

1339. REGAL THEATER
Vaudeville house. A TOBA theater. Manager: Charles Nickerson. The Regal opened on June 3, 1929 with the Billie Pierson show *Miss Broadway*.
References: *Chicago Defender*, "Ohio Theater Signs Up With TOBA Circuit," June 8, 1929.

Portsmouth

1340. LINCOLN THEATER
Picture house. Manager in 1921: W. F. McConnell.
References: Cahn, *Julius Cahn-Gus Hill Theatrical Guide*. *Film Daily Yearbook*, 1931, 1932. Hill, *Pages from the Harlem Renaissance*. Jackson, "List of Colored Theaters and Attractions," *Billboard*, August 6, 1921. Work, *Negro Yearbook, 1921–1922*.

Springfield

1341. BOOKER T. THEATER
541 Fair Street
Vaudeville house. A TOBA theater. Manager in 1928: C.S. Olinger.
References: *Official Theatrical World of Colored Artists*.

1342. LENOX THEATER
Picture house.
References: *Film Daily Yearbook*, 1949.

1343. LINCOLN THEATER
618 S. Center Street
Vaudeville and picture house. 300 seats. A TOBA theater. Manager in 1928: J.W. Hamilton.
References: *Film Daily Yearbook*, 1931–1933. *Official Theatrical World of Colored Artists*.

1344. SOUTHERN THEATER
Picture house. 300 seats.
References: *Film Daily Yearbook*, 1940–1949. *Motion Picture Herald*, July 15, 1939.

1345. WASHINGTON THEATER
Picture house.

References: *Film Daily Yearbook*, 1931, 1932.

Toledo

1346. DIXIE THEATER
Picture house. 560 seats.
References: *Film Daily Yearbook*, 1945–1955.

1347. LOOP THEATER
417 Superior Street
Picture house. 750 seats.
References: *Film Daily Yearbook*, 1949–1955.

Waynesburg

1348. WAYNE THEATER
Picture house.
References: *Film Daily Yearbook*, 1949–1955.

Wilberforce

1349. WILBERFORCE THEATER
Picture house.

References: *Film Daily Yearbook*, 1931–1933.

Xenia

1350. ORPHEUM THEATER
Picture house. 500 seats. Manager in 1921: A. L. Binder.
References: Cahn, *Julius Cahn-Gus Hill Theatrical Guide*. Hill, *Pages from the Harlem Renaissance*. Jackson, "List of Colored Theaters and Attractions," *Billboard*, August 6, 1921. Work, *Negro Yearbook, 1921–1922*.

Youngstown

1351. MCGUFFEY THEATER
Picture house. According to *Film Daily Yearbook*, the McGuffey was closed from 1949 to 1951.
References: *Film Daily Yearbook*, 1949–1955.

1352. REGENT THEATER
Picture house.
References: *Film Daily Yearbook*, 1949–1955.

OKLAHOMA

Altus

1353. STATE THEATER
Picture house.
References: *Film Daily Yearbook*, 1947–1955.

Ardmore

1354. COLORED THEATER
Picture house. Manager in 1921: Tobe Crisp (African American).
References: Cahn, Julius Cahn, *Julius*

Cahn-Gus Hill Theatrical Guide. Hill, *Pages from the Harlem Renaissance.* Jackson, "List of Colored Theaters and Attractions," *Billboard,* August 6, 1921. Work, *Negro Yearbook, 1921–1922.*

1355. DREAMLAND THEATER
Picture house.
References: *Film Daily Yearbook,* 1931–1933.

1356. JEWEL THEATER
Main Street
Picture house. 325 seats.
References: *Film Daily Yearbook, 1940–1955. Motion Picture Herald, July 15, 1939.*

Bartlesville

1357. DELTA THEATER
Picture house.
References: *Film Daily Yearbook,* 1945–1948

Boley

1358. HALE THEATER
Picture house.
References: *Film Daily Yearbook,* 1931–1933, 1940. *Motion Picture Herald,* July 15, 1939.

1359. KING ED THEATER
Picture house.
References: *Film Daily Yearbook,* 1946–1955.

Broken Bow

1360. WONDERLAND THEATER
Picture house.
References: *Film Daily Yearbook,* 1931, 1932.

Chickasha

1361. LIBERTY THEATER
Picture house.
References: *Film Daily Yearbook,* 1931–1933.

1362. PASTIME THEATER
Picture house. Manager in 1921: William Johnson.
References: Cahn, *Julius Cahn-Gus Hill Theatrical Guide.* Hill, *Pages from the Harlem Renaissance.* Jackson, "List of Colored Theaters and Attractions," *Billboard,* August 6, 1921. Work, *Negro Yearbook, 1921–1922.*

1363. RITZ THEATER
Picture house. 328 seats.
References: *Film Daily Yearbook, 1949–1955.*

Cushing

1364. LITTLE HARLEM THEATER
1125 N. Central Street
Picture house. 125 seats.
Source: *Film Daily Yearbook,* 1946–1955.

1365. WONDERLAND THEATER
Picture house.
References: *Film Daily Yearbook,* 1931–1933.

Duncan

1366. RITZ THEATER
Picture house.
References: *Film Daily Yearbook,* 1947–1949

El Reno

1367. ROYAL THEATER
Picture house.
References: *Film Daily Yearbook,* 1949.

Enid

1368. MECCA THEATER
Picture house. 125 seats.
References: *Film Daily Yearbook*, 1949–1955.

1369. ROYAL THEATER
Picture house. 300 seats.
References: *Film Daily Yearbook*, 1949–1955.

Frederick

1370. IDEAL THEATER
Picture house.
References: *Film Daily Yearbook*, 1947–1955.

Howata

1371. REX THEATER
Picture house.
References: *Film Daily Yearbook*, 1947, 1948.

Hugo

1372. LINCOLN THEATER
Picture house. Manager in 1921: J. Townsend.
References: Cahn, *Julius Cahn-Gus Hill Theatrical Guide*. Hill, *Pages from the Harlem Renaissance*. Jackson, "List of Colored Theaters and Attractions," *Billboard*, August 6, 1921. Work, *Negro Yearbook, 1921–1922*.

Idabel

1373. DUNLAP THEATER
Picture house.
References: *Film Daily Yearbook*, 1931, 1932.

Langston

1374. COLORED NORMAL THEATER
Picture house.
References: *Film Daily Yearbook*, 1946–1948.

Lawton

1375. HARLEM THEATER
Picture house.
References: *Film Daily Yearbook*, 1945–1955.

McAlester

1376. EDWARDS THEATER
Picture house
References: *Film Daily Yearbook*, 1941.

1377. V THEATER
Picture house.
References: *Film Daily Yearbook*, 1949.

Muskogee

1378. DREAMLAND THEATER
203 S. 2nd Street
Vaudeville house. 423 seats. Owner and manager in 1921: Mrs. Lola T. Williams (African American).
References: Cahn, *Julius Cahn-Gus Hill Theatrical Guide*. Hill, *Pages from the Harlem Renaissance*. Jackson, "List of Colored Theaters and Attractions," *Billboard*, August 6, 1921. Peterson, *The African American Theatre Directory*. Sampson, *Blacks in Black and White*. Work, *Negro Yearbook 1921–1922*.

1379. GRAND THEATER
117 S. 2nd Street
Picture house. 423–569 seats.
References: *Film Daily Yearbook*, 1931–

1933, 1940–1955. *Motion Picture Herald*, April 24, 1937; July 15, 1939. Sampson, *Blacks in Black and White*.

1380. SILVER MOON AIR DOME THEATER
Vaudeville house.
References: Peterson, *The African American Theatre Directory*.

Nowata

1381. REX THEATER
200 N. Maple Street
Picture house. 675 seats.
References: *Film Daily Yearbook*, 1947–1955.

Oklahoma City

1382. ALDRIDGE THEATER
303–305 2nd Street NE
Vaudeville and picture house. 750–900 seats. Built in 1920. A TOBA theater. Managers in 1921: Breaux and Whitlow (African Americans). Manager in 1928: Zelia N. Breaux (African American). The management prided itself on presenting quality entertainment. In a *Chicago Defender* article, the managers were quoted as stating "upon the Aldridge's picture screen, nothing but the highest grade of motion picture features are utilized." In April, 1921, Fisher's Fun Festival played at the Aldridge. Count Basie and Gonzelle White's band performed here in the late 1920s. In the 1940s and 1950s, the Aldridge was a motion picture theater.
References: Basie, *Good Morning Blues*. *Chicago Defender*, "The Aldridge Theater," November 13, 1927. *Film Daily Yearbook*, 1931–1933, 1940–1955. Hill, *Pages from the Harlem Renaissance*. Jackson, "Foreword to the List of Colored Theaters and Attractions," *Billboard*, August 6, 1921; "The Theater Owners' Booking Association," *Billboard*, December 16, 1922. *Motion Picture Herald*, April 24, 1937; July 15, 1939. *Official Theatrical World of Colored Artists*. Sampson, *Blacks in Black and White*. Work, *Negro Yearbook 1921–1922*.

1383. EASTSIDE THEATER
Picture house.
References: *Film Daily Yearbook*, 1947, 1948,

1384. JEWEL THEATER
904 4th Street NE
Picture house. 325–405 seats.
References: *Film Daily Yearbook*, 1940–1955. *Motion Picture Herald*, July 15, 1939.

1385. TEMPLE THEATER
Picture house. Manager in 1921: J. J. Dawson.
References: Cahn, *Julius Cahn-Gus Hill Theatrical Guide*. Hill, *Pages from the Harlem Renaissance*. Jackson, "List of Colored Theaters and Attractions," *Billboard*, August 6, 1921. Work, *Negro Yearbook 1921–1922*.

Okmulgee

1386. DREAMLAND THEATER
Vaudeville house. Owner and Manager in 1921: Mrs. Lola. T. Williams (African American). In April 1921, the vaudeville show featured Fisher's Fun Festival. References: Jackson, "List of Colored Theaters and Attractions," *Billboard*, August 6 1921. Cahn, *Julius Cahn-Gus Hill Theatrical Guide*. Hill, *Pages from the Harlem Renaissance*. Work, *Negro Yearbook, 1921–1922*.

1387. DREW THEATER
417 E. 5th Street
Picture house. 312 seats.

Pawnee

1388. RITZ THEATER
Pawnee Street
Picture house. 300–400 seats.
References: *Film Daily Yearbook*, 1949–1955.

Sapulpa

1389. GEORGE R. THEATER
520 W. Johnston Street
Picture house. Manager in 1921: S. L. James.
References: Cahn, *Julius Cahn-Gus Hill Theatrical Guide*. Hill, *Pages from the Harlem Renaissance*. Jackson, "List of Colored Theaters and Attractions," *Billboard*, August 6, 1921. Work, *Negro Yearbook, 1921–1922*.

1390. RITZ THEATER
Picture house.
References: *Film Daily Yearbook*, 1949–1955.

Tulsa

1391. DIXIE THEATER
Picture house.
References: *Film Daily Yearbook*, 1931–1933, 1940. *Motion Picture Herald*, July 15, 1939.

1392. DREAMLAND THEATER
133 N. Greenwood Avenue
Vaudeville and picture house. 300 seats. A TOBA theater. Owner and manager in 1921: Mrs. Lola T. Williams (African American). Manager in 1928: W. M. Cherry. In April 1921, the vaudeville show at the Dreamland featured acts such as Ridley and Ridley, Lemone, Lemone and Grant, and the Jones and Burney Trio. Several months later on June 14, a race riot broke out in Tulsa and the Dreamland was burned down. It was rebuilt and reopened by the owner, Mrs. Lola Williams. In 1927, Count Basie played piano here for Gonzelle White and the Big Jazz Jamboree. The Dreamland continued as a black theater through the 1950s.
References: Brophy, *Reconstructing the Dreamland*. Cahn, *Julius Cahn-Gus Hill Theatrical Guide*. *Film Daily Yearbook*, 1931, 1932, 1940–1955. Hill, *Pages from the Harlem Renaissance*. Hirsch, *Riot and Remembrance*. Jackson, "List of Colored Theaters and Attractions," *Billboard*, August 6, 1921; "The Theater Owners' Booking Association," *Billboard*, December 16, 1922. Madigan, *The Burning*. *Motion Picture Herald*, April 24, 1937; July 15, 1939. *Official Theatrical World of Colored Artists*. Sampson, *Blacks in Black and White*. Work, *Negro Yearbook, 1921–1922*.

1393. PEORIA THEATER
Picture house.
References: *Film Daily Yearbook*, 1948–1955.

1394. REGAL THEATER
Picture house.
References: *Film Daily Yearbook*, 1946–1955.

1395. REX THEATER
Picture house. 400 seats.
References: *Film Daily Yearbook*, 1940–1955. *Motion Picture Herald*, April 24, 1937; July 15, 1939. Sampson, *Blacks in Black and White*.

Wewoka

1396. NORTHSIDE THEATER

Dreamland Theater, Tulsa, Oklahoma, after the 1921 Tulsa race riot (Tulsa Historical Society)

Picture house.
References: *Film Daily Yearbook*, 1949–1955.

1397. PALACE THEATER
Picture house.
References: *Film Daily Yearbook*, 1949–1955.

PENNSYLVANIA

Blair Station

1398. CHESTER THEATER
Picture house.
References: *Film Daily Yearbook*, 1944–1949.

1399. PARK THEATER
Picture house.
References: *Film Daily Yearbook*, 1940–1955. *Motion Picture Herald*, July 15, 1939.

Chester

1400. RIO THEATER
Picture house. 583 seats.
References: *Film Daily Yearbook*, 1940–1955. *Motion Picture Herald*, July 15, 1939.

1401. ROXY THEATER
Picture house.
References: *Film Daily Yearbook*, 1950–1955.

Harrisburg

1402. PRINCESS THEATER
1130 N. 6th Street
Picture house. Manager in 1921: Bernard Shiff.
References: Cahn, *Julius Cahn-Gus Hill Theatrical Guide*. Hill, *Pages from the Harlem Renaissance*. Jackson, "List of Colored Theaters and Attractions," *Billboard*, August 6, 1921.

1403–4. STAR THEATER
1205 N. 3rd Street
Picture house. Manager in 1921: Bernard Shiff. The theater was torn down in the 1970s to make way for a housing subdivision.
References: *Film Daily Yearbook*, 1955. Cahn, *Julius Cahn-Gus Hill Theatrical Guide*.

Philadelphia

APEX THEATER *see* Joy Theater

AUDITORIUM THEATER *see* North Pole Theater

1405. BOOKER T. THEATER
1030 Fairmount Avenue
Vaudeville and picture house. 500 seats. The Booker T. was built in 1921.
References: *Film Daily Yearbook*, 1943–1955. Glazer, *Philadelphia Theatres, A–Z*.

1406. CIRCLE THEATER
4662 Frankford Avenue
Vaudeville house. 2,991 seats. Architects: Hoffman and Henon. In 1911, the Circle was part of the S. H. Dudley vaudeville circuit. In 1916 it joined the Southern Consolidated vaudeville circuit.
References: Glazer, *Philadelphia Theatres, A–Z*. Peterson, *The African American Theatre Directory*.

1407. COLONIAL THEATER
1025 W. Moyamensing Avenue
Vaudeville and picture house. 954 seats. According to Glazer, it was in business from 1910 to 1989.
References: *Film Daily Yearbook*, 1943–1955. Glazer, *Philadelphia Theatres, A–Z*.

1408. COLUMBIA THEATER
1328 Columbia Avenue
Vaudeville and picture house. 884 seats. Manager: W. A. Downlevy. The Columbia was part of the S. H. Dudley vaudeville circuit. Masingdale and Crosby played there in 1914.
References: Peterson, *The African American Theatre Directory*.

1409. DENBOW'S COULTER THEATER
312 W. Coulter Avenue
Vaudeville and picture house. 300 sets. According to Glazer, Denbow's was in business from 1924 to 1934.
References: Glazer, *Philadelphia Theatres, A–Z*.

1410. DIXIE THEATER
1224 Point Breeze Avenue
Picture house. 500 seats. Built around 1912. In April 1945, the Dixie was showing *Jane Eyre, Texas Rangers Ride Again. Swa-*

Circle Theater, Philadelphia, Pennsylvania, 1929 (Glazer Collection, Athenaeum of Philadelphia)

nee River, and *As Thousands Cheer*. In March 1955, the film *Carmen Jones* was shown. In September 1955, features included *East of Eden*, starring Julie Harris and Raymond Massey, and *Smoke Signal*, starring Dana Andrews and Piper Laurie.

References: *Film Daily Yearbook*, 1941–1955. *Motion Picture Herald*, July 15, 1939. *Philadelphia Tribune*, July 16, 1955.

1411. DOUGLASS THEATER
4410 Fairmount Avenue
Picture house. 490 seats. Active from 1915 to 1947. In 1925 Hewitt Bundy became the first African American movie operator at the Douglass and the youngest person licensed as movie operator in Philadelphia.

References: *Chicago Defender*, "Race Movie Operator For Douglass Theater," November 21, 1925. *Film Daily Yearbook*, 1940–1947. Glazer, *Philadelphia Theatres, A–Z*. *Motion Picture Herald*, July 15, 1939.

DUNBAR THEATER *see* Lincoln Theater

1412. FANS THEATER
4032–4034 Market Street
Picture house. 1,809 seats.
References: *Film Daily Yearbook*, 1950–1955.

FOREPAUGH'S THEATER *see* Four Paws Theater

1413. FORREST THEATER
Girard Avenue at 9th Street
Picture house. 500 seats. Bessie Smith performed here in the 1930s. According

178 Pennsylvania

Columbia Theatre, Philadelphia, Pennsylvania (Glazer Collection, Athenaeum of Philadelphia)

to Glazer, the Forrest was converted into a supermarket in the late 1940s.

References: Albertson, *Bessie*. *Film Daily Yearbook*, 1933, 1940–1942, Glazer, *Philadelphia Theatres, A–Z*. *Motion Picture Herald*, July 15, 1939.

1414. FOUR PAWS THEATER
253–259 N. 8th Street

Picture house. 1,300 seats. Also called Forepaugh's Theater. The theater was built in 1877 and opened as the Bijou. According to Glazer, the Four Paws looked like a three-story Victorian factory building. The house had a stock company from 1892 to 1907. Actors such as John L. Sullivan performed here. Then it featured vaudeville shows from 1908 to 1913, when the management switched to motion pictures. According to Glazer, in the 1920s, "it was a policy of the theater to present Cecil B. DeMille's *King of Kings* every Good Friday, a custom which lasted thirteen years." In 1960 the theater was demolished.

References: *Film Daily Yearbook*, 1955. Glazer, *Philadelphia Theaters, A–Z*.

GAYETY THEATER *see* New Garden Theater

GIBSON'S BROAD STREET THEATER *see* Lincoln Theater

GIBSON'S THEATER *see* Standard Theater

1415. GLADSTONE THEATER
1136 S. 17th Street

Picture house. Manager in 1921: M.B. Browsky.

References: Cahn, *Julius Cahn-Gus Hill Theatrical Guide*. Work, *Negro Yearbook*,

1921–1922. Jackson, "List of Colored Theaters and Attractions," *Billboard,* August 6, 1921.

1416. GLOBE THEATER
5901 Market Street
Picture house. 720 seats. Architects: Hoffman and Henon. Built in 1910. Also known as the New Globe. In 1945, the Globe featured the films *That Night In Rio,* starring the Andrews Sisters, *Topper,* starring Cary Grant, *Snow White And The Seven Dwarfs,* and *Tales of Manhattan,* starring Ethel Waters, Rochester, and Edward G. Robinson.
References: *Film Daily Yearbook,* 1940–1947. *Motion Picture Herald,* July 15, 1939.

1417. HAVERFORD THEATER
Picture house. Architect: H.N. Housekeeper. It opened in 1912 as the Haverford, a two-story building with a yellow brick façade. Morris Gerson bought the Haverford in 1928 and reopened it as the Sixtieth Street Theater. It closed in 1931, reopening once more as the Haverford until its demise in 1957.
References: Glazer, *Philadelphia Theaters, A–Z. Film Daily Yearbook,* 1950–1955.

1418. JEWELL THEATER
Picture house.
References: *Film Daily Yearbook,* 1933.

1419. JOY THEATER
Haverford Avenue at 51st Street
Nickeldeon and picture house. 499 seats. Also called the Apex. The house, a yellow brick building, was originally a nickeldeon. It was renamed the Joy in the 1940s when it began to be known as a "black theater." The house was converted into a church in the 1950s.
References: *Film Daily Yearbook,* 1940–1955. Glazer, *Philadelphia Theatres, A–Z. Motion Picture Herald,* July 15, 1939.

1420. KEYSTONE THEATER
937 South Street
Picture house. 490 seats. Architect: Joseph Levin. Manager in 1921: M. B. Browsky. The Keystone was built in 1919.
References: Cahn, *Julius Cahn-Gus Hill Theatrical Guide. Film Daily Yearbook,* 1931–1933. Glazer, *Philadelphia Theatres, A–Z.* Jackson, "List of Colored Theaters and Attractions," *Billboard,* August 6, 1921. Work, *Negro Yearbook, 1921–1922.*

1421. LINCOLN THEATER
Lombard and Broad Streets
Vaudeville, picture and drama house. Also known as the Dunbar and Gibson's Broad Street. 1,400 seats. Active from 1919 to 1955. A TOBA theater. Black owned and managed. Manager in 1921: Grant Williams (African American). Originally built by African Americans Josia Diggs, Edward C. Brown, and Andrew Stevens Jr. When the theater was called the Dunbar, singer Bessie Smith appeared here with her revue, *How Come?* in 1923. In 1928 John T. Gibson bought the theater and afterwards it began to feature motion pictures. Some of the many presentations at the Dunbar included theatrical productions by the Lafayette Players, and the musical comedies *Shuffle Along, Liza* and *How Come?* The vaudeville act Butterbeans and Susie and Bessie Smith were featured performers in the revue *Hot Stuff of 1933.* As the Lincoln, the house featured motion pictures. The theater is no longer standing but a Pennsylvania state historical marker commemorates its site.
References: Albertson, *Bessie.* Cahn, *Julius Cahn-Gus Hill Theatrical Guide. Film Daily Yearbook,* 1931–1933. Glazer, *Philadelphia Theatres, A–Z.* Harrison, *Black Pearls.* Hill, *Pages from the Harlem Renaissance.* Jackson, "List of Colored Theaters and Attractions," *Billboard,* August 6, 1921. Peterson, *The African American Theatre Directory; African American Stage Performers.* Work, *Negro Yearbook, 1921–1922.*

Keystone Theater, Philadelphia, Pennsylvania (Glazer Collection, Athenaeum of Philadelphia)

NEW FORREST THEATER *see* Forrest Theater

1422. NEW GARDEN THEATER
237–245 N. 8th Street
Picture house. 700–800 seats. Architect: George Plowman. Also called the Star and the Gayety. According to Glazer,

Pennsylvania 181

Lincoln Theater, Philadelphia, Pennsylvania (Glazer Collection, Athenaeum of Philadelphia)

"Roman columns formed the entrance to this theatre. Knotted garland and floral decorations contrasted with simplicity of the under two floors of the façade. The interior had two balconies and minimal décor." The house opened in 1892 as the Star and in 1907 became the Gayety, featuring burlesque shows and boxing matches! "In 1930 the theatre was wired for sound and became the New Garden, a moving picture theater. The theater was torn down in 1953.

References: *Film Daily Yearbook*, 1941–1955. Glazer, *Philadelphia Theatres, A–Z*. *Motion Picture Herald*, July 15, 1939.

1423. NEW JEWEL THEATER
1826–1830 W. Norris Street
Picture house. 500 seats. Also called the Norris. According to Glazer, "originally a brick faced structure, the Norris was covered with an imitation stone when it was re-named in the 1930's." It opened as a movie theatre in 1912 and closed in 1947.

References: *Film Daily Yearbook*, 1950–1955. Glazer, *Philadelphia Theatres, A–Z*.

1424. NIXON GRAND THEATER
28 S. 52nd Street
Vaudeville and picture house. 1,870 seats. Architect: J. D. Allen. In the 1930s, Count Basie and Duke Ellington brought their orchestras here. A feud between Billie Holiday and Ethel Waters kept Holiday from appearing here with Duke Ellington and the Brown Sisters. According to Glazer, the Nixon Grand was active from about 1910 to 1984.

References: Basie, *Good Morning Blues*. *Film Daily Yearbook*, 1940–1942. Glazer, *Philadelphia Theatres, A–Z*. Hajdu, *Lush Life*. Holiday, *Lady Sings the Blues*. *Motion Picture Herald*, July 15, 1939.

182 Pennsylvania

Nixon Grand, also called the Nixon Theater, Philadelphia, Pennsylvania (Glazer Collection, Athenaeum of Philadelphia)

1425. NORTH POLE THEATER
1426 South Street
Vaudeville house. Built in 1909. Owner in 1919: John T. Gibson. Primarily a vaudeville house but silent films may have been shown there. In 1910, the Florence

Olympia Theater, Phildelphia, Pennsylvania (Glazer Collection, Athenaeum of Philadelphia)

Mills Sisters Trio and the Hill Sisters performed here.

References: Bradshaw, *Born with the Blues.* Glazer, *Philadelphia Theatres, A–Z.* Mapp, *Blacks in the Performing Arts* Peterson, *The African American Theatre Directory.* Peterson, *Profiles of African American Stage Performers.*

1426. OLYMPIA THEATER
711 S. Broad Street
Picture house. 500 seats. Active from 1912 to 1929. Manager in 1921: Mr. Swartzman.

References: Jackson, "List of Colored Theaters and Attractions," *Billboard,* August 6, 1921. Work, *Negro Yearbook, 1921–1922.*

1427. PEARL THEATER
2047 Ridge Avenue
Picture house. 1,400 seats. Architect: J. K. Long. The Pearl was in business from about 1927 to 1963. In 1929 Bessie Smith sang here. During the 1930s, the bands of Count Basie, Cab Calloway, Earl Hines, and Bennie Moten were crowd pleasers at the Pearl. In April 1945, the big draw at the Pearl was *Thirty Seconds over Tokyo,* starring Spencer Tracy and Van Johnson. In July 1945, the Pearl showed *That Night In Rio,* starring Alice Faye and Carmen Miranda; *I'll Be Seeing You,* starring Ginger Rogers and Joseph Cotten; *Murder My Sweet,* starring Dick Powell and Claire Trevor; and *Keys of the Kingdom,* starring Gregory Peck and Thomas Mitchell.

Pearl Theater, Philadelphia, Pennsylvania (Glazer Collection, Athenaeum of Philadelphia)

References: Albertson, *Bessie. Film Daily Yearbook,* 1931, 1932, 1940–1955. Calloway, *Of Minnie the Moocher and Me.* Dance, *The World of Earl Hines.* Glazer, *Philadelphia Theatres, A–Z. Philadelphia Tribune. Motion Picture Herald,* July 15, 1939.

1428. REX THEATER
2127 South Street
Picture house. 475 seats. Owner in 1921: D. Starkman.
References: *Film Daily Yearbook,* 1931–1933, 1940–1955. Jackson, "List of Colored Theaters and Attractions," *Billboard,* August 6, 1921. *Motion Picture Herald,* July 15, 1939. Work, *Negro Yearbook, 1921–1922.*

1429. ROYAL THEATER
1524 South Street
Picture house. 1,200 seats. Architect: Frank E. Hahn. Built in 1919. The exterior of the Royal was made of brick and stone done in Georgian style architecture. The central box office was decorated in Rococo style. In its early years, the Royal exhibited films such as *Little Annie Rooney*, with Mary Pickford, *The Eagle*, featuring Rudolf Valentino, and Cecil B. DeMille's *The Road to Yesterday*. It also showed early black films such as Oscar Micheaux's 1922 film *Son of Satan*, and the 1926 film *A Prince of His Race*, featuring the Colored Players Company of Philadelphia. The theater advertised itself as "America's Finest Photoplay House." Later on the Royal showed regular Hollywood movies. In April 1945, for instance, the Royal featured *Main Street after Dark*, with Edward Arnold, and *Ministry of Fear*, starring Majorie Reynolds and Ray Milland. The Royal is remembered for its stage shows with performers such as Bessie Smith, Pearl Bailey, Cab Calloway, and others who appeared in the "Black and Tan Revues." In the 1920s the Colored Motion Picture Operators Union was formed at the Royal, and it became one of the first major African American theaters to have an all black staff. In 1980 the Royal was placed on the National Register of Historic Places. Kenny Gamble of the famed rhythm and blues songwriting team of Gamble and Huff indicated an interest in restoring the Royal, but as of 2003 the theater had not been restored.
References: Cahn, *Julius Cahn-Gus Hill Theatrical Guide. Film Daily Yearbook,* 1931–1933, 1940–1955. Jackson, "List of Colored Theaters and Attractions," *Billboard,* August 6, 1921. *Philadelphia Tribune,* April 7, 1945. *Motion Picture Herald,* July 15, 1939. Simms, *Simms' Blue Book. Philadelphia Tribune,* Wilson, Kendall, "Royal Theater Gets Federal Boost," September 19, 2000: Section A 1, 4.

1430. RUBY THEATER
Fairmount Avenue at Franklin Street
Picture house. 560 seats. Also called the Fairmount. Manager in 1922: Mr. Wack.
References: *Film Daily Yearbook,* 1950–1955. Glazer, *Philadelphia Theatres, A–Z.* Work, *Negro Yearbook, 1921–1922.*

1431. STANDARD THEATER
1124 South Street
Vaudeville, musical and picture house. 1,500 seats. Also known as Gibson's Theater. Architect: J. J. Hitchler. Built in 1899. Demolished in 19?? A TOBA theater. Owner and manager in 1921: John T. Gibson (African American). Although not a performer at the Standard, in 1921 Josephine Baker auditioned for the show *Shuffle Along* at this house. Actual performers at the Standard included Bessie Smith, Butterbeans and Susie, the Whitman Sisters, Buck and Bubbles, Mamie Smith, the Gonzzelle White band, the Nicholas Brothers, and Ethel Waters. The

New Standard Theatre

South St. above Eleventh,

ER ....Lessee and Manager
'RONG ....Business Manager

THOMAS ASHTON, Treasurer.

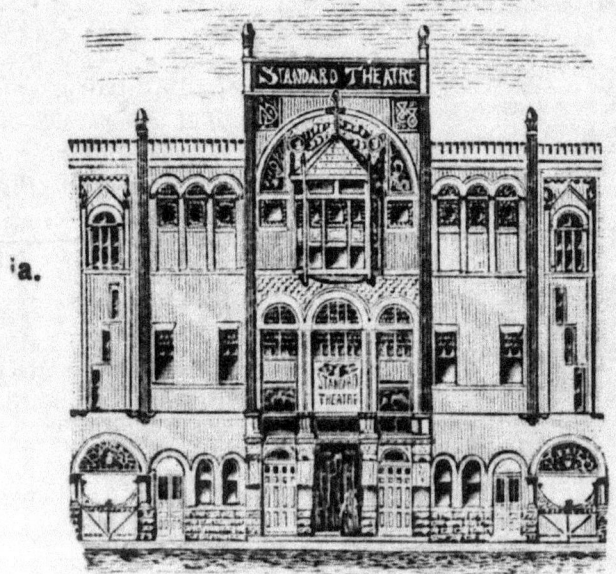

Presenting
Weekly the Best
and Strongest
Attractions
At Popular
Prices.

s, Thursdays, Saturdays,

es of Admission, 15, 25, 50, 75 and $1 00.

ESERVED SEATS, 50 Cents.

nd Sterling Attractions Will Always
be Our Motto.

Mr. Graydon, in his "Memoirs," speaks with praise
of the various members of this company, especially

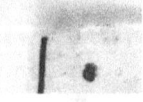

Standard Theater, also known as the New Standard, Philadelphia, Pennsylvania (Glazer Collection, Athenaeum of Philadelphia)

vaudeville bill for the week of May 16, 1921 included the singing acrobatic dancers Lula Coates and Crackjacks, Mabel Whitman and her Dixie Boys, comedians Dudley and Dudley, blues singer Bessie Smith, and the Bob Russell Company. In June 1923, the vaudeville show consisted of the Six Little Darlings, the singing and dancing team of Gold and Goldie, comedian Sandy Burns, comics Brown and Bell, the singing Wallace Trio, and the aerial acrobat act The Weldoras. In February 1924, the vaudeville show included the singing and dancing team of Cornell and Ward, the acrobat act the DeHaven Trio, comedians Jines and Jacqueline, the dance act of the Tasmania Trio, comics Pugh and Barker, singer Edmonia Henderson, and the Sandy Burns theater company. The Duke Ellington band played here in 1927. In 1929 Louis Armstrong and Bessie Smith's revue *Steamboat Days* as a big draw. In the 1930s, Count Basie, Gonzelle White, and the comedians Sandy Burns and Ashes were featured performers. During its motion picture theater heyday in July 1945, the Standard was showing the film *Murder My Sweet*, starring Dick Powell and Claire Trevor.

References: Albertson, *Bessie*. Baker, *Josephine*. Basie, *Good Morning Blues*. Bradshaw, *Born with the Blues*. Cahn, *Julius Cahn-Gus Hill Theatrical Guide*. *Chicago Defender*, "The Standard," June 9, 1923; Henry Gang Jines, "Standard Theater," February 16, 1924. Collier, *Duke Ellington*. Collier, *Louis Armstrong*. *Film Daily Yearbook*, 1931, 1932, 1940–1955. Glazer, *Philadelphia Theatres, A–Z*. Harrison, *Black Pearls*. Hill, *Pages from the Harlem Renaissance*. Jackson, "List of Colored Theaters and Attractions," *Billboard*, August 6, 1921. *Motion Picture Herald*, July 15, 1939. Peterson, *The African American Theatre Directory*; *Profiles of African American Stage Performers*. Simms, *Simms' Blue Book*. Waters, *His Eye Is On the Sparrow*. Work, *Negro Yearbook, 1921–1922*.

STAR THEATER *see* New Garden Theater

1432. STRAND THEATER
1202 Girard Avenue
Picture house. 450 seats. Architects: Stucket and Sloan. Manager in 1921: H. Swartz. Originally the home of the Germantown YMCA, the Strand was a movie theater from 1918 until 1958, when it became a church.

References:. Cahn, *Julius Cahn-Gus Hill Theatrical Guide*. *Film Daily Yearbook, 1940–1955*. Glazer, *Philadelphia Theatres, A–Z*. Jackson, "List of Colored Theaters and Attractions," *Billboard*, August 6, 1921. *Motion Picture Herald*, July 15, 1939. Work, *Negro Yearbook, 1921–1922*.

1433. UPTOWN THEATER
2240 N. Broad Street
Picture and musical house. 2,146 seats. Architects: Magaziner, Eberhard and Harris. Built circa 1929.

References: *Architecture,* "Uptown Theater, Philadelphia, Pa." Glazer, *Philadelphia Theatres, A–Z*.

1434. VOGUE THEATER
1905 W. Columbia Avenue
Picture house. 499 seats.
References: *Film Daily Yearbook*, 1950–1955. Glazer, *Philadelphia Theatres, A–Z*.

1435. YORK STREET PALACE THEATER
26th and York Streets.
Nickeldeon and picture house. 499 seats. Also known as the York Palace. Architects: Hoffman and Henon. According to Glazer, "the York started as a large nickelodeon operation in 1912. Hoffman and Henon transformed the bare premises

Uptown Theater, Philadelphia, Pennsylvania (Glazer Collection, Athenaeum of Philadelphia)

into a standard type theatre in 1927, creating a lobby and a proscenium stage effect. Moving pictures on a single and double basis were shown here until 1949."

References: *Film Daily Yearbook*, 1950. Glazer, *Philadelphia Theatres, A–Z*.

Pittsburgh

1436. AVENUE THEATER
809 Liberty Avenue
Picture house. 300–500 seats
References: *Film Daily Yearbook*, 1950–1955.

1437. BURKE THEATER
Picture house.
References: *Film Daily Yearbook*, 1933.

1438. CENTRE SQUARE THEATER
1712 Centre Avenue
Picture house.
References: *Historic Sites Survey of Allegheny County*. Work, *Negro Yearbook, 1921–1922*.

1439. CHESTER THEATER
Picture house.
References: *Film Daily Yearbook*, 1943–1947.

1440. ELMORE THEATER
2312 Centre Street
Vaudeville and picture house. 1,000 seats. A TOBA theater. Manager in 1928: Ben Engleberg. In March 1924, Virginia Liston and Sam H. Gray's company played here.
References: *Chicago Defender*, "Elmore Theater," March 22, 1924. *Film Daily Yearbook*, 1931, 1932. *Official Theatrical World of Colored Artists*.

GOLDEN THEATER *see* Rhumba Theater

1441. LINCOLN THEATER
2424 Wylie Avenue
Picture house. Owner in 1922: Louis Moogeman. According to *Billboard*, "On November 25 [1922] Louis Moogeman opened the Lincoln Theater. R. Patton, a colored contractor was responsible for the structural work."
References: *Billboard*, "Two New Theaters," December 16, 1922.

1442. NEW GRANADA THEATER
20019 Centre Avenue
Picture and musical house. Also known as the Pythian Theater. 850 seats. Built circa 1929. In April, 1935, Louis Deppe and the Moonlight Harbor Orchestra played here.
References: *Film Daily Yearbook*, 1940–1955. *Historic Sites Survey of Allegheny County*. *Motion Picture Herald*, July 15, 1939. *Pittsburgh Courier*, April 8, 1935.

1443. NEW HERRON THEATER
623 Herron Street
Picture house. 239–300 seats. Also known as the Pastime Theater.
References: *Film Daily Yearbook*, 1950–1955.

1444. PARK THEATER
551 Greenfield Avenue
Picture house.
References: *Film Daily Yearbook*, 1940. *Motion Picture Herald*, July 15, 1939.

PASTIME THEATER *see* New Herron Theater

1445. PERSHING THEATER
228 Collins Avenue
Drama and musical house. Owner: Quality Amusement Corp. Manager in 1921: Mr. Swartzman.
References: Cahn, *Julius Cahn-Gus Hill Theatrical Guide*. Hill, *Pages from the Harlem Renaissance*. Jackson, "List of Colored Theaters and Attractions," *Billboard*, August 6, 1921. Peterson, *The African American Theatre Directory*. Work, *Negro Yearbook, 1921–1922*.

New Granada Theater, Pittsburgh, Pennsylvania (Pittsburgh City Photographer Collection, Archives Service Center, University of Pittsburgh)

PYTHIAN THEATER *see* New Granada Theater

1446. RHUMBA THEATER
53 Fullerton Avenue
Picture house. 300 seats. Also known as the Golden. In April 1935 the theater featured Richard Cortex in *White Cockatoo*, John Wayne in *Trail Beyond*, Buck Jones in *Treason*, and Ginger Rogers in *Romance in Manhattan*.
References: *Film Daily Yearbook*, 1940–1955. *Motion Picture Herald*, July 15, 1939. *Pittsburgh Courier*, April 8, 1935.

1447. ROOSEVELT THEATER
1862–68 Centre Avenue
Vaudeville, musical and picture house. 1,300 seats. Bessie Smith sang here in 1933. In April 1935, the Roosevelt featured the films *Society Doctor*, starring Chester Morris and Virginia Bruce, *Roberta*, with Fred Astaire, Ginger Rogers, and Irene Dunn, and *Santa Fe*, with Ken Maynard. In 1936, Billy Strayhorn's musical *Fantastic Rhythm* played here.
References: Albertson, *Bessie. Film Daily Yearbook*, 1933, 1941–1955. Hajda,

Roosevelt Theater, Pittsburgh, Pennsylvania (Pittsburgh City Photographer Collection, Archives Service Center, University of Pittsburgh)

Lush Life. Historic Sites Survey of Allegheny County. Pittsburgh Courier, April 8, 1935.

1448. ROXY THEATER
Picture house.
References: *Film Daily Yearbook*, 1943–1950.

1449. STAR THEATER
1417 Wylie Avenue
Vaudeville and picture house. Manager in 1914: Abe Minsky. Owner in 1921: Harry Tennebaum. Manager in 1921: Charles P. Stinson (African American). The Star featured vaudeville shows as part of the Dudley Circuit in the early 1910s and the Southern Consolidated Circuit from 1916 to 1921 and later as part of the TOBA in the 1920s. In 1914, Taylor Duo, Criswell and Bailey, and Susie Cook performed at the Star. In May, 1923, comedians Leroy Knox and Williams and Brown appeared here with blues singer Sarah Martin. In February 1924 the Star presented yodeler John Churchill, comedians Jines and Jacqueline, and blues singer Monette Moore. In March 1924, Bessie Smith sang here. Later on, musicians Laura Badge and Earl Hines performed at the Star.

References: Albertson, *Bessie*. Cahn, *Julius Cahn-Gus Hill Theatrical Directory*. *Chicago Defender*, May 12, 1923; February 9, 1924. Dance, *The World of Earl Hines*. Hill, *Pages from the Harlem Renaissance*. Jackson, "List of Colored Theaters and Attractions," *Billboard*, August 6, 1921; "The Theater Owners' Booking Association," *Billboard*, December 16, 1922. Jines, Henry Gang, "Star Theater," *Indianapolis Freeman*, January 31, 1914. Work, *Negro Yearbook, 1921–1922*.

1450. TRIANGLE THEATER
6276 Franksford Avenue
Picture house. 800–900 seats. Manager in 1921: David Adler. In April, 1935, the Triangle offered both films and stage shows. Motion pictures included *The Case of the Howling Dog*, with Warren William and Mary Astor, *What Every Woman Knows*, with Helen Hayes, *Have A Heart*, featuring James Dunn and Jean Parker, *The Lost Lady*, starring Barbara Stanwyck, and *Against the Law*, with John Mack Brown. Tuesday night was "Harlem Night," and Wednesday and Thursday evenings were amateur show nights. References: *Film Daily Yearbook*, 1940–1955. *Motion Picture Herald*, July 15, 1939. *Pittsburgh Courier*, April 8, 1935.

Rankin

1451. RANKIN THEATER
Picture house.
References: *Film Daily Yearbook*, 1950–1955.

1452. RITZ THEATER
Picture house.
References: *Film Daily Yearbook*, 1950–1955.

Steelton

1453. PALACE THEATER
190 N. Front Street
Picture house. Manager in 1921: C. I. Donley (African American).
References: Cahn, *Julius Cahn-Gus Hill Theatrical Guide*. Jackson, "List of Colored Theaters and Attractions," *Billboard*, August 6, 1921. Work, *Negro Yearbook*, 1921–1922.

Wewoka

1454. PITTMAN THEATER
Picture house.
References: *Film Daily Yearbook*, 1940–1942.

SOUTH CAROLINA

Aiken

1455. NEW COLORED THEATER
Picture house.
References: *Film Daily Yearbook*, 1940–1948. *Motion Picture Herald*, July 15, 1939.

Allendale

1456. TENT SHOW THEATER
Picture house.
References: *Film Daily Yearbook*, 1950–1955.

Anderson

1457. GRAND THEATER
Vaudeville house. A TOBA theater. Manager in 1921: R. Sloan Driscoll. In April, 1921, the vaudeville bill featured the Mills and Frisby Company.
References: Cahn, *Julius Cahn-Gus Hill Theatrical Guide*. Jackson, "List of Colored Theaters and Attractions," *Billboard*, August 6, 1921. Work, *Negro Yearbook, 1921–1922*.

1458. JORDAN THEATER
Picture house.
References: *Film Daily Yearbook*, 1949–1955.

Barnwell

1459. BARNWELL THEATER
Picture house. According to *Film Daily Yearbook*, the Barnwell was closed from 1949 through 1951.
References: *Film Daily Yearbook*, 1949–1955.

Bennettsville

1460. COLORED THEATER
Picture house.
References: Jackson, "List of Colored Theaters and Attractions," *Billboard*, August 6, 1921. *Motion Picture Herald*, April 24, 1937.

1461. HILL DRIVE-IN
Picture house. Owner: Dr. William H. Henderson.
References: *Film Daily Yearbook*, 1952–1955.

1462. LINCOLN THEATER
Picture house.
References: *Film Daily Yearbook*, 1931, 1932.

1463. PALACE THEATER
Picture house. 200 seats.
References: *Film Daily Yearbook*, 1940–1955. *Motion Picture Herald*, July 15, 1939. Sampson, *Blacks in Black and White*.

Bishopville

1464. SCHOOL THEATER
Picture house.
References: *Film Daily Yearbook*, 1931, 1932.

Bowman

1465. PEOPLE'S THEATER
Picture house.
References: *Film Daily Yearbook*, 1952–1955.

Camden

1466. COLORED THEATER
Picture house. Said to be black owned and managed.
References: Cahn, *Julius Cahn-Gus Hill Theatrical Guide*. Jackson, "List of Colored Theaters and Attractions," *Billboard*, August 6, 1921. Work, *Negro Yearbook, 1921–1922*.

1467. LINCOLN THEATER
Picture house.
References: *Film Daily Yearbook*, 1931, 1932.

Charleston

1468. COLUMBIA THEATER
Vaudeville and picture house. Manager in 1921: J.C. V. Cannon.
References: Cahn, *Julius Cahn-Gus Hill Theatrical Guide*. Jackson, "List of Colored Theaters and Attractions," *Billboard*, August 6, 1921.

1469. LINCOLN THEATER
601 King Street
Vaudeville house. 440–450 seats. A TOBA theater. Owner and manager in 1921: P. McClone (African American).
References: Cahn, *Julius Cahn-Gus Hill Theatrical Guide*. *Film Daily Yearbook*, 1931–1933, 1940–1955. Hill, *Pages from the Harlem Renaissance*. Jackson, "List of Colored Theaters and Attractions," *Billboard*, August 6, 1921; "The Theater Owners' Booking Association," December 16, 1922. *Motion Picture Herald*, April 24, 1937; July 15, 1939. Sampson, *Blacks in Black and White*. Work, *Negro Yearbook, 1921–1922*.

1470. MIDWAY THEATER
Picture house.
References: *Film Daily Yearbook*, 1952–1955.

1471. MILO THEATER
Vaudeville house. A TOBA theater. Owner and Manager in 1921: J. J. Miller (African American).
References: Cahn, *Julius Cahn-Gus Hill Theatrical Guide*. Jackson, "List of Colored Theaters and Attractions," *Billboard*, August 6, 1921. Peterson, *The African American Theatre Directory*. Work, *Negro Yearbook, 1921–1922*.

1472. OLYMPIC THEATER
Vaudeville house. Owner: Alex I. Easter. According to Peterson, the Olympic was in business during the 1910s.
References: Peterson, *The African American Theatre Directory*.

1473. PASTIME THEATER
Picture house.
References: *Film Daily Yearbook*, 1931, 1932.

Chester

1474. BROOKLYN THEATER
Picture house.
References: *Film Daily Yearbook*, 1950–1955.

Columbia

1475. CAPITOL THEATER
Picture house.
References: *Film Daily Yearbook*, 1931–1933, 1940–1955. *Motion Picture Herald*, July 15, 1939.

1476. CARVER THEATER
1519 Harden Street
Picture house. 543 seats.
References: *Film Daily Yearbook*, 1944–1955.

1477. LINCOLN THEATER
Vaudeville and picture house. 250–468 seats. Manager in 1921: W. H. Tolbutt. The Oscar Micheaux film *Within Our Gates* was shown here January 30, 31, 1920.
References: Bowser, *Writing Himself into History*. Cahn, *Julius Cahn-Gus Hill Theatrical Guide*. *Film Daily Yearbook*, 1931, 1932. *Chicago Defender*, "Milton Starr Buys Another Race Theater," January 11, 1930. Jackson, "List of Colored Theaters and Attractions," *Billboard*, August 6, 1921. Work, *Negro Yearbook, 1921–1922*.

NEW ROYAL THEATER *see* Royal Theater

1478. ROYAL THEATER

1012 Washington Street
Picture and vaudeville house. Also called the New Royal. 300 seats. A TOBA theater. Manager in 1921: L. T. Lester. Manager in 1928: Earl Pinkerson.
References: Cahn, *Julius Cahn-Gus Hill Theatrical Guide. Film Daily Yearbook,* 1931, 1932, 1940–1943. Hill, *Pages from the Harlem Renaissance.* Jackson, "List of Colored Theaters and Attractions," *Billboard,* August 6, 1921; "The Theater Owners' Booking Association," *Billboard,* December 16, 1922. *Motion Picture Herald,* April 24, 1937. *Official Theatrical World of Colored Artists.* Peterson, *The African American Theatre Directory.* Sampson, *Blacks in Black and White.* Simms, *Simms' Blue Book.* Work, *Negro Yearbook, 1921–1922.*

Conway

1479. HILLSIDE THEATER
Picture house.
References: *Film Daily Yearbook,* 1950–1955.

Denmark

1480. JOY THEATER
Picture house.
References: *Film Daily Yearbook,* 1950–1955.

Dillon

1481. PRINCESS ANN THEATER
Picture house.
References: *Film Daily Yearbook,* 1949–1955.

Florence

1482. ELITE THEATER
Vaudeville house. According to Peterson, this theater was in business from the 1910s through the 1920s.
References: Peterson, *The African American Theatre Directory.*

1483. LINCOLN THEATER
218 N. Dargon Street
Picture house. 300 seats.
References: *Film Daily Yearbook,* 1940–1955. *Motion Picture Herald,* July 15, 1939.

1484. PRINCESS THEATER
Vaudeville house. Manager in 1921: G. Brown (African American).
References: Cahn, *Julius Cahn-Gus Hill Theatrical Guide.* Jackson, "List of Colored Theaters and Attractions," *Billboard,* August 6, 1921. Work, *Negro Yearbook, 1921–1922.*

Greeleyville

1485. CARO TENT THEATER
Picture house.
References: *Film Daily Yearbook,* 1949–1955.

Greenville

1486. HARLEM THEATER
Picture house.
References: *Film Daily Yearbook,* 1955.

1487. LIBERTY THEATER
14 Spring Street
Vaudeville and picture house. 200–622 seats. Managers in 1921: Wilson and Kurtz. The Oscar Micheaux film *Within Our Gates* played here on March 12, 1920.
References: Bowser, *Writing Himself into History.* Cahn, *Julius Cahn-Gus Hill Theatrical Guide. Film Daily Yearbook,* 1933, 1940–1955. Jackson, "List of Colored Theaters and Attractions," *Billboard,*

August 6, 1921. *Motion Picture Herald*, April 24, 1937; July 15, 1939. Sampson, *Blacks in Black and White*.

Greenwood

1488. BIJOU THEATER
Picture house. Manger in 1921: Mr. Adams.
References: Cahn, *Julius Cahn-Gus Hill Theatrical Guide*. Jackson, "List of Colored Theaters and Attractions," *Billboard*, August 6, 1921.

1489. BREVARD THEATER
Picture house.
References: *Film Daily Yearbook*, 1931, 1932.

1490. DIXIE THEATER
Picture house. The Oscar Micheaux film *Within Our Gates* was shown at the Dixie January 29, 1920.
References: Bowser, *Writing Himself into History*.

Greer

1491. SUNNYSIDE THEATER
Picture house. According to *Film Daily Yearbook*, the Sunnyside was closed in 1950 and 1951.
References: *Film Daily Yearbook*, 1950–1955.

Laurens

1492. HARLEM THEATER
Picture house. According to *Film Daily Yearbook*, the Harlem was closed in 1950 and 1951.
References: *Film Daily Yearbook*, 1949–1955.

1493. LIBERTY THEATER
Picture house.
References: *Film Daily Yearbook*, 1931, 1932.

Marion

1494. LIBERTY THEATER
Picture house.
References: *Film Daily Yearbook*, 1949–1955.

Olar

1495. CAROLINA THEATER
Picture house. This was a portable tent theater.
References: *Film Daily Yearbook*, 1950–1955.

Orangeburg

1496. PALMETTO THEATER
Picture house. Manager in 1921: Mr. Brown. The Oscar Micheaux motion picture *Within Our Gates* was shown February 3, 1920.
References: Bowser, *Writing Himself into History*. Cahn, *Julius Cahn-Gus Hill Theatrical Guide*. Jackson, "List of Colored Theaters and Attractions," *Billboard*, August 6, 1921. Work, *Negro Yearbook, 1921–1922*.

1497. STATE THEATER
Picture house.
References: *Film Daily Yearbook*, 1949–1955.

Page Land

1498. CARVER THEATER
Picture house.
References: *Film Daily Yearbook*, 1949.

Rock Hill

1499. BROADWAY THEATER
Picture house. Owner and manager in 1921: W. S. Alston (African American).
References: Jackson, "List of Colored Theaters and Attractions," *Billboard*, August 6, 1921. Work, *Negro Yearbook, 1921–1922*.

1500. CARVER THEATER
Picture house.
References: *Film Daily Yearbook*, 1949–1955.

Saint George

1501. CHRISTI THEATER
Picture house. According to *Film Daily Yearbook*, the Christi was closed from 1949 through 1951.
References: *Film Daily Yearbook*, 1949–1955.

Spartanburg

1502. DIXIE THEATER
Vaudeville house. Owner in 1922: Mrs. M. Roth.
References: Jackson, "The Theater Owners' Booking Association," *Billboard*, December 16, 1922.

1503. DUNBAR THEATER
Picture house.
References: *Film Daily Yearbook*, 1931, 1932.

1504. LIBERTY THEATER
Picture house.
References: *Film Daily Yearbook*, 1949–1955.

1505. RITZ THEATER
226 Trimmier Street
Picture house. 576 seats.
References: *Film Daily Yearbook*, 1946–1955.

1506. STAR THEATER
Vaudeville and picture house. Said to be black owned and managed.
References: Cahn, *Julius Cahn-Gus Hill Theatrical Guide*. Jackson, "Additions to Theater List," *Billboard*, December 31, 1921.

1507. UNION THEATER
Picture house. 300 seats.
References: *Film Daily Yearbook*, 1940–1945. *Motion Picture Herald*, July 15, 1939.

Summerville

1508. SALISBURY THEATER
Picture house. 300 seats.
References: *Film Daily Yearbook*, 1949–1955.

Sumter

1509. COLORED THEATER
Vaudeville and picture house. Said to be black owned and managed.
References: Cahn, *Julius Cahn-Gus Hill Theatrical Guide*. Jackson, "List of Colored Theaters and Attractions," *Billboard*, August 6, 1921.

1510. GARDEN THEATER
Picture house.
References: *Film Daily Yearbook*, 1931, 1932.

1511. LYRIC THEATER
Picture house. 300 seats.
References: *Film Daily Yearbook*, 1940–1955. *Motion Picture Herald*, July 15 1939.

Walterboro

1512. GLOBE THEATER

Picture house.
References: *Film Daily Yearbook*, 1950–1955.

Ware Shoals

1513. Y.M.C.A.
Picture house.
References: *Film Daily Yearbook*, 1931, 1932.

TENNESSEE

Bolivar

1514. GRAND THEATER
Picture house. According to *Film Daily Yearbook*, the Grand was closed from 1949 through 1951.
References: *Film Daily Yearbook*, 1949–1955.

Brownsville

1515. GEM THEATER
Picture house.
References: *Film Daily Yearbook*, 1947–1955.

1516. NEW THEATER
Picture house.
References: *Film Daily Yearbook*, 1940.

Chattanooga

1517. AMUSU THEATER
106 W. Main Street
Vaudeville and picture house. 450–500 seats.
References: *Film Daily Yearbook*, 1931–1933, 1940–1955. Hill, *Pages from the Harlem Renaissance. Motion Picture Herald*, April 24, 1937; July 15, 1939. Sampson, *Blacks in Black and White*. Work, *Negro Yearbook, 1921–1922*.

1518. GRAND THEATER
201 E. 9th Street
Vaudeville and picture house. 1,000 seats. Managers in 1921: M. H. Silverman and R. Sloan Driscoll.
References: Cahn, *Julius Cahn-Gus Hill Theatrical Guide. Film Daily Yearbook*, 1931–1933. Jackson, "List of Colored Theaters and Attractions," *Billboard*, August 6, 1921. Work, *Negro Yearbook, 1921–1922*.

1519. HARLEM THEATER
220 W. 9th Street
Picture house.
References: *Film Daily Yearbook*, 1941–1955.

1520. LIBERTY THEATER
310 E. 9th Street
Vaudeville house. 500 seats. A TOBA theater. Manager in 1928: Sam E. Reevin. In April, 1921, performers at the Liberty

included the Hambone Jones Company, featuring S.H. Gray and Virginia Liston, the McGarr-DeGaston Company, Jack Ginger Wiggins — the champion six-minute dancer — and the All-Star Review Company. In March 1924, the vaudeville show consisted of blackface comics Rastus and Jones, Jines and Jacqueline, singer John Brighty, and DeLeach and Corbin — singers and dancers. Bessie Smith sang here in 1925. In 1926, Marie and Clint, Charles Anderson, Dudley and Byrd, and Snow and Snow appeared here.

References: Albertson, *Bessie*. *Baltimore Afro-American*, October 31, 1926. *Film Daily Yearbook*, 1945–1955. Hill, *Pages from the Harlem Renaissance*. Jackson, "List of Colored Theaters and Attractions," *Billboard*, August 6, 1921; "The Theater Owners' Booking Association," *Billboard*, December 16, 1922. *Official Theatrical World of Colored Artists*. *Chicago Defender*, Jines, Gang, "Liberty Theater," March 22, 1924. Sampson, *Blacks in Blackface*. Work, *Negro Yearbook, 1921–1922*.

1521. LINCOLN THEATER
Picture house.
References: *Film Daily Yearbook*, 1931, 1932.

1522. NEW GRAND THEATER
Picture house.
References: *Film Daily Yearbook*, 1940–1955. *Motion Picture Herald*, April 24, 1937; July 15, 1939. Sampson, *Blacks in Black and White*.

1523. NEW THEATER
Picture house.
References: *Film Daily Yearbook*, 1943, 1944.

1524. STAR THEATER
133 E. Main Street
Picture house. 250 seats. Independent Theatres, Inc. operated this theater. References: Hill, *Pages from the Harlem Renaissance*. Work, *Negro Yearbook, 1921–1922*.

Columbia

1525. GEM THEATER
Picture house.
References: *Film Daily Yearbook*, 1947–1955.

Dyersburg

1526. SAVOY THEATER
Picture house. According to *Film Daily Yearbook*, the Savoy was closed from 1949 through 1951.
References: *Film Daily Yearbook*, 1947–1955.

Franklin

1527. GEM THEATER
Picture house.
References: *Film Daily Yearbook*, 1947–1955.

Halls

1528. HALLS THEATER
Picture house.
References: *Film Daily Yearbook*, 1949.

Jackson

1529. BARRETT'S THEATORIUM
Vaudeville house. Owner: Richard D. Barrett.
References: Peterson, *The African American Theatre Directory*.

1530. GEM THEATER
Vaudeville and picture house. A TOBA

theater. Manager in 1928: E. L. Drake.
References: *Film Daily Yearbook,* 1947–1955. *Official Theatrical World of Colored Artists.*

1531. PALACE THEATER
Picture house. 600 seats. Manager in 1927: M. F. Davis.
References: *Chicago Defender,* "New Theater Opens, November 15, 1927. *Film Daily Yearbook,* 1931, 1932.

Knoxville

1532. BOOKER T. THEATER
Picture house.
References: *Film Daily Yearbook,* 1952–1955.

1533. DIXIE THEATER
Picture house. Manager in 1921: Charles Roth.
References: Cahn, *Julius Cahn-Gus Hill Theatrical Guide.* Jackson, "List of Colored Theaters and Attractions," *Billboard,* August 6, 1921. Work, *Negro Yearbook, 1921–1922.*

1534. GEM THEATER
102 E. Vine Avenue
Vaudeville and picture house. 795 seats. A TOBA theater. Manager in 1921: M.C. Kennedy.
References: *Film Daily Yearbook,* 1931–1933, 1940–1955. Jackson, "List of Colored Theaters and Attractions, *Billboard,* August 6, 1921. *Motion Picture Herald,* April 24, 1937; July 15, 1939. *Official Theatrical World of Colored Artists.* Sampson, *Blacks in Black and White.* Work, *Negro Yearbook, 1921–1922.*

1535. GRAND THEATER
Picture house.
References: *Film Daily Yearbook,* 1947–1955.

1536. RITZ THEATER
Picture house. According to *Film Daily Yearbook,* the Ritz was closed from 1949 through 1951.
References: *Film Daily Yearbook,* 1947–1952.

Lewisburg

1537. SOUTHERN AIRE DRIVE-IN
Picture house. 300 cars.
References: *Film Daily Yearbook,* 1953–1955.

Martin

1538. CAPITOL THEATER
Picture house.
References: *Film Daily Yearbook,* 1949.

Memphis

1539. ACE THEATER
997 Mississippi Avenue
Picture house. 250–700 seats.
References: *Film Daily Yearbook,* 1940–1955. *Motion Picture Herald,* April 24, 1937; July 15, 1939. Sampson, *Blacks in Black and White.*

1540. CHURCH'S PARK THEATER
329–331 Beal Avenue
Vaudeville house. Also called the Auditorium. Owner: Robert E. Church. Lew Henry organized a resident stock theater company here in 1901. In 1915, the Park's program had Jones and Jones, comedians, Anna Holt, singer, and Doe Doe Green, comedian.
References: *Indianapolis Freeman,* "At Church's Park Theater," January 9, 1915. Peterson, *The African American Theatre Directory.* Simms, *Simms' Blue Book.*

1541. DAISY THEATER
329–331 Beal Avenue

Picture house. 600 seats. Manager in 1921: Joe Macire.
References: Cahn, *Julius Cahn-Gus Hill Theatrical Guide*. *Film Daily Yearbook*, 1931–1933, 1940–1955. Jackson, "List of Colored Theaters and Attractions," *Billboard*, August 6, 1921. *Motion Picture Herald*, April 24, 1937; July 15, 1939. Simms, *Simms' Blue Book*. Sampson, *Blacks in Black and White*. Work, *Negro Yearbook, 1921–1922*.

1542. ESQUIRE THEATER
Picture house.
References: *Film Daily Yearbook*, 1947–1955.

1543. GEM THEATER
Vaudeville house. According to Peterson, this theater was in business during the early 1900s.
References: Peterson, *The African American Theatre Directory*.

1544. GEORGIA THEATER
663 Mississippi Avenue
Picture house. 600 seats
References: *Film Daily Yearbook*, 1941–1955.

1545. GRAND THEATER
32 Beal Avenue
Picture house. 700 seats. Manager in 1921: Samuel Zarilla.
References: Cahn, *Julius Cahn-Gus Hill Theatrical Guide*. *Film Daily Yearbook*, 1931–1933, 1940–1948. Jackson, "List of Colored Theaters and Attractions," *Billboard*, August 6, 1921. *Motion Picture Herald*, April 24, 1937; July 15, 1939. Sampson, *Blacks in Black and White*. Work, *Negro Yearbook, 1921–1922*.

1546. HARLEM THEATER
1248 Florida Avenue
Picture house.
References: *Film Daily Yearbook*, 1940–1955. *Motion Picture Herald*, April 24, 1937; July 15, 1939. Sampson, *Blacks in Black and White*.

1547. HYDE PARK THEATER
Picture house.
References: *Film Daily Yearbook*, 1949–1954.

1548. LINCOLN COLORED DRIVE-IN
1700 Cincinnati Street
Picture house. 410 cars. Owner: Hamrick Theatre Service.
References: *Film Daily Yearbook*, 1953–1955.

1549. METROPOLITAN THEATER
Vaudeville house. The house was part of the Colored Consolidated Time vaudeville circuit. In February 1914, the vaudevillians Goodbar and Lewis, C.S. Thompson, and Tim and Hester Moore performed here.
References: *Indianapolis Freeman*, "On Colored Consolidated Time," January 31, 1914.

1550. NEW DAISY THEATER
Picture house. It is not certain that this was a different building from the Daisy.
References: *Film Daily Yearbook*, 1943–1955.

1551. PALACE THEATER
324–331 Beal Avenue
Vaudeville house. 1,000 seats. A TOBA theater. Manager in 1921: A. Barasso. In April 1921, the Palace offered Tim Moore's Chicago Follies and the Cooper and Lamar Company. In the 1930s Gonzelle White's band and Count Basie performed here.
References: Basie, *Good Morning Blues*. *Film Daily Yearbook*, 1931, 1932, 1940–1955. Hill, *Pages from the Harlem Renaissance*. Jackson, "List of Colored Theaters and Attractions," *Billboard*, August 6, 1921; "The Theater Owners' Booking Association, *Billboard*, December 16,

1922. *Official Theatrical World of Colored Artists*. Sampson, *Blacks in Black and White*. Simms, *Simms' Blue Book*. Work, *Negro Yearbook, 1921–1922*.

1552. SAVOY THEATER
1320 Thomas Street
Picture house. 590 seats.
References: *Film Daily Yearbook*, 1940–1955. *Motion Picture Herald*, July 15, 1939.

1553. VENUS THEATER
336 Beal Avenue
Vaudeville house. A TOBA theater. Manager in 1921: Samuel Zarilla. Manager in 1922: A. Barrasso.
References: Hill, Pages from the Harlem Renaissance. Jackson, "List of Colored Theaters and Attractions," *Billboard*, August 6, 1921; "The Theater Owners' Booking Association," *Billboard*, December 16, 1922.

Morristown

1554. DIXIE THEATER
Picture house.
References: *Film Daily Yearbook*, 1931, 1932.

Mount Pleasant

1555. LYRIC THEATER
Picture house. 440 seats.
References: *Film Daily Yearbook*, 1949–1955.

Nashville

1556. ACE THEATER
1123 Charlotte Avenue
Picture house. 431 seats.
References: *Film Daily Yearbook*, 1940–1955. *Motion Picture Herald*, July 15, 1939.

1557. BIJOU THEATER
423 N. 4th Avenue
Vaudeville house. 800 seats. A TOBA theater. Owner in 1921: Milton Starr. Manager in 1925: Harry Plater. In April, 1921, the Bijou offered Frank Montgomery's vaudeville company in *Hello 1921*. The musical starred Florence McClain and comedians Walker and Butler. Also in 1921 the Sandy Burns Company and the McGarr-DeGaston Company performed. From 1923 to 1925, Bessie Smith appeared regularly here. In 1926 during a midnight matinee, the Bijou became a segregated theater. Manager Milton Starr allowed whites to sit on the main floor and directed African Americans to sit in the balcony. In the 1920s Ethel Waters performed here often. In October 1926, the Susie Sutton Company played here. Bob Stark's Tennesseans appeared in November 1927. Gonzelle White and Count Basie were here in the 1930s.
References: Albertson, *Bessie. Baltimore Afro-American*, October 31, 1926. Basie, *Good Morning Blues. Chicago Defender*, "Nashville Theater Pulls Off Jim Crow Performance," May 8, 1926; Dave Peyton, "The Musical Bunch," November 12, 1927; "Harry Plater to Manage Bijou Theater, Nashville, Tenn.," September 5, 1928; "Bijou Opens Again," December 1, 1928. *Film Daily Yearbook*, 1931–1933, 1940–1955. Hill, *Pages from the Harlem Renaissance*. Jackson, "List of Colored Theaters and Attractions," *Billboard*, August 6, 1921; "The Theater Owners' Booking Association," *Billboard*, December 16, 1922. *Motion Picture Herald*, April 24, 1937; July 15, 1939. *Official Theatrical World of Colored Artists*. Peterson, *African American Theater Directory*. Sampson, *Blacks in Black and White*. Waters, *His Eye Is On the Sparrow*. Work, *Negro Yearbook 1921–1922*.

1558. GEM THEATER
1003 S. 1st Avenue
Picture house. 510 seats.
References: *Film Daily Yearbook*, 1941–1955.

1559. LINCOLN THEATER
424¼ Cedar Street
Picture house. 440 seats. Said to be black owned and managed.
References: Cahn, *Julius Cahn-Gus Hill Theatrical Guide*. *Film Daily Yearbook*, 1931, 1932, 1955. Jackson, "List of Colored Theaters and Attractions," *Billboard*, August 6, 1921. *Motion Picture Herald*, April 24, 1937. Sampson, *Blacks in Black and White*. Work, *Negro Yearbook, 1921–1922*.

1560. RITZ THEATER
1714 Jefferson Street
Picture house. 664–800 seats.
References: *Film Daily Yearbook*, 1940–1955. *Motion Picture Herald*, April 24, 1937; July 15, 1939.

1561. ROYAL THEATER
Vaudeville and picture house. A TOBA theater. In 1925 the Bijou Amusement Company remodeled this former Masonic Temple and converted it into a theater.
References: *Chicago Defender*, "New T.O.B.A. House For Nashville, Tenn.," September 19, 1925.

1562. STAR THEATER
314 Cedar Street
Picture house. Said to be black owned and managed.

References: Cahn, *Julius Cahn-Gus Hill Theatrical Guide*. Jackson, "List of Colored Theaters and Attractions," *Billboard*, August 6, 1921. Simms, *Simms' Blue Book* Work, *Negro Yearbook, 1921–1922*.

Newbern

1563. PALACE THEATER
Picture house.
References: *Film Daily Yearbook*, 1949.

Shelbyville

1564. WEST END THEATER
Picture house.
References: *Film Daily Yearbook*, 1949–1955.

Sumter

1565. LYRIC THEATER
Picture house.
References: *Film Daily Yearbook*, 1949–1955.

Union City

1566. HARLEM THEATER
Picture house. According to *Film Daily Yearbook*, the Harlem was closed from 1949 through 1951.
References: *Film Daily Yearbook*, 1949–1955.

TEXAS

Abilene

1567. ASH STREET THEATER
Picture house.

References: *Film Daily Yearbook*, 1930–1933.

1568. DIXIE THEATER
Picture house.

References: *Film Daily Yearbook*, 1930–1933.

1569. GRAND THEATER
Picture house. According to *Film Daily Yearbook*, the Grand was closed in 1949–1951.
References: *Film Daily Yearbook*, 1944–1955.

Amarillo

1570. HARLEM THEATER
Picture house.
References: *Film Daily Yearbook*, 1946–1955.

1571. HARMONY THEATER
Picture house.
References: *Film Daily Yearbook*, 1949–1955.

Athens

1572. FRANKS THEATER
Picture house.
References: *Film Daily Yearbook*, 1930–1933.

Austin

1573. CARVER THEATER
521 E. 6th Street
Picture house.
References: *Film Daily Yearbook*, 1955.

1574. DIXIE-DALE THEATER
References: Cahn, *Julius Cahn-Gus Hill Theatrical Guide*. Jackson, "List of Colored Theaters and Attractions," *Billboard*, August 6, 1921. Work, *Negro Yearbook, 1921–1922*.

1575. DUNBAR THEATER
Picture house.

References: *Film Daily Yearbook*, 1930–1933.

1576. HARLEM THEATER
1800 E. 12th Street
Picture house. 750 seats.
References: *Film Daily Yearbook* 1940–1955. *Motion Picture Herald*, April 24, 1937; July 15 1939. Murray, *Negro Handbook of 1942*. Sampson, *Blacks in Black and White*.

1577. LIBERTY BELL THEATER
Picture house.
References: *Film Daily Yearbook*, 1949–1955.

1578. LINCOLN THEATER
302 E. 6th Street
Picture house.
References: *Film Daily Yearbook*, 1930–1933.

1579. LYRIC THEATER
419 E. 6th Street
Vaudeville house. A TOBA theater. Owner in 1924: Dr. Everett A. Givens. In December 1927, the show "Sugarfoot Sam from Alabam" was at the Lyric.
References: *Chicago Defender*, "Sugarfoot Sam," December 3, 1927. *Official Theatrical World of Colored Artists*.

Ballinger

1580. RITZ THEATER
Picture house.
References: *Film Daily Yearbook*, 1947, 1948.

Bastrop

1581. TOWER THEATER
Picture house. 886 seats.
References: *Film Daily Yearbook*, 1949–1955.

Baytown

1582. BAYTOWN HUMBLE CLUB
Picture house.
References: *Film Daily Yearbook*, 1930–1933.

Beaumont

1583. GEM THEATER
2060 Irving Avenue
Picture house. 300 seats. Manager in 1953: Jefferson Amusement Company.
References: *Film Daily Yearbook, 1940–1955. Motion Picture Herald*, April 24, 1937; July 15, 1939. Sampson. *Blacks in Black and White.*

1584. JOYLAND THEATER
Picture house.
References: *Film Daily Yearbook*, 1930–1933.

1585. LEE'S TENT THEATER
Vaudeville house. Manager in 1921: Ed Lee (African American).
References: Cahn, *Julius Cahn-Gus Hill Theatrical Guide.* Jackson, "List of Colored Theaters and Attractions," *Billboard,* August 6, 1921. Work: *Negro Yearbook, 1921–1922.*

1586. LINCOLN THEATER
Vaudeville house. Also known as the Joyland. Owners in 1921: Clemmon Brothers. Manager in 1928: Lawrence Fontana. In April, 1921, the Lincoln featured the Cooper and Lamar Company, the Watts Brothers, Sherman and Sherman, and Lewis and Wilson.
References: Cahn, *Julius Cahn-Gus Hill Theatrical Guide.* Jackson, "List of Colored Theaters and Attractions," *Billboard,* August 6, 1921; "The Theater Owners'-Booking Association," *Billboard,* December 16, 1922. *Official Theatrical World of Colored Artists.* Peterson, *The African American Theatre Directory.* Work, *Negro Yearbook, 1921–1922.*

1587. NEW REX THEATER
Picture house.
References: *Film Daily Yearbook*, 1930–1933.

1588. PASTIME THEATER
Picture house.
References: Cahn, *Julius Cahn-Gus Hill Theatrical Guide.* Jackson, "List of Colored Theaters and Attractions," *Billboard,* August 6, 1921. Work, *Negro Yearbook, 1921–1922.*

1589. REX THEATER
Picture house.
References: *Film Daily Yearbook,* 1949, 1950.

1590. RITZ THEATER
2040 Irving Avenue
Picture house. Manager in 1941: Floyd Adams.
References: *Film Daily Yearbook,* 1941–1955.

1591. STAR THEATER
680 Forsythe Street
Picture house. 718 seats.
References: *Film Daily Yearbook,* 1946–1955.

1592. VERDUN THEATER
468 Forsythe Street
Picture house. Manager in 1921: A. N. Adams (African American).
References: Cahn, *Julius Cahn-Gus Hill Theatrical Guide.* Jackson, "List of Colored Theaters and Attractions," *Billboard,* August 6, 1921. Work, *Negro Yearbook, 1921–1922.*

Beeville

1593. AZTECA THEATER
Picture house.

References: *Film Daily Yearbook*, 1947–1955.

Big Spring

1594. RIO THEATER
309 NW 4th Street
Picture house. Manager in 1951; James Robb.
References: *Film Daily Yearbook*, 1955.

Bonham

1595. STAR THEATER
Picture house. Manager in 1921: Charles Jordan (African American).
References: Cahn, *Julius Cahn-Gus Hill Theatrical Guide*. Jackson, "List of Colored Theaters and Attractions," *Billboard*, August 6, 1921. Work, *Negro Yearbook, 1921–22*. *Film Daily Yearbook*, 1930–1933.

Breckenridge

1596. BUCKAROO THEATER
112 W. Walter Street
Picture house. 375 seats.
References: *Film Daily Yearbook*, 1952–1955.

Brownfield

1597. QUEEN THEATER
1125 Elizabeth Street, SE
Picture house.
References: *Film Daily Yearbook*, 1947–1950, 1955.

1598. RIO THEATER
Picture house. 450 seats.
References: *Film Daily Yearbook*, 1955.

1599. RITZ THEATER
Picture house.
References: *Film Daily Yearbook*, 1949.

Bryan

1600. LIBERTY THEATER NO. 1
Picture house.
References. *Film Daily Yearbook*, 1930–1933.

1601. LIBERTY THEATER NO. 2
Picture house.
References: *Film Daily Yearbook*, 1931–1933.

1602. STAR THEATER
Picture house. Managers in 1921: Queen and Baylor.
References: *Film Daily Yearbook*, 1955. Jackson, "List of Colored Theaters and Attractions," *Billboard*, August 6, 1921.

1603. STARLIGHT THEATER
Picture house.
References: *Film Daily Yearbook*, 1955.

Caldwell

1604. MATZONIAN THEATER
Buck Street
Picture house. 350 seats.
References: *Film Daily Yearbook*, 1952–1955.

Camden

1605. HARLEM THEATER
Picture house.
References: *Film Daily Yearbook*, 1940–1955. *Motion Picture Herald*, July 15, 1939.

Childress

1606. PALACE THEATER

212 Main Street
Picture house. 650 seats.
References: *Film Daily Yearbook*, 1947–1955.

Clarksville

1607. COZY THEATER
Picture house.
References: *Film Daily Yearbook*, 1930–1933.

1608. PRINCESS THEATER
Picture house. Manager in 1921: J.S. Thorton.
References: Cahn, *Julius Cahn-Gus Hill Theatrical Guide*. Jackson, "List of Colored Theaters and Attractions," *Billboard*, August 6, 1921. Work, *Negro Yearbook, 1921–22*.

1609. RUNDLA THEATER
Picture house.
References: *Film Daily Yearbook*, 1949–1955.

Cleburne

1610. DIXIE THEATER
Picture house.
References: *Film Daily Yearbook*, 1930–1933.

1611. DREAMLAND THEATER
Picture house.
References: *Film Daily Yearbook*, 1930–1933.

Cleveland

1612. HARLEM THEATER
Picture house.
References: *Film Daily Yearbook*, 1947–1955.

Coleman

1613. GEM THEATER
Picture house.
References: *Film Daily Yearbook*, 1949–1955.

Conroe

1614. DUGAN THEATER
Picture house.
References: *Film Daily Yearbook*, 1930–1933.

1615. HARLEM THEATER
References: *Film Daily Yearbook*, 1946–1955.

Corpus Christi

1616. GALVAN THEATER
Picture house.
References: *Film Daily Yearbook*, 1930–1933.

1617. HARLEM THEATER
110 N. Staples Street
Picture house. 673 seats.
References: *Film Daily Yearbook*, 1944–1949.

Corsiciana

1618. STARLIGHT THEATER
112 N. Commerce Street
Picture house. *Film Daily Yearbook*, 1947–1955.

1619. TEX THEATER
Picture house.
References: *Film Daily Yearbook*, 1947, 1948.

Crandall

1620. PRINCESS THEATER
Picture house. 300 seats.

References: *Film Daily Yearbook, 1952–1955.*

Dallas

1621. CARVER THEATER
1846 Singleton Boulevard
Picture house.
References: *Film Daily Yearbook,* 1952–1955.

1622. CENTURY THEATER
2300 Metropolitan Avenue
Picture house. 500 seats.
References: *Film Daily Yearbook,* 1940–1955. *Motion Picture Herald,* July 15 1939.

1623. CIRCLE THEATER
Picture house.
References: *Film Daily Yearbook,* 1930–1933.

1624. CLUB ALABAMA THEATER
Picture house.
References: *Film Daily Yearbook,* 1950–1955.

1625. ELLA B. MOORE THEATER
428 N. Central Avenue
Vaudeville house. A TOBA theater. Owner in 1928: Ella B. Moore. Manager in 1928: Chintz Moore (African American). The Dusty Murray Company played here in 1926. Blues singer Ida Cox sang here in 1930.
References: *Baltimore Afro-American,* October 31, 1926. *Chicago Defender,* "Ella B. Moore Theater Takes On New Life," September 27, 1929. *Film Daily Yearbook,* 1930–1933. Harrison, *Black Pearls.* Sampson, *Blacks in Blackface. Official Theatrical World of Colored Artists.*

1626. GRAND CENTRAL THEATER
405 N. Central Avenue
Picture house. Manager in 1921: Jack Harris.
References: Cahn, *Julius Cahn-Gus Hill Theatrical Guide. Film Daily Yearbook,* 1930–1933. Jackson, "List of Colored Theaters and Attractions," *Billboard,* August 6, 1921. Simms, *Simms' Blue Book.* Work, *Negro Yearbook, 1921–1922.*

1627. HARLEM THEATER
2407 Elm Street
Picture house. 500 seats.
References: *Film Daily Yearbook,* 1940–1955. *Motion Picture Herald,* July 15, 1939.

1628. HIGH SCHOOL THEATER
3211 Cochran Street
References: Simms, *Simms' Blue Book.*

1629. LINCOLN THEATER
5414 Bexer Street
Picture house. 450 seats.
References: *Film Daily Yearbook,* 1948–1955.

1630. MAMMOTH THEATER
2401–03 Elm Street
Picture house. Manager in 1922: C.S. Scott.
References: Cahn, *Julius Cahn-Gus Hill Theatrical Guide.* Jackson, "List of Colored Theaters and Attractions," *Billboard,* August 6, 1921. Work, *Negro Yearbook, 1921–1922.*

1631. MAPLE THEATER
5206 Maple Street
Picture house. 800 seats.
References: *Film Daily Yearbook,* 1949–1955.

1632. PALACE THEATER
Picture house.
References: *Film Daily Yearbook,* 1930–1933.

1633. PARK THEATER
420 N. Central Avenue
Vaudeville and picture house. 500 seats. A TOBA theater. Manager in 1921: Chintz Moore (African American). The

musical comedy *Cotton Blossoms* appeared at the Park in 1923. In February 1924 the vaudeville show featured John Long, the Dixiana Girls Company, DeGaston and Yeun, Happy Ferguson, and Kid and Eva. The Park was advertised as "the only theater in the United States playing T.O.B.A. time that gets top for admission: ten cents."

References: Cahn, *Julius Cahn-Gus Hill Theatrical Guide*. *Film Daily Yearbook*, 1949–1955. Hill, *Pages from the Harlem Renaissance*. Jackson, "List of Colored Theaters and Attractions," *Billboard*, August 6, 1921. *Chicago Defender*, Wyatt D. James, "Dallas Notes," June 9, 1923; James, "In Dallas, Texas," February 9, 1924. Peterson, *The African American Theatre Directory*. Simms, *Simms' Blue Book*. Work, *Negro Yearbook, 1921–1922*.

1634. STAR THEATER
1401 E. 8th Street
Picture house. 510 seats.
References: *Film Daily Yearbook*, 1930, 1947–1955.

1635. STATE THEATER
3217 Thomas Avenue
Picture house. 600 seats.
References: *Film Daily Yearbook*, 1931–1933, 1940–1955. *Motion Picture Herald*, July 15, 1939.

Dennison

1636. DREAMLAND THEATER
Picture house. Manager in 1921: P. Woods (African American).
References: Cahn, *Julius Cahn-Gus Hill Theatrical Guide*. *Film Daily Yearbook*, 1930–1933. Jackson, "List of Colored Theaters and Attractions," *Billboard*, August 6, 1921. Work, *Negro Yearbook, 1921–1922*.

1637. HARLEM THEATER
Vaudeville theater. 210 seats.
References: *Motion Picture Herald*, April 24, 1937. Sampson, *Blacks in Black and White*.

Denton

1638. DREAMLAND THEATER
Picture house. 423 seats.
References: *Film Daily Yearbook*, 1952–1955.

1639. HARLEM THEATER
Picture house. According to *Film Daily Yearbook*, the Harlem was closed in 1949, 1950, and 1951.
References: *Film Daily Yearbook*, 1947–1955.

1640. PALACE THEATER
Picture house. 363 seats.
References: *Film Daily Yearbook*, 1952–1955.

1641. TEXAS THEATER
Picture house. 834 seats.
References: *Film Daily Yearbook*, 1952–1955.

Edna

1642. EAST HARLON THEATER
Picture house. According to *Film Daily Yearbook*, the East Harlon was closed in 1950 and 1951.
References: *Film Daily Yearbook*, 1950–1955.

1643. QUEEN THEATER
Picture house.
References: *Film Daily Yearbook* 1930–1933.

El Paso

1644. ALCAZAR THEATER

Picture house.
References: *Film Daily Yearbook*, 1946–1948.

1645. MURRAY THEATER
Picture house. According to *Film Daily Yearbook*, the Murray was closed in 1949–1951.
References: *Film Daily Yearbook*, 1949–1955.

Ennis

1646. BELVA THEATER
Picture house.
References: *Film Daily Yearbook*, 1930–1933.

1647. COLORED THEATER
References: Cahn, *Julius Cahn-Gus Hill Theatrical Guide*. Jackson, "List of Colored Theaters and Attractions," *Billboard*, August 6, 1921. Work, *Negro Yearbook*, 1921–1922.

Fort Worth

1648. COMO THEATER
5531 Bonnell Street
Picture house. 500 seats.
References: *Film Daily Yearbook*, 1947–1955.

1649. DOUGLAS THEATER
Picture house. Manager in 1921: S. Lewis.
References: Cahn, *Julius Cahn-Gus Hill Theatrical Guide*. Jackson, "List of Colored Theaters and Attractions," *Billboard*, August 6, 1921.

1650. GRAND THEATER
1110 Forbes Avenue
References: *Film Daily Yearbook*, 1940–1955. *Motion Picture Herald*, July 15, 1939.

1651. JOY THEATER
Picture house.
References: *Film Daily Yearbook*, 1950–1955.

1652. RITZ THEATER
909 Calhoun Street
Picture house. 566 seats.
References: *Film Daily Yearbook*, 1940–1955. *Motion Picture Herald*, July 15, 1939.

1653. ROSEDALE THEATER
206–208 Rosedale Street
Picture house. 500 seats.
References: *Film Daily Yearbook*, 1947–1955.

1654. WASHINGTON THEATER
Picture house.
References: Cahn, *Julius Cahn-Gus Hill Theatrical Guide*. Jackson, "List of Colored Theaters and Attractions," *Billboard*, August 6, 1921. Work, *Negro Yearbook*, 1921–1922.

Galveston

1655. BOOKER T. THEATER
Picture house.
References: *Film Daily Yearbook*, 1949–1955.

1656. CARVER THEATER
2521 Market Street
Picture house. 650 seats.
References: *Film Daily Yearbook*, 1941–1955.

1657. DIXIE THEATER
Picture house.
References: *Film Daily Yearbook*, 1930–1933, 1943–1955.

1658. DIXIE 3 THEATER
Picture house.
References: Cahn, *Julius Cahn-Gus Hill Theatrical Guide*. *Film Daily Yearbook*,

1940–1942. Jackson, "List of Colored Theaters and Attractions," *Billboard*, August 6, 1921. *Motion Picture Herald*, July 15, 1939. Work, *Negro Yearbook, 1921–1922*.

1659. LIBERTY THEATER
Vaudeville and picture house. 400 seats. Owner in 1921: James Brown. The Liberty had four dressing rooms and an orchestra with piano, coronet, and drums. The Jackson and Rector Company played here in 1926.
References: *Baltimore Afro-American*, October 31, 1926. Hill, *Pages from the Harlem Renaissance*. Jackson, "The Theater Owners' Booking Association," *Billboard*, December 16, 1922. Peterson, *The African American Theatre Directory*. Sampson, *Blacks in Blackface*.

1660. LINCOLN THEATER
413–5 25th Street
Vaudeville house. A TOBA theater. Said to be Black owned and operated. In March 1915, the Lincoln's vaudeville bill consisted of Baby Floyd Seals, comedian, Bonnie Bell Drew, singer, Porter and Porter, comedians, and J. C. Boone, singer.
References: Cahn, *Julius Cahn-Gus Hill Theatrical Guide*. *Indianapolis Freeman*, W. A. Davis, "Lincoln Theatre, Galveston, Texas," March 27, 1915. Jackson, "List of Colored Theaters and Attractions," *Billboard*, August 6, 1921. Peterson, *The African American Theatre Directory*. Work, *Negro Yearbook, 1921–1922*.

1661. PRINCESS THEATER
2621 Avenue D
Picture house. 500 seats. Owner in 1921: A. B. Mendell.
References: Cahn, *Julius Cahn-Gus Hill Theatrical Guide*. *Film Daily Yearbook*, 1930–1933. Hill, *Pages from the Harlem Renaissance*. Jackson, "List of Colored Theaters and Attractions," *Billboard*, August 6, 1921*.* Work, *Negro Yearbook, 1921–22*.

1662. RIALTO THEATER
Vaudeville house. A TOBA theater. Manager in 1928: A. Martini.
References: *Official Theatrical World of Colored Artists*.

1663. STAR THEATER
Picture house.
References: Cahn, *Julius Cahn-Gus Hill Theatrical Guide*. Hill, *Pages from the Harlem Renaissance*. Jackson, "List of Colored Theaters and Attractions," *Billboard*, August 6, 1921. Work, *Negro Yearbook, 1921–1922*.

Gilmer

1664. LITTLE HARLEM THEATER
Picture house.
References: *Film Daily Yearbook*, 1949–1955.

Gladewater

1665. LIBERTY THEATER
Picture house.
References: *Film Daily Yearbook*, 1949–1955.

Greenville

1666. GRAND THEATER
Picture house.
References: *Film Daily Yearbook*, 1940, 1941. *Motion Picture Herald*, July 15, 1939.

1667. JOY THEATER
Picture house.
References: *Film Daily Yearbook*, 1942–1948.

1668. PASTIME THEATER
Vaudeville house. 400 seats. Said to be Black owned and operated.
References: *Film Daily Yearbook*, 1930–1933. Hill, *Pages from the Harlem Renaissance*. Jackson, "List of Colored Theaters and Attractions," *Billboard*, August 6, 1921. Work, *Negro Yearbook, 1921–1922*.

Hearne

1669. HAPPY HOUR THEATER
Picture house.
References: *Film Daily Yearbook*, 1930–1933.

Hill

1670. JONES THEATER
Picture house.
References: *Film Daily Yearbook*, 1955.

1671. PALACE THEATER
Picture house. Manager in 1921: H. D. Jackson.
References: Cahn, *Julius Cahn-Gus Hill Theatrical Guide*. Work, *Negro Yearbook, 1921–1922*.

Hillsboro

1672. GARDNER THEATER
Picture house.
References: *Film Daily Yearbook*, 1930–1933.

1673. JONES THEATER
Picture house.
References: *Film Daily Yearbook*, 1949–1955.

1674. PALACE THEATER
Picture house.
References: Cahn, *Julius Cahn-Gus Hill Theatrical Guide*. Jackson, "List of Colored Theaters and Attractions," *Billboard*, August 6, 1921.

Honey Island

1675. ACE THEATER
Picture house.
References: *Film Daily Yearbook*, 1949–1955.

1676. LINCOLN THEATER
Picture house.
References: *Film Daily Yearbook*, 1930–1933.

Houston

1677. AMERICAN THEATER
609–11 San Felipe Street
Vaudeville house. 500 seats. A TOBA theater. Manager in 1921: Charles Caffey. Manager in 1928: Paul Barraco. The house was part of the Southern Consolidated Vaudeville Circuit from 1916 to 1921.
References: Cahn, *Julius Cahn-Gus Hill Theatrical Guide*. Hill, *Pages from the Harlem Renaissance*. Jackson, "List of Colored Theaters and Attractions," *Billboard*, August 6, 1921. *Official Theatrical World of Colored Artists*. Peterson, *The African American Theatre Directory*.

1678. BEST THEATER
212 Main Street
Vaudeville house. A TOBA theater. Owner in 1921: Paul Barraco. The Dusty Murray Company performed here in 1926.
References: *Baltimore Afro-American*, October 31, 1926. Peterson, *The African American Theatre Directory*. Sampson, *Blacks in Blackface*.

1679. BOOKER T. THEATER
Vaudeville and picture house. 1,500

seats. Owner: Paul Barrasso. Manager: Victor Abram. The stage of the Booker T. was 20 × 30 feet. The theater had five dressing rooms and a four-piece orchestra.
References: Hill, *Pages from the Harlem Renaissance*. Peterson, *The African American Theatre Directory*.

1680. CLINTON THEATER
Picture house.
References: *Film Daily Yearbook*, 1945–1955.

1681. DELUXE THEATER
3303 Lyons Street
Picture house. 740 seats.
References: *Film Daily Yearbook*, 1941–1955.

1682. DOWLING THEATER
2110 Dowling Street
Picture house. 796 seats.
References: *Film Daily Yearbook*, 1941–1955.

1683. HOLMAN THEATER
Picture house. According to *Film Daily Yearbook*, the Holman was closed in 1950 and 1951.
References: *Film Daily Yearbook*, 1942–1955.

1684. IDEAL THEATER
514 Milam Street
Vaudeville house. 330 seats. Manager in 1921: Elmore Martin.
References: Hill, *Pages from the Harlem Renaissance*. Work, *Negro Yearbook, 1921–1922*.

1685. LINCOLN THEATER
711 Prairie Street
Picture house. 594–750 seats. Manager in 1921: Olen Pullum DeWalt (African American). The Lincoln had a 20 × 24-foot stage, 18 sets of lines, two dressing rooms, and a gallery. Blues singer Victoria Spivey played piano here.
References: Cahn, *Julius Cahn-Gus Hill Theatrical Guide*. *Film Daily Yearbook*, 1930–1933, 1940–1955. Harrison, *Black Pearls*. Hill, *Pages from the Harlem Renaissance*. Jackson, "List of Colored Theaters and Attractions," *Billboard*, August 6, 1921. *Motion Picture Herald*, July 15, 1939. Work, *Negro Yearbook, 1921–1922*.

1686. LYONS THEATER
4036 Lyons Street
Picture house. 500 seats.
References: *Film Daily Yearbook*, 1940–1955. *Motion Picture Herald*, July 15, 1939.

1687. ODIN THEATER
2705 Odin Avenue
Picture house. Manager in 1921: Alex Shulman.
References: Cahn, *Julius Cahn-Gus Hill Theatrical Guide*. Jackson, "List of Colored Theaters and Attractions," *Billboard*, August 6, 1921. Work, *Negro Yearbook, 1921–1922*.

1688. PARK THEATER
2813 Dowling Street
Picture house. 440 seats.
References: *Film Daily Yearbook*, 1940–1955. *Motion Picture Herald*, July 15, 1939.

1689. PARKVIEW THEATER
Dowling Street
Picture house.
References: *Film Daily Yearbook*, 1930–1933.

1690. PASTIME THEATER
Picture house. 500 seats.
References: *Film Daily Yearbook*, 1930–1933, 1940–1955. Hill, *Pages from the Harlem Renaissance*. *Motion Picture Herald*, July 15, 1939.

1691. PEOPLES THEATER
Vaudeville house. Manager: Frank

McKenzie. According to Peterson, this theater was in business during the 1900s.

References: Peterson, *The African American Theatre Directory*.

1692. RAINBOW THEATER
907 W. Dallas Street
Picture house. 600 seats.
References: *Film Daily Yearbook*, 1940–1955. *Motion Picture Herald*, July 15, 1939.

1693. RIO THEATER
Picture house.
References: *Film Daily Yearbook*, 1955.

1694. ROXY THEATER
2737 Lyons Street
Picture house. 600 seats.
References: *Film Daily Yearbook*, 1940–1955. *Motion Picture Herald, July 15, 1939*.

1695. SAINT ELMO THEATER
711 San Felipe Street
Picture house. 500 seats. Owner: H. Shulman.
References: *Film Daily Yearbook*, 1930–1933. Hill, *Pages from the Harlem Renaissance*. .

1696. WASHINGTON THEATER
2711 Odin Avenue
Vaudeville house. A TOBA theater. Manager in 1928: Paul Barraco. The famous Whitman Sisters headlined the vaudeville show in February 1924, along with dancer Little Albert, singer Bernice Ellis, and tenor Gene Thomas.
References: Cahn, *Julius Cahn-Gus Hill Theatrical Guide. Chicago Defender*, "Whitmans Hit," February 23, 1924. *Film Daily Yearbook*, 1930–1933. Jackson, "List of Colored Theaters and Attractions," *Billboard*, August 6, 1921. *Official Theatrical World of Colored Artists*. Work, *Negro Yearbook, 1921–1922*.

1697. ZOE THEATER
Picture house.
References: *Film Daily Yearbook*, 1930–1933.

Italy

1698. ACE THEATER
Picture house.
References: *Film Daily Yearbook*, 1947, 1948.

Jacksonville

1699. ALICE THEATER
Picture house.
References: *Film Daily Yearbook*, 1949–1955.

Lometa

1700. MAJESTIC THEATER
Picture house.
References: *Film Daily Yearbook*, 1950–1955.

Longview

1701. GREGG THEATER
Picture house. According to *Film Daily Yearbook*, the Gregg was closed in 1950.
References: *Film Daily Yearbook*, 1950.

1702. RITZ THEATER
Picture house.
References: *Film Daily Yearbook*, 1946–1955.

Lubbock

1703. PALACE THEATER
Picture house.
References: *Film Daily Yearbook*, 1950–1955.

1704. RITZ THEATER
1701 Avenue A
Picture house.
References: *Film Daily Yearbook*, 1945–1955.

Lufkin

1705. LINCOLN THEATER
Picture house. 350 seats. According to *Film Daily Yearbook*, the Lincoln was closed in 1950 and 1951.
References: *Film Daily Yearbook*, 1940–1955. *Motion Picture Herald*, April 24, 1937; July 15, 1939. Sampson, *Blacks in Black and White*.

Marlin

1706. COLORED THEATER
Picture house.
References: Cahn, *Julius Cahn-Gus Hill Theatrical Guide*. Jackson, "List of Colored Theaters and Attractions," *Billboard*, August 6, 1921. Work, *Negro Yearbook, 1921–1922*.

Marshall

1707. HARLEM THEATER
Picture house. According to *Film Daily Yearbook*, the Harlem was closed in 1949–1951.
References: *Film Daily Yearbook*, 1941–1955.

1708. LOMA THEATER
Picture house. According to *Film Daily Yearbook*, the Loma was closed in 1949.
References: *Film Daily Yearbook*, 1949–1955.

Martin

1709. MARTEX THEATER
Picture house. According to *Film Daily Yearbook*, the Martex was closed in 1950.
References: *Film Daily Yearbook*, 1949–1955.

McKinley

1710. RIO THEATER
Picture house.
References: *Film Daily Yearbook*, 1955.

Mexia

1711. LIBERTY THEATER
Picture house. 400 seats.
References: *Film Daily Yearbook*, 1952–1955.

1712. NATIONAL THEATER
Picture house.
References: *Film Daily Yearbook*, 1952–1955.

Mineola

1713. ALAMO THEATER
Picture house.
References: *Film Daily Yearbook*, 1930–1933.

Morehead

1714. COZY THEATER
Picture and vaudeville house. Manager in 1921: W. A. Hoggs.
References: Jackson, "List of Colored Theaters and Attractions," *Billboard*, August 21, 1921. Cahn, *Julius Cahn-Gus Hill Theatrical Guide*.

Mount Pleasant

1715. LIBERTY THEATER

Picture house.
References: *Film Daily Yearbook*, 1930–1933.

1716. LINCOLN THEATER
Picture house.
References: *Film Daily Yearbook*, 1949–1955.

Nacogdoches

1717. GLENN THEATER
Picture house. 250 seats. Also known as the Glynn.
References: *Film Daily Yearbook*, 1940–1955. *Motion Picture Herald*, July 15, 1939.

GLYNN THEATER *see* Glenn Theater

1718. HARLEM THEATER
Picture house. 250 seats.
References: *Motion Picture Herald*, April 24, 1937. Sampson, *Blacks in Black and White*.

1719. SHAWNEE THEATER
Picture house.
References: *Film Daily Yearbook*, 1930–1933.

Nacona

1720. CONA THEATER
Picture house.
References: *Film Daily Yearbook*, 1946, 1947.

Navasota

1721. DIXIE THEATER
Picture house. 250 seats.
References: *Motion Picture Herald*, April 24, 1937. *Film Daily Yearbook*, 1955. Sampson, *Blacks in Black and White*.

1722. HARLEM THEATER
Picture house.
References: *Film Daily Yearbook*, 1949–1955.

1723. QUEEN THEATER
Picture house.
References: *Film Daily Yearbook*, 1930–1933.

Odessa

1724. HARLEM THEATER
Picture house.
References: *Film Daily Yearbook*, 1949–1955.

Orange

1725. AQUA FALLS THEATER
Picture house.
References: *Film Daily Yearbook*, 1949–1955.

1726. COLORED THEATER
Picture house.
References: Cahn, *Julius Cahn-Gus Hill Theatrical Guide*. Jackson, "List of Colored Theaters and Attractions," *Billboard*, August 6, 1921. Work, *Negro Yearbook*, 1921–1922.

1727. DRAGON THEATER
1112 2nd Street
Picture house. 350 seats.
References: *Film Daily Yearbook*, 1946–1955.

1728. LIBERTY THEATER
Picture house.
References: *Film Daily Yearbook*, 1930–1933.

Palestine

1729. HARLEM THEATER

Picture house.
References: *Film Daily Yearbook*, 1950–1955.

Pampa

1730. WOODS THEATER
Picture house.
References: *Film Daily Yearbook*, 1949–1955.

Paris

1731. ALHAMBRA THEATER
552 E. Tucker Street
Vaudeville and picture house. 300–450 seats.
References: Cahn, *Julius Cahn-Gus Hill Theatrical Guide*. *Film Daily Yearbook*, 1930–1933, 1940–1955. Jackson, "List of Colored Theaters and Attractions," *Billboard*, August 6, 1921. *Motion Picture Herald*, April 24, 1937, July 15, 1939. Murray, *Negro Handbook of 1942*. Sampson, *Blacks in Black and White*. Work, *Negro Yearbook, 1921–1922*.

1732. DIXIE THEATER
Picture house.
References: *Film Daily Yearbook*, 1940–1955. *Motion Picture Herald*, July 15, 1939.

Pittsburg

1733. LINCOLN THEATER
Picture house.
References: *Film Daily Yearbook*, 1930.

Port Arthur

1734. DREAM THEATER
Vaudeville and picture house.
References: Cahn, *Julius Cahn-Gus Hill Theatrical Guide*. Jackson, "List of Colored Theaters and Attractions," *Billboard*, August 6, 1921. *Official Theatrical World of Colored Artists*. Work, *Negro Yearbook, 1921–1922*.

1735. DREAMLAND THEATER
Vaudeville and picture house. 554 seats. A TOBA theater. Manager in 1928: Lawrence Fontana.
References: *Film Daily Yearbook*, 1930–1933, 1940–1942, 1955. *Motion Picture Herald*, April 24, 1937; July 15, 1939. Sampson, *Blacks in Black and White*.

1736. HOLLYWOOD THEATER
Picture house. 850 seats.
References: *Film Daily Yearbook*, 1946–1955.

1737. LINCOLN THEATER
Picture house.
References: *Film Daily Yearbook*, 1941–1955. *Motion Picture Herald*, July 15, 1939.

1738. MAJESTIC THEATER
Picture house.
References: *Film Daily Yearbook*, 1930–1933.

1739. RINK THEATER
Vaudeville house. Manager in 1922: Jim Brown.
References: Hill, *Pages from the Harlem Renaissance*. Jackson, "The Theater Owners' Booking Association," *Billboard*, December 16, 1922.

1740. VICTOR THEATER
Picture house.
References: *Film Daily Yearbook*, 1930–1933.

Poth

1741. TEX THEATER

Picture house. 265 seats.
References: *Film Daily Yearbook*, 1952–1955.

Prairie View College

1742. AUDITORIUM THEATER
Picture house. 800 seats.
References: *Film Daily Yearbook*, 1940–1947. *Motion Picture Herald*, April 24, 1937; July 15, 1939. Sampson, *Blacks in Black and White*.

Rusk

1743. QUEEN THEATER
Picture house. Manager in 1921: Ed Conley (African American).
References: Cahn, *Julius Cahn-Gus Hill Theatrical Guide*. Jackson, "List of Colored Theaters and Attractions," *Billboard*, August 6, 1921. Work, *Negro Yearbook*, 1921–1922.

San Angelo

1744. REX THEATER
Picture house.
References: *Film Daily Yearbook*, 1952–1955.

San Antonio

1745. ALAMO DRIVE-IN
Picture house. 350 cars. Owner: Statewide D-I Theaters.
References: *Film Daily Yearbook*, 1949–1955.

1746. AMERICAN THEATER
San Felipe Street
Picture and vaudeville house. Manager in 1921: Charles Coffey.
References: Cahn, *Julius Cahn-Gus Hill Theatrical Guide*. Work, *Negro Yearbook*, 1921–1922.

1747. BELLINGER THEATER
Vaudeville house. A TOBA theater.
References: *Film Daily Yearbook*, 1930–1933. Hill, *Pages from the Harlem Renaissance*. Jackson, "The Theater Owners' Booking Association," *Billboard*, December 16, 1922.

1748. CAMEO THEATER
619 E. Commerce Street
Picture house. 600 seats.
References: *Film Daily Yearbook*, 1941–1955.

1749. DREAMLAND THEATER
416 E. Commerce Street
Vaudeville house. A TOBA theater. Manager in 1921: A. N. Sack.
References: Cahn, *Julius Cahn-Gus Hill Theatrical Guide*. Hill, *Pages from the Harlem Renaissance*. Work, *Negro Yearbook*, 1921–1922.

1750. HELLINGER THEATER
Vaudeville and picture house. 550 seats. Manager: Luke Scott (African American). The Hellinger had five dressing rooms and 17 sets of lines.
References: Hill, *Pages from the Harlem Renaissance*.

1751. MISSION DRIVE-IN THEATER
Picture house.
References: *Film Daily Yearbook*, 1949.

1752. RITZ THEATER
Picture house.
References: *Film Daily Yearbook*, 1949–1955.

Sherman

1753. ANDREWS THEATER
Picture house. Said to be black owned and operated.

References: Cahn, *Julius Cahn-Gus Hill Theatrical Guide*. *Film Daily Yearbook*, 1930–1933. Jackson, "List of Colored Theaters and Attractions," *Billboard*, August 6, 1921. Work, *Negro Yearbook, 1921–1922*.

1754. RIO THEATER
Picture house.
References: *Film Daily Yearbook*, 1952–1955.

Somerville

1755. LYON THEATER
Caldwell Hives
Picture house. 325 seats.
References: *Film Daily Yearbook*, 1952–1955.

Taylor

1756. DIXIE AIRDROME
Picture house.
References: *Film Daily Yearbook*, 1940. *Motion Picture Herald*, July 15, 1939.

1757. RINK THEATER
Picture house. Manager in 1921: J. W. Lewis.
References: Cahn, *Julius Cahn-Gus Hill Theatrical Guide*. Jackson, "List of Colored Theaters and Attractions," *Billboard*, August 6, 1921. Work, *Negro Yearbook, 1921–1922*.

1758. STAR THEATER
Picture house.
References: *Film Daily Yearbook*, 1930–1933.

Temple

1759. DUNBAR THEATER
307 S. 8th Street
Picture house. 300 seats.
References: *Film Daily Yearbook*, 1947–1955.

1760. RINK THEATER
Picture house. Manager in 1921: J. J. Dawson (African American).
References: Cahn, *Julius Cahn-Gus Hill Theatrical Guide*. Jackson, "List of Colored Theaters and Attractions," *Billboard*, August 6, 1921. Work, *Negro Yearbook, 1921–1922*.

Terrell

1761. HARLEM THEATER
Picture house.
References: *Film Daily Yearbook*, 1948–1955.

Texarkana

1762. DREAMLAND THEATER
Vaudeville house. The Dreamland was part of the combined TOBA and Managers and Performers vaudeville circuits.
References: Hill, *Pages from the Harlem Renaissance*.

1763. HARLEM THEATER
Picture house.
References: *Film Daily Yearbook*, 1947, 1948.

1764. PALACE THEATER
Picture house.
References: *Film Daily Yearbook*, 1940–1955. *Motion Picture Herald*, July 15, 1939.

Thorndale

1765. QUEEN THEATER
Picture house.
References: *Film Daily Yearbook*, 1952–1955.

Trinity

1767. DIXIE THEATER
Picture house.
References: *Film Daily Yearbook*, 1930–1933.

Tyler

1768. KARUMU THEATER
Picture house. 316 seats. According to *Film Daily Yearbook*, the Karumu was closed in 1949–1951.
References: *Film Daily Yearbook*, 1948–1955.

1769. LONGS THEATER
Picture house. Said to be black owned and operated.
References: Cahn, *Julius Cahn-Gus Hill Theatrical Guide*. Jackson, "List of Colored Theaters and Attractions," *Billboard*, August 6, 1921. Work, *Negro Yearbook*, 1921–1922.

1770. PALACE THEATER
305 N. Spring Street
Picture house. 300 seats.
References: *Film Daily Yearbook*, 1940–1955. *Motion Picture Herald*, April 24, 1937; July 15, 1939. Sampson, *Blacks in Black and White*.

1771. STAR THEATER
Picture house.
References: *Film Daily Yearbook*, 1930–1933.

Vernon

1772. MECCA THEATER

1766. RIO THEATER
Picture house. 350 seats.
References: *Film Daily Yearbook*, 1955.

Picture house.
References: *Film Daily Yearbook*, 1955.

Victoria

1773. DIAMOND THEATER
Picture house.
References: *Film Daily Yearbook*, 1930–1933.

1774. HARLEM THEATER
Picture house.
References: *Film Daily Yearbook*, 1948–1955.

Waco

1775. ALOHA THEATER
Picture house.
References: *Film Daily Yearbook*, 1948–1955.

1776. GAYETY THEATER
117 Bridge Street
Vaudeville and picture house. A TOBA theater. Manager in 1919: M. L. Gardner. Manager in 1921: W. H. Leonard. Manager in 1928: J. A. Lemke.
References: Cahn, *Julius Cahn-Gus Hill Theatrical Guide*. *Film Daily Yearbook*, 1930–1933. Jackson, "List of Colored Theaters and Attractions," *Billboard*, August 6, 1921. *Official Theatrical World of Colored Artists*. Peterson, *The African American Theatre Directory*. Work, *Negro Yearbook*, 1921–1922.

1777. GEM THEATER
206 S. Side Square
Picture house. 558 seats. Advertised as an "exclusive colored theatre."
References: *Film Daily Yearbook*, 1940–1955.

1778. MAJESTIC THEATER
Picture house. Manager in 1921: M. L. Gardner.

Gem Theater, Waco, Texas (Library of Congress, Prints and Photographs Division)

References: Cahn, *Julius Cahn-Gus Hill Theatrical Guide*. Jackson, "List of Colored Theaters and Attractions," *Billboard*, August 6, 1921. Work, *Negro Yearbook, 1921–1922*.

1779. PALACE THEATER
Picture house.
References: *Film Daily Yearbook*, 1941.

Waxahachie

1780. LINCOLN THEATER
Picture house. According to *Film Daily Yearbook*, the Lincoln was closed in 1949 and 1950.
References: *Film Daily Yearbook*, 1930–1933, 1947–1955.

Wichita Falls

1781. ISIS THEATER
Picture house. 776 seats. According to *Film Daily Yearbook*, the Isis was closed in 1949–1951.
References: *Film Daily Yearbook*, 1949–1955.

1782. LYRIC THEATER
Picture house.
References: *Film Daily Yearbook*, 1930–1933.

1783. VICTORY THEATER
Picture house. Manager in 1921: E. C. Lewis
References: Cahn, *Julius Cahn-Gus Hill Theatrical Guide*. Jackson, "List of Colored Theaters and Attractions," *Billboard*, August 6, 1921. Work, *Negro Yearbook, 1921–1922*.

VIRGINIA

Accomac

1784. BOOKER T. THEATER
Picture house. 325 seats.
References: *Film Daily Yearbook*, 1940–1955. *Motion Picture Herald*, April 24, 1937; July 15, 1939. Murray, *Negro Handbook of 1942*. Sampson, *Blacks in Black and White*.

Alexandria

ALPHA PALACE *see* Virginia Theater

1785. CAPITOL THEATER
Picture house. 300 seats. Manager in 1934: Sidney Lust.
References: *Film Daily Yearbook*, 1940–1955. Headley, *Motion Picture Exhibition in Washington, D.C. Motion Picture Herald*, April 24, 1937; July 15, 1939. Sampson, *Blacks in Black and White*.

1725. CARVER THEATER
1120 Queen Street
Picture house. 684 seats. Also called King's Palace. Architect: John Z. Zink. According to Headley, the Carver opened in 1948 and operated until 1953. "The corner entrance was flanked by curved brick walls and topped by a glass brick tower. Hand-painted murals on the auditorium walls portrayed the life of George Washington Carver.... The Carver was planned as the first-run African American theater in Alexandria; second-run films, cowboy films, and serials were going to be shown at the Capitol." As of 1993, the building was being used as a church.
References: *Film Daily Yearbook*, 1949–1955. Headley, *Motion Picture Exhibition in Washington, D.C.*

1787. DUDLEY THEATER
Vaudeville and picture house. Manager: Sherman H. Dudley (African American).
References: Cahn, *Julius Cahn-Gus Hill Theatrical Guide. Film Daily Yearbook*, 1931, 1932. Hill, *Pages from the Harlem Renaissance*. Jackson, "Additions to Theater List," *Billboard*, December 31, 1921.

1788. LINCOLN THEATER
1101–1103 Queen Street
Picture and vaudeville house. Architect: Henry A. Bramlow. Also known as the Olympic. Managers in 1921: Irving Hicks and Clay Smith. Late in 1921, a local black group brought the theater. By 1930 Abe Lichtman leased the theater and changed its name to Olympic. The Lincoln ended up as an auto parts store.
References: Cahn, *Julius Cahn-Gus Hill Theatrical Guide. Film Daily Yearbook*, 1930–1933. Headley: *Motion Picture Exhibition in Washington D.C.* Jackson, "List of Colored Theaters and Attractions," *Billboard*, August 6, 1921. Work, *Negro Yearbook, 1921–1922*.

OLYMPIC THEATER *see* Lincoln Theater

1789. VIRGINIA THEATER
516–518 S. Pitt Street
Picture house. 1,133 seats. Architect: William J. Noble. Manager in 1919: Sherman S. Dudley. Manager in 1921: R. Shapiro. Headley described the theater as

"an unheated wood frame building." Around 1922, a new owner — Edward A. Barrett — changed the name of the theater to Alpha Palace.
References: Cahn, *Julius Cahn-Gus Hill Theatrical Guide*. Headley, *Motion Picture Exhibition in Washington, D.C.* Jackson, "List of Colored Theaters and Attractions," *Billboard*, August 6, 1921. Work, *Negro Yearbook, 1921–1922*.

Arlington

1790. ARLINGTON THEATER
Sycamore Street
Vaudeville house.
References: *Simms' Blue Book*.

Ashland

1791. CAB THEATER
Picture house.
References: *Film Daily Yearbook*, 1950–1955.

1792. OLD ASHLAND THEATER
Picture house.
References: *Film Daily Yearbook*, 1949.

Berkeley

1793. LIBERTY THEATER
Vaudeville house. Manager in 1921: M. H. Harkesen.
References: Cahn, *Julius Cahn-Gus Hill Theatrical Guide*. *Film Daily Yearbook*, 1930–1932. Jackson, "List of Colored Theaters and Attractions," *Billboard*, August 6, 1921. Work, *Negro Yearbook, 1921–1922*.

1794. LINCOLN THEATER
Picture house.
References: *Film Daily Yearbook*, 1933, 1940–1944. *Motion Picture Herald*, July 15, 1939.

1795. RITZ THEATER
Picture house. During the week of July 2, 1955, the Ritz showed the films *Cannibal Attack*, starring Johnny Weissmuller, and *Vera Cruz*, featuring Burt Lancaster and Gary Cooper.
References: *Norfolk Journal-Guide*, July 2, 1955. *Film Daily Yearbook*, 1944–1955.

1796. ROYAL THEATER
Picture house.
References: *Film Daily Yearbook*, 1944–1955.

Birds Nest

1797. MALLIE THEATER
Picture house.
References: *Film Daily Yearbook*, 1950–1955.

Bluefield

1798. LEE THEATER
519 Virginia Avenue
Picture house. 419 seats.
References: *Film Daily Yearbook*, 1949–1955.

Cape Charles

1799. CARVER THEATER
Picture house. 360 seats.
References: *Film Daily Yearbook*, 1949–1955.

Chase City

1800. HARDY THEATER
State Highway 49

Picture house. 300 seats.
References: *Film Daily Yearbook*, 1949–1955.

1801. MECCA THEATER
Main Street
Picture house. 600 seats.
References: *Film Daily Yearbook*, 1949–1955.

1802. ROXY THEATER
Picture house.
References: *Film Daily Yearbook*, 1949–1955.

Cheapside

1803. BOOKER T. THEATER
Picture house.
References: *Film Daily Yearbook*, 1950–1955.

1804. NEW THEATER
Picture house. This may have been the Booker T.
References: *Film Daily Yearbook*, 1949.

Danville

1805. COLUMBIA THEATER
Vaudeville house. Manager in 1914: W. A. Donleavy. The Columbia was on the Dudley vaudeville circuit. In early 1914, the Columbia featured the performers Hendricks and Leo, and Charles H. Clarke.
References: *Indianapolis Freeman*, "What's What on the Dudley Circuit," January 31, 1914.

1806. DIXIE THEATER
Vaudeville house. According to Peterson, the Dixie was part of the Dudley circuit from 1911 to 1916.
References: Peterson, *The African American Theatre Directory*.

1807. HIPPODROME THEATER
215 N. Union Street
Vaudeville house. A TOBA theater. Owner in 1921: James D. Henry. Manager in 1921: W. A. Donleavy. The house was part of the combined TOBA and M&P vaudeville circuit.
References: Cahn, *Julius Cahn-Gus Hill Theatrical Guide*. *Film Daily Yearbook*, 1930–1932. Hill, *Pages from the Harlem Renaissance*. Jackson, "List of Colored Theaters and Attractions," *Billboard*, August 6, 1921; "The Theater Owners' Booking Association," December 16, 1922.

1808. LINCOLN THEATER
Picture house.
References: *Film Daily Yearbook*, 1933.

1809. RITZ THEATER
Picture house. 554 seats.
References: *Film Daily Yearbook*, 1950–1955.

Emporia

1810. JOYNER THEATER
Picture house. 300 seats.
References: *Film Daily Yearbook*, 1949–1955.

1811. ROXY THEATER
Picture house.
References: *Film Daily Yearbook*, 1949–1955.

Exmore

1812. ROXY THEATER
Picture house.
References: *Film Daily Yearbook*, 1944–1955.

Gloucester

1813. AUDITORIUM THEATER

Picture house.
References: *Film Daily Yearbook*, 1949–1955.

Goshen

1814. MELODY THEATER
Picture house.
References: *Film Daily Yearbook*, 1949–1955.

Hampton

1815. BASIE THEATER
Picture house.
References: *Film Daily Yearbook*, 1949–1955.

1816. LINCOLN THEATER
Vaudeville and picture house. Manager: George C. Bacchus.
References: Cahn, *Julius Cahn-Gus Hill Theatrical Guide*. *Film Daily Yearbook*, 1941–1949, 1955. Work, *Negro Yearbook, 1921–1922*.

1817. LYRIC THEATER
Vaudeville and picture house. Manager: George C. Bacchus.
References: Cahn, *Julius Cahn-Gus Hill Theatrical Guide*. *Film Daily Yearbook*, 1940–1955. Jackson, "List of Colored Theaters and Attractions," *Billboard*, August 6, 1921. *Motion Picture Herald*, July 15, 1939. Work, *Negro Yearbook, 1921–1922*.

Hopewell

1818. ARLINGTON THEATER
Picture house.
References: *Film Daily Yearbook*, 1950–1955.

Kenbridge

1819. FREE STATE THEATER
Broad Street
Picture house. 483 seats.
References: *Film Daily Yearbook*, 1949–1955.

Lynchburg

1820. BOSTON THEATER
Vaudeville house on the Dudley circuit. Manager: C. C. Andrews. The Whitman Sisters played there in 1914.
References: *Chicago Defender*, November 30, 1914. Peterson, *The African American Theatre Directory*. Sampson, *Blacks in Blackface*.

1821. EMPIRE THEATER
Vaudeville house. Manager in 1921: C. K. Smith.
References: Cahn, *Julius Cahn-Gus Hill Theatrical Guide*. Jackson, "List of Colored Theaters and Attractions," *Billboard*, August 6, 1921. Work, *Negro Yearbook, 1921–1922*.

1822. FORD'S THEATER
Vaudeville house. Manager in 1914: R. F. Johnson. Ford's was part of the Dudley vaudeville circuit. The Burtons appeared here in 1914.
References: *Indianapolis Freeman*, "What's What on the Dudley Circuit," January 31, 1914.

1823. HARRISON THEATER
905 5th Street
Picture house. 393 seats. Owners: Lichtman Theaters. Manager in 1941: Lorenzo Feels. In July 1955, the Harrison featured the motion pictures *Ten Wanted Men*, starring Randolph Scott, *Sign of the Pagan*, with Jack Palance and Jeff Chandler, *Silver Star*, with Edgar Buchanan and Marie Windsor, and *World for Ransom*, starring Dan Duryea.

Martinsville

1824. DUBOIS THEATER
Picture house. Manager in 1921: H. Ball.
References: Cahn, *Julius Cahn-Gus Hill Theatrical Guide*. Jackson, "List of Colored Theaters and Attractions," *Billboard*, August 6, 1921. Work, *Negro Yearbook, 1921–1922*.

1825. FAYETTE STREET AUDITORIUM
Picture house.
References: *Film Daily Yearbook*, 1930–1933.

1826. REX THEATER
Fayette Street
Picture house. 350 seats.
References: *Film Daily Yearbook*, 1944–1955.

1827. WEST END THEATER
Fayette Street
Picture house. 400 seats.
References: *Film Daily Yearbook*, 1952–1955.

Montrose

1828. MONTROSE THEATER
Picture house.
References: *Film Daily Yearbook*, 1949–1955.

Newport News

1829. CAPITOL THEATER
Picture house.
References: *Film Daily Yearbook*, 1930–1932.

1830. CARVER THEATER
3105 Chestnut Avenue
Picture house. 350 seats. According to *Film Daily Yearbook*, the Carver was closed in 1950.
References: *Film Daily Yearbook*, 1949–1955.

1831. COLONIAL THEATER
1414 Wanule Avenue
Vaudeville and picture house. The Colonial was part of the combined TOBA and M&P vaudeville circuit.
References: *Film Daily Yearbook*, 1930–1932. Hill, *Pages from the Harlem Renaissance*. Jackson, "The Theater Owners' Booking Association," *Billboard*, December 16, 1922.

1832. DIXIE THEATER
2129 Jefferson Avenue
Picture house. 800 seats.
References: *Film Daily Yearbook*, 1930–1933, 1940–1955. *Motion Picture Herald*, July 15, 1939.

1833. DUDLEY THEATER
Vaudeville house on the S. H. Dudley circuit. Named for owner Sherman H. Dudley, a black entertainer who performed with Williams and Walker. Manager in 1911: Leigh Whipper.
References: Hill, *Pages from the Harlem Renaissance*. Peterson, *The African American Theatre Directory*; *Profiles of African American Stage Performers*. Smith, *Bert Williams*.

1834. JEFFERSON THEATER
632 25th Street
Picture house. 355 sears. Owned by Lichtman Theaters. Manager in 1941: Ernest L. Lewin. During the week of July 2, 1955, the Jefferson was showing the film *Underwater!* starring Jane Russell.
References: *Film Daily Yearbook*, 1940–1955. *Motion Picture Herald*, April 24, 1937; July 15, 1939. Sampson, *Blacks in Black and White*.

1835. LINCOLN THEATER
20th Street and Jefferson Avenue
Vaudeville house. Manager in 1921: W. L. Mosely.
References: Cahn, *Julius Cahn–Gus Hill Theatrical Guide*. Jackson, "List of Colored Theaters and Attractions," *Billboard*, August 6, 1921. Work, *Negro Yearbook, 1921–1922*.

1836. LYRIC THEATER
Vaudeville house. During the week of April 12, 1915, dancers George Stamper and Lula Lawson were at the Lyric, along with Martin and Motley's Merrymakers.
References: *Indianapolis Freeman*, April 17, 1915.

1837. MOTON THEATER
2101 Jefferson Avenue
Picture house. 557 seats. Manager in 1941: Isaac M. Burden. During the week of July 2, 1955, the Moton was showing the films *The Wild One*, starring Marlon Brando, and *Destry*, starring Audie Murphy.
References: *Film Daily Yearbook*, 1944–1955. *Norfolk Journal–Guide*, July 2, 1955.

Norfolk

1838. ATTUCKS THEATER
1010–12 Church Street
Vaudeville, picture, and drama house. A TOBA theater. Built in 1919 by the Twin City Amusement Company. It later was controlled by the Quality Amusement Company. Managers in 1921: Rufus Byars and Billy Pierce (African Americans). During the week of January 3, 1921, the Attucks featured Douglas Fairbanks in the picture *His Majesty the American*, along with the comedy *The Bone Dry Blues*. A local African American group — the Southland Singers — performed at the 9:30 p.m. show on Wednesday and Thursday. On Saturday there was a matinee for children starring the Hambone Jones Company. During the week of October 17, 1921, the vaudeville group known as The Smarter Set — featuring J. Homer Tutt, Amon Davis, and Salem Tutt Whitney — played the Attucks. According to Peterson, "although this theatre had a policy of permitting whites to attend Friday midnight performances on an integrated basis, this policy was soon dropped after the City of Norfolk passed an ordinance forbidding such practices in November 1922." Jazz musician Sidney Bechet and blues singer Bessie Smith performed together in the 1923 musical *How Come?* According to Walker, the Crispus Attucks Cultural Center, Inc., a non-profit organization, is raising funds to restore the Attucks Theater.
References: Albertson, *Bessie*. Cahn, *Julius Cahn–Gus Hill Theatrical Guide*. *Film Daily Yearbook*, 1930–1933. Hill, *Pages from the Harlem Renaissance*. Jackson, "List of Colored Theaters and Attractions," *Billboard*, August 6, 1921. *Norfolk Journal–Guide*, January 3, 1921; October 17, 1921. Peterson, *The African American Theatre Directory*. Walker, "The Attucks Theatre," Crispus Attucks Cultural Center website. Work, *Negro Yearbook 1921–1922*.

1839. BOOKER T. THEATER
Picture house. 1,200 seats. Manager in 1941: Hugo Harrison. During the week of July 2, 1955, the movies *Port of Hell*, starring Dane Clark, and *Rage at Dawn*, featuring Randolph Scott, were playing at the Booker T.
References: *Film Daily Yearbook*, 1940–1955. *Motion Picture Herald*, April 24, 1937; July 15, 1939. *Norfolk Journal–Guide*, July 2, 1955. Sampson, *Blacks in Black and White*.

1840. CARVER THEATER

Attucks Theater, Norfolk, Virginia (SoulOfAmerica.com)

Picture house. Manager in 1941: Robert J. Moye. During the week of July 2, 1955, the Carver was playing the movies *House of Wax*, starring Vincent Price and Phyllis Kirk, and *Guns Ablaze*, with Walter Houston and Andy Devine. According to *Film Daily Yearbook*, the Carver was closed in 1950.
References: *Film Daily Yearbook*, 1944–1955. *Norfolk Journal–Guide*, July 2, 1955.

1841. COLONIAL THEATER
120 W. Tazewell
Picture house. 1,100 seats.
References: Hill, *Pages from the Harlem Renaissance*.

1842. COLUMBIA THEATER
Picture house.
References: *Film Daily Yearbook*, 1930–1932.

1843. CRESTWOOD THEATER
Main Street
Picture house. 215 seats.
References: *Film Daily Yearbook*, 1950–1955.

1844. DOZIER THEATER
Picture house. Owner in 1923: J.E. Reese.
According to Bowser, "J.E. Reese opened the Dozier Theater to Colored patrons after the house had been dark for a long time. However, 'local white citizens did not approve.' On opening day, the theater was picketed and patrons were 'warned away.' At the evening's performance, 'a shot was fired from a shotgun and the audience was stampeded; the next day an injunction against operating the theater for Negroes was granted. This despite the fact that it is a Negro neighborhood."
References: *Baltimore Afro-American*, March 23, 1923. Bowser, *Writing Himself into History*.

1845. DUNBAR THEATER
660 Church Street
Picture house. 400 seats. During the week of July 2, 1955, the Dunbar was showing the movies *The Far Country*, starring James Stewart, Ruth Roman, Corrine Calvet, and Walter Brennan, *Suddenly*, featuring Frank Sinatra, and Alfred Hitchcock's thriller *Rear Window*, with Grace Kelly and James Stewart.
References: *Film Daily Yearbook*, 1949–1955. *Norfolk Journal–Guide*, July 2, 1955.

1846. GEM THEATER
815 Church Street
Picture house. 487 seats.
References: *Film Daily Yearbook*, 1944–1955.

1847. GLOBE THEATER
Vaudeville house. The Globe was part of the Dudley vaudeville circuit.
References: Hill, *Pages from the Harlem Renaissance*.

1848. LENNOX THEATER
706–708 Church Street
Picture house. 500 seats.
During the week of July 2, 1955, the film *There's No Business Like Show Business* played at the Lennox.
References: *Film Daily Yearbook*, 1944–1955. *Norfolk Journal–Guide*, July 2, 1955.

1849. MANHATTAN THEATER
623 E. Queen Street
Picture house. 500 seats. Owned by Lichtman Theaters. Manager in 1941: James L. White. According to *Film Daily Yearbook*, the Manhattan was closed in 1950 and 1951.
References: *Film Daily Yearbook*, 1930–1933, 1940–1955. *Motion Picture Herald*, April 24, 1937; July 15, 1939. Sampson, *Blacks in Blackface*.

1850. MOTON THEATER
Picture house. During the week of July

2, 1955, the Moton was showing Cecil DeMille's *Reap the Wild Wind*, starring John Wayne and Susan Hayward, and the western *The Redhead and the Cowboy*, with Glenn Ford, Rhonda Fleming, and Edmond O'Brien. On Saturday, there was a "kiddie show" consisting of cartoons and the pictures *Sioux City Sue*, starring Gene Autry, and *Canadian Mounties versus the Atomic Invaders*.

References: *Norfolk Journal–Guide*, July 2, 1955.

1851. PALACE THEATER
830 Church Street
Vaudeville house. A TOBA theater. Manager: Hoffheimer Corporation.

References: Cahn. *Julius Cahn–Gus Hill Theatrical Guide*. Hill, *Pages from the Harlem Renaissance*. Jackson, "List of Colored Theaters and Attractions," *Billboard*, August 6, 1921; "The Theater Owners' Booking Association," *Billboard*, December 16, 1921. Work, *Negro Yearbook, 1921–1922*.

1852. REGAL THEATER
828 Church Street
Picture house. 875–1,000 seats. Manager in 1941: Joseph M. Rowley. During the week of July 2, 1955, the Regal showed the films *Smoke Signals*, starring Dana Andrews and Piper Laurie, and *The She-Wolf*, featuring Kerima and introducing actress May Britt.

References: *Film Daily Yearbook*, 1933, 1940–1955. *Motion Picture Herald*, April 24, 1937; July 15, 1939. *Norfolk Journal–Guide*, July 2, 1955. Sampson, *Blacks in Black and White*.

1853. STAR THEATER
Picture house.
References: *Film Daily Yearbook*, 1930–1933.

Parksley

1854. GEORGES THEATER
Picture house. According to *Film Daily Yearbook*, the Georges was closed in 1949 and 1950.
References: *Film Daily Yearbook*, 1949–1955.

1855. LOUISE THEATER
Picture house. 260 seats.
References: *Film Daily Yearbook*, 1945–1955.

Petersburg

1856. DUDLEY THEATER
109 Harrison Street
Vaudeville house. Manager: Sherman H. Dudley (African American). The house was part of the Dudley circuit and later the combined TOBA and Managers and Performers vaudeville circuit.

References: Cahn, *Julius Cahn–Gus Hill Theatrical Guide*. *Film Daily Yearbook*, 1930–1932. Hill, *Pages from the Harlem Renaissance*. Jackson, "List of Colored Theaters and Attractions," *Billboard*, August 6, 1921; "The Theater Owners' Booking Association," *Billboard*, December 16, 1922. Work, *Negro Yearbook, 1921–1922*.

1857. GEM THEATER
222 Halifax Street
Picture house. 415 seats. Manager: John G. Vaughn (African American). The Gem was owned by Lichtman Theaters. During Christmas week of 1941, the house was showing the motion picture *Belle Starr*, with Randolph Scott, Gene Tierney, Louise Beavers, Clarence Muse, and Stymie Beard. During the week of July 2, 1955, the Gem featured the movies *Run for Cover*, starring James Cagney, *A Star Is Born*, starring Judy Garland and James

Mason, and *The Outcast*, with John Derek and Joan Evans.
References: *Film Daily Yearbook*, 1944–1955. *Norfolk Journal-Guide*, December 1941, July 2, 1955.

1858. IDLE HOUR THEATER
112–114 Halifax Street
Picture house. 360 seats. Also known as Barney's Idle Hour.
References: *Film Daily Yearbook*, 1930–1933, 1940–1955. *Motion Picture Herald*, July 15, 1939.

1859. RIALTO THEATER
108 South Avenue
Picture house. Manger in 1921: O. R. Johnson (African American).
References: Cahn, *Julius Cahn-Gus Hill Theatrical Guide*. Jackson, "List of Colored Theaters and Attractions," *Billboard*, August 6, 1921. Work, *Negro Yearbook, 1921–1922*.

1860. STATE THEATER
Picture house.
References: *Film Daily Yearbook*, 1940. *Motion Picture Herald*, July 15, 1939.

Portsmouth

1861. BLAND THEATER
Picture house. Owned by Litchman Theaters. Manager in 1941: George W. Riddick. According to *Film Daily Yearbook*, the Bland was closed in 1950 and 1951.
References: *Film Daily Yearbook*, 1944–1955.

1862. CAPITOL THEATER
608 Effington Street
Picture house. 500–835 seats. Owned by Litchman Theaters. Manager in 1941: Marc A. Terrell.
References: *Film Daily Yearbook*, 1930–1933, 1940–1955. Hill, *Pages from the Harlem Renaissance*. Jackson, "Additions to Theater List," *Billboard*, December 31, 1921. *Motion Picture Herald*, April 24, 1937; July 15, 1939. Sampson, *Blacks in Black and White*.

1863. CARVER THEATER
Picture house.
References: *Film Daily Yearbook*, 1949–1955.

1864. COLONIAL THEATER
Picture house.
References: Cahn, *Julius Cahn-Gus Hill Theatrical Guide*.

1865. LINCOLN THEATER
Picture house. Manager in 1921: John Mills.
References: Cahn, *Julius Cahn-Gus Hill Theatrical Guide*. Jackson, "List of Colored Theaters and Attractions," *Billboard*, August 6, 1921. Work, *Negro Yearbook, 1921–1922*.

1866. LYRIC THEATER
907 High Street
Picture house. 540 seats.
References: *Film Daily Yearbook*, 1944–1955.

1867. PORTSMOUTH THEATER
Picture house.
References: Hill, *Pages from the Harlem Renaissance*.

1868. QUEEN THEATER
Picture house.
References: *Film Daily Yearbook*, 1949–1955.

Richmond

1869. BOOKER T. THEATER
118 Broad Street
Picture and vaudeville house. 900 seats. Owned by Lichtman Theaters. Manager in 1941: R. L. Ward. The open-

ing feature films in 1933 were *I Cover the Waterfront*, starring Claudette Colbert, and *Flying Down to Rio*, featuring Fred Astaire, Ginger Rogers, and Etta Moten. During Christmas week of 1941, the Booker T. was showing *Weekend Havana*, starring Alice Faye, John Payne, Carmen Miranda, and Cesar Romero.

References: *Film Daily Yearbook*, 1940–1955. *Motion Picture Herald*, April 24, 1937; July 15, 1939. Peterson, *The African American Theatre Directory*. Sampson, *Blacks in Black and White*.

1870. BROADWAY OPEN AIR THEATER

Picture house. Also known as the Open Air. According to *Film Daily Yearbook*, the Broadway Open Air was closed in 1949. This may have been a drive-in.

References: *Film Daily Yearbook*, 1949–1955.

1871. DIXIE THEATER

Vaudeville house. This theater was original on the Dudley vaudeville circuit.

References: Hill, *Pages from the Harlem Renaissance*.

1872. GLOBE THEATER

510 N. 2nd Street

Picture house. 500 seats. Owned by Lichtman Theaters. Manager in 1921: Ray Hollenger. Manager in 1941: Thomas Thompson. During Christmas week of 1941, the Globe was showing *Blondie Goes Latin*, starring Penny Singleton and Arthur Lake, *Dude Cowboy* featuring Tim Holt, and *Footsteps in the Dark*, starring Errol Flynn.

References: Cahn, *Julius Cahn-Gus Hill Theatrical Guide*. *Film Daily Yearbook*, 1930–1933, 1940–1955. Jackson, "List of Colored Theaters and Attractions," *Billboard*, August 6, 1921. *Motion Picture Herald*, April 24, 1937; July 15, 1939. Sampson, *Blacks in Black and White*. Work, *Negro Yearbook 1921–1922*.

1873. GREEN'S OPERA HOUSE

Vaudeville house. The house was part of the S. H. Dudley Circuit. The vaudeville act Nit and Tuck performed here in November 1914.

References: *Chicago Defender*, November 30, 1914. Peterson, *The African American Theatre Directory*. Sampson, *Blacks in Blackface*.

1874. HIPPODROME THEATER

528 N. 2nd Street

Vaudeville and picture house. 850–900 seats. A TOBA theater. Manager in 1921: Charles Somma. Manager in 1941: Lorenzo Minor. The Hippodrome was part of the combined TOBA and M & P circuit.

References: Cahn. *Julius Cahn-Gus Hill Theatrical Guide. Film Daily Yearbook*, 1930–1933, 1940–1955. Hill, *Pages from the Harlem Renaissance*. Jackson, "List of Colored Theaters and Attractions," *Billboard*, August 6, 1921. *Motion Picture Herald*, April 24, 1937; July 15, 1939. Work, *Negro Yearbook 1921–1922*.

1875. LENOX THEATER

Picture house.

References: *Film Daily Yearbook*, 1949–1953.

1876. LINCOLN THEATER

1919 Hull Street

Picture house. 325 seats.

References: *Film Daily Yearbook*, 1940–1955. *Motion Picture Herald*, April 24, 1937; July 15, 1939. Sampson, *Blacks in Black and White*.

1877. RAYO THEATER

Vaudeville house. Manager in 1921: Ray Hollenger.

References: Cahn, *Julius Cahn-Gus Hill Theatrical Guide*. Jackson, "List of Colored Theaters and Attractions," *Billboard*, August 6, 1921. Work, *Negro Yearbook 1921–1922*.

REGENCY THEATER *see* Walker Theater

1878. ROBINSON THEATER
2901–03 Q Street
Picture house. 600 seats. Owned by Lichtman Theaters. Manager in 1941: Howard Lucas.
During Christmas week of 1941, the Robinson was showing the picture *The Devil Commands*, with Boris Karloff, and *Aloma of the South Seas*, starring Dorothy Lamour and Jon Hall.
References: *Film Daily Yearbook*, 1940–1949. *Motion Picture Herald*, April 24, 1937; July 15, 1939. Sampson, *Blacks in Black and White*.

1879. STAR THEATER
514 Louisiana Street
Picture house. 200 seats.
References: *Motion Picture Herald*, April 24, 1937. Sampson, *Blacks in Black and White*.

1880. WALKER THEATER
116 W. Broad Street
Picture house. 386–392 seats. Also known as the Regency. Owned by Lichtman Theaters.
Manager in 1941: Walter Shivers. During Christmas week of 1941 the Walker was showing the film *Ladies in Retirement*, starring Ida Lupino.
References: *Film Daily Yearbook*, 1940–1949. *Motion Picture Herald*, April 24, 1937; July 15, 1939. *Norfolk Journal-Guide*, December 27, 1941. Sampson, *Blacks in Black and White*.

Roanoke

1881. BOSTON THEATER
Vaudeville house. The Boston was on the Dudley and later the Southern Consolidated vaudeville circuits.
References: Hill, *Pages from the Harlem Renaissance*. Peterson, *The African American Theatre Directory*.

1882. HAMPTON THEATER
Picture house. Manager in 1921: C. F. Tolliver. Also called the Strand.
References: Cahn. *Julius Cahn-Gus Hill Theatrical Guide. Film Daily Yearbook*, 1930–1933. Jackson, "List of Colored Theaters and Attractions," *Billboard*, August 6, 1921. Peterson, *The African American Theatre Directory*. Work, *Negro Yearbook, 1921–1922*.

1883. HIPPODROME THEATER
Vaudeville house. Manager in 1914: W. J. Goulter. The Hippodrome was part of the S. H. Dudley Circuit. In November 1914, the vaudeville show featured the acts Davis and Green and Brown and Pinkey.
Sources: *Chicago Defender*, November 30, 1914. Sampson, *Blacks in Blackface*.

STRAND THEATER *see* Hampton Theater

1884. VIRGINIAN THEATER
38 Centre Avenue NW
Picture house. 500–531 seats. In December 1941, Virginian audiences saw *Sun Valley Serenade*, starring Sonja Henie, John Payne, the Nicholas Brothers, Dorothy Dandridge, and Glenn Miller's Orchestra; another holiday feature was the comedy *Caught in the Draft*, starring Bob Hope and Dorothy Lamour. In July 1955, the Virginian featured the following pictures: *Six Bridges to Cross*, starring Tony Curtis; *The Americano*, starring Glenn Ford; *Drive a Crooked Road*, with Mickey Rooney; and *The Desparado*, starring John Wayne.
References: *Film Daily Yearbook*, 1940–1955. *Motion Picture Herald*, April 24, 1937; July 15, 1939. *Norfolk Journal-Guide*, December 27, 1941; July 2, 1955. Sampson, *Blacks in Black and White*.

Sedley

1885. CARVER THEATER
Picture house.
References: *Film Daily Yearbook*, 1954–1955.

1886. SEDLEY THEATER
Picture house. 233 seats.
References: *Film Daily Yearbook*, 1949–1955.

Staunton

1887. SUNNYSIDE THEATER
Vaudeville house. Owner: Mrs. R. L. Pannel. According to Peterson, the Sunnyside was in business during the early 1900s.
References: Peterson, *The African American Theatre Directory*.

Suffolk

1888. BROADWAY THEATER
Picture house.
References: *Film Daily Yearbook*, 1930–1932, 1940. *Motion Picture Herald*, April 24, 1937; July 15, 1939. Sampson, *Blacks in Black and White*.

1889. CARVER THEATER
Picture house.
References: *Film Daily Yearbook*, 1944–1950.

1890. LENOX THEATER
Picture house.
References: *Film Daily Yearbook*, 1954, 1955.

1891. LINCOLN THEATER
Picture house.
References: *Film Daily Yearbook*, 1954, 1955.

1892. ROBINSON THEATER
Picture house.
References: *Film Daily Yearbook*, 1954, 1955.

1893. WALKER THEATER
Picture house.
References: *Film Daily Yearbook*, 1954, 1955.

Tazewell

1894. CLINCH THEATER
Main Street
Picture house. 450 seats.
References: *Film Daily Yearbook*, 1949–1955.

1895. VALLEY THEATER
Picture house. 350 seats.
References: *Film Daily Yearbook*, 1949–1955.

Trebernville

1896. MALLIE THEATER
Picture house. 350 seats.
References: *Film Daily Yearbook*, 1949–1955.

Williamsburg

1897. APOLLO THEATER
References: *Film Daily Yearbook*, 1940. *Motion Picture Herald*, April 24, 1937; July 15, 1939. Sampson, *Blacks in Black and White*.

1898. BRUTON HEIGHTS THEATER
Picture house. 392 seats. According to *Film Daily Yearbook*, the Bruton Heights was closed from 1949 through 1951.
References: *Film Daily Yearbook*, 1949–1955.

WASHINGTON

Seattle

1899. ATLAS THEATER
412 Maynard Street
Picture house. 420 seats.
References: *Film Daily Yearbook*, 1949–1955.

WEST VIRGINIA

Bluefield

1900. BLUEFIELD INSTITUTE
Picture house.
References: *Film Daily Yearbook*, 1930–1932.

1901. EMPIRE THEATER
293 Bland Street
Vaudeville and picture house. Manager in 1921: C.C. Cole (African American).
References: Jackson, "Additions to Theater List," *Billboard*, December 31, 1921.

1902. FIELDS THEATER
Picture house. 290 seats.
References: *Film Daily Yearbook*, 1949–1955.

Charleston

1903. ARMORY THEATER
408 Capitol Street
Musical and drama house. Said to play "colored companies."
References: Cahn, *Julius Cahn-Gus Hill Theatrical Guide*. Jackson, "List of Colored Theaters and Attractions," *Billboard*, August 6, 1921. Work, *Negro Yearbook*, 1921–1922.

1904. FERGUSON THEATER
833 Capital Avenue
Picture house. 362–500 seats.
References: *Film Daily Yearbook*, 1930–1933, 1940–1955. Hill, *Pages from the Harlem Renaissance. Motion Picture Herald*, April 24, 1937; July 15, 1939. Sampson, *Blacks in Black and White*.

1905. PALACE THEATER
Picture house.
References: *Film Daily Yearbook*, 1955.

Clarksburg

1906. KELLY MILLER THEATER
Picture house. According to *Billboard*, this theater featured "race films."
References: Cahn, *Julius Cahn-Gus Hill Theatrical Guide*. Jackson, "List of

Colored Theaters and Attractions," *Billboard*, August 6, 1921. Work, *Negro Yearbook, 1921–1922*.

Huntington

1907. CARVER THEATER
Picture house.
References: *Film Daily Yearbook*, 1955.

1908. DREAMLAND THEATER
Picture and vaudeville house. Owner in 1921: Dr. Adams.
References: Cahn, *Julius Cahn-Gus Hill Theatrical Guide*. Jackson, "Additions to Theater List," *Billboard*, December 31, 1921.

1909. FOX THEATER
Picture house. 275 seats.
References: Cahn, *Julius Cahn-Gus Hill Theatrical Guide*. *Film Daily Yearbook*, 1940–1955. *Motion Picture Herald*, April 24, 1937; July 15, 1939. Sampson, *Blacks in Black and White*.

1910. HENTON THEATER
Vaudeville and picture house. Manager in 1921: J. B. Henton (African American).
References: Cahn, *Julius Cahn-Gus Hill Theatrical Guide*. Jackson, "Additions to Theater List," *Billboard*, December 31, 1921.

1911. HUNTINGTON THEATER
Picture house.
References: *Film Daily Yearbook*, 1930.

1912. LINCOLN THEATER
Picture house.
References: *Film Daily Yearbook*, 1931, 1932.

Institute

1913. INSTITUTE THEATER
Picture house.
References: *Film Daily Yearbook*, 1930–1932.

Keyser

1914. LEWIS THEATER
Picture house.
References: *Film Daily Yearbook*, 1940–1955.

Laredo

1915. LAREDO THEATER
Picture house.
References: *Film Daily Yearbook*, 1940–1955. *Motion Picture Herald*, July 15, 1939.

Logan

1916. GEM THEATER
Picture house. According to *Film Daily Yearbook*, the Gem was closed from 1950 to 1955.
References: *Film Daily Yearbook*, 1940–1955.

Montgomery

1917. EMPIRE THEATER
Picture and vaudeville house. Manager in 1921: R. S. Shields.
References: Cahn, *Julius Cahn-Gus Hill Theatrical Guide*. Jackson, "Additions to Theater List," *Billboard*, December 31, 1921.

Northfork

1918. CLARK THEATER
Vaudeville house. Manager: F. E. Alexander (African American).

References: Cahn, *Julius Cahn-Gus Hill Theatrical Guide*. Jackson, "List of Colored Theaters and Attractions," *Billboard*, August 6, 1921. Work, *Negro Yearbook 1921–1922*.

Wheeling

1919. ALDON THEATER
Picture house.
References: *Film Daily Yearbook*, 1949–1955.

1920. FEDO THEATER
Picture house.
References: *Film Daily Yearbook*, 1950–1955.

1921. TEMPLE THEATER
Picture house.
References: *Film Daily Yearbook*, 1940–1948. *Motion Picture Herald*, July 15, 1939.

WISCONSIN

Milwaukee

1922. REGAL THEATER
704 W. Walnut Street
Picture house. According to Trotter, "By the late 1930s, [the Regal] had shifted from a predominately white audience to a predominately black clientele and received billing in the *Wisconsin Enterprise Blade* as 'our theater.' Many Afro-Americans, especially middle-class blacks, refused to patronize the Regal "because of noise caused by children and lack of supervision."
References: *Film Daily Yearbook*, 1947–1955. Trotter, *Black Milwaukee*.

APPENDIX 1

Numbers of Theater Buildings

Total Number of African American Theaters Selected Years, 1909–1955

(Sources used do not permit an unbroken run of dates.)

Year	Number
1909	112
1921	346
1922	253
1925	425
1930	461
1931	455
1932	445
1933	400
1937	232
1939	388
1940	397
1941	389
1942	403
1943	411
1944	425
1945	422
1946	480
1947	559
1948	619
1949	911
1950	971
1951	959
1952	1,072
1953	992
1954	1,037
1955	1,036

(Sources: *Indianapolis Freeman*, March 13, 1909. Jackson, "List of Colored Theaters and Attractions," *Billboard*, August 6, 1921, December 16, 1922. *Film Daily Yearbook*, 1930–1933, 1940–1955. *Motion Picture Herald*, April 24, 1937; January 24, 1939. Work, *Negro Yearbook*, 1921–1922; 1925–1926.

States with the Most African American Theaters, 1900–1955

The tallies shown below reflect the total number of theaters for black audiences that a given state had during the period 1900–1955. This does not, however, mean that in some particular year a state contained the total number of theaters recorded here. The numbers show the *total* number of African American theaters documented in each state during the period of this book's coverage. The numbers of houses vary greatly from year to year and from state to state. These numbers provide some insight into what states were most likely to provide or permit entertainment venues for their African American population. They demonstrate that Southern states more than Northern states tended to have "all-black" theaters despite the fact that Southern black theaters were not as famous as those in the North.

1. Texas — 215
2. Florida — 189
3. North Carolina — 157
4. Georgia — 114
5. Virginia — 113
6. Louisiana — 98

7. Alabama — 88
8. Mississippi — 81
9. Ohio — 74
10. New York — 71
11. Illinois — 68
12. South Carolina — 57

Cities with the Most African American Theaters, 1900–1955

The following tallies reflect major cities' total number of theaters catering to African American audiences during the period 1900 through 1955. This does not, however, mean that at any given time a city had the high number of theaters listed here. The numbers show the *total* number of African American theaters documented in each city during the period of this book's coverage. The numbers of houses varied greatly from year to year and from city to city. It is interesting to compare this list with the immediately preceding one, which shows that the states with the most African American theaters in the early twentieth century were in the South. In contrast, this table records that of the top 20 American cities with African American theaters, 11 were in the North. Of the top five cities, three were north of the Mason-Dixon Line. This suggests that while Northern cities witnessed the building of many black theaters, the South had *overall* more theaters for its African American population, in both rural and urban areas.

1. New York, New York (Bronx, Brooklyn, Manhattan) — 60
2. Chicago, Illinois — 49
3. Detroit, Michigan — 48
4. District of Columbia — 34
5. Baltimore, Maryland — 34
6. Philadelphia, Pennsylvania — 31
7. Saint Louis, Missouri — 30
8. Indianapolis, Indiana — 22
9. Houston, Texas — 21
10. Atlanta, Georgia — 20
11. Cleveland, Ohio — 20
12. Los Angeles, California — 18
13. Pittsburgh, Pennsylvania — 18
14. New Orleans, Louisiana — 17
15. Dallas, Texas — 15
16. Norfolk, Virginia — 15
17. Cincinnati, Ohio — 14
18. Newark, New Jersey — 13
19. Jacksonville, Florida — 13
20. Kansas City, Missouri — 12

APPENDIX 2

Architects

Adler, Darmark
Backoff, George W.
Bamlow, Henry A.
Bates, Edward T.
Beall, F.E.
Bowers, James A.
Callis and Callis
Charles, Stewart
Childs, George S.
Clafflin, Fuller
Cowan, John
Crane, C. Howard
Denny, C.
Dowrick, James A.
Emmart, Paul
Flaks, Kalm
Geare, Reginald
Gray, W.B.
Greenbaum and Evartt
Hahn, Frank E.
Hales, George P.
Haller, N.T.
Hallet, Morris
Harrison, David
Hattan, I. J.
High, Wallace
Hitchler, J. J.
Hoffman and Henon
Hollabird and Roche
Hughes, T. Cecil
Hurlburt, George C.
Hurlehane, F.A.
Jones, C. Clark
Julien, Philip M.
Kahn, Albert
Kalischer, Mark D.
Klein, William J.
Kourkoulis, James
Laferty, J.E.
Lamb, Thomas W.
Levey, Alexander J.
Levin, Joseph
Lockart, E.A.
Lockwood and Poundstone
Long, J. K.
McAuley, Hugh
Magaziner, Eberhard and Harris
Melby, J.A.
Midner and Eisen
Milburn, Herster and Co.
Mizner, Addison Cairns
Morstein, Harry
Myerberg, Julius
Noble, William J.
Page, Harvey L.
Pietsch, Theodore W.
Pittman, W. Sidney
Plowman, George
Pottle, George V.
Plager, W.S.
Proctor, F. B.
Ramish, Adolph
Root, John Wellborn
Rubish and Hunter
Russell, Stanislaus
Santmeyer, George R.
Smith, Harry T.
Smith, Wilson Porter
Speiden, Albert
Speiden, William L.
Storck, J. Edward
Stratten, William B.
Stucket and Sloan
Tormey, F.E.
Turner, Samuel R.
Vaughn and Hattan
Warner, James H.
Wenig, Julius
Wetzell, B. C.
Wight, Oliver B.
Wilby, Ernest
Williams Brothers
Zink, John

APPENDIX 3

Owners and Managers

(* = *African American*)

ABC Theatrical Enterprises
Abram, Victor
Adams, A. N.*
Adams, Dr.
Adams, Floyd
Adams, George
Adams, Mr.
Adler, David
Alexander, F.E.*
Alston, W. S.*
Amazon Amusement Company
Andrews, C.C.
Angelos, George
Armstead, Thomas
Aronson, M. M.
Ascher Brothers
Atkinson, Sam
Atwood, C. K.
Austin, Benjamin
Austin, Buddy*
Bacchus, George C.
Bailey, Tom
Ball, H.
Barasso, A.
Barkett, M.
Barnes, Jerry C.
Barr, A.
Barr, Joseph W.
Barraco, Paul
Barrett, George
Barrett, James
Barrett, Richard D.*
Bartholomew, H.C.
Baum, S.
Beardreaux and Bennett
Beaux and Whitlow*
Bell, Otis
Bell, R. A.
Bell, Steve*
Benjamin, Arthur E.
Benjamin, Roy
Berheimer Theaters
Bernard, Thomas
Bijou Amusement Company
Binder, A. L.
Boehringer, Ernest
Bolansy, Bernard E.
Bolden, J.*
Bond, Monument
Bordeaux and Camp
Bottom, R. A.
Bowman, Mrs. Anna
Bramlow, H. A.
Breaux, Zelia N.*
Brecher, Leo
Brewer, Charles
Brown, Amanda
Brown, Edward C.*
Brown, Frank
Brown, G.*
Brown, G. F.
Brown, James
Brown, Jim
Brown, Mr.
Brown, Willis
Browsky, M. B.
Brunet, Paul H.
Buggs, Jim
Bunts, H. A.*
Burden, Issac M.
Burrell, Alfred A.
Byars, Rufus G.*
Caffey, Charles
Calhoun, Virgil
Camp, James F.
Campbell, Alan
Cannon, J. C. V.
Carey and Prestman
Carpentier, Curtis W.
Carr, Walter
Carter, Jack
Cattey, C. H.
Chappelle, Pat H.*
Chase, C.*
Chase, R.
Cherry, W. M.*
Church, Robert E.
Clemmon Brothers
Coffey, Charles
Cole, C. C.
Cole, R. W.
Coleman, Mr.*
Colfax, Mr.
Conley, Ed*
Costi, John
Cox, Lloyd H.
Craver, S. W.
Crawford, J. H.
Cremen, James
Crisp, Tobe*
Cross, Robert*
Crowd, Frank*

Crown Amusement
  Company
Cummings, Ernest L.
Cunningham, Arthur
Curry, Mrs.
Curthbert, J. H.*
Curtis, L. B.
Dabney, Ford*
Daley, William H.
Davis, Elijah
Davis, Wiley
Dawson, J. J.*
Delano, Peter
Derrick, Howard
DeWalt, Olen Pullum*
DiCharry, Jacques A.
Diggs, Josiah*
Dillon, F. O.*
Donleavy, W.A.
Donley, C. I.*
Dooley, Mr.*
Douglas, James S.*
Douglass, C. H.*.
Downes, Mrs. Marie
Doxey, F. B.
Drake, E. L.
Driscoll, R. Sloan
Dudley, E. B.*
Dudley, Sherman H.*
Dunn, J. J.
Duvall, Harry
Eckert, Peter
Edding, W. T.
Efigan, Chris
Eger, Henry F.
Ellington, Joseph A.
Elliott, R. A.
Elson, J.
Engleberg, Ben
Engler, P. A.
English, Charles
English, J.A.
Enterprise Amusement
  Company
Evans, Earl
Evans, Edward

Feels, Lorenzo
Fels, Lorenzo
Ferdon, M.A.
Fieldman, Manuel
Fields, Elijah N.*
Finklestein, Rubin
Flaks, Kalman
Flaks, M.
Fletcher, Mr.
Follies Amusement Com-
  pany
Fontana, Lawrence
Ford, G.*
Forster, Alex I.
Forster, Mrs. Bessie*
Fremont Amusement
  Company
Friedlander, Jacob
Gaither, Major Edward
  G.
Gardner, M. L.
Garner, G.C.
Gates, W. C.*
Gay Theater Properties
Gem Theater Company
Gentry, G.
George, Dr. S.*
George, S. H.
George, William
Geyser, R. S.
Gibson, John T.*
Gilmore and Saratoga
Givens, E. H.
Givens, Everett A.
Goldberg, Abraham
Goldman, Lawrence
Goode, Sam
Gordon, Charles F.
Gordon, Edward
Gordon, Mr.
Gosselin, Fred
Goulter, W. J.
Grott, Harold
Guggenheimer, A. S.
Gunn, William*
Haag, Jack

Hable, F. H.
Hadaway, R. Norris
Hall, Marvin E.
Hamburger, Alfred
Hamilton, J. W.
Hammond, Frank
Hammond, John
Hammond, O. C.
Hamrick Theatre Service
Harkensen, M. H.
Harwell, John C.
Harris, Jack
Harris, O. T.*
Harrison, Hugo
Hawkins, M. L.*
Hawkins, Oscar*
Hayes, Gus
Healy, R. A.
Heard, Sigman
Hendel, Harry
Henderson, John S.
Henderson, Dr. William
  H.
Hendricks, Alvin W.
Henry, James D.
Henry, Lew*
Henton, J. B.*
Herring, Robert
Hershenson, Henry
Hiawatha Amusement
  Company
Hicks, Irving
High, Wallace
Hill, Dr. J. Seth*
Hill, James
Hill, Lewis
Hill, Piddle
Hills Brothers
Hirschensoln, Harry
Hoffheimer Corporation
Hoggs, W. A.
Hollenger, Ray
Home, H. L.
Hopkins, John*
Horstein family
Horstein, M.

244 Appendix 3: Owners and Managers

Hortwicz, M. B.
Howard and Louisiana
Hubert, John A.
Hudnell, James H.
Hury, H. J.
Imwold, Charles H.
Israel, Louis
JML Amusement Company
Jackson, H. D.
Jackson, J. A.*
Jacobs, George
Jacoby, M.
Jaffe, Ben
James, S. L.
James, Thomas
James, Tom
Jefferson Amusement Company
Jennings, Josephine
Johnson, E. H.
Johnson, Mr.
Johnson, O. R.*
Johnson, R. F.
Johnson, William
Jones, C. I.
Jones, Charles B.
Jones, Tom
Jonn, W. T.
Joplin, Robert B.*
Jordan, Charles*
Kaplan, Mr.
Kelly, J.B.
Kelly, Wilbert M.
Kemp, Dirk
Kennedy, M. C.
Keyser, Karl K.
King and Covington*
King and Davis
King, Billy*
King, C. B.
King, J. H.
Kling, Billy*
Knights of Pythias Lodge*
Koppin, Henry S.

Korman Theaters
Koupolis, J. W.
Kramer, Sam
Krapf, R. C.
LaFrance, Clifford
LaMott, Ira J.
Leatherman, J. S.
Lee, Ed*
Lee, Henry H.
Lee, Mr.
Lee, Robert E.
Lee, Stanley
Lemke, J. A.
Leonard, W. H.
Lester, L. T.
Levin, Fred
Lewin, Ernest L.
Lewis, Cary B.
Lewis, E. C.
Lewis, E. L.
Lewis, J. W.
Lewis, S.*
Lichtman, Abe
Lichtman Theaters
Lightman, M. A.
Lightner Brothers*
Lively, Jack
Lockett, Frank
Lockett, S. L.*
Logan, G. W.*
Long, Leon
Love, G. S.
Love, G. W. K.
Lovely, W. J.
Lower, Peter
Lucas, Howard
Lust, Sidney
Lustgarten, Jack
Luting, Charles
McAfee, Mrs. Minnie*
McClone, P.*
McConnell, W. F.
McGehoe, J. B.*
McKenzie, Frank
Macire, Joe
Makover, A

Mancuso, S. B.
Marasco, Flore
Marshall, Jimmy
Martin, A.
Martin, Elmore*
Martin, M.*
Martin, Roy
Martin Theaters
Martini, A.
Mason, James
Melcher, Henry C.
Mendell, A. B.
Merriwether, M.
Miller, Fred*
Miller, George
Miller, H. B.
Miller, J. J.
Miller, Mrs. E. A.*
Mills, John
Minor, Lorenzo
Minsky, Abe
Mitchell, Luther K.*
Moffett, J.A. *
Monroe, A. G.*
Moogeman, Louis
Moore, C. Robert
Moore, Chintz*
Moorman, E. S.
Morgan, G. M.
Moser, J. H.
Moseley, Charles
Mosley, W. L.
Motts, Robert
Moye, Robert J.
Murray Brothers*
Murray, Raymond H.*
Muse, Clarence.*
Nathan, Joseph
Neil, O.
Nicholson, J.
Nickerson, Charles
Niquet, Otto "Dutch"
Nolte, Charles E.
Norris, Timothy P.
Olinger, S. C.
Owens, S. L.

Appendix 3: Owners and Managers

Owsley, Tim
Panama Amusement Company
Pannell, Mrs. R. L.
Parker, Alan
Parrett, Richard
Patterson, James
Patterson, William R.
Paul, Mr.
Peterson, Mrs.
Petray, T.W.
Phelps, Charles T.*
Pierce, Billy
Pinchback, Walter*
Pinkerton, Earl
Pitman, C.
Plater, Harry
Polies, Herman
Pond, E. H.
Pressly, Nathaniel
Privett, J. J.
Puryear, Dr. O.*
Queen and Baylor
Raine, Same J.
Rainey, W.M.*
Rankin, A. E.
Reaves, S. J.
Reese, J.E.
Reevin, Sam E.
Regan, David R.
Rhinehart, R. V.
Rhone, J. M.*
Richardson, Lee
Riddick, George W.
Roach, William C.*
Robb, James
Robins, Charles P.
Rome, J. L.
Rome Theater
Rosen, A.
Rosenthal, Fred
Ross, Mr.
Roth, Charles
Roth, Harry
Roth, Mrs. M.
Rowland, I. H.
Rowley, Joseph M.
Sachs, Benjamin
Sack, A. N.
Saegner Amusement Company
Sanders, Mr.*
Sappel, C. A.
Saulkins, Mr.
Savage, James W.
Savage, W.
Savannah Motion Picture Company
Scales, W. S.*
Schiffman, Frank
Schlen, Oscar
Schreiner, C. C.
Scott, C. S.
Scott, Luke*
Scott, Walter*
Seligman, Gus
Shapiro, R.
Shepard, John M.
Shields, R. S.
Shiff, Bernard
Shivers, Walter
Shook, Benjamin*
Shoubin, Samuel
Shulman, Alex
Shulman, H.
Silverman, M. H.
Simmons, C.
Simms, C. C.
Smith, Billy
Smith, C. K.
Smith, Clay
Smith, M. C.
Smith, Walter
Somma, Charles
Sovini, Mr.
Stallworth, Frank
Starkman, D.
Starr, Milton
Statewide D-I Theaters
Stein, Ben
Stephens, Shedrick S.
Stiles, W. J.
Stinson, Charles P.*
Stokes, Charles G.
Stone, E. S.*
Stone, Emsirdell S.
Styles, J.*
Sumter, W. S.*
Swartz, H.
Swartzman, Mr.
Sykes, Mr.*
Sylvester, J. H.
Tennelbaum, Harry
Terrell, Marc A.
Thomas Brothers*
Thompson, Thomas
Thorton, J. S.
Tinley, T. S.*
Toemnes, Walter
Tolburtt, W. H.
Toliver, C. F.
Tomko, George
Townsend, J.
Trimble, H.S.
Trueman, B. C.*
Turpin, Charles H.*
Victor, John H.
Wack, Mr.
Walker and Dorsey
Walton, Lester A.*
Ward, R. L.
Warley, William
Warrington, Mrs. Noah
Washington, James
Watkins, F. K.*
Wax, Abraham
Weinberg, Louis
Wethers, Carl T.
Wheeler, L.
Whippler, Morris
White, James L.
Williams, Grant*
Williams, Mrs. Lola T.*
Wilson and Kurtz
Wilson, Lucien*
Wilson, O. T.
Wood, Joe
Woodlen, George H.

Appendix 3: Owners and Managers

Woods, P.*
Wright, Delvin
Young, G. B.
Young, Vern U.
Zarigg, Bert
Zarilla, Samuel
Zarillo, Paul

(Sources: African Americans were identified by J. A. Jackson in his *Billboard* survey of August 6, 1922, and reprinted in Monroe Work's *Negro Yearbook, 1921–1922*.)

APPENDIX 4

African American Drive-in Theaters

Alabama

Huntsville — Regal
Lannett — Valley
Tuskegee — Eighty, Lincoln

Florida

Cocoa — Skyview
Daytona Beach — Palm
Fort Lauderdale — Brown's
Fort Myers — Lincoln
Hollandale — Hyde Park
Jacksonville — Skyview
Orlando — Washington Shores

Georgia

Columbus — Jet
Savannah — Highway 21

North Carolina

Greensboro — Sun
Henderston — Starlite
Winston-Salem — Park-Vu

South Carolina

Bennettville — Hill

Tennessee

Memphis — Lincoln Colored

Texas

San Antonio — Alamo

BIBLIOGRAPHY

"Adelphi Theatre, Chicago," *Architectural Forum*, Vol. 63 (July 1935): 56–57.

Albertson, Chris. *Bessie*. New York: Stein and Day, 1972.

Anderson, Jervis. *This Was Harlem: A Cultural Portrait, 1900–1950*. New York: Farrar Straus Giroux, 1982.

"Apollo Theatre, Cairo, Illinois," *Architectural Record*, Vol. 53 (June 1923): 533–43.

Armstrong, Louis. *Louis Armstrong in His Own Words: Selected Writings*. Edited with an introduction and appendix by Thomas Brothers. New York: Oxford University Press, 1999.

Baker, Josephine, and Bouillon, Jo. *Josephine*. Translated from the French by Mariana Fitzpatrick. New York: Marlowe and Company, 1977.

Basie, Count. *Good Morning Blues: The Autobiography of Count Basie as told to Albert Murray*. New York: Da Capo, 1995.

Berry, Faith. *Langston Hughes: Before and Beyond Harlem*. Westport, Conn.: L. Hill, 1983.

Bowser, Pearl, and Spence, Louise. *Writing Himself into History: Oscar Micheaux, His Silent Films, and His Audiences*. New Brunswick, N.J.: Rutgers University Press, 2001.

Bradford, Perry. *Born with the Blues: Perry Bradford's Own Story*. New York: Oak, 1965.

Brophy, Alfred A. *Reconstructing the Dreamland: The Tulsa Riot of 1921, Race, Reparations, and Reconciliation*. New York: Oxford University Press, 2002.

Brown, T. Allison. *A History of the New York Stage, from the First Performance in 1732 to 1901*. New York: B. Blom, 1964.

Cahn, Julius. *Julius Cahn–Gus Hill Theatrical Guide and Moving Picture Directory: 1922 Supplement*. New York: Columbia Theater, 1922.

Calloway, Cab, and Rollins, Bryant. *Of Minnie the Moocher and Me*. New York: Thomas Y. Crowell, 1976.

Carbine, Mary. "The Finest Outside the Loop: Motion Picture Exhibition in Chicago's Black Metropolis, 1905–1928" *Camera Obscura* 23 (May 1990): 9–41.

Chambers, Billy. "Colored Theaters in Birmingham, Alabama." *Billboard*, December 16, 1921: 89.

Collier, James Lincoln. *Duke Ellington*. New York: Collier, 1993.

———. *Louis Armstong: An American Genius*. New York: Oxford University Press, 1983.

Colin, Sid. *Ella: The Life and Times of Ella Fitzgerald*. London: Elm Tree, 1987.

Curtis, Nancy C. *Black Heritage Sites: An African American Odyssey and Finder's Guide*. Chicago: American Library Association, 1996.

Dabney, Wendell Phillips. *Cincinnati's Colored Citizen: historical, sociological and biographical*. New York: Negro Universities Press, 1970.

Dance, Stanley. *The World of Earl Hines*. New York: Charles Scribner's Sons, 1977.

DjeDje, Jacqueline Cogdell, and Meadows, Eddie S., eds. *California Soul: Music of African Americans in the West*. Berkeley: University of California Press, 1998.

Dodson, Howard; Moore, Christopher; and Yancy, Roberta. *The Black New Yorkers: The Schomberg Illustrated Chronology*. New York: John Wiley, 2000.

Driggs, Frank. *The Sound of Harlem*. Produced by Frank Driggs. Text by George Hoefer. New York: Columbia Records, c. 1964.

Film Daily Yearbook of Motion Pictures. Ed. J.W. Alicoate. New York: J. W. Alicoate, 1926–1955.

Fitzgerald, Sandra, and Goodwin, Maria R. *The Guide to Black Washington: Places and Events of Historical and Cultural Significance in the Nation's Capital*. New York: Hippocrene, 1990.

Fletcher, Tom. *100 Years of the Negro in Show Business*. New York: Burdge, 1954; reprint, Da Capo, 1984.

Fox, Ted. *Showtime at the Apollo*. New York: Da Capo, 1993.

Fraden, Rena. *Blueprints for a Black Federal Theatre, 1935–1939*. New York: Cambridge University Press, 1994.

Galbraith, Stuart, IV. *Motor City Marquees: A Comprehensive, Illustrated Reference to Motion Picture Theaters in the Detroit Area, 1906–1992*. Jefferson, N.C.: McFarland, 1994.

George-Graves, Nadine. *The Royalty of Negro Vaudeville: The Whitman Sisters and the Negotiation of Race, Gender, and Class in African American Theater, 1900–1940*. New York: St. Martin's, 2000.

Gillespie, Dizzy, with Al Frazer. *To Be or Not ... To Bop: Memoirs*. Garden City, N.Y.: Doubleday, 1979.

Glazer, Irvin R. *Philadelphia Theaters: A Pictorial Architectural History*. Philadelphia: Athenaeum of Philadelphia; New York: Dover, 1994.

_____. *Philadelphia Theaters A–Z: A Comprehensive Descriptive Record of 813 Theaters Constructed Since 1724*. New York: Greenwood, 1986.

Gottschild, Brenda Dixon. *Waltzing in the Dark: African American Vaudeville and Race Politics in the Swing Era*. New York: St. Martin's, 2000.

Green, Abel, and Laurie Joe, Jr. *Show Biz, from Vaude to Video*. New York: Holt, 1951.

Hajdu, David. *Lush Life: A Biography of Billy Strayhorn*. New York: North Point, 1996.

Harrison, Daphne Duval. *Black Pearls: Blues Queens of the 1920s*. New Brunswick, N.J.: Rutgers University Press, 1988.

Haskins, James. *Black Theater in America*. New York: Thomas Y. Crowell, 1982.

_____, and Biondi, Joanne. *Hippocrene U.S.A. Guide to the Historic Black South*. New York: Hippocrene, 1993.

Headley, Robert K., Jr. *Exit: A History of Movies in Baltimore*. University Park, Md.: Published by the author, 1974.

_____. *Motion Picture Exhibition in Washington, D.C.: An Illustrated History of Parlors, Palaces and Multiplexes in the Metropolitan Area, 1894–1997*. Jefferson, N.C.: McFarland, 1999.

Hill, Anthony D. *Pages from the Harlem Renaissance: A Chronicle of Performance*. New York: Peter Lang, 1996.

Historic Sites Survey of Allegheny County. Harrisburg: Pennsylvania Historical and Museum Commission, 1994.

Holiday, Billie, and Duffy, William. *Lady Sings the Blues*. Garden City, N.Y.: Doubleday, 1956.

Hirsch, James S. *Riot and Remembrance: The Tulsa Race War and Its Legacy*. Boston and New York: Houghton Mifflin, 2001.

Hughes, Langston, and Meltzer, Milton. *Black Magic: A Pictorial History of the Negro in American Entertainment*. Englewood Cliffs, N.J.: Prentice-Hall, 1967.

"The Intimate Theater Idea," *Architecture and Building*, Vol. 45 (March 1913): 107.

Jackson, J.A. "Additions to theater list since original compilation of July 1 was published in *The Billboard* August 6," *Billboard*, December 31, 1921.

_____. "Forward to the List of Colored Theaters and Attractions." *Billboard*, August 6, 1921: 63.

_____. "List of Colored Theaters and Attractions." *Billboard*, August 6, 1921: 63–64.

_____. "The Theater Owners Booking Association," *Billboard*, December 16, 1922: 88.

Jasen, David A., and Tichenor, Trebor Jay. *Rags and Ragtime: A Musical History*. New York: Dover, 1978.

Jones, William Henry. *Recreation and Amusement among Negroes in Washington, D.C.* Washington, D.C.: Howard University Press, 1927.

Keller, Bruce, ed. *The Harlem Renaissance: A Historical Dictionary for the Era*. New York: Methuen, 1984.

Kenny, William Howland. *Chicago Jazz: A Cultural History, 1904–1930*. Oxford, England: Oxford University Press, 1994.

Kuhn, Clifford M. *Living Atlanta: An Oral History of the City, 1914–1948*. Atlanta: Atlanta Historical Society; Athens: University of Georgia Press, 1990.

Madigan, Tim. *The Burning: Massacre, Destruction, and the Tulsa Race Riot of 1921*. New York: St. Martin's, 2001.

"The Lyric Theater in Newark, N.J.," *Architects and Builders' Magazine*, December 1908: 108–112.

Mitchell, Loften. *Black Drama: The Story of the American Negro in the Theatre*. New York: Hawthorn, 1967.

Moore, Jacqueline M. *Leading the Race: The Transformation of the Black Elite in the Nation's Capital, 1880–1920*. Char-

lottesville: University Press of Virginia, 1999.
Murray, Florence, ed. *The Negro Handbook.* New York: Wendell Malliet, 1942.
"The National Theater, Detroit, Michigan." *American Architect.* Vol. 102 (July 3, 1912).
Negro Yearbook see Work, Monroe N.
"Negroes Movie-Conscious; Support 430 Film Houses." *Motion Picture Herald* January 24, 1942: 33–34.
Newman, Richard. "The Lincoln Theatre." *American Visions* 6 (August 1991): 29–32.
Newman, Scott. "Metropolitan Theater." Website. http://www.suba.com/~scottn/explore/sites/theaters/met.htm
_____. "Vendome Theater." Website. http://www.suba.com/~scottn/explore/sites/theaters/vendome.htm
Official Theatrical World of Colored Artists, National Guide and Directory. New York: Theatrical World, 1928.
Peterson, Bernard L. Jr., *The African American Theatre Directory, 1816–1960: A Comprehensive Guide to Early Black Theatre Organizations, Companies, Theatres, and Performing Groups.* Westport, Conn.: Greenwood, 1997.
_____. *Profiles of African American Stage Performers and Theatre People, 1816–1960.* Westport, Conn.: Greenwood, 2001.
Pfeffer, Murray L. *My Harlem Reverie.* Website: The Great American Big Bands Database. http://www/mfp/met/.WWW/harlem.html
Pruter, Robert. *Chicago Soul.* Urbana: University of Illinois Press, 1991.
Riis, Thomas L. "Pink Morton's Theater, Black Vaudeville, and the T.O.B.A.: Recovering the History, 1910–30." In: Josephine Wright, ed. *New Perspectives on Music: Essays in Honor of Eileen Southern.* Detroit: Harmonie Park, 1992: 229–243.
Russell, Ross. *Bird Lives! The High Life and Hard Times of Charlie "Bird" Parker.* New York: Charterhouse Publishers, 1973.
Sampson, Henry T. *Blacks in Black and White: A Source Book on Black Films.* Second Edition. Lanham, Md.: Scarecrow, 1995.
_____. *Blacks in Blackface: A Source Book on Early Black Musical Shows.* Metuchen, N.J.: Scarecrow, 1980.
Savage, Beth L., ed. *African American Historic Places.* Washington, D.C.: Preservation Press, c. 1994.
Schiffmann, Jack. *Uptown: The Story of Harlem's Apollo Theatre.* New York: Cowles, 1971.
Shortridge, "The Indiana Theatre: Pat Past, Uncertain Future." *Marquee* 7 (Fourth Quarter, 1975): 3–8.
Simms, James N. *Simms' Blue Book and National Negro Business and Professional Directory.* Chicago: Published by the author, 1923.
Smith, Eric Ledell. *Bert Williams: A Biography of the Pioneer Black Comedian.* Jefferson, N.C.: McFarland, 1992).
Thompson, George A., Jr. *A Documentary History of the African Theatre.* Chicago: Northwestern University Press, 1998.
Thompson, Sister Mary Francesca. "The Lafayette Players: 1915–1932." Ph.D. dissertation, University of Michigan, 1932.
Thurman, Wallace. *Negro Life in New York's Harlem: A Lively Picture of a Popular and Interesting Section.* Girard, Kansas: Haldemann-Julius, 1925.
Touart, Paul. "African-American Heritage in Worcester County Maryland: Segregation." Website: Worcester County, Maryland. http://www.skipjack.net/le_shore/visit-worcester/african-american/segregation.html
Trotter, Joe William, Jr. *Black Milwaukee: The Making of an Industrial Proletariat, 1915–45.* Urbana: University of Illinois Press, 1985.
"Two New Theaters," *Billboard.* December 16, 1922: 88.
"232 Negro Theatres, One and One-Half Percent of All Houses." *Motion Picture Herald* April 24, 1937: 78, 80.
"U.S. Lists 388 Negro Theatres, An Increase of 156 in Two Years." *Motion Picture Herald* July 15, 1939: 41, 44.
"Uptown Theatre, Philadelphia, Pa.," *Architecture,* Vol. 60 (November 1929): 107).
Waller, Gregory. *Main Street Amusements: Movies and Commercial Entertainment in a Southern City.* Washington and London: Smithsonian Institution Press, 1995.
Waller, Maurice, and Calabrese, Anthony. *Fats Waller.* New York: Schirmer, 1977.
Walker, Stacy, and Christian, Denise. "The Attucks Theatre." Website: Crispus Attucks Cultural Center. http://helios.whro.org/cl/attucks/history.html
Walton, Lester A. "Benefit at Alhambra a Success." *New York Age,* August 6, 1918: 6.

Waters, Ethel, and Samuels, Charles. *His Eye Is on the Sparrow: An Autobiography.* Garden City, N.Y.: Doubleday, 1950.

Wilson, Kendall. "Royal Theater Gets Federal Boost." *Philadelphia Tribune*, September 19, 2000: 1–4A.

Work, Monroe N. *Negro Yearbook: An Annual Encyclopedia of the Negro, 1912.* Tuskegee, Ala.: Tuskegee Institute, 1912.

_____. *Negro Yearbook: An Annual Encyclopedia of the Negro, 1921–1922.* Tuskegee, Ala.: Negro Yearbook Publishing Company, 1922.

_____. *Negro Yearbook: An Annual Encyclopedia of the Negro, 1925–1926.* Tuskegee, Ala.: Negro Yearbook Publishing Company, 1926.

Young, Artee Felicita. "Lester Walton: Black Theater Critic." Ph.D. dissertation, University of Michigan, 1980.

INDEX

*References are to entry numbers except for those with p. or pp., indicating page numbers. References in **boldface** are to photographs.*

A and M College Theater (Tallahassee, FL) 414
Aaron and Robinson 802
Abbeville, AL 1
Aberdeen, NC 1120
Abilene, TX 1567, 1567, 1568
Accents 592
Accomac, VA 1784
Ace Theater (Tuscaloosa, AL) 83; (Auburndale, FL) 247; (Belle Glade, FL) 253; (Cocoa, FL) 269; (Homestead, FL) 310; (Miami, FL) 338; (Pahokee, FL) 363; (Sanford, FL) 402; (Saratoga, FL) 406; (Seminole, FL) 412; (Alexandria, LA) 670; (Ferriday, LA) 692; (Hammond, LA) 696; (New Orleans, LA) 722; (Natchez, MS) 939; (Burlington, NC) 1137; (Memphis, TN) 1539; (Nashville, TN) 1556; (Honey Island, TX) 1675; (Italy, TX) 1698
Ada Meade Theater (Lexington, KY) 655
Adams, Dr. 1908
Adams, George 1015
Adams, Mr. 1488
Adams Theater (Newark, NJ) 1032; (Pinehurst, NC) 1227
Adelphia Theater (Chicago, IL) 552
Adler, David 1450
Advertising of black theaters pp. 2-3
After Thirty Years (film) 1111
Against the Law (film) 1450
Aiken, SC 1455
Ailena Theater (Los Angeles, CA) 152
Airdome Theater (DC) 209; (Cocoa, FL) 272; (Jacksonville, FL) 312; (Atlanta, GA) 441; (Columbus, GA) 478; (Indianapolis, IN) 623
Airdome theaters pp. 3-4
Akron, OH 1279
Alabama Bound (musical) 566
Alabama Tin Band 1101
Aladdin Theater (Baltimore, MD) 776
Alameda Theater (Sacramento, CA) 179
Alamo Drive-in (San Antonio, TX) 1745
Alamo Theater (DC) p. 4, 210; (New Roads, LA) 739; (Opelousas, LA) 741; (Jackson, MS) 914; (Meridan, MS) 934; (Mineola, TX) 1713
Alan Theater (Atlantic City, NJ) 1026
Albany, GA 412
Albaugh's Opera House 217
Albemarle, NC 1121
Albert, Little 1696
Alcazar Theater (El Paso, TX) 1644
Aldon Theater (Wheeling, WV) 1919
Aldridge Theater (Oklahoma City, OK) 1382
Alewine Theater (Louisville, MS) 930
Alexander, F. E. 1918
Alexander City, AL 2, 3
Alexandria, LA 670-675
Alexandria, VA 1785-1789
Algretta, Priscilla 476
Alhambra Theater (Detroit, MI) 820; (Omaha, NE) 1013; (New York, NY) 1084; (Paris, TX) 1731
Ali, Bardu 164
Ali Baba and the Forty Thieves (film) 838
Alice Theater (Vinton, LA) 763; (Jacksonville, TX) 1699
All Star Review Company 733, 1520
Allen, J.D. 1424
Allendale, SC 1456
Aloha Theater (Waco, TX) 1775
Alpha Theater (Cleveland, OH) 1294
Alpine Theater (Concord, NC) 1154
Alston, W. S. 1499
Altus, OK 1353
Amarillo, TX 1570, 1571
Amazon Amusement Company 789
Ameche, Don 725
American Beauty (film) 164
American Romance (film) 820
American Theater (San Francisco, CA) 187; (DC) 211, 243; (E. St. Louis, IL) 603; (Baltimore, MD) p. 3, 772; (Jackson, MS) 915; (Houston, TX) 1677; (San Antonio, TX) 1746

The Americano (film) 1884
Americus, GA 436, 437
Amite, LA 676
Amite Theater (Jackson, MS) 916
Amith Hall (Southern Pines, NC) 1253
Amo Theater (Chicago, IL) 553
Amusu Theater (Chattanooga, TN) 1517
Amytis Theater (St. Louis, MO) 981
Anco Theater (New York, NY) 1085
Anderson, Charles 733
Anderson, Charlie 514, 1520
Anderson, Eddie "Rochester" 1416
Anderson, Mary 802
Anderson, SC 1457, 1458
Andrews, C. C. 1820
Andrews, Dana 1410, 1852
Andrews, Ernie 164
Andrews Sisters 1416
Andrews Theater (Sherman, TX) 1753
Angelos, George 464
Annapolis, MD 768, 769, 770
Annex Theater (Ruleville, MS) 944
Anniston, AL 4, 5, 6
Anthony Theater (Baltimore, MD) 773
Antler Club 786
Apalachicola, FL 245
Apex Theater (Topeka, KS) 650; (Philadelphia, PA) 1419
Apollo Theater (Chicago, IL) 554; (Detroit, MI) 821; (Atlantic City, NJ) 1027; (Brooklyn, NY) 1064; (New York, NY) 1086, p. **143**; (Cleveland, OH) 1295; (Williamsburg, VA) 1897
Apopka, FL 246
Aqua Falls Theater (Orange, TX) 1725
Arbuckle, Fatty 777
Arcade Theater (Wauchula, FL) 426; (Atlanta, GA) 442; (Baldwin, LA) 677; (Ferriday, LA) 693; (Patterson, LA) 745; (Detroit, MI) 822: Ardmore, OK 1354, 1355, 1356
Architects of black theaters p. 5, p. 241

253

254 INDEX

Arena Playhouse (Baltimore, MD) 774; p. **103**
Arena Players Company 774, 1305
Arena Theater (Baltimore, MD) 774, p. 103
Arganta Theater (Little Rock, AR) 115
Arizona and the Horseman (film) 574, 585
Arkadelphia, AR 91
Arlington, VA 1790
Arlington Theater (Arlington, VA); (Hopewell, VA) 1818
Armory Theater (Charleston, WV) 1903
Armstead, Thomas 927
Armstrong, Louis 230, 556, 579, 580, 592, 597, 804, 853, 1431
Arnet, Billy 733
Arnold, Edward 1429
Aronson, M. M. 1014
Arrant, 1288
Art Theater (Montgomery AL) 61; (Brooklyn, NY) 1065
Arthur, Jean 726
Artistics 592
As Thousands Cheer (film) 1410
Asbury, John C. p. 1, p. 6n3
Asbury Park, NJ 1024, 1025
Ascher Brothers 584
Ash Street Theater (Abilene, TX) 1567
Ashby Theater (Atlanta, GA) 443
Asheboro, NC 1122
Asheville, NC 1123, 1134, 1125, 1126
Ashland, VA 1791, 1792
Assembly Theater (St. Louis, MO) 982
Astaire, Fred 728, 1447, 1869
Astor, Mary 1450
Astor Theater (New Rochelle, NY) 1058; (Chapel Hill, NC) 1143
Athens, GA 438, 439, 440
Athens, TX 1572
Atkinson, Sam 552
Atlanta, GA 441–460
Atlanta Daily World (newspaper) p. 6n11
Atlanta Independent (newspaper) 444
Atlantic City, NJ 1026, 1027, 1028
Atlantic Records 1086
Atlas Theater (Chicago, IL) 554; (Indianapolis, IN) 628; (Seattle, WA) 1899
Attapulcus, GA 461
Attucks Theater (Norfolk, VA) p. 5, 1838, p. **228**
Atwood, L. K. 915
Aubert Theater (St. Louis, MO) 983

Auburn, AL 7.
Auburndale, FL 248, 249
The Auction Block (film) 1093
Auditorium Theater (Atlanta, GA) 444; (Princess Anne, MD) 811; (Beaufort, NC) 1132; (Memphis, TN) 1540; (Prairie View, TX) 1742; (Gloucester, VA) 1813
Augusta, GA 462, 463, 465, 466
Aulander, NC 1127
Austin, Benjamin 1001
Austin, Buddy 313, 323
Austin, TX 1573–1579
Austin Theater (Jacksonville, FL) 313
Autry, Gene 1850
Avalon Theater (Los Angeles, CA) 153; (Loughman, FL) 337
Avenue, MD 771
Avenue Theater (Sanford, FL) 403; (Chicago, IL) 556; (Indianapolis, IN) 624; (Pittsburgh, PA) 1436;
Avon Park, FL 250, 251
Avon Theater (Avon Park, FL) 250; (Saratoga, FL) 408
Ayden, NC 1128
Aztec Theater (San Diego, CA) 184
Azteca Theater (Beeville, TX) 1593

Bacchus, George C. 1816
Back to God's Country (film)
Backoff, George W. 1037
Baden, NC 1129
Badge, Laura 1449
Badman's Territory (film) 737
Bailey, Charles P. 453
Bailey, NC 1130
Bailey, Pearl 661, 1429
Bailey, Roy 627
Bailey, Tom 446
Bailey Theater (Tallulah, LA) 757
Bailey's Eighty One Theater 446
Bailey's Royal 459
Bainbridge, GA 467
Baker, Josephine 984, 1431
Baker Theater (Gadsden, AL) 38
Bakerfield, CA 145, 146
Baldwin, LA 677
Ball, H. 1824
Ballin, Hugo 597
Ballin, Mabel 597
Ballinger, TX 1580
Baltimore, MD 772–805
Baltimore Afro-American (newspaper) 213, 772, 777, 780, 793, 801, 802, 804, 805
Bamboo Theater (Monroeville, AL) 60
Banco Theater (Brooklyn, NY) 1066

Bancroft, George 597
Band Box Theater (DC) 213
Bara, Theda 166
Barasso, A. 1551, 1553
Barbara Theater (Los Angeles, CA) 154
Barkett, M. 64
Barnes, Jerry C. 209
Barnesville, GA 468
Barney's Idle Hour Theater (Petersburg, VA) 1858
Barnwell, SC 1459
Barnwell Theater (Barnwell, SC) 1459
Barr, Joseph W. 643
Barraco, Paul 1677, 1678, 1696
Barrett, George 476
Barrett, James H. 1315
Barrett, Richard 982
Barrett, Richard D. 1529
Barrett's Theatorium (Jackson, TN) 1529
Barriscale, Bessie 801
Barry, Don 724
Barrymore, Lionel 725, 1101
Bartholomew, H. C. 429
Bartlesville, OK 1357
Barton, MD 806
Bartow, FL 252.
Basehart, Richard 731
Basie, Count 164, 446, 514, 592, 733, 788, 804, 831, 853, 968, 984, 1042, 1084, 1086, 1093, 1103, 1382, 1392, 1424, 1427, 1431, 1551, 1557
Basie Theater (Hampton, VA) 1815
Bastrop, LA 678
Bastrop, TX 1581
Bates, Edward T. 798
Bath, NC 1131
Batman, Chapter 1 (film) 722
Baton Rouge, LA 679, 680, 681, 682
Battle, George E. 229
Baxley, GA 469
Bay City, MI 819
Baytown, TX 1582
Baytown Humble Club (Baytown, TX) 1582
Beal, Eddie 159, 164
Beale Street Theater (Hughes, AR) 114
Beall, F.E. 805
Beamon, B. B. 446
Beard, Stymie 1857
Beaudreaux and Bennett 733
Beaufort, NC 1132, 1133, 1134, 1135
Beaumont, TX 1583–1592
Beautiful Liar (film) 574
Beavers, Louise 1857
Bechet, Sidney 1838
Beecher Theater (Cincinnati, OH) 1280
Beechwood Theater (Detroit, MI) 823

INDEX

Beeville, TX 1593
Behind Prison Walls (film) 827
Belafonte, Harry 661, 662
Belmont Theater (Pensacola, FL) 374
Bell, Otis 636
Bell, R. A. 914
Bell, Steven 664
Belle Glade, FL 253, 254, 255, 256
Belle Starr (film) 1857
Bellinger Theater (San Antonio, TX) 1747
Belva Theater (Ennis, TX) 1646
Belzoni, MS 878
Benbow, William 968
Benjamin, Arthur 808, 848
Bennett, Edith 802
Bennettsville, SC 1460, 1461, 1462, 1463
Ben's Theater (Haines City, FL) 304
Benson, Al 59
Berheimer Theaters 241
Berkeley, VA 1793–1796
Berkland Theater (Aberdeen, NC) 1120
Berlin, MD 807
Bern Theater (New Bern, NC) 1219
Bernard, Thomas 239
Berry, Wallace 725
Bessemer, AL 8, 9, 10, 11, 12
Bessie Smith and Her Yellow Girl Revue 1103
Bessie Theater (Florence, AL) 34
Best Theater (Houston, TX) 1678
Betrayed (film) 725
Bickford, Charles 838
Biddle Theater (Baltimore, MD) 775
The Bigamist (film) 661
Big Spring, TX 1594
Biggs, Verona 585
Bijou Amusement Company 1561
Bijou Stock Company 314
Bijou Theater (Fresno, CA) 147; (Jacksonville, FL) 317; (Detroit, MI) p. 4, 824; (Greenwood, MS) 899; (Philadelphia, PA) 1414; (Greenwood, SC) 1488; (Nashville, TN) 1557
Bilbrew, Kitty 16
Bill Robinson Theater (Los Angeles, CA) 155
The Billboard (newspaper) 1315, 1441
Billy Young Shoulder Shakers 1273
Biloxi, MS 879
Biltmore Theater (Mount Vernon, NY) 1057
Binder, A. L. 1350
Birmingham, AL 13, 14, 15, 16, 17, 18, 19, 20, 21, 22, 23

Birmingham (AL) Reporter (newspaper) p. 2
Birmingham Theater (Birmingham, AL) 13
Birds Nest, VA 1797
Bishop, Andrew 566
Bishopville, SC 1464
Black, Clarence H. 590
Black entrepreneurs p. 2
Black film industry p. 2, p. 6n10
Black Patti's Troubadours 915
The Black Perspective in Music (periodical) p. 6n7
The Black Widow (film) 724
Blackbirds of 1926 (musical) 1084
Blackbirds of 1929 (musical) 1084
Blackmon, Ted 1101
Blackshear, GA 470
Bladesboro, NC 1136
Blair Station, PA 1398, 1399
Blair's Theater (West Helena, AR) 141
Bland Theater (Portsmouth, VA) 1861
Bledsoe, Jules 1101
Blondie Goes Latin (film) 1872
Blue Bird Theater (Chicago, IL) 557; (New York, NY) 1087
Blue Fox (film) 574
Blue Heaven Theater (Marianna, AR) 121
Blue Jacket's Honor (film) 574
Blue Mouse Theater (DC) 212
Bluefield, VA 1798
Bluefield, WV 1900, 1901, 1902
Bluefield Institute (Bluefield, WV) 1900
Blythville, AL 92, 93
Boardman, Eleanor 1093
Bob Stark's Tennesseans 1557
Boehringer, Ernest 680
Bogalusa, LA 683, 684
Bogart, Humphrey 662
Boisy Legge Trio 801
Bolansy, Bernard E. 1312
Bolden, J. 1246
Buley, OK 1358, 1359
Bolivar, TN 1514
Bon Ami Theater (Opelousas, LA) 742
Bond, Monument 805
Bond Theater (Houma, LA) 700
The Bone Dry Blues (comedy) 1838
Bonham, TX 1595
Bonnie Theater (Amite, LA) 676
Booker T. Theater (Mobile, AL) 52; (Texarkana, AR) 134; (DC) 213; (Annapolis, MD) 768; (Baltimore, MD) p. 3, 776; (Detroit, MI) 825; (Cleveland, MS) 890; (Jackson, MS) 917; (Asheville, NC) 1123;
Booker T. Washington Theater (Vicksburg, MS) p. 4, 953; (St. Louis, MO) 984; (Durham,

NC) 1157; (Reidsville, NC) 1236; (Rocky Mount, NC) 1241; (Springfield, OH) 1341; (Philadelphia, PA) 1405; (Knoxville, TN) 1532; (Galveston, TX) 1655; (Houston, TX) 1679; (Accomac, VA) 1784; (Cheapside, VA) 1803; (Norfolk, VA) 1839; (Richmond, VA) 1869
Boone, J. C. 1660
Boone Theater (Columbia, MO) 960
Bordeaux, Luke S. 733
Bordeaux and Camp 723
Bordeaux Theater (New Orleans, LA) 723
Border River (film) 728
Boston Road Theater (Bronx, NY) 1059
Boston Theater (Lynchburg, VA) 1820; (Roanoke, VA) 1881
Bostwick, Marie 1294
Bosworth, Hobart 164
Bottom, R. A. 1272
Boulevard Theater (Lake Charles, LA) 706
Bowers, James A. 776
Bowery Boys 445, 448, 458
Bowery to Bagdad (film) 458
Bowman, Mrs. Anna 639
Bowman, SC 1465
Bowser, Pearl p. 1, p. 6n2, n5, n10, p. 7n18
Boyd, Bill 731
Boyd and Boyd 733
Bradentown, FL 257
Bradford, Perry 588, 1103
Brady, Scott 728
Bramlow, Henry A. 1788
Branch Theater (Baxley, GA) 469
Brando, Marlon 724, 727, 1837
Brandon, MS 880
The Breaking Point (film) 802
Breaux, Zelia N. p. 3, 1382
Breaux and Whitlow 1382
Brecher, Leo 1084, 1097
Breckenridge, TX 1596
Brennan, Walter 1845
Brent, George 448
Brevard Theater (Greenwood, SC) 1489
Brevoort Theater (Brooklyn, NY) 1067
Brewer, Charles 448, 458
Bridgeport, CT 202
Bright Road (film) 662
Brighty, John 1520
Britt, May 1852
Broadway Garden Theater (Baltimore, MD) 798
Broadway Open Air Theater (Richmond, VA) 1870
Broadway Rastus (musical) 566, 1027
Broadway Strand Theater

(Chicago, IL) 558; (Detroit, MI) 826
Broadway Theater (DC) 214; (Ocala, FL) 353; (E. St. Louis, IL) 603; (Gary, IN) 618; (Indiana Harbor, IN) 621; (Buffalo, NY) 1049; (Rock Hill, SC) 1499; (Suffolk, VA) 1888
Broken Bow, OK 1360
Broken Lance (film) 731
Bronx, NY 1059–1063
Bronx Theater (Bronx, NY) 1060
Brookdale Drive-in (Charlotte, NC) 1144
Brookhaven, MS 881, 882
Brooklyn, NY 1064–1083
Brooklyn Theater (Perry, FL) 381; (Lumberton, NC) 1216; (Wilmington, NC) 1266; (Chester, SC) 1474
Brophy, Alfred L. p. 7n18
Brown, Amanda L. 638
Brown, "Babe" 805
Brown, Charles 164
Brown, Edward C. p. 3, 1075, 1421
Brown, Frank 235
Brown, G. 1484
Brown, G. F. 133
Brown, James 1659
Brown, Jim 1739
Brown, John Mack 1450
Brown, Louis N. 233
Brown, R. B. "Happy" 19
Brown, Willie 17
Brown and Bell 1431
Brown and Navarro 588
Brown and Pinkey 1883
Brown and Struffin 582, 845
Brown Sisters 1424
Brown Theater (Bastrop, LA) 678
Brown v. Board of Education (U.S. Supreme Court decision) p. 5, p. 7n19
Browne, Sam 164
Brownfield, TX 1597, 1598, 1599
Brown's Drive-in (Fort Lauderdale, FL) 287
Brownsville, GA 471
Brownsville, TN 1515, 1516
Browsky, M. B. 1415, 1420
Bruce, Virginia 1447
Bruner, Paul H. 726
Brunswick, GA 472, 473, 474, 475, 476
The Brute (film) 222
The Brute Maker (film) 166
Bruton Heights Theater (Williamsburg, VA) 1898
Bryan, TX 1600, 1601, 1602, 1603
Bryant, Willie 230, 1101
Bubbles (film) 802
Buchanan, Edgar 1823

Buck and Bubbles 1431
Buckaroo Theater (Breckenridge, TX) 1596
Buckingham Theater (Tampa, FL) 418
Buffalo, NY 1049–1055
Buffalo Theater (Garysburg, NC) 1176
Buggs, James 473, 476
The Bull's Eye (film) 582
Bunche Theater (Miami, FL) 339
Bundy, Hewitt p. 3, 1411
Bunnell, FL 258
Bunts, H. A. 544
Burden, Issac M. 1837
Burgess Theater (Raleigh, NC) 1230
Burke Theater (Pittsburgh, PA) 1437
Burland Theater (New York, NY) 1088
Burlington, NC 1137, 1138, 1139
Burns, Sandy 660, 1287, 1431, 1557
Burns and Ashes 1431
Burrell, Alfred A. 4
Burtons 1822
Bush, Anita 514, 1093
Butler, Billy 566
Butler, David 1103
Butler Theater (St. Inigoes, MD) 813
Butlers 627
Butterbeans and Susie 514, 1041, 1421, 1431
Byars, Rufus G. p.3, 214, 222, 226, 229, 1838
Bymn, J. T. 1105

Cab Theater (Ashland, VA) 1791
Caffey, Charles 1677
Cagney, James 1857
Cairo, IL 548, 549, 550, 551
Caldwell, TX 1604
Calhoun, Rory 459, 659
Calhoun, Virgil 119
Call of Home (film) 589
Call of the Wild (film) 574
Callia, Henry 19, 514
Callis and Callis 780
Calloway, Blanche 804
Calloway, Cab 230, 802, 831, 853, 861, 1101, 1427, 1429
Calvet, Corrine 1845
Cambridge, MD 808
Camden, AL 24
Camden, AR 94, 95
Camden, NJ 1029, 1030
Camden, SC 1466, 1467
Camden, TX 1605
Cameo Theater (San Antonio, TX) 1748
Camera Obscura (periodical) p. 6n4
Cameron, NC 1140
Camerphone Theater (Omaha, NE) 1014

Camilla, GA 477
Camille (film) 164
Camp Hill, AL 25
Campbell, Alvin 213
Campobello Theater (Ybor City, FL) 433
Canadian Mounties versus the Atomic Invaders (film) 1850
Cannibal Attack (film) 735, 1795
Cannon, J. C. V. 1468
Canova, Judy 832
Canton, MS 883
Cape Charles, VA 1799
Capitol Theater (St. Petersburg, FL) 396; (Tallahassee, FL) 415; (Indianapolis, IN) 625; (Brooklyn, NY) 1068; (Columbia, SC) 1475; (Martin, TN) 1538; (Alexandria, VA) 1785; (Newport News, VA) 1829; (Portsmouth, VA) 1862
Carbine, Mary p. 6n3
Carey Theater (Baltimore, MD) 777
Carlsbad, NM 1047
Carmen Jones (film) 661, 1410
Caro Tent Theater (Greelyville, SC) 1485
Carolina Theater (Fort Valley, GA) 498; (Sanford, NC) 1248; (Olar, SC) 1495
Carpenter, Charlie 579
Carpenter, Curtis W. 164
Carroll, IA 645
Carter, Benny 164, 853
Carter, Jack 233
Carter, Paul 733
Carter and Mitchell 1287
Carter Theater (Cleveland, OH) 1296
Carver, George Washington p. 3
Carver Theater (Abbeville, AL); (Birmingham, AL) 14, **p. 11;** (Dothan, AL) 29; (Gadsden, AL) 39; (Montgomery, AL) 62; (Pritchard, AL) 74; (Sheffield, AL) 77; (DC) 215; (Lake City, FL) 328; (Leesburg, FL) 335; (Orlando, FL) 358; (St. Augustine, FL) 392; (Tampa, FL) 419; (Atlanta, GA) 445; (Decatur, GA) 491; (Gainsville, GA) 500; (Waycross, GA) 543; (New Orleans, LA) 724; (Baltimore, MD) 779; (Detroit, MI) 828; (Kansas City, MO) 962; (St. Louis, MO) 985; (Durham, NC) 1158; (Gadsden, NC) 1174; (Kinston, NC) 1205; (Roanoke Rapids, NC) 1246; (Williamston, NC) 1265; (Columbia, SC) 1476; (Page Land, SC) 1498; (Rock Hill, SC) 1500; (Austin, TX) 1575; (Dallas, TX) 1621; (Fort

INDEX 257

Worth, TX) 1656; (Alexandria, VA) p. 3, 1725; (Cape Charles, VA) 1799; (Newport News, VA) 1830; (Norfolk, VA) 1840; (Portsmouth, VA) 1863; (Sedley, VA) 1885; (Suffolk, VA) 1889; (Huntington, WV) 1907
Cary, Bessie 220
The Case of the Howling Dog (film) 1450
Case Theater (Dania, FL) 275; (Delray Beach, FL) 281; (Fort Lauderdale, FL) 288; (Pompano, FL) 385
Casino Theater (St. Louis, MO) 986; (Oxford, NC) 1226
Castle, Mary 728
Castle, Peggy 724
Castle Theater (Kansas City, KS) 647; (Detroit, MI) 827; (Kansas City, MO) 962
Cat Women of the Moon (film) 726
Cathcart, Jack 456
Catherine Theater (Detroit, MI) 828
Cato, Minto 1101
Cattle Queen of Montana (film) 735
Cauger, MS 884
Cauger Theater (Cauger, MS) 884
Caught in the Draft (film) 1884
Cavern Theater (Carlsbad, NM) 1047
Cedar Theater (Cleveland, OH) 1297
Cent Odeon Theater (Detroit, MI) 824
Central Theater (Los Angeles, CA) 156; (Hollopaw, FL) 307; (Saratoga, FL) 407; (Tampa, FL) 420
Centre Square Theater (Pittsburgh, PA) 1438
Century Theater (Dallas, TX) 1622
Chadwick and Crippen 217
Champion Theater (Birmingham, AL) 15
Chandler, Gene 592
Chandler, Jeff 1823
Chandu the Magician (film) 786
Chaney, Lon 585, 595
Chapel Hill, NC 1141, 1142
Chaplin, Charlie 1018
Chappelle, James 418
Chappelle, Lewis 418
Chappelle, Pat H. 418
Chappelle Brothers Circuit 418
Charles, Steward 221
Charles Theater (Bunnell, FL) 258
Charleston, MS 885
Charleston, MO 959
Charleston, SC 1468–1473
Charleston, WV 1903, 1904, 1905

Charlotte, NC 1143–1151
Charwood Theater (St. Joseph, MO) 977
Chase, Plimpton B. 216
Chase, R. 314
Chase City, VA 1800, 1801, 1802
Chase's Theater (DC) 216
Chatham Theater (New York, NY) 1089
Chattanooga, TN 1517–1524
Cheapside, VA 1803, 1804
Chelsea Theater (DC) 217
Chenault, Lawrence 597, 801
Cherry, W. M. 1392
Chester, PA 1400, 1401
Chester, SC 1472
Chester Theater (Blair Station, PA) 1398; (Pittsburgh, PA) 1439
Chic Theater (Detroit, MI) 829
Chicago, IL 552–601
Chicago Defender (newspaper) p. 6n14, 435, 556, 566, 585, 592, 595, 597, 1382
Chicago Follies (musical) 733, 1551
Chickasha, OK 1361, 1362, 1363
Chief Crazy House (film) 443
Childress, TX 1606
Childs, George S. 792
Childs, James H. 234
Chinese Parrot (film) 164
Christi Theater (St. George, SC) 1501
Christmas Revels (revue) 1098
Church, Robert E. 1540
Churchill, John 1449
Church's Park Theater (Memphis, TN) 1540
Chutes Amusement Park 187
Cincinnati, OH 1280–1293
Cinex Theater (Detroit, MI) 851
Circle Theater (Camden, AR) 93; (New Orleans, LA) 725; (St. Louis, MO) 987; (Philadelphia, PA) 1406, p. 177; (Dallas, TX) 1623
Claffin, Fuller 837
Clark, Charles 1805
Clark, Dane 1839
Clark, James H. 1315
Clark, June 1107
Clark, W. T. 318
Clark Stock Company 1315
Clark Theater (Northfolk, WV) 1918
Clarksburg, WV 1906
Clarksdale, MS 886, 887, 888, 889
Clarksville, TX 1607, 1608, 1609
Classic Theater (Dayton, OH) 1327
Clay Street Theater (Annapolis, MD) 769
Clay Theater (Detroit, MI) 821
Claybrooks 865
Clearwater, FL 259, 260, 261, 262

Cleburne, TX 1610, 1611
Clements, Stanley 737
Clemmons Brothers 1586
Cleveland, MS 890
Cleveland, OH 1294–1313
Cleveland, TX 1612
Clewiston, FL 263, 264, 265
Clifford and Jackson 802
Clinch Theater (Tazewell, VA) 1894
Clinton, NC 1152
Clinton Theater (Houston, TX) 1680
Club Alabama Theater (Dallas, TX) 1624
Cochran, Steve 724
Cocoa, FL 266, 267, 268, 269, 270, 271
Coffey, Charles 1746
Colbert, Claudette 1869
Cole, C. C. 1901
Cole, Nat King 164, 804, 853
Cole, R. W. 673
Coleman, TX 1613
Coleman Brothers 1101, 1132
Coleran, NC 1153
Colfax, Mr. 225
College Theater (Talladega, AL) 80; (Greensboro, NC) 1181
Colonial Theater (Greenville, NC) 1185; (Philadelphia, PA) 1407; (Newport News, VA) 1831; (Norfolk, VA) 1842; (Portsmouth, VA) 1864
Colorado Theater (Smackover, AR) 131
Colored Annex Theater (Winter Garden, FL) 431
Colored Consolidated Vaudeville Circuit 579, 580, 627, 663, 984, 1288, 1294, 1315, 1330, 1549
Colored High School Theater (Auburn, AL) 7
Colored Motion Picture Operators Union 1429
Colored Normal Theater (Langston, OK) 1374
Colored Player Film Corporation p. 2
Colored Players Company 1429
Colored Theater (Huntsville, AL) 44; (Daytona Beach, FL) 276; (St. Augustine, FL) 393; (Cordele, GA) 485; (Homer, LA) 698; (Scotlandville, LA) 750; (Detroit, MI) 830; (Vicksburg, MS) 954; (Beaufort, NC) 1133; (Greenville, NC) 1186; (Kingston, NC) 1202; (Lake Washington, NC) 1210; (New Bern, NC) 1220; (Ardmore, OK) 1354; (Bennettsville, SC) 1460; (Camden, SC) 1466; (Sumter, SC) 1509; (Ennis, TX) 1647; (Marlin, TX) 1706; (Orange, TX) 1726

258 INDEX

Colp, IL 602
Columbia, MS 891
Columbia, MO 960
Columbia, SC 1475–1478
Columbia, TN 1525
Columbia Theater (Chicago, IL) 559; (Indianapolis, IN) 626–27; (Detroit, MI) p. 4, 831; (Kansas City, MO) 964; (New York, NY) 1090; (Philadelphia, PA) 1408, p. **178**; (Charleston, SC) 1468; (Danville, VA) 1805; (Norfolk, VA) 1842
Columbus, GA 478–484
Columbus, MS 892
Columbus, OH 1314–1326
Comet Theater (St. Louis, MO) 988; (Brooklyn, NY) 1069
Community Theater (Hope, AR) 107; (Prescott, AR) 128; (Texarkana, AR) 134; (St. Petersburg, FL) 395;
Como Theater (Fort Worth, TX) 1648
Compton, Betty 555
Cona Theater (Nacona, TX) 1720
Concord, NC 1154, 1155, 1156
Conley, Ed 1743
Conquest of Space (film) 446
Conroe, TX 1614, 1615
Conway, SC 1479
Cook, Susie 1449
Cook's Scenic Highway Theater (Scotlandville, LA) 751
Cooper, Gary 735, 1795
Cooper, Ralph 735, 1098
Cooper and Lamar Company 1551, 1586
Coral Gables, FL 272
Cordele, GA 485, 486, 487
Corey, Harry 801
Cortex, Richard 1446
Cornell and Ward 1431
Corona, NY 1056
Corpus Christi, TX 1616, 1617
Corsiciana, TX 1618, 1619
Cort Theater (Chicago, IL) 560
Costi, John 769
Cottoe, Joseph 1427
Cotton Blossoms (musical) 1633
Cotton Plant, AR 96.
Court Theater (Newark, NJ) 1033
Coushatta, LA 685
Covington, GA 488, 489
Cowan, John 791
Cox, Ida 660, 1086, 1625
Cox, Lloyd H. 1330
Cozy Theater (Clarksville, TX) 1607; (Morehead, TX) 1714
Crabbe, Buster 827
Crain, Jeanne 832
Crampton and Bailey 1288
Crandall, TX 1620

Crandall Theater Corporation 233
Crane, C. Howard 820, 823, 828, 831, 837, 861
Craver, S. W. 1149
Crawford, J. H. 613
Crawford, Joan 566, 661
Crawford, Samuel 81
Crawfordsville, AR 97
Crazy Over Horses (film) 445
Cremen, J. C. 777
Crescent Amusement Company 222
Crescent Theater (New York, NY) 1091
Crestwood Theater (Norfolk, VA) 1843
Crimson Skull (film) 1093
Crisfield, MD 809
Crisp, Tobe 1354
Crispus Attucks Cultural Center Inc. 1838
Criswell and Bailey 1449
Criterion Theater (St. Louis, MO) 989
Crosby, Bing 820
Cross City, FL 273
Crowd, Frank 317, 377
Crowley, LA 686, 687
Crown Amusement Company 780
Crown Garden Theater (Indianapolis, IN) 627, 644; (Columbus, OH) 1314
Crown Theater (Camp Hill, AL) 25; (Cleveland, OH) 1298
Crump, Jesse 660
Crystal Springs, MS 893
Crystal Theater (Daytona Beach, FL) 277; (Dublin, GA) 496
Culbert, J. H. 277
Cunningham, Arthur 754
Curry, Mrs. 669
Curtis, Tony 1884
Cushing, OK 1364, 1365
Cutout and Willie Eldridge 733

Dabney, Ford 227
Dade City, FL 274
Daisy Theater (Memphis, TN) 1451
Dakota (film) 827
Dallas, TX 1621–1635
Daly, William H. 778
Daly Theater (Baltimore, MD) 778
The Damsel in Distress (film) 780
Dandridge, Dorothy 661, 662, 1884
Dania, FL 275
Daniels and Walton 556
Dantino, Helmut 722
Danville, VA 1805–1809
The Dare Devil (film) 801
Darkel Theater (Los Angeles, CA) 157
Darktown Frolics (musical) 1051

Davis, Amon 566, 1838
Davis, Bette 838
Davis, Elijah 455
Davis, M. F. 1531
Davis, Sam 1331
Davis, Wiley 209
Davis and Green 1883
Davis Brothers 226
Davison Theater (Detroit, MI) 852
Dawn at Socorro (film) 660
Dawson, J.J. 1385, 1760
Dawson, GA 490
Dayton, OH 1327–1332
Daytona Beach, FL 276, 277, 278, 279
Dead End (film) 662
Dean, Priscilla 585, 595
Deanwood Theater (DC) 242
DeBurg Sisters 556
DeCarlo, Yvonne 728
Decatur, AL 26, 27, 28
Decatur, GA 491, 492, 493, 494
Decatur Theater (Bainbridge, GA) 467
Dee, Frances 838
Dee, Ruby 831
DeGaston, Galle 1086
DeGaston and Yuen 582, 1633
DeHaven Trio 1431
Deland, FL 280.
Delano Theater (High Point, NC) 1195
DeLeach and Corbin 1520
Della Rosa Theater (Lake Wales, FL) 333
Dells 592, 1086
Deloach and Corbin 733
Delora Theater (E. St. Louis, IL) 603
Delray Beach, FL 281
Delray Theater (Delray Beach, FL) 282
Delta Theater (Bartlesville, OK) 1357
Deluxe Roosevelt Theater (Baltimore, MD) 803
Deluxe Theater (Los Angeles, CA) 158; (E. St. Louis, IL) 606; (New York, NY) 1092; (Houston, TX) 1681
De Mille, Cecil 1111, 1414, 1429, 1850
Denbow's Coulter Theater (Philadelphia, PA) 1409
Denmark, SC 1480
Denniston, TX 1636
Denny, C. 225
Denton, TX 1638, 1639, 1640, 1641
Denver, CO 201
Deppe, Lois 592, 1442
Derrick, Howard 212
De Ridder, LA 688, 689
Des Moines, IA 646
Desiree (film) 724, 727
Desmond, Cleo 566

INDEX 259

DeSoto Theater (Lake City, FL) 329
The Desparado (film) 1884
Destry (film) 1837
Detroit, MI 820–868
Detroit Arcade Theater (Detroit, MI) 822
Devine, Andy 1840
DeWalt, Olen Pullum 1685
Diamond Theater (Tuscaloosa, AL) 84; (Omaha, NE) 1015; (Victoria, TX) 1773
Diane Theater (Baltimore, MD) 779
Dicharry, Jacques A. 731
Dick and Dick 805
Diggs, Josiah 780, 1421
Dillon, F. O. 660
Dillon, SC 1481
Dixiana Girls 1633
Dixie Airdome (Taylor, TX) 1756
Dixie Belle Theater (Tupelo, MS) 952
Dixie Theater (Birmingham, AL) 16; (Gadsden, AL) 40; (Jackson, AL) 40; (Blythville, AR) 92; (Malvern, AR) 119; (DC) 218; (Clearwater, FL) 259; (Goulds, FL) 303; (Sebring, FL) 409; (West Palm Beach, FL) 429; (Barnesville, GA) 468; (Columbus, GA) 479; (Macon, GA) 513; (Sandersville, GA) 523; (Louisville, KY) 658; (Lake Charles, LA) 707; (New Orleans, LA) 726; (Pocomoke City, MD) 810; (Charleston, MS) 885; (Greenwood, MS) 900; (Hattiesburg, MS) 907; (Indianola, MS) 910; (Inverness, MS) 911; (Itta Bena, MS) 913; (Sunflower, MS) 949; (Bath, NC) 1131; (Burlington, NC) 1138; (Charlotte, NC) 1145; (Hnderson, NC) 1190; (New Bern, NC) 1221; (Plymouth, NC) 1228; (Tarboro, NC) 1257; (Cincinnati, OH) 1281; (Toledo, OH) 1346; (Tulsa, OK) 1391; (Philadelphia, PA) 1410; (Greenwood, SC) 1490; (Spartanburg, SC) 1502; (Knoxville, TN) 1533; (Morristown, TN) 1554; (Abilene, TX) 1567; (Cleburne, TX) 1610; (Galveston, TX) 1657; (Navasota, TX) 1721; (Paris, TX) 1732; (Trinity, TX) 1767; (Danville, VA) 1806; (Newport News, VA) 1832; (Richmond, VA) 1871
Dixie-Dale Theater (Austin, TX) 1574
Dixie 3 Theater (Galveston, TX) 1658

Dixieland Blues Blowers 164
Dixieland Theater (Gainsville, GA) 501
Doc Cheatham's Jazz Syncopators 1302
Dodge Theater (Eastman, GA) 497
Doing Time (film) 777
Donaldsonville, LA 690
Donleavy, Brian 820
Donleavy, W. A. 1805, 1807
Donley, C. I. 1453
Dooley, H. 555
Dooley and Robinson 984
Dothan, AL 29, 20
Dothan Theater (Dothan, AL) 30
Douglas, GA 495
Douglas Theater (Indianapolis, IN) 628; (Baltimore, MD) 804; (St. Louis, MO) 990; (New York, NY) 1093, 1095, 1112; (Fort Worth, TX) 1649
Douglass, C. H. 515
Douglass, Frederick p. 3
Douglass, George 803
Douglass, James A. 134
Douglass Theater (Macon, GA) 514, p. 70; (Philadelphia, PA) 1411
Dove, Billie 164
Dowling Theater (Houston, TX) 1682
Downes, Mrs. Marie p. 3, 1103
Downlevy, W. A. 1408
Dowrich, James A. 242
Doxey, F. B. 654
Doxey Theater 654
Dozier Theater (Norfolk, VA) 1844
Dragon Theater (Orange, TX) 1727
Drake, E. L. 1530
Drake Walker's Bombay Girls 968, 984, 1302
Dream Theater (St. Petersburg, FL) p. 5, 396; (Columbus, GA) 480; (Port Arthur, TX) 1734
Dreamland Theater (Opelika, AL) 69; (Troy, AL) 82; (Stamps, AR) 132; (Texarkana, AR) 136; (DC) 219; (Savannah, GA) 524; (Monroe, LA) 719; (Baden, NC) 1129; (Ardmore, OK) 1355; (Muskogee, OK) p. 3, 1378; (Okmulgee, OK) p. 3, 1386; (Tulsa, OK) p. 3, p. 5, p. 7n18, p. **175**, 1392; (Cleburne, TX) 1611; (Dennison, TX) 1636; (Denton, TX) 1638; (Port Arthur, TX) 1735; (San Antonio, TX) 1749; (Texarkana, TX) 1762; (Huntington, WV) 1908
Drew, Bonnie Bell 1660
Drew, Lane 660

Drew Theater (Okmulgee, OK) 1387
Drew-Vels 592
Driscoll, R. Sloan 1457, 1518
Drive a Crooked Road (film) 1884
Drive-in theaters p. 4, p. 247
Drumbeat (film) 458
Drums Across the River (film) 728
Dublin, GA 496
Dubois Theater (Martinville, VA) 1824
Dude Cowboy (film) 1872
Dudley, E. B. 833, 866
Dudley, Sherman H. p. 2–3, p. 6n7, 211, 220, 223, 226, 236, 1051, 1787, 1833, 1856
Dudley and Byrd 514, 1520
Dudley and Dudley 1431
Dudley Theater (DC) 220; (Detroit, MI) 866; (St. Joseph, MO) 978; (Alexandria, VA) 1787; (Newport News, VA) 1833; (Petersburg, VA) 1856
Dudley Vaudeville Circuit p. 2, 212, 216, 220, 223, 226, 230, 512, 866, 1132, 1222, 1267, 1406, 1409, 1449, 1805, 1806, 1820, 1822, 1871, 1873, 1881, 1883
Dugan Theater (Conroe, TX) 1614
Duke Theater (Detroit, MI) 832
Dunbar, Paul Laurence p. 3, 802
Dunbar Theater (North Birmingham, AL) 68; (Lake City, Florida) 327; (Columbus, GA) 481; (Savannah, GA) 524; (Wichita, KS) 652; (Baltimore, MD) 780; (Detroit, MI) 833; (Sanford, NC) 1249; (Statesville, NC) 1256; (Winston-Salem, NC) 1272; (Columbus, OH) 1315; (Lockland, OH) 1336; (Philadelphia, PA) 1421; (Spartanburg, SC) 1503; (Austin, TX) 1575; (Temple, TX) 1759; (Norfolk, VA) 1835
Dunbar Theater 1 (DC) 221
Dunbar Theater 2 (DC) p. 5, p. **39**, 222
Duncan, OK 1366
Dunick Theater (Indianapolis, IN) 629
Dunlap Theater (Idabel, OK) 1373
Dunn, Irene 1447
Dunn, J. J. 79
Dunn, James 1450
Duo, Taylor 1449
Durham, NC 1157–1162
Duryea, Dan 1823
Duvall, Harry 777
Dyersburg, TN 1526

260 INDEX

The Eagle (film) 1111, 1429
Eagle Theater (New York, NY) 1094; (Asheville, NC) 1124; (High Point, NC) 1195
Earle, AR 98.
Earle Theater (Atlantic City, NJ) 1028
East Chicago, IN 617
East End Theater (Baton Rouge, LA) 679
East Harlon Theater (Edna, TX) 1642
East Hickory, NC 1163
East of Eden (film) 1410
East St. Louis, IL 603–610
Easter, Alex I. 1472
Eastman, GA 497
Eastman Theater (Decatur, GA) 492
Eastside Theater (Savannah, GA) 526; (Detroit, MI) 834; (Oklahoma City, OK) 1383
Eblon Theater (Kansas City, MO) 965
Ebony Film Company 589
Ebony Parade (film) 831
Echo Theater (Detroit, MI) 835
Eckert, Peter 1095
Eckstein, Billy 592, 853
Edding, W. T. 1129
Eddy, Nelson 725
Eden Theater (Baltimore, MD) 781
Edenton, NC 1164
Edgar Hayes and His Symphonic Harmonists 1084
Edgemont Theater (Dayton, OH) 1328
Edington, Bessie 984
Edna, TX 1642, 1643
Edwards and Edwards 660
Edwards and Hardee 984
Edwards Theater (McAlester, OK) 1376
Efigan, Chris 1006
Egan, Richard 737
Egypt Theater (Eustis, FL) 284
Eighth Avenue Theater (Birmingham, AL) 16, p. **13**
Eighty Drive-in (Tuskegee, AL) 86
Eighty-One Theater (Atlanta, GA) 446
El Dorado, AR 99, 100, 101
El Dorado Theater (Pensacola, FL) 375
El Paso, TX 1644, 1645
El Rey Theater (Oakland, CA) 171
El Reno, OK 1367
Elba Theater (Chicago, IL) 561
Electric Mills, MS 894
Electric Theater (Pensacola, FL) 376
Elite Theater (Decatur, AL) 26; (Florence Villa, FL) 285; (Cordele, GA) 486

Elizabeth City, NC 1165, 1166, 1167
Elizabeth Theater (Lake Washington, NC) 1211
Elizabethtown, NC 1168
Elks Lodge 786
Ella B. Moore Theater (Dallas, TX) 1625
Ellington, Edward "Duke" 787, 804, 832, 853, 1101, 1424, 1431
Ellington, Joseph 445
Elliott, R. A. 112
Elliott Theater (River Rouge, MI) 874
Ellis, Bernice 1696
Ellis Theater (San Francisco, CA) 188
Elm, NC 1169
Elm Theater (Elm, NC) 1169
Elmont Theater (Mount Airy, NC) 1218
Elmore, Eugene 1091
Elmore Theater (Pittsburgh, PA) 1440
Elson, J. 42
Embassy Theater (Hickory, NC) 1194
Emmart, Paul 795
Empire Circuit 211
Empire Theater (Reno, NV) 1021; (Lynchburg, VA) 1821; (Bluefield, WV) 1901; (Montgomery, WV) 1917
Emporia, VA 1810, 1811
Empress Theater (Jacksonville, FL) 314; (Columbus, OH) 1316
Emroe Theater (Indianapolis, IN) 630
The End of the World (film) 555
Enfield, NC 1170
Engleburg, Ben 1440
Engler, P.A. 15, 18, 19
English, Charles 628
English, J. A. 65.
English Theater (Indianapolis, IN) 631
Enid, OK 1368, 1369
Ennis, TX 1646, 1647
Ensley, AL 31.
Enterprise Amusement Company 126
Enterprise Theater (Pine Bluff, AR) 126
Ephraim Johnson from Norfolk (play) 317
Erie Theater (Cleveland, OH) 1299
Esquire Theater (Memphis, TN) 1542
Essex Theater (Newark, NJ) 1034
Eunice, LA 691
Eustis, FL 284
Evans, Earl 463
Evans, Edward 230
Evans, Mrs. S. Clarissa p. 1

Exhibit Theater (Columbus, OH) 1317
Exmore, VA 1812

F and M Liberty Theater (Eunice, LA) 691
Fairbanks, Douglas 1838
Fairfield, AL 32
Fairmount Theater (Philadelphia, PA) 1430
Fairview Theater (El Dorado, AR) 99
Fairyland Theater (Bessemer, AL) 8; (DC) 223
Family Theater (Jackson, MI) 872; (Cleveland, OH) 1300
Famous Theater (Birmingham, AL) 18; (Atlanta, GA) 447
Fan Theater (Tallahassee, FL) 416
Fans Theater (Philadelphia, PA) 1412
Fantastic Rhythm (musical) 1447
The Far Country (film) 1845
Farfield Theater (Detroit, MI) 836
Farmsville, NC 1172
Favorite Theater (DC) 224
Faye, Alice 725, 1427, 1869
Fayette, AL 33
Fayette Street Auditorium (Martinville, VA) 1825
Fayetteville, NC 1173
Federal Theater Program 1101
Fedo Theater (Wheeling, WV) 1920
Feels, Lorenzo 1823
Fenway Theater (Bronx, NY) 1061
Ferbee and McCann 733
Ferguson, Happy 1291, 1633
Ferguson and Ferguson 733
Ferguson Theater (Charleston, WV) 1904
Ferriday, LA 692, 693
Fieldman, Manuel 570
Fields Theater (Sheffield, AL) 78; (Bluefield, WV) 1902
The Fight Never Ends (film) 831
Fighting Colleen (film) 166
Film Daily Yearbook p. 5
Finklestein, Rubin 968
Finley T. Spencer 229, 235
First National Pictures 780
Fisher's Fun Festival 117, 1382, 1386
Fitzgerald, Ella 1086, 1098
Five Du-Tones 592, 1086
Five Stairsteps 592
Flaks, Kalman 793
Flaks, Karem 772
Flaks, M. 793
The Flame of Youth (film) 772
Fleming, Rhonda 1850
Fletcher, Darrow 592
Fletcher, Dusty 374, 1086, 1101
Fletcher, Mr. 1024

INDEX 261

Flint, MI 869, 870
Florence, AL 34, 35, 36
Florence, SC 1482, 1483, 1484
Florence Mills Theater (Los Angeles, CA) 159
Florence Mills Sisters Trio 1425
Florence Villa, FL 285
Florida Amusement Company 225
Florida City, FL 286
Florida Theater (DC) 225; (Ocala, FL) 354
Flying Down to Rio (film) 1869
Flynn, Errol 1872
Follette's Monkeys 556
Folly Theater (Crystal Springs, MS) 893
Fonda, Henry 725
Fontaine, Joan 241, 661
Fontana, Lawrence 1586, 1735
Footsteps in the Dark (film) 1872
For His Mother's Sake (film) 555, 590
Foraker Theater (DC) 226
Ford, Francis 777
Ford, G. 729
Ford, Glenn 722, 731, 1850, 1884
Ford Dabney Theater (DC) 227
Ford's Opera House (DC) p. 4, 235
Ford's Theater (New Bern, NC) 1222; (Lynchburg, VA) 1822
Forepaugh's Theater (Philadelphia, PA) 1414
Forest City, AR 102
Forest Theater (Detroit, MI) 837
Forrest, Sally 458, 459
Forrest Theater (Atlanta, GA) 448; (Philadelphia, PA) 1413
Forster, Little Clarence 660
Forster Photoplay Company p. 2
Fort Deposit, AL 37
Fort Deposit Theater (Fort Deposit, AL) 37
Fort Lauderdale, FL 287, 288, 289, 290
Fort Myers, FL 291, 292, 293, 294
Fort Pierce, FL 295, 296, 297
Fort Smith, AR 103
Fort Valley, GA 498, 499
Fort Worth, TX 1648–1654
Foster, Bessie 34
Fountain Theater (Chicago, IL) 562; (Cleveland, OH) 1301
The Four Bobs 1101
Four Faces West (film) 838
Four Guns to the Border (film) 659
Four Paws Theater (Philadelphia, PA) 1414
Four Star Theater (Chicago, IL) 563
Fox, William 1103
Fox Theater (Bogalusa, LA) 683; (Huntington, WV) 1909

Francis and Phillips 556
Francis Joins the WACs (film) 735
Frank D. Reeves Municipal Center (DC) 213
Frank Theater (Valdosta, GA) 538
Frankfort, KY 653
Franklin, LA 694, 695
Franklin, TN 1527
Franklin Theater (Chicago, IL) 564; (Grand Rapids, MI) 871; (Omaha, NE) 1016; (New York, NY) 1095
Franks Theater (Athens, TX) 1572
Frederick, OK 1370
Free State Theater (Kenbridge, VA) 1819
Freeman, H. Lawrence 1091
Freeman Theater (Cincinnati, OH) 1282
Fremont Amusement Company 782
Fremont Theater (Baltimore, MD) 782
Fresno, CA 147, 148, 149
Friedlander, Jacob 803
Frolic Theater (Bessemer, AL) 9; (Birmingham, AL) 15, 19; (Lexington, KY) p. 3; (Jacksonville, FL) 315
Fulton Theater (Baltimore, MD) 783
Fun Theater (Crowley, LA) 686; (Lafayette, LA) 702
Funny Folks (revue) 418

Gable, Clark 566, 725
Gadsden, AL 38, 39, 40, 41, 42
Gadsden, NC 1174, 1175
Gaiety Theater (Elizabeth City, NC) 1165; (Gadsden, NC) 1175
Gainesville, FL 298, 299, 300, 301, 302
Gainesville, GA 500, 501, 502, 503, 504
Gaither, Major Edward G. 1283
Gaither Theater (Cincinnati, OH) 1283
Galax Theater (Decatur, AL) 27
Gallo Theater (New Orleans, LA) 727
Galvan Theater (Corpus Christi, TX) 1616
Galveston, TX 1655–1663
Gamble, Kenny 1429
Gamble and Huff 1429
Gambler from Natchez (film) 659
Gans, Joe 827
Gant and Perkins 556
Garden Theater (Indiana Harbor, IN) 622; (Newark, NJ) 1035; (Trenton, NJ) 1045; (Sumter, SC) 1510
Gardner, Ava 737

Gardner, M. L. 1776, 1778
Gardner Theater (Hillsboro, TX) 1672
Garland, Judy 838, 1857
Garner, G. C. 452
Garrett, Jo Ann 592
Gary, IN 618, 619, 620
Garysburg, NC 1176
Gastonia, NC 1177, 1178
Gates, W.C. 557
Gay Theater (Birmingham, AL) 20; (Hurtsboro, AL) 49; (Crawsfordsville, AR) 97
Gay Theater Properties 13, 19, 20
Gaye, Lisa 728
Gayety Theater (Mobile, AL) 53; (Los Angeles, CA) 160; (Columbus, OH) 1316; (Philadelphia, PA) 1422; (Waco, TX) 1776
Geare, Reginald W. 222, 244
Gem Amusement Company 966
Gem Theater (Anniston, AL) 4; (Camden, AL) 24; (Montgomery, AL) 63; (Pritchard, AL) 75; (Hope, AR) 109; (Little Rock, AR) 116; (Osceola, AR) 124; (Oakland, CA) 172; (DC) 228; (Jacksonville, FL) 316; (Brownsville, GA) 471; (Fort Valley, GA)) 499; (Indianapolis, IN) 632; (Carroll, IA) 645; (New Orleans, LA) 728; (Saginaw, MI) 875; (Grenada, MS) 902; (Kansas City, MO) 966; (New York, NY) 1096; (Greensboro, NC) 1182; (Reidsville, NC) 1237; (Cincinnati, OH) 1284; (Brownsville, TN) 1515; (Columbia, TN) 1525; (Franklin, TN) 1527; (Jackson, TN) 1530; (Knoxville, TN) 1534; (Memphis, TN) 1543; (Nashville, TN) 1558; (Beaumont, TX) 1583; (Coleman, TX) 1613; (Waco, TX) 1777, p. **221**; (Norfolk, VA) 1846; (Petersburg, VA) 1857; (Logan, WV) 1916
Gentlemen and Guns (film) 827
Gentry, D. 216, 217
George, S. H. 667
George, William 777
George R Theater (Sapulpa, OK) 1389
Georges Theater (Parksley, VA) 1854
Georgetown-on-the-Aisle 212
Gerson, Morris 1417
Gertrude McCoy Theater (Baltimore, MD) 783
Gey Lew Theater (Indianapolis, IN) 644
Geyser, R. S. 623
Georgia-Alabama Theater (Opelika, AL) 79

262 INDEX

Georgia Theater (Memphis, TN) 1544
Get Rich Quick Wallingford (film) 597
Gibson, Hoot 595
Gibson, John T. 1421, 1425, 1431
Gibson's Broad Street Theater (Philadelphia, PA) 1421
Gibson's Theater (Philadelphia, PA) 1431
Gibson's Famous Midgets 1051
Gil Theater (Lafayette, LA) 703
The Gilded Lily (film) 555
Giles and Gulfport 1041
Gillespie, Dizzy 592
Gillis Theater (Independence, MO) 961
Gilmer, TX 1664
Gilmore Theater (Baltimore, MD) 784
Gilmore and Saratoga 784
Gilmore-Douglass Theater (Baltimore, MD) 784
Gilpin, Charles 588
Gilreatti, Money 15
Giroffi, Massimo 722
Givens, Dr. Everett A. 1579
Gladewater, TX 1665
Gladstone Theater (Philadelphia, PA) 1415
Glasco and Glasco 514
Glaum, Louise 780
Glenn and Bogsdale 984
Glenn Theater (Nacogdoches, TX) 1717
Globe Amusement Company 239
Globe Theater (San Pedro, CA) 197; (Jacksonville, FL) 317; (Covington, GA) 488; (Savannah, GA) 527; (Chicago, IL) 565; (St. Louis, MO) 991; (Kingston, NC) 1203; (New Bern, NC) 1223; (Wilson, NC) 1270; (Cleveland, OH) 1302; (Philadelphia, PA) 1416; (Walterboro, SC) 1512; (Norfolk, VA) 1847; (Richmond, VA) 1872
Gloucester, VA 1813
Glynn Theater (Nacogdoches, TX) 1717
Go West Young Man (film) 166
Gog (film) 737
Gold and Goldie 1431
Goldberg, Abraham 725
The Golden Gift (film) 589
Golden Nugget Theater (Belle Glade, FL) 254; (Pahokee, FL)
Golden Terrace Theater (Marrero, LA) 717
Golden Theater (Pittsburgh, PA) 1446
Goldfield Theater (Baltimore, MD) 785
Goldfield Theater No. 1 (Baltimore, MD) 790

Goldfield Theater No. 2 (Baltimore, MD) 785
Goldman, L. 968
Goldman, Lawrence E. 972
Goldsboro, NC 1179, 1180
Gone with the Wind (film) 233
Goodale, OH 1333
Goodale Theater (Columbus, OH) 1318
Goodbar and Lewis 579, 1549
Goode, Sam 552
Gorcey, Leo 735
Gordon, Charles S. 754
Gordon, Edward 358
Goselin, Fred 226
Goshen, VA 1814
Goulds, FL 303.
Goulter, W. J. 1883
Governor Theater (New York, NY) 1089
Graham, Maggie 805
Grahame, Gloria 659
Granada Theater (Detroit, MI) 838
Grand Central Theater (Cleveland, OH) 1303; (Dallas, TX) 1626
Grand Larceny (film) 597
Grand Rapids, MI 871
Grand Theater (Birmingham, AL) 21; (Cocoa, FL) 270; (Fort Myers, FL) 291; (Fort Pierce, FL) 295; (Chicago, IL) 556, 566; (Mounds, IL) 613; (Louisville, KY) 659; (Alexandria, LA) 671; (Baton Rouge, LA) 680; (Houma, LA) 701; (Jackson, MS) 918; (Charlotte, NC) 1146; (Muskogee, OK) 1379; (Anderson, SC) 1457; (Bolivar, TN) 1514; (Chattanooga, TN) 1518; (Knoxville, TN) 1535; (Memphis, TN) 1545; (Abilene, TX) 1569; (Fort Worth, TX) 1650; (Greenville, TX) 1666
Grant, Cary 241, 1416
Grant Theater (Detroit, MI) 840
Gratiot Theater (Detroit, MI) p. 4, 841
Gray, GA 505
Gray, S. H. 1520
Gray, Sam 984
Gray, Sam H. 1440
Gray, W. B. 216
Gray and Dunlop 1288
Gray Theater (Gray, GA) 505
Greater Osage Theater (Plaquemine, LA) 746
Greeleyville, SC 1485
Green, Ada 476
Green, Doe Doe 1540
Green, Hazel 784
Green, Silas 476
Green and Lane 733
Green Frog Theater (Tallulah, LA) 758

Green River Theater (Scotland, AR) 130
Green Theater (Sulphur, LA) 755; (Jonestown, MS) 923
Greenbaum and Evart 782
Green's Opera House (Richmond, VA) p. 4, 1873
Greensboro, NC 1181, 1182, 1183, 1184
Greenville, AL 43
Greenville, AR 104
Greenville, MS 895
Greenville, NC 1185–1189
Greenville, SC 1486, 1487
Greenville, TX 1666, 1667, 1668
Greenwood, DE 204
Greenwood, MS 899, 900, 901
Greenwood, SC 1488, 1489, 1490
Greenwood Theater (Greenwood, DE) 204
Greer, SC 1491
Gregg Theater (Longview, TX) 1701
Grenada, MS 902, 903
Gresham, Jones 1075
Grice and Coleman 801
Griffin, GA 506
Griffin Theater (Griffin, GA) 506
Grott, Harold 786
Groveland Theater (Chicago, IL) 567
Guerilla Girl (film) 722
Guggenheimer, A. S. 527, 532
Gulfport, MS 904, 905, 906
Guns Ablaze (film) 1840
The Gunsalus Mystery (film) 597
The Guttersnipe (film) 585

Haag, Jack 579
Hadaway, R. Norris 13
Hahn, Frank E. 1429
Hail the Woman (film) 590
Haines City, FL 304, 305
Hale Theater (Boley, OK) 1358
Hales, George p. 213
Hall, Huntz 735
Hall, Jon 820, 838
Hall, Marvin E. 682
Haller, N. T. 243
Hallett, Morris 237
Halls, TN 1528
Halls Theater (Halls, TN) 1528
Haltnorth Theater (Cleveland, OH) 1304
Hamburger, Alfred 601
Hamilton, OH 1334, 1335
Hamilton, J. W. 1343
Hamilton Theater (Natchez, MS) 940; (New York, NY) 1097
Hammerstein I, Oscar 1098
Hammond, LA 696, 697
Hammond, Frank 589, 590, 597
Hammond, Johnny 597
Hammond, O.C. 589, 597

INDEX 263

Hampton, Lionel 164
Hampton, VA 1815, 1816, 1817
Hampton and Hampton 9
Hampton Theater (Roanoke, VA) 1882
Hamrick Theatre Service 1548
Hanen, Juanita 772
Happy Hour Theater (Hearne, TX) 1669
Hardy Theater (Chase City, VA) 1800
Harkesen, M. H. 1793
Harlem Frolics (revue) 968, 1103
Harlem Opera House (New York, NY) p. 4, 1086, 1098, p. **145**
Harlem Park Methodist Episcopal Church 786
Harlem Strutters 374
Harlem Theater (Mobile, AL) 54; (Camden, AR) 95; (Forest City, AR) 102; (Newport, AR) 122; (Turrell, AR) 137; (West Memphis, AR) 144; (Bartow, FL) 252; (Clearwater, FL) 260; (Clewiston, FL) 263; (Miami, FL) 340; (Mulberry, FL) 349; (Port St. Joe, FL) 388; (St. Petersburg, FL) 397; (Americus, GA) 436; (Athens, GA) 438; (Atlanta, GA) 449; (Augusta, GA) 462; (Lithonia, GA) 511; (Sycamore, GA) 534; (Thomaston, GA) 535; (E. St. Louis, IL) 607; (De Ridder, LA) 688; (Donaldsonville, LA) 690; (Lake Providence, LA) 712; (Sulphur, LA) 756; (Thibodaux, LA) 761; (Baltimore, MD) 786, p. **106**; (Belzoni, MS) 878; (Biloxi, MS) 879; (Canton, MS) 883; (Clarksdale, MS) 886; (Greenville, MS) 895; (Leland, MS) 928; (Ruleville, MS) 945; (Kinloch Park, MO) 975; (Lawton, OK) 1375; (Greenville, SC) 1486; (Laurens, SC) 1492; (Chattanooga, TN) 1519; (Memphis, TN) 1546; (Union City, TN) 1566; (Amarillo, TX) 1570; (Austin, TX) 1576; (Camden, TX) 1605; (Cleveland, TX) 1612; (Conroe, TX) 1615; (Corpus Christi, TX) 1617; (Dallas, TX) 1627; (Dennison, TX) 1637; (Marshall, TX) 1707; (Nacogdoches, TX) 1718; (Navasota, TX) 1722; (Odessa, TX) 1724; (Palestine, TX) 1729.
Harmony Theater (Chicago, IL) 568; (Amarillo, TX) 1571; (Denton, TX) 1639; (Terrell, TX) 1761; (Texarkana, TX) 1763; (Victoria, TX) 1774
Harper, Leonard 1041

Harris, Alice 1101
Harris, Charles 793
Harris, Jack 1626
Harris, Julie 1410
Harris, O. T. 1303
Harris, Paul 802
Harris, Shead 19
Harris and Harris 514, 733
Harris and Turner 1270
Harrisburg, PA 1402, 1403-4
Harrison, David 773
Harrison, Hugo 1839
Harrison Theater (Lynchburg, VA) 1823
Hart, William B. 595
Harvard Theater (Winsboro, LA) 767
Harwell, John C. 11
Hattiesburg, MS 907, 908
Hatton, Isaiah J. p. 5, 222
Have a Heart (film) 1450
Haver, Phyllis 1103
Haverford Theater (Philadelphia, PA) 1417
Hawkins, Erskine 853
Hayden, Sterling 559, 727
Hayes, Gabby 731
Hayes, Helen 1450
Hazel Theater (Plant City, FL) 383
Hawkins, M. L. 610
Hawkins, Oscar 1238
Hayward, Susan 1850
Headin' West (film) 595
Headland, AL p. 5
Healy, R. A. 582
Heard, Sigman 214
Hearne, TX 1669
Heflin, Van 724, 726
Hegaman, Lucille 556
Helena, AR 105, 106
Hellens, Jake 865
Hellinger Theater (San Antonio, TX) 1750
Hello 1921 (musical) 1557
Hell's Island (film) 448
Henderson, Edmonia 143
Henderson, John S. 1330
Henderson, KY 654
Henderson, NC 1190, 1191, 1192
Hendricks, Alvin W. 634
Hendricks and Leo 1805
Henie, Sonja 1884
Henry, James D. 1807
Henry, Lew p. 3, 220, 1286, 1287, 1291, 1540
Henry Dixon Jazzland Girls 514
Henry Theater (Leaksville, NC) 1213
Henry Wooden's Bon Tons 805
Henton, J. B. 1910
Henton Theater (Huntington, WV) 1910
Her Own Money (film) 590
Here Come the Waves (film) 820
Here We Go Again (film) 728
Herring, Robert 1266

Hersford, NC 1193
Heston, Charlton 725
Hiawatha Amusement Company 229
Hiawatha Theater (DC) 229; (Paducah, KY) 667
Hickory, NC 1194
Hicks, Irving 1788
Hicks, Mary 1291
High Point, NC 1195, 1196, 1197
High School Theater (Dallas, TX) 1628
High Society (film) 448
Highlands Theater (Gastonia, NC) 1177; (Wadesboro, NC) 1258
Highway 21 Drive-in (Savannah, GA) 528
Hightower, Charles 733
Hill, Dr. J. Seth 317, 377
Hill, James 641
Hill, Lewis 641
Hill, TX 1670, 1671
Hill Brothers 626
Hill Drive-in (Bennettsville, SC) 1461
Hill Sisters 446, 582, 1132, 1425
Hill Theater (Baltimore, MD) 787
Hillsboro, TX 1672, 1673, 1674
Hillside Theater (Conway, SC) 1479
Hilltop Theater (Apalachicola, FL) 245
Hines, Earl "Fatha" 579, 597, 853, 1032, 1086, 1427, 1449
Hippodrome Theater (Alexandria, LA) 672; (Shreveport, LA) 752; (Baltimore, MD) 788; (Detroit, MI) 842; (Cincinnati, OH) 1285; (Columbus, OH) 1319; (Danville, VA) 1807; (Richmond, VA) 1874; (Roanoke, VA) 1883
Hirschensohn, Harry 435
His Majesty O'Keefe (film) 443
His Majesty the American (film) 1838
Hitchcock, Alfred 241, 1845
Hitchler, J. J. 1431
Hite, Les 164
Hobbs, NM 1048
Hoffheimer Corporation 1851
Hoffman and Henon 1406, 1416, 1434
Hoggs, W. A. 1714
Holbrook Theater (Detroit, MI) 843
Holiday, Billie 230, 1086, 1424
Hollabird and Roche 554
Hollandale, FL 306
Hollandale, MS 909
Hollenger, Ray 1872, 1877
Hollopaw, FL 307
Hollywood, FL 308, 309
Hollywood Theater (Kansas

City, MO) 967; (Chapel Hill, NC) 1141; (Port Arthur, TX) 1736
Holman Theater (Houston, TX) 1683
Holmes and his Peacock Track Strutters 63
Holt, Anna 1540
Holt, Tim 1872
Home Theater (Baltimore, MD) 789
Homer, LA 698, 699
Homestead, FL 310, 311
The Homesteader (film) 1015, 1018
Honey Island, TX 1675, 1676
Hope, Bob 1884
Hope, Boots 845
Hope, AR 107, 108, 109, 110, 111, 112, 113
Hopewell, VA 1818
Hopkins, John 208
Hopkins Theater (Farmsville, NC) 1172
Horne, H. L. 1012
Horne, Lena 853, 861
Hornstein, M. 801
Hortense Theater (Indianapolis, IN) 633
Hortwicz, M. B. 1302
Hot Chocolates (musical) 1084
The Hot Mikado (show) 1101
Hot News (film) 737
Houma, LA 700, 701
House of Wax (film) 1840
House on Telegraph Hill (film) 731
Houston, TX 1677–1697
Houston, Walter 1840
How Come? (revue) 1421, 1838
Howard and Louisiana 731
Howard Theater (DC) 230, p. 42; (Atlanta, GA) 456; (Brooklyn, NY) 1070
Howata, OK 1371
Howell Theater (Palatka, FL) 368
Hoxey, Jack 780
Hub Theater (Los Angeles, CA) 161
Hubert, John A. 642
Hudnell, James H. 227
Hughes, Howard 459
Hughes, T. Cecil 1037
Hughes, AR 114
Hugo, OK 1352
Human Desire (film) 722, 731
Hunt, Harry 117
Hunter, Eddie 1091
Hunter, Glen 1103
Huntington, WV 1907–1912
Huntington Theater (Huntington, WV) 1911
Huntsville, AL 44, 45, 46, 47, 48
Hurlehane, F. A. 220
Hurtig and Seamon's Burlesque 1086

Hurtig and Seamon's Music Hall 1086
Hurtsboro, AL 49
Hury, H. J. 19, 20
Hutton, Betty 820
Hyde Park Drive-in (Hollandale, FL) 306
Hyde Park Theater (Memphis, TN) 1547

I Cover the Waterfront (film) 1869
Idabel, OK 1373
Ideal Theater (Frederick, OK) 1370; (Houston, TX) 1684
Idle Hour Theater (Petersburg, VA) 1858
I'll Be Seeing You 1427
Imperial Theater (Haines City, FL) 305; (Chicago, IL) 569
Imwold, Charles H. 782
Independence, MO 961
Independent Theatres, Inc. 1524
Indiana Harbor, IN 621, 622
Indiana Theater (Chicago, IL) 570; (Indianapolis, IN) 634
Indianapolis, IN 623–644
Indianapolis Freeman (newspaper) p. 2, p. 6n8, 1315
Indianola, MS 910
Institute, WV 1913
Institute Theater (Institute, WV) 1913
The Insurance Agents (show)
Inner City Broadcasting Corporation 1086
International Sweethearts of Rhythm 853
Interstate Theater (Stuttgart, AR) 133
Inverness, MS 911, 912
Irene (film) 725
Iroquois Theater (New Orleans, LA) 729
Irving Theater (Chicago, IL) 571
Isis Theater (Wichita Falls, TX) 1781
Island of Lost Men (film) 731
Israel, Louis 1302
Italy, TX 1698
Itta Bena, MS 913

Jackson, AL 50, 51
Jackson, GA 509
Jackson, H. D. 1671
Jackson, J. A. 1315, 1316
Jackson, MI 872
Jackson, MS 914–922
Jackson, NC 1198
Jackson, TN 1529
Jackson and Rector 1659
Jackson Theater (Jackson, NC) 1198
Jackson, Wilson and Johnson 733
Jacksonville, FL 312–323
Jacksonville, NC 1199

Jacksonville, TX 1699
Jacobs, George 785
Jade Theater (Los Angeles, CA) 162
Jaffee, Ben 9
James, S. L. 1389
James, Thomas 989, 997
James Theater (Cotton Plant, AR) 96; (Goldsboro, NC) 1180
Jane Eyre (film) 1410
Jasper, FL 325
Jaws of Steel (film) 164
Jaxon Theater (Brunswick, GA) 472
Jazz Lips, Fritz, Jr. 733
Jean Theater (Baltimore, MD) 789; (Seaboard, NC) 1250
Jeepers Creepers (film) 731
Jefferson Amusement Company 1583
Jefferson Theater (New York, NY) 1099; (Newport News, VA) 1834
Jenkins and Jenkins 845
Jennings, Josephine 530
Jesse James' Women (film) 724
Jest-A-Mere Theater (St. Louis, MO) 992
Jet Drive-in (Columbus, GA) 482
Jewel Theater (DC) 231; (Detroit, MI) 844; (New York, NY) 1100; (Ardmore, OK) 1356; (Oklahoma City, OK) 1384
Jewell Theater (Indianapolis, IN) 635; (Philadelphia, PA) 1418
Jim Crow establishments pp. 1–2
Jines and Jacqueline 660, 1291, 1315, 1431, 1449, 1520
Jive Drive-in (Columbus, GA) 482
JML Amusement Company 770
Joe Palooka Fighting Mad (film) 838
John Mason's Dixie Beach Girls 660, 866
Johnny Guitar (film) 727
Johnny Lee Long and His Dixiana Girls 968, 984
John's Theater (Columbia, MS) 891
Johnson, E. H. 865
Johnson, Haven 164
Johnson, Jack 481, 585, 827
Johnson, James P. 1112
Johnson, Mr. 566
Johnson, O. T. 1859
Johnson, R. F. 1222, 1822
Johnson, Van 1427
Johnson, William 1362
Johnson and Johnson 663
Johnson and Lee 1291, 1315
Jolly Theater (New Orleans, LA) 730
Jones, Buck 212, 1446

INDEX 265

Jones, C. Clark
Jones, C. I. 1226
Jones, Charles B. 54, 55
Jones, Clarence 556, 585, 597
Jones, Garbage 1101
Jones, Hambone 1520, 1838
Jones, Jennifer 725
Jones, Maggie 9
Jones, Sam 476
Jones, Tom 992
Jones and Burney Trio 1392
Jones and Chatman 633
Jones and Jones 627, 1540
Jones Theater (Hill, TX) 1670; (Hillsboro, TX) 1673
Jonestown, MS 923
Jonn, W.T. 1235
Joplin, Robert B. 1052
Jordan, Charles 1595
Jordan, Joe 588, 984
Jordan, Louis 831
Jordan Theater (Anderson, SC) 1458
The Journey's End (film) 597
Joy Theater (Osceola, AR) 125; (Chicago, IL) 572; (Philadelphia, PA) p. 4, 1419; (Denmark, SC) 1480; (Fort Worth, TX) 1651; (Greenville, TX) 1667
Joyland Theater (Beaumont, TX) 1584
Joyner Theater (Emporia, VA) 1810
Jug Theater (West Helena, AR) 142
Julian Theater (Vinton, LA) 764
Julien, Philip M. 239
The Jungle Princess (film) 772

Kahn, Albert 851, 867
Kalischer, Mark 552
Kane Theater (Baltimore, MD) 798
Kannapolis, NC 1200
Kansas City, KS 647, 648, 649
Kansas City, MO 962–974
Kaplan, Mr. 1303
Karumu House Theater (Cleveland, OH) 1305, p. **166**
Karumu Players 1305
Karamu Theater (Tyler, TX) 1768
Kearney, F. T. 223
Keith Vaudeville Circuit 1084
Keith's Hamilton Theater (New York, NY) 1097
Kelford, NC 1201
Kelly, Gene 838
Kelly, Grace 1845
Kelly, J. B. 447
Kelly, Wilbert M. 21
Kelly Miller Theater (Clarksburg, WV) 1906
Kemp, Dirk 585
Kenbridge, VA 1819
Kennedy, M. C. 1534

Kenton, Stan 804
Kerima 1852
Ketchel, Stanley 585
Key West, FL 326
Keys of the Kingdom (film) 1427
Keyser, Karl K. 343
Keyser, WV 1914
Keystone Babies (film) 156
Keystone Theater (Philadelphia, PA) 1420, p. **180**
Kid and Eva 1633
Kid Thomas Company 20
Kilbride, Perry 724
King, Billy 566
King, C. B. 57
King, J. H. 57
King and Davis 573
King Ed Theater (Boley, OK) 1358
King of Kings (film) 1414
King Theater (Cleveland, OH) 1306
King's Palace Theater (Alexandria, VA) 1725
Kingston, NC 1202, 1203, 1204
Kinky Doo Trio 663
Kinloch, IL 611
Kinloch Park, MO 975, 976
Kinloch Theater (Kinloch, IL) 611
Kinston, NC 1205–1209
Kirk, Phyllis 1840
Kirkwood, Joe 838
Kismet Theater (Brooklyn, NY) 1071
Kissimmee, FL 327
Klein, William J. 592
Kling, Billy 971, 974
Knickerbocker Theater (Columbus, OH) 1316
Knight, Atella p. 6n7
Knights of Pythias Lodge 734, 786, 1323
Knox, Leroy 1449
Knoxville, TN 1532–1536
Koppin, Henry S. 845
Koppin Theater (Detroit, MI) 845
Korman Pictures 825, 827
Kosciusko, MS 924
Koupolis, James M. 964
Kourkoulis, James 775
Kramer, Sam 164
Krapf, R. C. 1329
Kum-C Theater (Detroit, MI) 846

Laclede Theater (St. Louis, MO) 994
Ladd, Alan 458, 726, 737
Ladies in Retirement (film) 1880
Lady in the Lake (film) 832
Lafayette, LA 702, 703, 704, 705
Lafayette Players 164, 556, 566, 1421
Lafayette Theater (Baltimore, MD) 791; (New York, NY) 1041, 1101, p. **147**; (Winston-Salem, NC) 1273
Laferty, J.E. 798
LaFrance, Clifford 722
LaGrange, GA 510
Lake, Arthur 1872
Lake Charles, LA 706, 707, 708, 709, 710, 711
Lake City, FL 328, 329
Lake Providence, LA 712, 713
Lake Theater (South Bay, FL) 413; (Chicago, IL) 573; (Lake Charles, LA) 708; (Lake Providence, LA) 713; (Omaha, NE) 1017
Lake Wales, FL 333, 334
Lake Washington, NC 1210
Lakeland, FL 330, 331, 332
Lamas, Fernando 731
Lamb, Thomas W. 788, 1109
LaMott, Ira J. 242
Lamour, Dorothy 735, 838, 1884
Lancaster, Burt 443, 1795
Lance, Major 592
Landi, Elissa 1101
Langston, OK 1374
Langston Theater (DC) 232
La Place, LA 714
La Place Theater (La Place, LA) 714
Laredo, WV 1915
Laredo Theater (Laredo, WV) 1915
Largo Theater (Los Angeles, CA) 163, p. **29**
Lark, David 1075
Late Hour Dancers (show) 1101, 1103
Laurel, DE 205
Laurel, MS 925, 926, 927
Laurens, SC 1492, 1493
Laurie, Piper 1410, 1852
Laurinburg, NC 1212
Lawson, Lula 1836
Lawton, OK 1375
Leaksville, NC 1213
Leatherman, J.S. 214
Lee, Clarence 582, 866
Lee, Ed 1585
Lee, Gypsy Rose 820
Lee, Henry H. 798
Lee, Mr. 775
Lee, Robert R. 773
Lee, S. Charles p. 6n15
Lee and Wright 514
Lee Theater (Bluefield, VA) 1798
Lee's Tent Theater (Beaumont, TX) 1585
Leesburg, FL 335
Leide, Enrico 456
Leland, MS 928, 929
Lemcone Theater (Elizabethtown, NC) 1168
Lemke, J. A. 1776
Lemone, Lemone and Grant 1392

Lennox Theater (Norfolk, VA) 1848
Lenoir, NC 1214
Lenox Theater (Atlanta, GA) 450; (Augusta, GA) 463; (Baltimore, MD) 792, p. **108**; (Detroit, MI) 847; (Washington, NC) 1259; (Springfield, OH) 1342; (Richmond, VA) 1875; (Suffolk, VA) 1890
Leon Theater (Tallahassee, FL) 417
Leonard, W. H. 1776
Leron Theater (Enfield, NC) 1170
Lester, L.T. 1478
Let Freedom Ring (film) 725
Leve, Bessie 166
Levi, Fred 14
Levin, Joseph 1420
Levon Theater (Aulander, NC) 1127
Levy, Alexander L. 592
Levy, Syd 753
Lewin, Ernest L. 1834
Lewis, Cary 579
Lewis, E. C. 1783
Lewis, E. L. 1223
Lewis, J. W. 1757
Lewis, S. 1649
Lewis and Wilson 1586
Lewis Theater (San Francisco, CA) 189; (Keyser, WV) 1914
Lewisburg, TN 1537
Lexington, KY p. 3, 655, 656, 657
Lexington Leader (newspaper) p. 6n13
The Liar (play) 164
Liberty Bell Theater (Austin, TX) 1577
Liberty City, FL 336
Liberty Theater (Talladega, AL) 81; (Greenville, AR) 104; (San Francisco, CA) 190; (Stockton, CA) 198; (Hollywood, FL) 308; (Liberty City, FL) 336; (Miami, FL) 341; (Columbus, GA) 483; (Griffin, GA) 507; (Valdosta, GA) 539; (Lovejoy, IL) 612; (Pikesville, KY) 668; (Alexandria, LA) 73; (Detroit, MI) p. 4, 848; (Minneapolis, MN) 876; (McComb, MS) 932; (Greenville, NC) 1187; (Raleigh, NC) 1231; (Chickasha, OK) 1361; (Greenville, SC) 1487; (Laurens, SC) 1493; (Marion, SC) 1494; (Spartanburg, SC) 1504; (Chattanooga, TN) 1520; (Galveston, TX) 1659; (Gladewater, TX) 1665; (Houston, TX) 1685; (Mexia, TX) 1711; (Mount Pleasant, TX) 1715; (Orange, TX) 1728; (Berkeley, VA) 1793
Liberty Theater No. 1 (Bryan, TX) 1600

Liberty Theater No. 2 (Bryan, TX) 1601
Lichtman, Abe 240, 804, 1788
Lichtman Theaters 212, 213, 214, 230, 238, 1823, 1834, 1849, 1857, 1861, 1862, 1869, 1872, 1878
Lido Theater (Indianapolis, IN) 636-37; (New York, NY) 1102
Life's Darn Funny (film) 555
Lightman, M. A. 117
Lightner Arcade Theater (Raleigh, NC) 1232
Lightner Brothers 1232
Lillian Russell (film) 725
Lincoln, Abraham p. 3
Lincoln, Elmo 156
Lincoln Colored Drive-in (Memphis, TN) 1548
Lincoln Drive-in (Tuskegee, AL) 87; (Fort Myers, FL) 292
Lincoln-Howard Corporation 233
Lincoln Motion Picture Company p. 2, 1018
Lincoln Park Theater (Rockville, MD) 812
Lincoln Square Theater (Kansas City, MO) 969
Lincoln Theater (Bessemer, AL) 10; (Mobile, AL) 55; (Los Angeles, CA) 164, p. **50**; (Oakland, CA) 171; (Stockton, CA) 199; (DC) 233, p. **44**; (Bradentown, FL) 257; (Clearwater, FL) 261; (Clewiston, FL) 264; (Delray Beach, FL) 282; (Fort Pierce, FL) 296; (Gainsville, FL) 298; (Homestead, FL) 311; (Jacksonville, FL) 318; (Jasper, FL) 325; (Key West, FL) 326; (Miami, FL) 342; (Orlando, FL) 359; (Palatka, FL) 369; (Panama City, FL) 372; (Pensacola, FL) 377; (Plant City, FL) 384; (Punta Gorda, FL) 389; (St. Petersburg, FL) 398; (Sanford, FL) 404; (Tampa, FL) 421; (Atlanta, GA) 451; (Gainsville, GA) 502; (Griffin, GA) 508; (Cairo, IL) 548; (Chicago, IL) 574; (E. St. Louis, IL) 607; (Des Moines, IA) 646; (Louisville, KY) 660; (Winchester, KY) 669; (New Orleans, LA) 731; (Rustin, LA) 748; (Baltimore, MD) p. 3, 793; (Crisfield, MD) 809; (Greenville, MS) 896; (Laurel, MS) 926; (Kansas City, MO) 968; (Kinloch Park, MO) 976; (St. Louis, MO) 995; (New York, NY) p. 4, 1103; (Burlington, NC) 1139; (Charlotte, NC) 1147; (Kinston, NC) 1206; (Raleigh, NC)

1234; (Whiteville, NC) 1262; (Winston-Salem, NC) 1274; (Cincinnati, OH) p. 3, 1286; (Portsmouth, OH) 1340; (Springfield, OH) 1342; (Hugo, OK) 1372; (Philadelphia, PA) 1421, p. **181**; (Pittsburgh, PA) 1441; (Bennettsville, SC) 1462; (Camden, SC) 1467; (Charleston, SC) 1469; (Columbia, SC) 1477; (Florence, SC) 1483; (Chattanooga, TN) 1521; (Nashville, TN) 1559; (Austin, TX) 1578; (Beaumont, TX) 1586; (Dallas, TX) 1629; (Galveston, TX) 1660; (Honey Island, TX) 1676; (Lufkin, TX) 1705; (Mount Pleasant, TX) 1716; (Pittsburg, TX) 1733; (Port Arthur, TX) 1737; (Waxahachie, TX) 1780; (Alexandria, VA) 1788; (Berkeley, VA) 1794; (Danville, VA) 1808; (Hampton, VA) 1816; (Newport News, VA) 1835; (Portsmouth, VA) 1865; (Richmond, VA) 1876; (Suffolk, VA) 1891; (Huntington, WV) 1912
Lincoln No. 2 Theater (Baltimore, MD) 772
Lincolnton, NC 1215
Lindy Theater (Brooklyn, NY) 1072
Liston, Virginia 1440, 1520
Lithonia, GA 511
Little Annie Rooney (film) 1429
Little Broadway Theater (E. St. Louis, IL) 609
Little Harlem Theater (Inverness, MS) 912; (Cushing, OK) 1364; (Gilmer, TX) 1664
Little Herman 731
Little Lord Fauntleroy (film) 556
Little Minister (film) 589
Little Rock, AR 115, 116, 117
Lively, Jack 396
Liza (musical) 1421
Liza and Her Shuffling Band 1086
Lockhart, E. A. 781
Lockett, S. L. 444.
Lockland, OH 1336, 1337, 1338
Lockwood and Poundstone 435
Loew's Brevoort Theater (Brooklyn, NY) 1067
Loew's 116th Street Theater (New York, NY) 1106
Logan, G. W. 1162
Logan, WV 1916
Loma Theater (Marshall, TX) 1708
Lometa, TX 1700
Long, J. K. 1427
Long, John 1633

Long, Leon 66
Long and Jackson 984
Long Beach, CA 150, 151
Long View, TX 1701, 1702
Longs Theater (Tyler, TX) 1769
Look Out Sister (film) 831
Loop Theater (Toledo, OH) 1347
Lorraine, Marjorie 1288
Los Angeles, CA 152, 153, 154, 155, 156, 157, 158, 159, 160, 161, 162, 163, 164, 165, 166, 167, 168, 169
Los Angeles Sentinel (newspaper) 164
The Lost Lady (film) 1450
Lou, Mandy 1101
Lou Ann Theater (Opelousas, LA) 743
Loughman, FL 337
Louis, Joe 929
Louis Theater (Chicago, IL) 575, (St. Joseph, MO) 979
Louise Theater (Parksley, VA) 1855
Louisianne Theater (Lake Charles, LA) 709
Louisville, GA 512
Louisville, KY 658–664
Louisville, MS 930
Love, Bessie 1093
Love, G. S. 480
Love, G. W. 970
Lovejoy, IL 612
Loveland Theater (Pompano, FL) 387
Lovely, W. J. 11
Love's Theater (Kansas City, MO) 970
Lowe, Edward 786
Lowe's Palace (Brunswick, GA) 473
Loyal Theater (Omaha, NE) 1018
Lubbock, TX 1703, 1704
Lucas, Howard 1878
Lucille Hagamin and Her Sunny Land Cotton Pickers 1103
Lufkin, TX 1705
Lula Coates and Crackerjacks 1431
Lumberton, NC 1216, 1217
Luna Park Theater (Atlanta, GA) 452
Lupino, Ida 661, 724, 832, 1880
Lust, Sidney 1785
Lustgarten, Jack 1291
Lutcher, LA 715
Luther K. Mitchell Theater (New Orleans, LA) 732
Lux Theater (Starkville, MS) 948
Luxor Theater (Newark, NJ) 1036
Lyceum Theater (Fresno, CA) 148; (Chicago, IL) 576; (Buffalo, NY) 1049; (Cincinnati, OH) p. 3, 1287

Lying Lips (film) 728
Lynchburg, VA 1820–1823
Lynn Theater (Chicago, IL) 577
Lyon, James 15
Lyon Theater (Somerville, TX) 1755
Lyons Theater (Houston, TX) 1686
Lyric Theater (Sacramento, CA) 180; (San Francisco, CA) 187; (San Jose, CA) 196; (New Haven, CT) 203; (Miami, FL) 343; (Ocala, FL) 355; (Perry, FL) 381; (Lexington, KY) 656; (Louisville, KY) 661; (New Orleans, LA) 733; (Jackson, MS) 919; (McComb, MS) 933; (Kansas City, MO) 971; (Camden, NJ) 1029; (Newark, NJ) 1037; (Wilmington, NC) 1267; (Cincinnati, OH) 1287; (Hamilton, OH) 1334; (Sumter, SC) 1511; (Mount Pleasant, TN) 1555; (Sumter, TN) 1565; (Austin, TX) 1579; (Wichita Falls, TX) 1782; (Hampton, VA) 1817; (Newport News, VA) 1836; (Portsmouth, VA) 1866

Ma and Pa Kettle at Home (724)
Mabel Whitman and Her Dixie Boys 1431
Mabley, Jackie "Moms" 592
Macbeth (play) 1101
Maceo Theater (DC) 234; (Tampa, FL) 422
Macire, Joe 1541
Mack, Baby 164
Macon, GA 513, 514, 515, 516
Macon, MS 933
Macon Theater (Tuskegee, AL) 88
Made in Harlem (revue) 1103
Madison Theater (Pahokee, FL) 370; (Baltimore, MD) 794
Madlin Theater (Chicago, IL) 578
Magaziner, Eberhard and Harris 1433
Magnolia, AR 118
Magnolia Theater (Cocoa, FL) 266; (Waynesboro, GA) 545
Mahandra 556
Main, Majorie 724
Main Street After Dark (film) 1429
Main Theater (Cleveland, OH) 1307
Majestic Theater (Montgomery, AL) 64 ; (Hope, AR) 110; (San Francisco, CA) 191; (DC) 235; (Lometa, TX) 1700; (Port Arthur, TX) 1738; (Waco, TX) 1778
Make It Snappy (musical) 556
Makeover, Joseph 213, 239

Malden, Karl 725
Mallie Theater (Birds Nest, VA) 1797; (Trebernville, VA) 1896
Malone, Dorothy 445, 446
Malvern, AR 119, 120
Mammoth Theater (Dallas, TX) 1630
The Man I Love (film) 832
Man Who Wouldn't Take (film) 735
Managers and Performers Vaudeville Circuit 104, 323, 355, 374, 396, 423, 439, 464, 480, 530, 906, 1807, 1831, 1856, 1874
Managers of black theaters p. 3, pp. 242–246
Mancuso, S. B. 706
Manhattan Theater (Rocky Mount, NC) 1242; (Norfolk, VA) 1849
A Man's Duty (film) 1018
Mansfield, LA 716
Maple Theater (Dallas, TX) 1631
Marquee Theater (Oakland, CA) 174
Marquette Theater (St. Louis, MO) 996
Maraco, Flore 344
Margie (film) 832
Marianna, AR 121
Marie and Clint 1520
Marihuana (film) 662
Marion, SC 1494
Markham, Dewey "Pigmeat" 164, 735, 1084
Marlin, TX 1706
Marrero, LA 717
The Marriage of William Ash (film) 555
Mars Theater (East Chicago, IN) 617
Marshall, Jimmy 164
Marshall, TX 1707, 1708
Marshall, Tillie 1291
Martex Theater (Martin, TX) 1709
Martin, E. A. 393
Martin, Elmore 1684
Martin, M. 212
Martin, Roy 483
Martin, Sarah 514, 984, 1449
Martin, TN 1538
Martin, TX 1706
Martin and Motley's Merrymakers 1836
Martin and Walker Company 582
Martin Luther King Performing Arts Center (Columbus, OH) 1323
Martin Theatres 482
Martini, A. 1662
Martinson and Nibur 1091
Martinville, VA 1824–1827
The Marvelows 592, 1086
Mary Mack's Merry Makers of Mirth 984, 1287

Masingdale and Crosby 1408
Mason, James 615
Mason, James (actor) 1857
Mason, John 660
Mason, Shirley 772
Mason and Zudora 556
Massey, Raymond 1410
Matthews, Artie 984
Matthews and Matthews 733
Mature, Victor 443, 725
Matzonian Theater (Caldwell, TX) 1604
The Mauraders (film) 446
Maurin Theater (Reserve, LA) 747
May, Doris 777
Mayfair Theater (Detroit, MI) 849
Mayfield, KY 665
Maynard, Ken 1447
Mayo, Frank 166
The Mayor of Dixie (musical) 588
McAfee, Mrs. Minnie p. 3, 662
McAlester, OK 1376, 1377
McAuley, Hugh 212
McCarvers 1294
McClain, Florence 1557
McClain's Theater (Buffalo, NY) 1051
McClone, P. 1469
McComb, MS 931, 932
McComb Theater (Lafayette, LA) 705
McConnell, W. F. 1340
McCormick, John 164
McCrea, Joel 728, 838
McDow, Dude 801
McEvoy Theater (Buffalo, NY) 1052
McGarr-DeGaston Company 1520, 1557
McGarr-DeGaston Ragtime Steppers 984
McGehoe, J. B. 1237
McGhee, Howard 1032
McGuffey Theater (Youngstown, OH) 1351
McKenzie, Frank 454, 1691
McKinley, TX 1709
McKinley Theater (Baton Rouge, LA) 681
McKinney, Nina 164
McLaurin, Billie 1291
McLean, Douglas 777
McShann, Jay 1086
McTell, Katie 446
Mecca Theater (Enid, OK) 1368; (Vernon, TX) 1772; (Chase City, VA) 1801
Meer and Meer 1086
Meighan, Thomas 780
Melba Theater (Mount Bayou, MS) 938
Melby, J. A. 243
Melcher, Henry C. 1016
Melody Theater (Savannah, GA) 529; (Goshen, VA) 1814

Melrose Theater (Covington, GA) 489
Memphis, TN 1539–1553
Men of the West (film) 801
Mendall, A. B. 1661
Meridian, MS 934, 935, 936
Merry Mack's Merry Makers of Mirth 984, 1287
Metro Goldwyn Mayer Film Company 780
Metropolitan Theater (Chicago, IL) 579; (Newark, NJ) 1038; (Memphis, TN) 1549
Metts Theater (Gainsville, FL) 299
Mexia, TX 1711, 1712
Miami, FL 338–347
Micheaux, Oscar p. 2, p. 6n1, 222, 446, 463, 474, 480, 486, 499, 514, 523, 525, 544, 555, 597, 738, 754, 801, 1015, 1111, 1161, 1204, 1223, 1261, 1270, 1429, 1477, 1487, 1496
Micheaux Film Corporation p. 2
Michigan Theater (Chicago, IL) 580
Mid-City Theater (DC) 236
Middletown, OH 1339
Midget Theater (Dayton, OH) 1329
Midnite Ramble (show) 164
Midway Theater (Daytona Beach, FL) 277; (Perrine, FL) 380; (Chicago, IL) 580; (Charleston, SC) 1470
Milburn, Heister and Company 214
Mildner and Eisen 824
Miles Theater (Fairfield, AL) 32
Milford, DE 206
The Milky Waif (film) 728
Millard, Ray 725, 1429
Miller, Mrs. E. A. p. 3, 106
Miller, George 238, 586
Miller, Glenn 1884
Miller, H. B. 566, 582
Miller, Irvin C. 566, 1027
Miller, J. J. 1471
Miller, Stanley 845
Miller and Lyles 588, 1084
Millinder, Lucky 853
Mills, Florence 159, 1084
Mills, John 1865
Mills and Frisby Company 1457
Mills Brothers 725, 831, 853
Milo Theater (Charleston, SC) 1471
Milwaukee, WI 1922
Mindlin, LA 718
Mineola, TX 1713
Ministry of Fear (film) 1429
Minneapolis, MN 876
Minnehaha Theater (DC) 220
Minniefield, Pauline
Minor, Lorenzo 1874
Minsky, Abe 1149
Miranda, Carmen 1427, 1869

Miss Broadway (show) 1339
Mission Drive-in (San Antonio, TX) 1751
Mississippi Days (revue) 1101
Missourians 1101
Mitchell, Abbie 588
Mitchell, Luther K. 732
Mitchell, Thomas 1427
Mitchum, Robert 459
Mix, Tom 212, 585, 772, 801
Mixed houses pp. 1–2
Mobile, AL 52, 53, 54, 55, 56, 57, 58, 59
Modella Theater (Hollywood, FL) 309
Modern Theater (Miami, FL) 344
Moffett, J.A. 463
Mona, Prince Ali 476
Monogram Theater (Chicago, IL) 582; (Cambridge, MD) 808
Monroe, A. G. 530
Monroe, LA 719, 720
Monroe, Marilyn 459
Monroe Theater (Detroit, MI) 850
Monroeville, AL 60
Montalban, Ricardo 722
Montana Belle (film) 448
Monterey, CA 170
Montez, Maria 820, 838
Montgomery, AL 61, 62, 63, 64, 65, 66, 67
Montgomery, Frank 1557
Montgomery, Robert 832
Montgomery, WV 1917
Monticello Theater (Newark, NJ) 1039
Montrose, VA 1828
Montrose Theater (Montrose, VA) 1828
Moogeman, Louis 1441
Moonlight Harbor Orchestra 1442
Moonlight Theater (Miami, FL) 345
Moore, C. Robert 781
Moore, Chintz 1625, 1633
Moore, Ella B. 1625
Moore, Fred 19
Moore, Hester 579, 1549
Moore, Monette 1449
Moore, Tim 579, 1084, 1549, 1551
Moore, Tom 166, 1093
Moore Haven, FL 348
Moorman, E. S. 680
Morehead, TX 1714
Moreland, Mantan 831
Morella's Toy Shop 556
Moreno, Antonio 780
Morgan, G. M. 503
Morgan Theater (Baltimore, MD) 795
Morningside Theater (New York, NY) 1104

INDEX 269

Morris, Chester 1447
Morristown, NJ 1031
Morristown, TN 1554
Morstein, Harry 799
Morton Theater (Athens, GA) 439
Mosby, Curtis 164
Moseley, Charles 799
Mosely, W. L. 1835
Moser, J. H. 735
Moten, Benny 1101, 1427
Moten, Etta 1869
Moton Theater (Newport News, VA) 1837; (Norfolk, VA) 1850
Motown Records 1086
Mott, Lucretia 212
Mott Theater 212
Motts, Robert M. 588
Motts' Pekin Temple 588
Moultrie, GA 517, 518
Mounds, IL 613
Mount Airy, NC 1218
Mount Bayou, MS 937, 938
Mount Pleasant, TN 1555
Mount Pleasant, TX 1715, 1716
Mount Vernon, NY 1057
Movie Theater (St. Louis, MO) 997
Moye, Robert J. 1840
Mrs. Williams' Theater (Helena, AR) 105
Mulberry, FL 349
Mullins, Mamie 1103
Murder My Sweet (film) 1427, 1431
Murphy, Audie 728, 1837
Murphy, Mary 448
Murray, Dusty 1625, 1678
Murray, George 117
Murray, Raymond H. 222, 229
Murray Brothers 1101
Murray Theater (El Paso, TX) 1645
Muse, Clarence 164, 312, 1857
Muse and Pugh Stock Company 1091
Muskogee, OK 1378, 1379, 1380
Musu Theater (New Iberia, LA) 721
Myerberg, Julius 787
Myers Theater (Ayden, NC) 1128; (Coleran, NC) 1153
Mystery of 13 (film) 777

N.R.A. Theater (Chicago, IL) 583
Nacogdoches, TX 1717, 1718, 1719
Nacona, TX 1720
Naked Alibi (film) 660
Naming of black theaters p. 3
Nash, J. Carroll 731
Nashville, TN 1556–1562
Nassau, FL 350
Natchez, MS 939, 940, 941
Nathan, Joseph 574
National Theater (Wilmington, DE) 208; (Baltimore, MD) 781, 796; (Detroit, MI) 851; (Newark, NJ) 1040; (Mexia, TX) 1712
A Natural Born Shooter (film) 589
Navasota, TX 1721, 1722, 1723
Neagle, Anna 725
The Negro Soldier (film) 838
Nevada Theater (Reno, NV) 1022
New Albert Theater (Baltimore, MD) p. 4, 797
New Bay Theater (St. Paul, MN) 877
New Bern, NC 1219–1225
New Carver Theater (Baltimore, MD) 779
New Colored Theater (Raeford, NC) 1229; (Reidsville, NC) 1238; (Aiken, SC) 1455
New Daisy Theater (Memphis, TN) 1550
New Davison Theater (Detroit, MI) 852
New Dixie Theater (Bessemer, AL) 11
New Douglas Theater (New York, NY) 1093
New Douglass Theater (Macon, GA) 515
New Dunbar Theater (Savannah, GA) 525
New Elba Theater (Chicago, IL) 561
New Frazier Theater (Belle Glade, FL) 255
New Frolic Theater (Jacksonville, FL) 315
New Garden Theater (Philadelphia, PA) 1422
New Globe Theater (Philadelphia, PA) 1416
New Goldfield Theater (Baltimore, MD) 785
New Grand Theater (Chattanooga, TN) 1522
New Granada Theater (Pittsburgh, PA) 1442, p. **190**
New Haven CT 203
New Heights Theater (Lockland, OH) 1337
New Herron Theater (Pittsburgh, PA) 1443
New Iberia, LA 721
New Jewel Theater (Philadelphia, PA) 1423
New Kane Theater (Baltimore, MD) 798
New Lincoln Theater (Trenton, NJ) 1046
New Lyric Theater (Louisville, KY) 661
New Movie Theater (Clair County, IL) 614; (Laurel, MS) 925; (St. Louis, MO) 998; (Philadelphia, PA) 1419
New Orleans, LA p 2, 722–738
New Pekin Theater (Dayton, OH) 1329
New Progress Theater (San Francisco, CA) 187
New Queen Theater (Anniston, AL) 5; (Baltimore, MD) 799
New Rainbow Theater (Baltimore, MD) 800
New Ren Theater (Yazoo City, MS) 957
New Rex Theater (Winston-Salem, NC) 1275; (Beaumont, TX) 1587
New Roads, LA 739, 740
New Rochelle, NY 1058
New Royal Theater (Columbia, SC) 1478
New Smyrna Beach, FL 352
New Theater (Mobile, AL) 56; (Barton, MD) 806; (Jackson, MS) 920; (Elizabeth City, NC) 1166; (Columbus, OH) 1320; (Brownsville, TN) 1516; (Chattanooga, TN) 1523; (Cheapside, VA) 1804
New United Theater (Brooklyn, NY) 1073
New Waller Theater (Laurel, DE) 205
New Wonder Theater (Columbus, OH) 1321
New York, NY 1984–1118
New York Age (newspaper) 556
New York Follies (show) 808
Newark, NJ 1032–1044
Newbern, TN 1563
Newberry, FL 351
Newman, GA 519
Newport, AR 122
Newport News, VA 1829–1837
News Theater (Cocoa, FL) 271
Newsreel Theater (Long Beach, CA) 150; (Los Angeles, CA) 165
Newsreel theaters pp. 4–5
Nicholas Brothers 1431, 1884
Nicholson, J. 629
Nickelodeon theaters p. 4
Nickerson, Charles 1339
A Night in Chinatown (musical) 588
The Night Rose (film) 597
Niles, Dewyman 514
Ninety-One Theater (Atlanta, GA) 453
Nippon Theater (Sacramento, CA) 181
Niquet, Otto "Dutch" 793
Nit and Tuck 1873
Nixon, Marion 164
Nixon Grand Theater (Philadelphia, PA) 1423
No Adults Allowed (film) 728
Nolte, Charles E. 782
Noma 1086
Norfolk, VA 1838–1853

270 INDEX

Normand, Mabel 1018
Norris, Timothy P. 681
Norris Theater (Philadelphia, PA) 1423
North Birmingham, AL 68
North Little Rock, AR 123
North Pole Theater (Philadelphia, PA) 1425
Northfork, WV 1918
Northside Theater (Wewoka, OK) 1396
Northwestern Theater (Indianapolis, IN) 637
Norton and Margot 981
Norwood Theater (East Hickory, NC) 1163
The Notorious Mrs. Sands (film) 801
Nowata, OK 1381

Oakland, CA 171, 172, 173, 174, 175
Oakland Square Theater (Chicago, IL) 584
O'Brien, Edmond 661, 1850
O'Brien, Eugene 561
O'Brien, James 566
Ocala, FL 353, 354, 355, 356, 357
O'Connor, Donald 735
Odd Fellows' Auditorium (Atlanta, GA) 444
Odeon Theater (New York, NY) 1105, 1112
Odessa, TX 1724
Odin Theater (Houston, TX) 1687
Ogden Theater (Columbus, OH) 1322
Oklahoma City, OK 1382, 1383, 1384, 1385
Okmulgee, OK 1386, 1387
Okmulgee Park Theater (Columbus, GA) 484
Olar, SC 1495
Old Ashland Theater (Ashland, VA) 1792
Old Douglass Theater (Macon, GA) 514
Olestsky, Peter 791
Olinger, C. S. 1341
Olive Theater (Detroit, MI) 866
Olympia Theater (E. St. Louis, IL) 610; (St. Louis, MO) 999; (Philadelphia, PA) 1426, p. **183**
Olympic Theater (DC) 213; (Charleston, SC) 1472; (Alexandria, VA) 1788
Omaha, NE 1013, 1014, 1015, 1016, 1017, 1018
On the Reservation (play) 1315
One Hundred and Sixteenth Street Theater (New York, NY) 1106
Opelika, AL 69, 70
Opelousas, LA 741, 742, 743, 744

Open Air Theater (Richmond, VA) 1870
Open air theaters pp. 3–4
Opera House Theater (Cairo, IL) 549; (Franklin, LA) 694
Opera houses p. 4
Opollo Theater (Whiteville, NC) 1263
Orange, TX 1723–1728
Orangeburg, SC 1496, 1497
Orchestra Hall (Detroit, MI) 853
Orient Theater (New York, NY) 1107
Origin of black theaters p. 1
Original Dead End Boys 662
Orlando, FL 358, 359, 360, 361, 362
Orpheum Amusement Company 211
Orpheum Theater (Lexington, KY) 657; (Newark, NJ) 1041; (Xenia, OH) 1350
Osceola, AR 124, 125
Othello Theater (New Orleans, LA) 734
Our Gang 725
The Outcast (film) 1857
Outside the Law (film) 585, 595
Outten, Rudolph 815
Outten's Colored Theater (Snow Hill, MD) 815
Ovelton, John 19
Owen, Chester 832
Owens, S. L. 600
Owens and Owens, 220
Owensboro, KY 666
Owl Theater (Chicago, IL) 585
Owners of black theaters p. 3, pp. 242–246
Owsley, Tim 644
Oxford, NC 1226

Paducah, KY 667
Page, Harvey L. 216
Page Land, SC 1498
Pahokee, FL 363, 364, 365, 366, 367
Pal Theater (Newman, GA) 519
Palace Picture House (Louisville, KY) 662
Palace Theater (Ensley, AL) 31; (Greenville, AL) 43; (Hope, AR) 108; (Warren, AR) 139; (Pittsburg, AR) 176; (Seaford, DE) 207; (Cross City, FL) 273; (Fort Lauderdale, FL) 289; (Fort Myers, FL) 293; (Jacksonville, FL) 289; (St. Petersburg, FL) 399; (Tampa, FL) 423; (Augusta, GA) 464; (Brunswick, GA) 473; (Camilla, GA) 476; (Valdosta, GA) 540; (Louisville, KY) 662; (Lake Charles, LA) 708; (New Orleans, LA) 735; (Vicksburg, MS) 954; (St.

Joseph, MO) 980; (St. Louis, MO) 1000; (Springfield, MO) 1012; (Morristown, NJ) 1031; (Corona, NY) 1056; (Charlotte, NC) 1148; (Fayetteville, NC) 1173; (Gastonia, NC) 1178; (Greensboro, NC) 1183; (Kannapolis, NC) 1200; (Kingston, NC) 1204; (New Bern, NC) 1224; (Wilmington, NC) 1268; (Dayton, OH) 1330; (Wewoka, OK) 1397; (Steelton, PA) 1453; (Bennettsville, SC) 1463; (Jackson, TN) 1531; (Memphis, TN) 1551; (Newbern, TN) 1563; (Childress, TX) 1606; (Dallas, TX) 1632; (Denton, TX) 1640; (Hill, TX) 1671; (Hillsboro, TX) 1674; (Lubbock, TX) 1705; (Texarkana, TX) 1764; (Tyler, TX) 1770; (Waco, TX) 1779; (Norfolk, VA) 1851; (Charleston, WV) 1905
Palance, Jack 1823
Palestine, TX 1729
Palm Drive-in (Daytona Beach, FL) 278
Palm Theater (Sebring, FL) 410
Palmetto, FL 371
Palmetto Theater (Orangeburg, SC) 1496
Pampa, TX 1730
Panama (play) 79
Panama Amusement Company 556
Panama City, FL 372, 373
Panama Theater (Kansas City, MO) 972
Pannel, Mrs. R. L. 1887
Pansy (show) 1101
Paradise Theater (Avenue, MD) 771; (Detroit, MI) 853, p. **119**
Paramount Pictures 780
Paramount Theater (Newark, NJ) 1042
Paris, TX 1731, 1732
Park Theater (Clearwater, FL) 262; (Chicago, IL) 586; (Indianapolis, IN) 638; (Baltimore, MD) 798; (Detroit, MI) 853; (Blair Station, PA) 1399; (Pittsburgh, PA) 1443; (Dallas, TX) 1633; (Houston, TX) 1688
Park West Theater (New York, NY) 1108
Parker, Allen 1132
Parker, Charlie 230, 592, 1086
Parker, Jean 1450
Parker Theater (Blackshear, GA) 470
Parks, Jean 853
Parksley, VA 1854, 1855
Parnum, Franklin 585
Parkview Theater (Houston, TX) 1689

INDEX 271

Park-Vu Drive-In (Winston-Salem, NC) 1276
Pascagoula, MS 942
Pass, Leon 164
Pastime Theater (Chickasa, OK) 1362; (Pittsburgh, PA) 1443; (Charleston, SC) 1473; (Beaumont, TX) 1588; (Greenville, TX) 1668; (Houston, TX) 1690
Pastor, Bob 929
Patterson, James 464
Patterson, LA 745
Patterson, William R. 848
Patton, R. 1441
Paul, Mr. 595
Pawnee, OK 1388
Payne, John 448, 458, 1869, 1884
Pearl Theater (Philadelphia, PA) 1427, p. **184**
Peck, Gregory 1427
Peerless Theater (San Francisco, CA) 152; (Chicago, IL) 587; (Brooklyn, NY) 1074
Penn Theater (Reidsville, NC) 1239; (Rocky Mount, NC) 1243
Pensacola, FL 374, 375, 376, 377, 378, 379
People's Theater (Alexander City, AL) 2; (Kinston, NC) 1207; (Houston, TX) 1691
Pekin Players 588
Pekin Theater (Montgomery, AL) 65, p. **18**; (Brunswick, GA) 474; (Savannah, GA) 530; (Chicago, IL) p. 2, 588; (Springfield, IL) 615; (Cincinnati, OH) 1288; (Dayton, OH) 1331
Pendleton Theater (St. Louis, MO) 1001
Penrose Club 786
Peoples Theater (Brookhaven, MS) 881; (Kinston, NC) 1207; (Bowman, SC) 1465
Peoria Theater (Tulsa, OK) 1393
Perkins, Alberta 588
Perrine, FL 380
Perry, FL 381, 382
Perry Theater (Gainsville, FL) 300
Pershing Theater (Pittsburgh, PA) 1445
Petersburg, VA 1856–1860
Peterson, Mrs. 1015
Petray, T. W. 51
Peyton, Dave 566, 587, 592
Phantom Foe (film) 805
Phantom Riders (film) 725
Phelps, Charles T. 971, 978
Philadelphia, PA 1406–1434
Philadelphia Tribune (newspaper) p. 3, p. 3n3, p. 6n12, p. 7n20
Philbin, Mary 1103
Phoenix, AZ 90

Phoenix City, AL 71
Phoenix Theater (Chicago, IL) 589
Photo Theater (Huntsville, AL) 45
Pic Theater (Macon, GA) 516
Picayune, MS 943
Pickford, Mary 556, 1103, 1429
Pickford Theater (Chicago, IL) 590
Picto Theater (Huntsville, AL) 46
Piedmont, AL 72
Piedmont and Caswell 1286
Pierce, Billy 1838
Pierson, Billie 1339
The Pietchodore W. 793
Pigeon, Walter 725
Pike Theater (Birmingham, AL) 22; (Mobile, AL) 57
Pikesville, KY 668
Pinchback, Walter 239
Pine Bluff, AR 126, 127
Pinehurst, NC 1227
Pinkerson, Earl 1478
Pioneer Theater (Indianapolis, IN) 639
The Pirate (film) 838
Pitman, C. 992
Pittman, W. Sidney 229, 234
Pittman Theater (Wewoka, PA) 1454
Pittsburg, CA 176
Pittsburg, TX 1733
Pittsburgh, PA 1436–1450
Pix Theater (Jacksonville, FL) 319; (Detroit, MI) 855; (Leland, MS) 929
Plant City, FL 383, 384
Plantation Revue (musical) 566
Plantation Theater (Pahokee, FL) 365
Plaquemine, LA 746
Plateau, AL 73.
Plater, Harry 1557
Play Square (film) 574
Plaza Theater (Helena, AR) 106; (Little Rock, AR) 117; (Milford, CT) 206; (San Diego, CA) 185; (Tampa, FL) 424; (Colp, IL) 602; (Owensboro, KY) 666; (Baltimore, MD) 798; (Buffalo, NY) 1053; (South Jamaica, NY) 1119; (Greenville, NC) 1188
Pless, B. R. 1192
Plessy, Homer p. 1
Plessy v. Ferguson (U.S. Supreme Court decision) p. 1, p. 5; p. 6n1
Plowman, George 1422
Plymouth, NC 1228
Plymouth Theater (DC) 237
Pocomoke City, MD 810
Polies, Herman 340
Poli's Theater (DC) 217
Polo, Eddie 585

Pompano, FL 385, 386, 387
Pond, E. H. 359
Poor Relations (film) 555
Port Arthur, TX 1734–1740
Port Huron, MI 873
Port of Hell (film) 1839
Port St. Joe, FL 388
Porter and Porter 1660
Portsmouth, OH 1340
Portsmouth, VA 1861–1868
Portsmouth Theater (Portsmouth, VA) 1867
Possessed (film) 566
Poth, TX 1741
Powell, Dick 722, 838, 1427, 1431
Prairie View College, TX 1742
Preer, Evelyn 164, 597
Preminger, Otto 661
Prescott, AR 128
Pressly, Nathaniel 15
Preston, Robert 735
Price, Vincent 458, 459, 1840
Price and Jones 1331
Prince and Connie 514
The Prince Chap (film) 780
A Prince of His Own (film) 1429
Prince Theater (Pahokee, FL) 366; (Lake Charles, LA) 711
Princess Ann Theater (Dillon, SC) 1481
Princess Anne, MD 811
Princess Theater (Huntsville, AL) 47; (Piedmont, AL) 72; (Cocoa, FL) 267; (Lake City, FL) 330; (LaGrange, GA) 510; (Kansas City, KS) 648; (Bogalusa, LA) 684; (Kansas City, MO) 973; (Asheville, NC) 1125; (Harrisburg, PA) 1402; (Florence, SC) 1484; (Clarksville, TX) 1608; (Crandall, TX) 1620; (Galveston, TX) 1661
Priscilla Theater (Detroit, MI) 856
Pritchard, AL. 74, 75
Private Hell 36 (film) 724
Privett, J. J. 1270
Proctor, AR 129
Proctor, F. B. 230
Proctor Vaudeville p. 1
Public Theater (Chicago) 591
Puggsley, H. H. 1288
Pugh and Barker 143
Punta Gorda, FL 389
Pursley, T. B. 318
Puryear, Dr. O. 634
Putnam Theater (Brooklyn, NY) 1075; (Columbus, OH) 1323
Pythian Temple (New Orleans, LA) 736
Pythian Theater (Pittsburgh, PA) 1442

Quality Amusement Company 1075, 1445, 1838

Queen Amusement Company 798
Queen and Baylor 1602
Queen Theater (Birmingham, AL) 23; (Gadsden, AL) 42; (Clewiston, FL) 265; (Baltimore, MD) 799; (Clarksdale, MS) 887; (Brownfield, TX) 1597; (Edna, TX) 1643; (Navasota, TX) 1723; (Rusk, TX) 1743; (Thorndale, TX) 1765; (Portsmouth, VA) 1868
Queens Theater (St. Louis, MO) 1002
Quincy, FL 390
Quincy Theater (Cleveland, OH) 1308
Quitman, FL 391
Quitman, GA 520

Race houses p. 2–3
Race loyalty p. 3
Radio Theater (Baltimore, MD) 800
Raeford, NC 1229
Rage at Dawn (film) 448, 1839
Rainbow Theater (Baltimore, MD) 801; (Houston, TX) 1692
Rainey, Ma 446, 478, 484
Rainey, W. M. 484
Raisin' Cain (revue) 1084
Raleigh, NC 1230–1235
Raleigh Theater (Raleigh, NC) 1234
Ralston, Vera 827
Ramish, Adolf 164
Ramona Theater (Phoenix City, AL) 7; (Phoenix, AZ) 90
Randall, Jack 929
Rankin, A. E 107, 135
Rankin, PA 1451, 1452
Rankin Theater (Rankin, PA) 1451
Raphael Theater (DC) 238
Rastus and Jones 660, 1520
Raulerson's Theater (Lakeland, FL) 331
Rayo Theater (Richmond, VA) 1877
Reagan, Ronald 725
Realart Theater (De Ridder, LA) 689
Reap the Wild Wind (film) 1850
Rear Window (film) 1845
Received Payment (film) 589
Red Caps 853
Redd, Alton 155
The Redhead and the Cowboy (film) 1850
Redman, Don 1098
Reese, J. E. 1844
Reeves, S. J. 5
Reevin, Sam E. 1520
Regal Drive-In (Huntsville, AL) 48
Regal Theater (Chicago, IL) 592, p. **81**; (Indianapolis, IN) 640; (Kansas City, KS) 649; (St. Louis, MO) 1003; (Durham, NC) 1159–60; (Cincinnati, OH) 1289; (Dayton, OH) 1332; (Middletown, OH) 1339; (Tulsa, OK) 1394; (Norfolk, VA) 1852; (Milwaukee, WI) 1922
Regan, David R. 76
Regency Theater (Richmond, VA) 1880
Regent Theater (Baltimore, MD) 802, p. **111**; (Brooklyn, NY) 1076; (New York, NY) 1109; (Youngstown, OH) 1352
Regun Theater (New York, NY) 1110
Reidsville, NC 1236, 1237, 1238, 1239
Renaissance Casino (New York, NY) 1111
Renaissance Theater (New York, NY) 1111
Renard Moving Picture Parlor (Baltimore, MD) 797
Rendezvous Theater (Wilkesboro, NC) 1264
Rene and Florence 556
Renfro Theater (Charleston, MO) 959
Reno, NV 1021, 1022, 1023
Reno Theater (Reno, NV) 1023
Reo Theater (Brooklyn, NY) 1077
Republic Theater (DC) 239
Reserve, LA 747
Retina Theater (St. Louis, MO) 1004
Rex Theater (Alexander City, AL) 2; (Warren, AR) 140; (Oakland, CA) 175; (Fort Pierce, FL) 297; (Lake Wales, FL) 334; (Palmetto, FL) 371; (St. Petersburg, FL) 400; (Vero Beach, FL) 425; (Gainsville, GA) 503; (St. Martinsville, LA) 749; (Berlin, MD) 807; (Brookhaven, MS) 882; (Greenville, MS) 897; (Leland, MS) 929, p. **127**; (Yazoo City, MS) 958; (Beaufort, NC) 1134; (Charlotte, NC) 1149; (Durham, NC) 1161; (Winston-Sslem, NC) 1277; (Cincinnati, OH) 1290; (Howata, OK) 1371; (Nowata, OK) 1381; (Tulsa, OK) 1395; (Philadelphia, PA) 1428; (Beaumont, TX) 1589; (San Angelo, TX) 1744; (Martinville, VA) 1826
Reynolds, Marjorie 1429
Rhodes, Todd 832
Rhone, J. M. 126
Rhumba Theater (Pittsburgh, PA) 1446
Rialto Musical Show Theater (Florence, AL) 35
Rialto Theater (Sheffield, AL) 79; (Columbus, OH) 1324; (Galveston, TX) 1662; (Petersburg, VA) 1859
Richards Theater (Fayette, AL) 33; (Flint, MI) 869
Richardson, Lee 1335
Richmond, CA 177, 178
Richmond, VA 1869–1880
Rico Theater (Savannah, GA) 531
Riddick, George W. 1861
Ride Vaquero (film) 737
Ridge Theater (Sebring, FL) 411
Riding High (film) 838
Ridley and Ridley 1392
Rin Tin Tin 164
Rinehart, R. V. 31
Ring Champs of Yesteryear (film) 827
Ringgold, Muriel 805
Rink Theater (Port Arthur, TX) 1739; (Taylor, TX) 1757; (Temple, TX) 1760
Rio Theater (Malvern, AR); (Richmond, CA) 177; (Sacramento, CA) 182; (Baltimore, MD) 805; (Snow Hill, MD) 815; (Chester, PA) 1400; (Big Spring, TX) 1594; (Brownfield, TX) 1598; (Houston, TX) 1693; (McKinley, TX) 1709
Ritz Theater (Montgomery, AL) 66; (Magnolia, AR) 118; (North Little Rock, AR) 123; (Arcade, FL) 247; (Daytona Beach, FL) 279; (Florida City, FL) 286; (Jacksonville, FL) 320, p. **52**; (Miami, FL) 346, p. **54**; (Pensacola, FL) 378; (Wauchula, FL) 427; (Albany, GA) 434; (Augusta, GA) 465; (Decatur, GA) 493; (Thomasville, GA) 536; (Topeka, KS) 651; (Alexandria, LA) 674; (Hammond, LA) 697; (Monroe, LA) 720; (New Orleans, LA) 737; (Shreveport, LA) 753; (Tallulah, LA) 759; (Salisbury, MD) 814; (Port Huron, MI) 873; (Gulfport, MS) 904; (Jackson, MS) 921; (Meridian, MS) 935; (Omaha, NE) 1019; (Clinton, NC) 1152; (High Point, NC) 1197; (New Bern, NC) 1225; (Rocky Mount, NC) 1244; (Salisbury, NC) 1247; (Washington, NC) 1260; (Wilmington, NC) 1269; (Wilson, NC) 1271; (Akron, OH) 1279; (Chickasa, OK) 1363; (Duncan, OK) 1366; (Pawnee, OK) 1388; (Rankin, PA) 1452;

INDEX 273

(Spartanburg, SC) 1505; (Knoxville, TN) 1536; (Nashville, TN) 1560; (Ballinger, TX) 1580; (Beaumont, TX) 1590; (Brownfield, TX) 1599; (Fort Worth, TX) 1652; (Longview, TX) 1702; (Lubbock, TX) 1704; (San Antonio, TX) 1752; (Sherman, TX) 1754; (Thorndale, TX) 1766; (Berkeley, VA) 1795; (Danville, VA) 1809
River of No Return (film) 459
River Rouge, MI 874
Rivoli Theater (Douglas, GA) 495; (Cleveland, OH) 1309
The Road Demon (film) 772
The Road to Yesterday (film) 1429
Roanoke, VA 1881, 1882, 1883, 1884
Roanoke Rapids, NC 1240
Roberta (film) 1447
Robertson, Dale 458, 459, 659
Robeson Theater (Lumberton, NC) 1217
Robins, Charles P. 446
Robinson, Bill "Bojangles" 155, 164, 853, 861, 1084, 1101
Robinson, Edward G. 1416
Robinson Theater (Richmond, VA) 1878; (Suffolk, VA) 1892
Rock Hill, SC 1499, 1500
Rock Island Theater (Venice, IL) 616
Rockettes 164
Rockville, MD 812
Rocky Mount, NC 1241, 1242, 1243, 1244, 1245
Roeach, W. J. 737
Rogers, Ginger 728, 1427, 1446, 1447, 1869
Rogers, Roy 731
Rogers Theater (Detroit, MI) 857; (Brooklyn, NY) 1078
Roman, Ruth 1845
Romance in Manhattan (film) 1446
Rome, J. L. 785
Rome Theaters 785
Romero, Cesar 1869
Rooney, Mickey 1884
Roosevelt Theater (Dade City, FL) 274; (Jacksonville, FL) 321; (Gary, IN) 619; (Baltimore, MD) 803; (St. Louis, MO) 1005; (New York, NY) 1105, 1112; (Kinston, NC) 1208; (Winston-Salem, NC) 1278; (Cincinnati, OH) 1291; (Pittsburgh, PA) 1447, p. **191**
Rosalia Theater (DC) 240
Roscoe and Mitchell's Radio Girls 429, 805
Roscoe Montella Company 112
Rose Theater (Gainsville, FL) 301
Rosebud Theater (Los Angeles, CA) 166, p. **31**; (Detroit, MI) p. 4, 858
Rosedale Theater (Opelousas, LA) 744; (Fort Worth, TX) 1653
Rosen, A. 772
Rosenthal, Fred 561
Rosenwald School Theater (Welsh, LA) 765
Rosita (film) 1103
Ross, Clifford 984
Ross, Mr. 1038
Roth, Charles 1183, 1533
Roth, Harry 1124
Roth, Mrs. M. 1502
The Rough House (film) 777
Rowland, I. H. 226
Rowley, Joseph M. 1852
Roxboro, NC 1246
Roxbury, MA 818
Roxbury Theater (Roxbury, MA) 818
Roxy Theater (Selma, AL) 76; (Denver, CO) 201; (Lakeland, FL) 332; (Ocala, FL) 356; (Pensacola, FL) 379; (Quincy, FL) 390; (Americus, GA) 437; (Brunswick, GA) 475; (Gainsville, GA) 503; (Tifton, GA) 537; (Mansfield, LA) 716; (Tallulah, LA) 760; (Bay City, MI) 819; (Detroit, MI) 859; (Clarksdale, MS) 888; (Camden, NJ) 1030; (Concord, NC) 1135; (Greenville, NC) 1189; (Laurinburg, NC) 1212; (Lockland, OH) 1338; (Chester, PA) 1401; (Pittsburgh, PA) 1448; (Houston, TX) 1694; (Chase City, VA) 1802; (Emporia, VA) 1811; (Exmore, VA) 1812
Roy White's Stylish Slippers 660
Royal, Marshall 155, 159, 166
Royal Palm Theater (Greenville, MS) 898
Royal Theater (Fort Myers, FL) 294; (Panama City, FL) 373; (St. Petersburg, FL) 401; (Atlanta, GA) 459; (Baltimore, MD) 804, p. **112**; (Gulfport, MS) 905; (Picayune, MS) 943; (Omaha, NE) 1020; (Asbury Park, NJ) 1024; (Charlotte, NC) 1150; (Raleigh, NC) 1234; (Columbus, OH) 1325; (Goodale, OH) 1333; (El Reno, OK) 1367; (Enid, OK) 1369; (Philadelphia, PA) p. 5, p. 7n20, 1429; (Columbia, SC) 1478; (Nashville, TN) 1561; (Berkeley, VA) 1796
Rubish and Hunter 634, 643
Ruby Gentry (film) 725
Ruby Theater (Louisville, GA) 512; (Louisville, KY) 663; (Philadelphia, PA) 1429
Ruleville, MS 944, 945
Run for Cover (film) 1857
Rundla Theater (Clarksville, TX) 1609
Rupert Theater (Detroit, MI) 860
Rusk, TX 1743
Russell, Bill 164
Russell, Bob 1431
Russell, Jane 448, 1834
Russell, Sam "Bibo" 164
Russell, Stanislaus 777
Russell Theater (Detroit, MI) 861
Russell-Ownes-Brooks Stock Company 833
Rustin, LA 748
Ryan Theater (Fresno, CA) 149

Sachs, Benjamin 792, 801
Sack, A. N. 1749
Sacramento, CA 179, 180, 181, 182, 183
Saenger Amusement Company 671
Safari Drums (film) 722
Saginaw, MI 875
Sahara (film) 780
St. Augustine, FL 392, 393, 394
St. Clair County, IL 614
St. Cyr, Lili 458, 459
St. Elmo Theater (Houston, TX) 1695
St. George, SC 1501
St. Inigoes, MD 813
St. Joseph, MO 977, 978, 979, 980
St. Louis, MO 981–1011
St. Louis Blues (film) 1084
St. Martinsville, LA 749
St. Paul, MN 877
St. Petersburg, FL 395, 396, 397, 398, 399, 400, 401
Salisbury, MD 814
Salisbury, NC 1247
Salisbury Theater (Summerville, SC) 1508
Sambo, Little 777
Sampson, Henry T. p. 2, p. 6n9, n10
San Angelo, TX 1744
San Antonio, TX 1745–1752
San Diego, CA 184, 185, 186.
San Francisco, CA 187, 188, 189, 190, 191, 192, 193, 194, 195
San Jose, CA 196
San Pedro, CA 197
Sanders, Mr. 662
Sandersville, GA 523
Sanford, CA 402, 403, 404, 405
Sanford, NC 1248, 1249
Sangaree (film) 731
Santa Fe (film) 1447
Santa Fe Passage (film) 458
Santmeyer, George R. 226
Sappel, C. A. 422
Sapulpa, OK 1389, 1390

Saracen Blade (film) 722
Saratoga, FL 406, 407
Saskatchewan (film) 737
Saulkins, Mr. 585
Saunders, Jolly 582
Savage, James W. 332
Savannah, GA 524–532
Savannah Motion Picture Company 525
Savoia Theater (Columbus, OH) 1326
Savoy Theater (Blythville, AR) 93; (Earle, AR) 98; (El Dorado, AR) 100; (Los Angeles, CA) 167; (Nassau, FL) 350; (Detroit, MI) 862; (Clarksdale, MS) 889; (Laurel, MS) 927; (Macon, MS) 931; (Tunica, MS) 951; (Newark, NJ) 1043; (Buffalo, NY) 1054; (New York, NY) 1113; (Charlotte, NC) 1151; (Rocky Mount, NC) 1245; (Dyersburg, TN) 1526; (Memphis, TN) 1552
Scales, W. S. 1273, 1274
Schanze Theater (Baltimore, MD) 795
Schiffman, Frank 1086, 1098
Schlen, Oscar 784
Schoenlein, Gus 786
School Days (play) 1315
School Theater (Bishopville, SC) 1464
Schreiner, C. C. 57
Scotland, AR 130.
Scotlandville, LA 750, 751
Scott, C. S. 1630
Scott, Luke 1750
Scott, Randolph 445, 446, 448, 737, 1823, 1839, 1857
Scott, Walter 525
Scout Theater (Hobbs, NM) 1048
The Scrapper (film) 574
Sea Breeze, NC 1135
Seaboard, NC 1250
Seaford, DE 207
Seals, B. F. 899
Seals, Baby Floyd 1660
Seals and Mitchell's Melody Lane Girls 19, 733
Seals and White 1315
Seattle, WA 1899
Sebring, FL 408, 409, 410, 411
Secret Four (film) 574
Sedley, VA 1885, 1886
Sedley Theater (Sedley, VA) 1886
Segrave, Kerry p. 6n17
Segregation p. 1, p. 5
Seligman, Gus 315
Selma, AL 76
Selma, NC 1251
Seminole, FL 412
Senate Theater (Indianapolis, IN) 641

Senator Theater (DC) 241
Sennett, Mack 1018
Sequins 592
Shadows of the Past (film) 562
Shadows of the Sea (film) 589
Shane (film) 726
Shawnee Theater (Nacogdoches, TX) 1719
Sheffield, AL 77, 78, 79
Sheffield, Johnny 722
Shelby, MS 946
Shelby, NC 1252
Shelbyville, TN 1564
Shepard, John M. 342
Sherman, TX 1753, 1754
Sherman and Sherman 1586
The She-Wolf (film) 1852
Shields, R. S. 1917
Shiff, Bernard 1402, 1403–4
Shipma, Nell 155
Shipp, Jesse 588
Shook, Ben 863
Shook Theater (Detroit, MI) 863
Shore, MS 947
Shoubin, Samuel 795
Showboat Theater (Belle Glade, FL) 256; (Pahokee, FL) 367
Showcase Theater (Augusta, GA) 466
Shreveport, LA 752, 753, 754
Shuffle Along (musical) 1421, 1431
Shulman, Alex 1687
Sign of the Pagan (film) 1823
Silk Hosiery (film) 802
Silver City Theater (Alexandria, LA) 675
Silver Moon Airdome Theater (Muskogee, OK) 1380
Silver on the Sage (film) 731
Silver Palace Theater (Sacramento, CA) 183
Silver Star (film) 1823
Silver Star Theater (West Helena, AR) 143
Silver Theater (San Francisco, CA) 193
Silverman, M. H. 1518
Simmons, C. 802, 804
Simmons, Jean 724, 727
Simms, C. C. 915
Simms and Warfield 802
Simtec and Wylie 1086
Sinatra, Frank 1845
Singing in the Corn (film) 832
Singleton, Penny 1872
Sins of Rome (film) 722
Sioux City Sue (film) 1850
Sipp, Margie 446
Six Bridges to Cross (film) 1884
Six Little Darlings 1431
Sixtieth Street Theater (Philadelphia, PA) 1417
Sky King Theater (Mobile, AL) 58
Sky View Drive-in (Cocoa, FL)

268; (Jacksonville, FL) 322; (Orlando, FL) 360;
Skydome Theater (Miami, FL) 347
Sledge and Sledge 9
Smackover, AR 131
Smart Set p. 2
Smarter Set 1838
Smith, Bessie 9, 19, 31, 230, 446, 453, 514, 556, 566, 733, 784, 804, 968, 984, 1041, 1084, 1086, 1098, 1101, 1103, 1291, 1302, 1413, 1421, 1427, 1429, 1431, 1447, 1449, 1520, 1557, 1838
Smith, Billie 1314
Smith, C. K. 1821
Smith, Clara 480, 582, 845, 1084
Smith, Clay 1788
Smith, Harry T. 854
Smith, Kent 838
Smith, M.C. 91
Smith, Mamie 1431
Smith, W. H. 588
Smith, Walter 620
Smith, Willie "The Lion" 1107
Smith, Wilson Porter 786
Smith and King 793
Smoke Signals (film) 1410, 1852
Snow and Snow 1520
Snow Hill, MD 815, 816
Snow White and the Seven Dwarfs (film) 1416
Society Doctor (film) 1447
Soft Boiled (film) 585
Some Wild Oats (film) 574
Somerville, TX 1755
Somma, Charles 1874
Son of Satan (film) 1429
Son of Sinbad (film) 458, 459
Son of Tarzan (film) 805
The Song and Dance Man (film) 1093
South Baltimore Club 786
South Bay, FL 413
South Jamaica, Long Island, NY 1119
Southern Aid Society of Virginia 222
Southern Aire Drive-in (Lewisburg, TN) 1537
Southern Amusement Company 444
Southern Consolidated Vaudeville Circuit 57, 323, 439, 512, 1302, 1406, 1497, 1449, 1677, 1881
Southern Pines, NC 1253
Southern Theater (Springfield, OH) 1344
Southland Singers 1838
Sovini, Mr. 1112
Spartanburg, SC 1502–1507
The Speedmakers (farce)
Speiden, Albert 228
Speiden, William L. 228

INDEX 275

Spence, Louise p. 6n2, n5
Spencer Theater (Kelford, NC) 1201
Spindale, NC 1254
Spivey, Victoria 1103, 1685
The Sport of the Gods (film) 802
Spring Hope, NC 1255
Springfield, IL 615
Springfield, MO 1012
Springfield, OH 1341–1345
The Square Deal Man, (film) 585, 595
Stafford, Eddie 566
Stage Struck (film) 1111
Stallworth, Frank 9
Stamper, George 1836
Stamps, AR 132.
Standard Theater (Cairo, IL) 550; (Chapel Hill, NC) 1142; (Cleveland, OH) p. 4, 1310; (Philadelphia, PA) 1431, p. **186**
Standing, Wyndham 597
Stanley Theater (Philadelphia, PA) p. 1
Stanwyck, Barbara 735, 1450
A Star Is Born (film) 1857
Star Theater (Anniston, AL) 6; (Bessemer, AL) 12; (Tuscaloosa, AL) 85; (El Dorado, AR) 101; (New Smyrna Beach, FL) 352; (Quitman, FL) 391; (Sanford, FL) 405; (Dawson, GA) 490; (Moultie, GA) 518; (Quitman, GA) 520; (Savannah, GA) 532; (Swainsboro, GA) 533; (Waycross, GA) 544; (Chicago, IL) 593; (Crowley, LA) 687; (New Roads, LA) 740; (Shreveport, LA) 754; (Annapolis, MD) 770; (Baltimore, MD) 800, 805; (Gulfport, MS) 906; (Hattiesburg, MS) 908; (Meridian, MS) 935; (Natchez, MS) 941; (Pascagoula, MS) 942; (Shelby, MS) 946; (Shore, MS) 947; (St. Louis, MO) 1006; (Buffalo, NY) 1055; (Asheville, NC) ; (Greenville, NC) 1191; (Roxboro, NC) 1246; (Harrisburg, PA) 1403–4; (Pittsburgh, PA) 1449; (Spartanburg, SC) 1506; (Chattanooga, TN) 1524
Stark, Bob 1557
Starkman, D. 1428
Starkville, MS 948
Starlight Drive-in (Henderson, NC) 1192; (Nashville, TN) 1562; (Beaumont, TX) 1591; (Bryan, TX) 1602; (Dallas, TX) 1634; (Galveston, TX) 1663; (Taylor, TX) 1758; (Tyler, TX) 1771; (Norfolk, VA) 1853; (Richmond, VA) 1879

Starlight Theater (Cameron, NC) 1140; (Bryan, TX) 1603; (Corsiciana, TX) 1618
Starr, Milton, 31, 463, 1235, 1557
Starr Theater (Jacksonville, NC) 1199
Stars Over Texas (film) 831
State Theater (Montgomery, AL) 67, p. **19**; (Asbury Park, NJ) 1025; (Brooklyn, NY) 1079; (Hertsford, NC) 1193; (Kinston, NC) 1209; (Cincinnati, OH) 1292; (Altus, OK) 1353; (Orangeburg, SC) 1497; (Dallas, TX) 1635; (Petersburg, VA) 1860
State-Harrison Theater (Chicago, IL) 594
States Theater (Chicago, IL) 595
Statesville, NC 1256
State-wide D-I Theaters 1745
Station Theater (Newark, NJ) 1044
Station West (film) 722
Staunton, VA 1887
Stax Records 1086
Steamboat Days (revue) 1302, 1431
Steelton, PA 1453
Stein, Ben 514
Stemmons and Stemmons 793
Sten, Anna 838
Stephens, Shedrick S. 640
Stevens, Andrew, Jr. 1421
Stevens, George 726
Stewart, James 1845
Stewart, Sammy 579, 601
Stiles, W. J. 474
Stinson, Charles P. 1449
Stockton, CA 198, 199, 200
Stokes, Charles G. 62
Stone, Emsirdell S. 644
Stone and Stone 1294
Stone Theater (Detroit, MI) 864
Storck, J. Edward 230, 785
Storefront theaters p. 4
Stormy Weather (film) 853, 861
Straine, Doc 164
Strand Theater (Stockton, CA) 200; (Bridgeport, CT) 202; (DC) 242; (Jacksonville, FL) 323; (Orlando, FL) 361; (Albany, GA) 435; (Atlanta, GA) 460; (West Point, GA) 546; (Gary, IN) 620; (St. Louis, MO) 1007; (Asheboro, NC) 1122; (Philadelphia, PA) 1432; (Roanoke, VA) 1882
Stratton, William B. 844
Strayhorn, Billy 1447
Stringer Theater (Avon Park, FL) 25651
Strong Circuit Theater (Proctor, AR) 129
Struffin and Brown 793
Stucket and Sloan 1432

Studio Theater (Richmond, CA) 178
Stuttgart, AR 133
Subway Theater (Brooklyn, NY) 1080
Suddenly (film) 1845
Suffolk, VA 1888–1893
Sugar Foot Greene from New Orleans (show) 117
Sugar Foot Sam from Alabam' (show) 1579
Sullivan, John L. 1414
Sulphur, LA 755, 756
Summerville, SC 1508
Sumner Theater (Brooklyn, NY) 1081
Sumter, SC 1509, 1510, 1511
Sumter, TN 1565
Sumter, W. S. 317, 377
Sun Drive-in (Greensboro, NC) 1184
Sun Theater (St. Louis, MO) 1008
Sun Valley Serenade (film) 1884
Sunbeam Theater (Cleveland, OH) 1311
Sunbeams 1331
Sunflower, MS 949
Sunnyside Theater (Greer, SC) 1491; (Staunton, VA) 1887
Sunset Theater (New York, NY) 1115
Sunshine Sammy Revue 802
Supreme Theater (Brooklyn, NY) 1075
Suspicion (film) 241
Sutton, Percy 1086
Sutton, Susie 235, 1557
Swainsboro, GA 553
Swanee River (film) 1410
Swanson, Gloria 1111
Swartz, H. 1432
Swartzman, Mr. 1426, 1445
Sweatman, Wilbur 230, 566, 582, 1091
Sycamore, GA 534
Sykes, Mr. 28
Sykes Theater (Decatur, AL) 28
Sylvan Theater (DC) 243
Symbol of the Unconquered (film) 525, 801

Tales of Manhattan (film) 1416
Tall Man Riding (film) 445
Tall, Tan, and Terrific 831
Talladega, AL 80, 81
Tallahassee, FL 414, 416, 417
Tallulah, LA 757, 758, 759, 760
Talmadge, Constance 1093
Talmadge, Norma 164, 801
Tampa, FL 418, 419, 420, 421, 422, 423, 424
Tarboro, NC 1257
Tarzan and the Amazons (film) 820
Tarzan of the Apes (film) 156
Tasmania Trio 1431

276 INDEX

Tate, Erskine 579, 597
Taylor, Robert 737
Taylor, TX 1756, 1757, 1758
Taylor Theater (Edenton, NC) 1164
Tazewell, VA 1894, 1895
Tchula, MS 950
Tchula Theater (Tchula, MS) 950
Temple, TX 1759, 1760
Temple of Venus (film) 1103
Temple Theater (Fort Smith, AR) 103; (San Francisco, CA) 194; (Baton Rouge, LA) 682; (New Orleans, LA) 738; (Cleveland, OH) 1312; (Oklahoma City, OK) 1385; (Wheeling, WV) 1921
The Ten Commandments (film) 1111
Ten Wanted Men (film) 1823
Tennebaum, Harry 1449
Tent Show (Brandon, MS) 880
Tent Theater (Kansas City, MO) 974
Tent theaters p. 4
Tent Show Theater (Allendale, SC) 1456
Tenth Street Theater (West Point, GA) 547
Terrace Theater (Chicago, IL) 596
Terrell, Marc A. 1862
Terrell, TX 1761
The Test (play) 588
Tetche Theater (Franklin, LA) 695
Tex Theater (Corsiciana, TX) 1619; (Poth, TX) 1741
Texarkana, AR 134, 135, 136
Texarkana, TX 1762, 1763, 1764
Texas Rangers Ride Again (film) 1410
Texas Theater (Denton, TX) 1641
That Night in Rio (film) 1416, 1427
Theater Owners Booking Association (TOBA) p. 6n7, 5, 9, 19, 20, 31, 57, 104, 109, 111, 112, 212, 226, 230, 239, 242, 323, 355, 374, 423, 435, 446, 464, 480, 530, 566, 574, 582, 618, 660, 680, 733, 754, 793, 802, 805, 845, 866, 898, 906, 919, 936, 968, 984, 1086, 1103, 1124, 1149, 1183, 1223, 1266, 1273, 1274, 1286, 1287, 1291, 1302, 1303, 1339, 1341, 1343, 1382, 1392, 1421, 1431, 1440, 1449, 1457, 1469, 1471, 1478, 1520, 1530, 1534, 1551, 1553, 1557, 1561, 1579, 1633, 1660, 1662, 1677, 1696, 1735, 1747, 1749, 1762, 1776, 1807, 1831, 1838, 1851, 1856, 1874
Theby, Rosemary 777

There's No Business Like Show Business (film) 1848
Thibodaux, LA 761
Thirty-five Drive-in (Jackson, MS) 922
Thirty Seconds Over Tokyo (film) 1427
Thomas, Andrew J. 211, 230
Thomas, Margaret Ward 556
Thomas and Breeden 733
Thomas Brothers 230
Thomaston, GA 535
Thomasville, GA 536
Thompson, C. S. 1549
Thompson, Sadie 164
Thompson, Thomas 1872
Thompson, Walter 801
Thoms, Gene 1696
Thorndale, TX 1765, 1766
Thorton, J. S. 1608
Three Russian Girls (film) 838
Three Stooges 731
Thunderbolt Jack (film) 780, 805
Thundering West (film) 929
Tierney, Gene 724, 1857
Tiffany Theater (Brooklyn, NY) 1082
Tifton, GA 537
Tiger Band (film) 805
Tilden Theater (Flint, MI) 870
Tillie's Punctured Romance (film) 1018
Tinley, T. S. 1287
Tivoli Theater (Los Angeles, CA) 168
Tobias, Josephine 1288
Tobias Theater (Moore Haven, FL) 348
Toemnes, Walter 346
Tolbutt, W. H. 1477
Toledo, OH 1346, 1347
Tolliver, C. F. 1882
Tom Baxter's Place (Jacksonville, FL) 324
Tompkins Theater (Brooklyn, NY) 1083
Top Hat (film) 728
Topeka, KS 650, 651
Topper (film) 1416
Tormey, F. E. 783
Touchdown (film) 574
Tower Theater (Mindlin, LA) 718; (Bronx, NY) 1062; (Bastrop, TX) 1581
Townsend, J. 1372
Tracy, Spencer 731, 1427
Tracy Theater (Long Beach, CA) 151
Trader Tom of China, Chapter 2 (film) 722
The Trail Beyond (film) 1446
Treason (film) 1446
Trebernville, VA 1896
Trenton, NJ 1045, 1046
Trevor, Claire 1427, 1431
Triangle Theater (Pittsburgh, PA) 1450

Trigger Smith (film) 929
Trinity, TX 1767
Troy, AL 82
Troy, NY p. 1
Trueman, B. C. 110
Truman Theater (Hope, AR) 111
The Tryst (opera) 1091
Tufts, Sonny 726
Tulsa, OK 1391–1395
Tunica, MS 951
Tupelo, MS 952
Turner, Lana 725
Turner, Samuel R. 236
Turpin, Charles H. 984
Turpin, Thomas M. J. 984
Turrell, AR 137, 138
Turrell Theater (Turrell, AR) 138
Tuskegee, AL 86, 87, 88, 89
Tuskegee Institute Theater (Tuskegee, AL) 89
Tutt, Homer 1838
Twenty Mule Team (film) 725
Twenty-three and One-half Hours Leave (film) 777
Twin Amusement Company 1838
Twinkle Drive-in (Auburndale, FL) 249
Two Johns Theater (Indianapolis, IN) 642
Two Kinds of Women (film) 589
Tyler, TX 1768–1771
Typhoon (film) 735

U.S. Theater (Cleveland, OH) 1313
Underwater! (film) 1834
Union City, TN 1566
Union Theater (Grenada, MS) 903; (Spartanburg, SC) 1507
Unique Theater (San Francisco, CA) 195; (Mayfield, KY) 665; (Detroit, MI) 865
United Artists Theater (Louisville, KY) 662
Uptown Theater (Cairo, IL) 551; (Baltimore, MD) 795; (St. Louis, MO) 1009; (Philadelphia, PA) 1432, p. **188**

V Theater (McAlester, OK) 1377
Valdosta, GA 538, 539, 540
Valentine, Maggie p. 6n15, n16
Valentino, Rudolph 1111, 1429
Valley Drive-in (Lanett, AL) 51
Valley Theater (Tazewell, VA) 1895
Vaudette Theater (Detroit, MI) 866
Vaughn, John G. 1857
Vaughn, Sarah 1086
Vaughn and Hattan 229
The Veiled Mystery (film) 780
Vendome Theater (Hope, AR) 112; (Chicago, IL) 597; (St. Louis, MO) 1010; (Hamilton, OH) 1335

INDEX 277

Venice, IL 616
Venus Theater (St. Louis, MO) 1011; (Memphis, TN) 1553
Vera Cruz (film) 1795
Verdun Theater (Beaumont, TX) 1592
Vernon, TX 1772
Vernon Theater (Los Angeles, CA) 169
Vernot, Henry 802
Vero Beach, FL 425
Vesta Theater (Pine Bluff, AR) 127
Vicksburg, MS 953, 954, 955
Victor, John H. 642
Victor Theater (Brunswick, GA) 476; (Port Arthur, TX) 1740
Victoria, TX 1773, 1774
Victoria Theater (Washington, NC) 1261; (Cincinnati, OH) 1293
Victory Theater (San Diego, CA) 186; (Fort Lauderdale, FL) 290; (Chicago, IL) 598; (Louisville, KY) 664; (New York, NY) 1116; (Albemarle, NC) 1121; (Wichita Falls, TX) 1783
Vidalia, GA 541
Vidalia, LA 762
Vidalia Theater (Vidalia, LA) 762
Villa Theater (Winter Haven, FL) 423
Vinton, LA 763, 764
Virginia Theater (Bakersfield, CA) 145; (Chicago, IL) 599; (Alexandria, VA) 1789
Virginian Theater (Roanoke, VA) 1884
Vista Theater (Bakersfield, CA) 146
Vogue Theater (Philadelphia, PA) 1434
Vondell Club 786
Vontastics 592

W. Lee Theater (Newberry, FL) 351
Wack, Mr. 1430
Waco, TX 1775–1779
Wages of Sin (film) 662
Wadesboro, NC 1258
Waldorf, MD 817
Waldorf Theater (Waldorf, MD) 817
Walker, Aida Overton 1084
Walker, Billy 805
Walker, Madame C. J. 643
Walker and Butler 1557
Walker and Dorsey 1018, 1020
Walker Theater (Indianapolis, IN) 643, p. **87**; (Richmond, VA) 1880; (Suffolk, VA) 1893
Wallace Trio 1431
Waller, Gregory p. 6n13
Waller, Thomas "Fats" 579, 1086, 1101, 1112

Wall's Opera House (DC) 235
Walsh, Judy 735
Walterboro, SC 1512
Walthall Theater (Greenwood, MS) 901
Walton, G. W. 318
Walton, Lester 1101
Wapie the Killer 156
Ward, R. L. 1869
Ware Shoals, SC 1513
Warfield Theater (Detroit, MI) 867
Warley, William 660
Warner, James H. 226
Warner Brothers 780
Warren, AR 139, 140
Warwick, GA 542
Washington, Booker T. 213
Washington, Dinah 592
Washington, DC p. 2, 209–244
Washington, James 240
Washington, NC 1259, 1260, 1261
Washington Bee (newspaper) 235
Washington Shores Drive-in (Orlando, FL) 362
Washington Theater (Mobile, AL) 59; (Plateau, AL) 73; (Apopka, FL) 246; (Deland, FL) 280; (Indianapolis, IN) 644; (Electric Mills, MS) 894; (New York, NY) 1117; (Elizabeth City, NC) 1167; (Shelby, NC) 1252; (Springfield, OH) 1345; (Fort Worth, TX) 1654; (Houston, TX) 1696
Waters, Ethel 5, 9, 20, 230, 446, 556, 566, 582, 1101, 1416, 1424, 1431, 1557
Waters Theater (Coushatta, LA) 683
Watkins, F. K. 1161, 1162
Watt, Ernest 805
Watt and Ringgold 805
Watts and Willis 1267
Watts Brothers 1586
Wauchula, FL 428
Wauchula Theater (Wauchula, FL) 428
Waxahachie, TX 1780
Waycross, GA 543, 544
Wayne, John 827, 1446, 1850, 1884
Waynesboro, GA 545
Waynesburg, OH 1348
W.E. Lee Theater (Gainsville, FL) 302
Weaver Brothers 731
Webb and Simmons 582
Weekend in Havana (film) 1869
Weinberg, Louis 556
Weismuller, Johnny 735, 820, 1795
Welch, Jack S. 754
Weldoras 1431
Wells, Mordecai, and Taylor 1101
Welsh, LA 765

Wenig, Julius 212, 217, 223
West End Theater (Arkadelphia, AR) 91; (Lutcher, LA) 715; (New York, NY) 1118; (Lenoir, NC) 1214; (Shelbyville, TN) 1564; (Martinville, VA) 1827
West Helena, AR 141, 142, 143
West Memphis, AR 144
West of the Water Tower (film) 1103
West Palm Beach, FL 429, 430
West Point, GA 546, 547
Western Theater (Chicago, IL) 660
The Westerner (film) 735
Westmore Theater (Concord, NC) 1156
Westside Theater (Ocala, FL) 357
Wethers, Carl T. 679
Wetzell, B.C. 822
Wewoka, OK 1396, 1397
Wewoka, PA 1454
What Every Woman Knows (film) 1450
Wheeler, L. 1266
Wheeling, WV 1919, 1920, 1921
Whipper, Leigh 802, 1041, 1833
Whippler, Morris 1267
White, Anna 1291, 1315
White, Clarence 15
White, Gonzelle 446, 514, 733, 968, 1382, 1392, 1431, 1551, 1557
White, James L. 1849
White, Roy 660
White Cockatoo (film) 1446
White Fire (film) 728
White Savage (film) 820
Whiteville, NC 1262, 1263
Whitman, Bert 1331
Whitman Sisters 230, 312, 566, 592, 731, 1084, 1101, 1103, 1431, 1696, 1820
Whitney, Salem Tutt 1838
Whitney and Tutt 1302
Why Announce Your Marriage? (film) 590
Why Go Home? (film) 156
Wichita, KS 652
Wichita Falls, TX 1781, 1782, 1783
Widmark, Richard 731
Wiener, Ike 237
The Wiff Woff Wabblers (musical) 566
Wiggins, Jack Ginger 733, 1520
Wight, Oliver B. 781
Wilberforce, OH 1349
Wilberforce Theater 1349
Wilby, Ernest 851
The Wild One (film) 1837
Wilkes, Mattie 597, 801
Wilkesboro, NC 1264
Willard, Jess 827
Willard Theater (Chicago, IL) 601

Williams, Bert 227, 1084
Williams, Ethel 556
Williams, Grant 1421
Williams, Mrs. Lola T. p. 3, 1378, 1386, 1392
Williams, Percy G. 1084
Williams, Warren 1450
Williams and Brown 793, 1449
Williams and Richardson 805
Williams and Walker 1086, 1833
Williams Brothers 867
Williamsburg, VA 1897, 1898
Williamston, NC 1265
Willie Toosweet Company 57, 733, 919
Willis, Charles 164
Willis Theater (Detroit, MI) 868; (Bronx, NY) 1063
Wilmington, DE 208
Wilmington, NC 1266, 1267, 1268, 1269
Wilson, Eddie p. 4, 44
Wilson, Edith 1084
Wilson, Kendall p. 7n20
Wilson, Lucien 113
Wilson, NC 1270, 1271
Wilson, O. T. 1187
Wilson, T. Finley 786
Wilson and Kurtz 1487
Wilson Dam Theater (Florence, AL) 36
Wilson's Airdome Theater (Hope, AR) 113

Winchester, KY 669
Windsor, Marie 1823
Winn Theater (Winfield, LA) 766
Winnfield, LA 766
Winona, MS 956
Winsboro, LA 767
Winston-Salem, NC 1272–1278
Winter Meeting (film) 838
Winters, Shirley 737
Wisconsin Enterprise Blade (newspaper) 1922
Within Our Gates (film) 446, 463, 474, 480, 486, 499, 514, 523, 544, 555, 738, 754, 1018, 1126, 1161, 1204, 1223, 1261, 1270, 1477, 1487, 1496
The Woman Gives (film) 801
A Woman There Was (film) 166
A Woman's Face (film) 661
A Woman's Place (film) 1093
Women owners and managers of black theaters p. 3
Wonder Music Company 793
Wonderful Thing (film) 589, 590
Wonderland Theater (Durham, NC) 1162; (Broken Bow, OK) 1360; (Cushing, OK) 1365
Wong, Anna Mae 731
Wonit Theater (Bladenboro, NC) 1136
Woods, P. 1636
Woolden, George H. 792, 801

Works Progress Administration 1101
World for Ransom (film) 1823
Wright, Delvin 338
Wyer, E. M. 595
Wynn, Keenan 446

Xenia, OH 1350

Yazoo City, MS 957, 958
The Yellow Ticket (film) 1101
Yiddish Theater (Detroit, MI) 833
YMCA (Ware Shoals, SC) 1513
York Palace Theater (Philadelphia, PA) 1435
York Street Palace Theater (Philadelphia, PA) p. 4, 1435
York Theater (DC) 244
Young, LaBlanch 582
Young, Vern U. 618
Young, Walter 19
Youngstown, OH 1351, 1352

Zarilla, Samuel 1545, 1553
Zarrigg, Bert 626
Zink, John J. 215, 232, 241
Zink, John Z. 1725
Zoe Theater (Houston, TX) 1697

www.ingramcontent.com/pod-product-compliance
Lightning Source LLC
Chambersburg PA
CBHW081542300426
44116CB00015B/2726